A Particular Kind
of Fool

A Particular Kind
of Fool

Noel Whitcomb

An Anthony Blond Book
London   New York

First published in Great Britain by Quartet Books Limited 1990
A member of the Namara Group
27/29 Goodge Street
London W1P 1FD

Copyright © 1990 by Noel Whitcomb
The author hereby asserts his moral
right and paternity of the work

'Herrings for Breakfast' by Cassandra (Sir William Connor)
is published by kind permission of the *Daily Mirror*

British Library Cataloguing in Publication Data

Whitcomb, Noel
    A particular kind of fool.
    1. Great Britain   Journalism.   Biographies
    I. Title
    070.92
            ISBN 0-7043-2761-9

Printed and bound in Great Britain by
BPCC Hazell Books
Aylesbury, Bucks, England
Member of BPCC Ltd.

for Sally

Most fools can get a book published,
but it takes a particular kind of fool
to hold down a job on a daily paper.

Evelyn Waugh, *Ninety-Two Days*

Preface

I did not set out to write a book about newspapers. All I had in mind was to write the story of one man who, from time to time during a long career in newspapers, kept suspecting that he had made a ghastly mistake on the day when he took a taxi to Fleet Street in search of a job. That seemed to sum up the comedy of my life – the tale of a tailormade misfit.

Of course I realized that this approach might be said to owe a small debt to the Theatre of the Absurd – a character constantly finding himself out of harmony with his surroundings and struggling in vain against his destiny, a journalist forever waiting for Godot – but I had no such grandiose pretensions. The most I hoped to do was to give an amusing account of the life and times of one newspaperman who worked during a period that is already becoming shadowy.

Being of part-Irish extraction, I naturally began my story at the end.

However, having written the book I now find that the reader will probably be groping about with a torch during the early pages, trying to find the background to it all. Rather than risk the possibility that he or she may throw the book out of the window in bemused fury before reaching the funny bits, I decided to write this preface explaining the circumstances that led up to the end of the affair.

In spite of all my good resolutions this unavoidably entails offering a brief resumé of the state of play in Fleet Street immediately prior to my exit, and although these details will be familiar to many readers they provide a necessary setting for my comedy – a Greek chorus, perhaps, or what we in newspapers used to call 'a situationer'.

In the early 1980s British national newspapers were in an appalling financial and industrial mess, and Fleet Street was drifting up the creek without a paddle. Rapacious union bosses had seized the ship and were encouraging mutiny in the crew. Disaster in the shape of widespread bankruptcy loomed ahead. There seemed to be no way of preventing a titanic crash. That was the moment when two raiders jumped aboard and, in the nick of time, snatched the industry back from the white waters of chaos: Rupert Murdoch and Robert Maxwell.

Maxwell, who had started life as a poor and uneducated Czechoslovakian peasant, was regarded by some at the time as a bit of a flash-Harry who used the wiliness of the street trader in the world of high finance, but there was another side to him: he was hooked on newpapers; he saw himself romantically in the role of the great editor-proprietor, wearing the mantle of his hero, Maxwell Aitken, lst Baron Beaverbrook. He had already transformed the British printing industry, after bitter and savage battles with the workers and their unions, and he had made previous attempts to buy a national newspaper, three times being beaten to the post by the far richer Rupert Murdoch, who had picked up the *Sun*, the *News of the World, The Times* and the *Sunday Times* in the process.

Of all the newpapers that were in trouble, the *Daily Mirror* was deepest in the quagmire. It employed far too many people, it was spending far too much money, and it was an industrial can of worms. Its owners, Reed International, were out of patience with the way it conducted its affairs and they wanted to get rid of it. Rupert Murdoch was not interested – he had enough troubles of his own – so Robert Maxwell saw his chance at last. Few at the *Mirror* wanted Maxwell to succeed in taking over the paper because many of them, workers and executives alike, detested the man; more to the point, Reed International had publicly announced that they would not sell the Mirror Group Newspapers to any single individual, a promise that was made with Maxwell specifically in mind.

However, businessmen's promises are made to be broken, and so, in a cloak-and-dagger sequence of clandestine negotiations behind closed doors in Piccadilly, Maxwell took the trick. The prelude to that certain midnight when the owners of the *Mirror* signed the contract to sell, and Maxwell arose from the table as the winner, would make a gripping play; it was a cat-and-mouse game of plot and counter-plot, of shadowy scurryings across Piccadilly from Reed International's offices to the Ritz, where Maxwell was sitting in his spider's web, awaiting the moment to pounce; of urgent and supposedly top-secret board meetings at the *Mirror*, whose directors – mere pawns in the game – were desperately seeking ways to frustrate Maxwell's ambitions, unaware that there was a mole in their midst who was reporting their stratagems back to Maxwell.

It was a City-slicker drama to quicken the pulses of young hopeful *arbitrageurs*, and it ended with a handshake at midnight when Maxwell, exultant in victory, was requested by Les Carpenter, chief executive of Reed International, not to visit the *Mirror* building until the following morning because if the news leaked out while the presses were still rolling it might result in another industrial stoppage. But Maxwell walked down to his car and drove straight to the *Daily Mirror*. He called in *Mirror* directors for a meeting at 3 a.m. and made it clear that he was the boss from that moment on.

To watch Maxwell, as I did, stomping round his newly conquered *Daily Mirror* empire, hardly able to contain his excitement, was like watching an acquisitive child on Christmas morning. Building by building, floor by floor, room by room, he unwrapped it all as if it were a pillowcase full of presents that he had longed for; which, indeed, it was. For weeks he seldom slept for more than two hours out of the twenty-four, usually less, sometimes not at all. He had Fleet Street power at last, and seemed hooked on the spurious glamour of an old-fashioned dream in which he would assign his ace reporters to big stories, chewing a large cigar with the cynical sophistication of Walter Matthau in the part of the relentless editor in Hecht and MacArthur's *The Front Page*, boss and pal of his Hildy Johnson-type newshounds who always got the story that beat the world. He dreamed of becoming the greatest press baron of them all. But dreams are only dreams. It did not work out like that.

Maxwell's business activities in the past had been rooted in publishing, but publishing of a different kind; he knew little about the way newspapers work; so for a while he became something of a laughing-stock, partly because pictures of him were so frequently printed in the paper. It was all very funny unless you happened to be working there. If you happened to be working there it was like sitting on a ticking bomb. Although he had been a millionaire before, Maxwell had never been a rich millionaire: during some of his previous attempts to buy a newspaper, stretching over a period of fifteen years, there had been doubts in the minds of some people whether he could raise enough money; other businessmen who at one time or another had been concerned in negotiations to buy national newspapers – men such as Sir James Goldsmith, Lord Weinstock, Rupert Murdoch and Tiny Rowland – were generally acknowledged to be easily rich enough, but doubts had been expressed at times about the extent of Maxwell's funds. This was largely because much of Maxwell's personal fortune was held, perfectly legally, in trusts in Leichtenstein, a tax haven where the law provides for great secrecy to surround such financial arrangements: so it was not easy for outsiders to ascertain how much Maxwell was worth, and the lack of available evidence left some businessmen unsure whether Maxwell could support his bids with cash. According to a passage in Joe Haines' book, *Maxwell*, which was written with Maxwell's assistance and published by one of his companies, even in the late stages of 'Maxwell's negotiations with Reed International, when his bid of £113,000,000 for Mirror Group Newspapers had been accepted, Maxwell's offer to pay by means of a banker's draft from the National Westminster Bank was rejected; Sir Robert Clark, the chairman of Hill Samuel, had to be contacted late that night to give a cheque for the purchase price on Maxwell's behalf to Warburg's, Reed's bankers, before the deal was finalized.

With hindsight it is clear that Maxwell picked up an incredible bargain. But at the time, as Maxwell admitted in a television interview, he regarded the price he paid as an enormous sum of money; and he was acutely aware that unless he could pull the business round with great speed and defeat the unions he could face ruin.

The problem was that the *Daily Mirror* had become more accustomed to spending money than earning it. But Maxwell waded in and stopped the rot. As a result he soon became a rich millionaire, because the ownership of national newspapers confers tremendous creditworthiness on any man, and creditworthiness was what Maxwell had lacked before in the wheeler-dealer days when he had unwisely been scorned contemptuously as the Bouncing Czech. Always a breathtaking gambler, he used his new status as a press card for entry to the *salles privées* of the City, where the big games are played. In short order he became nearly as rich as his old rival, Rupert Murdoch; but wealth was the only point of similarity between the two press barons, because Murdoch, unlike Maxwell, was a newspaperman.

Rupert Murdoch had been weaned on printer's ink. The print was his family business. His father, Sir Keith Murdoch, was a distinguished Australian journalist who became an owner of newspapers. Young Rupert had been sent to Oxford to finish his formal education and then to Fleet Street to learn his trade on Lord Beaverbrook's *Daily Express*. Upward he soared in the world of international newspapers until some experts began comparing him with Northcliffe, Hearst and Beaverbrook – a comparison that sounds less effusive when you recall what an unholy trinity of vindictive paranoiacs those three men were; naturally a great deal of hatred and envy came his way as he became more powerful, but there was one fact that nobody could deny: he knew his work: he could do the job of every man on his payroll.

So, in those turbulent days of the chaotic 1980s, while Robert Maxwell stumbled his way round his newly acquired newspapers in a blaze of personal publicity, Rupert Murdoch lay low, like Brer Rabbit, and said nuffin'. Secretly he was making plans to defeat the print unions. Few people at the time believed that this was possible. It had been tried so often before. The union bosses were too deeply entrenched. They had become the mafia godfathers who controlled every game that was played in the street. However, taking a leaf out of the book of good old reliable Nathan Detroit who ran the oldest-established permanent floating crap game in New York, Murdoch shifted the venue of the game overnight to Wapping, thereby defeating the outraged print unions at a stroke and bringing Fleet Street's ramshackle house of cards tumbling down.

It was a famous victory, and others among the new generation of press barons followed Murdoch's banner eastward towards the Isle of Dogs, a shabby paradise where it was summertime and the living was easy because the rates were low and the running costs were as cheap as a tabloid editor's morals. This geographical shift coincided with the consolidation in British national newspapers of electronic technology which had been evolving for twenty years elsewhere but had been outlawed in Fleet Street by the Luddite unions. So the Wapping *Risorgimento* was represented as a new dawn. The recent past was as out of date as the horse and cart. Fleet Street soon became merely another thoroughfare of no more specific identity than Putney High Street. However, apart from the updating of its technical mechanics, the trade that had once flourished there continued with little change.

Some singularly loathsome newspapers were produced, but there was nothing new in that: where there's muck there's brass, and always has been. Popular newspapers have always been careful to follow slavishly the tastes and preferences of their readers, and consequently in any age a society gets the newspapers it deserves; at a time when spitefulness, envy, violence and sex are matters that engross the minds of the masses, those are the junk-food dishes that are served up daily by unscrupulous editors. Of course, many honest and talented journalists were still around, as always before, but in spite of all the excitement about a new dawn newspapers of all kinds continued to include among their editors and senior executives as fine a collection of hypocrites as ever played Happy Families in a whorehouse; among their proprietors they still boasted as crafty a *galère* of entrepreneurs as ever parlayed a ten-dollar bill into a billion; on their reporting staffs they still employed a gallimaufry of chancers, male and female, who would eagerly sell their grandmothers into the white-slave trade for the promise of two columns on the splash: there is no new technology in human nature, and the human factor in printing has changed little since the days of Johann Gutenberg.

That was the world I left behind when I walked out of Maxwell's *Mirror* building at Holborn Circus. It was not a premature exit. Maxwell or no Maxwell, it was time for me to call it a day. My love-hate affair with the *Daily Mirror* had started in its skittish days when jubilant crowds were mafficking in the streets to celebrate the end of the Second World War, and I had stuck by the old girl through thick and thin – with a few deviations on the side – right through to the sombre days of her decline when the circulation of the *Mirror* under Maxwell's rule was dropping like a lead balloon, raucous mobs were fighting in the streets around Murdoch's successful plant at Wapping, and the knell of Fleet Street was tolling from St Bride's.

By coincidence, those four decades neatly encompass a period in the history of British popular newspapers that is as specifically identifiable as the Georgian period in furniture or the Gothic in architecture; it was a period different in character from the Northcliffe era which preceded it, and even more different from the Murdoch era that followed it: it was a period apart, as recognizably separate in its way as the *belle époque* or Scott Fitzgerald's Jazz Age. The essence of its difference lay in the nature of its extravagance. Never before in the centuries of printing history in Fleet Street had the managers of the public prints behaved with such egregious profligacy. There had been spurts of big spending before, such as the time between the wars when Lord Southwood of the *Daily Herald* and his contemporaries had spent fortunes on circulation battles, seeking to buy readers by offering them expensive free gifts, but that was advertising; the wanton prodigality of my period stemmed from a different philosophy, a knowledge that we were all living under the volcano: like the dissolute Romans during the last days of Pompeii, we knew that our world would one day be engulfed by a cataclysm. Presided over by its Caesars – its Caligulas and its Neros – Fleet Street wallowed in Saturnalia, declining inexorably into the decadence that ultimately destroyed it.

It was tawdry, of course, and bogus, because that is the nature of the game; yet any fun-seeking lad like myself who wandered by chance into that blaring Fleet Street funfair and found to his excitement that he was being whirled around faster and faster on the hurtling gallopers of its

xiv

carousel would have echoed the schmaltzy words that William Wordsworth wrote – with a similarly romantic misunderstanding of the reality – about the French Revolution: 'Bliss was it in that dawn to be alive, but to be young was very heaven!' It was the era of magnificent nonsense.

It began in the earnest but down-at-heel second half of the 1940s, when the war ended and our circus came to town; it careered on through the flibbertigibbet fifties and the sex-shop-and-pseudo-psychology sixties, on through the politics-of-envy and industrial anarchy of the seventies and into the yuppy eighties of the early Thatcher years: we played to packed houses, ignoring the fact that the notices had already been posted backstage, and we laughed all the way to the bank until the bank suddenly shut its doors. We were all touched by the madness which was endemic during that period in Fleet Street, like the inhabitants of the French village who all went mad together when a hallucinatory drug was introduced by accident into their bread.

As a reporter I did most of the things that roustabout newsmen do in every age: at one time or another I found myself being bombed out of hotels, shot at in the streets, eluding undercover cops in Cairo, dodging down alleyways in South America to shake off secret agents and playing gin rummy with a couple of deposed kings (Umberto of Italy and Peter of Yugoslavia) and an assortment of grand dukes on a balcony in Estoril. I was smuggled across mountains into a country for which I had no entry papers, led blindfold to the lair of a terrorist chief, was duped by the KGB in Vienna and was propositioned for a job as a spy by the head of an East German trade delegation in a hotel in Russell Square. I shivered in a morgue in Rio while investigating the mysterious death of an acquaintance and was frisked for firearms by the Revd Ian Paisley in the porch of a church in Belfast. None of these escapades will be detailed in this book because they are all bread-and-butter incidents in any newsman's life and, in any case, to make more than a passing mention of such shenanigans would be like a commercial traveller showing his case of samples but knowing that they are not the goods that the customer will get. The writing of any account of my life is more likely to cause the fruity bouquet of Galahad Threepwood's memoirs to arise from the word-processor than the sharp tang of James Bond's aftershave. It has not been the sort of life that I envisaged when I was a lad.

I was a fairly typical middle-class boy in the 1930s, keen on cricket and girls, dreaming the usual Walter Mitty daydreams of scoring a century at Lord's or bringing the house down at Drury Lane with my new play and taking Jessie Matthews out to supper afterwards. My future was no more than a misty horizon in a Turner seascape but I imagined it as something vaguely literary, something connected with poetry. If, in my school cap, I had wandered along Brighton pier and visited Gypsy Lee the fortune-teller, and she had told me that I would spend much of my life working for the *Daily Mirror*, I would have asked her for my money back. Indignantly. It was on the cards that I might become a journalist because that was my family trade, but not the sort of journalist from whose exploits you could cobble up the libretto for a Broadway musical – that was a life for a scaramouch.

What I did not realize then was the extent to which my future would be shaped by the fact that I would constantly find myself requiring far larger quantities of disposable cash than would normally be reflected in my sort of pay-check; this is not an uncommon trait, of course, although many men who have it end up assisting the Fraud Squad with their inquiries. I never had any inclination – nor the nerve, I may say – to become another Raffles, but I kept needing what Errol Flynn used to call 'a nett income fit for my gross habits', so I had to find some legal way of supporting my habit of living above my income. After a few shaky starts I eventually found this when I joined the *Daily Mirror*, which in its munificent days behaved like an indulgent rich uncle to its favoured employees, allowing them to spend its money with the abandon of maharajahs. It was not so much a job, more a private bank. The *Mirror* averted what might otherwise have been a Micawber problem for me, and although I never had any illusions about the paper I did my best to justify its liberality.

Most newspaper historians agree that there was a stretch of some twenty years, starting around the early 1950s, when the *Daily Mirror* was a cleverly produced, responsibly edited and surprisingly well-written paper. But anyone with a long memory or a shelf of books on the subject knows that no popular newspaper has ever had much in common with Little Lord Fauntleroy: the tabloids have always been artful dodgers, street urchins that gleefully endangered the blood pressure of the *bourgeoisie*; they have always been as beguilingly sly as a covey of Galway horse-copers, and they are exasperating things to work for because you are never completely sure what they will do with the words you send them; sometimes they make you look an awful fool. Which is why, from time to time during what may smilingly be called my career, I decided that enough was enough, and either through irritation with my own pusillanimity or through fury with the outrageous duplicity of the newspaper I made up my mind to get out and do something different. Sometimes I nearly succeeded, but never quite, and for a most peculiar

fifty, a ca~~~ ~~~ ~~~ ~~~, and a ~~~
that seemed to make it a sensible move for me ~~~ ~~~ ~~~
had no other job in mind but I was determined to start a new sort of life
while there was still time. I was reasonably fit and financially secure.
What had I to lose?

I wrote a note of resignation, put it in my pocket, and was striding
down Fleet Street to deliver it when I was suddenly struck by a
remarkably good idea. St Paul described a similar experience. It was not
just an ordinary idea, it was an idea that would unquestionably captivate
any popular newspaper. I paused. What should I do – waste it? Forget
about it and press on? Deliver my resignation and get out? Well . . . yes
and no. What I decided to do was to mention the idea when I handed in
my portfolio and offer it to the *Daily Mirror* as a parting gift for old times'
sake.

This grandiose gesture misfired, of course, and the result was that I
was persuaded to put my idea into operation for the *Daily Mirror*. The
idea itself had nothing complex about it; it was simply that I should
launch a club for horse-racing enthusiasts, which I christened the *Daily
Mirror* Punters Club. This developed into the biggest sporting association
of its kind in the world, with a membership of 600,000 people, all of
whom had to buy the *Daily Mirror* to find out what was going on in the
way of club activities. Among its most popular activities the club
pioneered foreign travel in luxury to the races in the world's most
glamorous places, and tens of thousands of readers came on these
enjoyable trips, which the club sold at bargain prices. The *Mirror*'s
circulation shot up. Everybody was happy. Including, and most
particularly, me.

In the process of running the club as its president I became the owner
of several successful racehorses, and entertained my friends in private
boxes at the races when they ran, for all of which the grateful
newspaper picked up the bills. Furthermore, as another bonus under this
new arrangement, I took my wife travelling round the world in leisurely
style and mandarin comfort, occupying the best suites in the most
luxurious hotels; we wandered at will through Europe, America, India,
Australia, South-East Asia, the Caribbean islands, Japan and all over the
Far East. It was all sumptuously elegant. The duties associated with this
princely lifestyle were not arduous. Apart from writing a weekly

Who could be surprised that when this happened to me I abandoned for the time being all further thoughts about getting out? Candide had arrived in El Dorado.

Comic scenarios of this kind, farcical cameos in the style of Feydeau or Ben Travers, highlighting the wonderfully fatuous way in which old Fleet Street conducted its affairs under the aegis of Lord Copper and his ilk, are no longer to be found in British newspapers. Life is more serious now. So newspapermen of my kind, professionals but dilettanti with a penchant for the exotic and a grotesquely high running cost, have become virtually extinct – a fate which even conservationists might call poetic justice. We happy few who devoted our lives to the pursuit of the ridiculous are already suitable for exhibition in the V & A, collectors' items from a bygone age, as quaint as Beau Nash, George Thurston or the Edwardian Country Lady because we, too, lived in the foreign country of the past where they did things differently.

Our frolicsome reign of piracy on the seas of printer's ink ended when the new fleet of newspaper proprietors, led by Rupert Murdoch with Captain Maxwell floundering in his frothy wake, sailed in and captured British newspapers, scuppering their old Spanish customs and imposing economic discipline on their unruly crews, forcing them to eat ships' biscuits instead of their accustomed diet of Bollinger and Beluga, and hanging their ringleaders from the yard-arm: it was rumoured that they all perished, with no survivors, but Candide was washed up on the wilder shores of Kensington and lived to tell this tale.

Campden Hill Square, London

1

A life does not end with a dramatic exit from
the stage, or the perfect conclusion of a
comedy or of a tragedy.

Peter Levi, *The Life and Times of
William Shakespeare*

On the day when the volcano erupted I was entertaining friends to
luncheon in a box at York races. It was a beautiful day. The summer sun
was shining on the green of the Knavesmire, York's ancient and
supremely elegant racecourse, and a few early arrivals among the horses
engaged to race that afternoon were being led round the pre-parade
ring. A tranquil scene, perhaps almost menacingly idyllic because it is
well known that on such a day as this Fate is invariable lurking behind a
tree and twirling a bicycle chain, lying in wait to wallop the unwary.

A waiter switched on the television for the BBC one o'clock news,
and there on the screen I saw him, a mountain of a man, stepping from
his red Rolls Royce in the *Daily Mirror* vanway, beaming triumphantly,
waving a big cigar, the new emperor come to claim his conquered
kingdom.

'That's my new boss,' I said. 'Robert Maxwell. He bought the *Daily
Mirror* last night.'

My guests watched in silence, momentarily embarrassed. They were
Yorkshire countryfolk, sporting farmers and horsemen, the sort of
people I like best.

One of them, Anthony Barker, said, 'He doesn't look like a racing
man.'

'He isn't,' I said.

Another, Frank Mallory, remarked drily, 'He doesn't look the sort
of chap from whom one would care to buy a secondhand car, either.
I'd lay a fair bit of six to four that you're going to have trouble with
him.'

The waiter asked, 'Shall I serve the strawberries now, sir?'

'Yes, if you would,' I nodded. 'And put a few more bottles of

Bollinger on ice – if there are any messages for me we may have to celebrate a hasty retirement.'

We backed four winners that afternoon when the lamps were going out all over Fleet Street. It was like the ball on the eve of Waterloo.

I had met Maxwell a few times during the years of his rise to fortune and his fall from favour in 1971 when he had been severely criticized in a Department of Trade and Industry report, and there was no doubt in my mind that he and I were not what Bertram Wooster would have described as twin souls. When he asked me to go and see him some time after his arrival at the *Mirror*, I walked along the corridor prepared for a *High Noon* shoot-out. As I sauntered into his office, a room I knew well but upon which he had already stamped his own neo-megabuck style of furnishing, he lumbered to his feet and waved a sheet of paper at me.

'Mr Whitcomb,' he growled, 'I understand that you have been one of the stars around here.'

I stifled an impulse to reply, in the words of Sean O'Casey, 'What is the stars? A darlin' question, Captain.' It was not a moment for flippancy. Maxwell's eyebrows were drawing together like two black spaniels snarling at each other. So I replied, 'Ah.' Not a witty response, but not provocative.

'I have here,' he went on, still waving the sheet of paper, 'a set of figures which show that it is costing me one million pounds a year to employ you on this paper. One million pounds a year, out of my pocket.'

I itched to ask him how he could get a million pounds into his pocket, even in a roomy suit like that, but money is to Maxwell what music was to Mozart, no joking matter, so I addressed myself directly to his onslaught.

'That's nonsense,' I said. 'Certainly I spend a lot of money, but much of it comes back to the paper in revenue. Our racing travel operations alone turned over two million pounds last year.'

'Yes,' he said, 'but not enough of it was profit. Lousy business. I'm not interested in anything less than twenty-five per cent nett. But I'll tell you what I'll do – I'll buy a travel agency for you to run if you gear the profits to more than twenty-five per cent.'

'Thanks,' I said, 'but I don't want a travel agency. I'm not a travel agent. And in any case if we put up the profits of our racing travel to twenty-five per cent the whole thing would collapse. It is successful because it is good value for money. That policy was agreed by the previous management because the primary purpose in setting it up was to attract new readers to the paper. And it worked.'

'If my grandmother had balls she'd be my grandfather,' said Maxwell.

I looked at him, puzzled, wondering what this was supposed to mean. (Later I discovered that this was one of his favourite witticisms, and he used it to point out that circumstances alter cases – *autre temps, autres moeurs*.) 'Here are the figures,' he went on, pushing the sheet of paper across the desk and getting up to walk across the room behind me.

I cast an eye over the figures and immediately saw that they were inaccurate, so I turned in my chair to tell him so. He was standing by a table that had a large cheeseboard on it, stacked with foreign cheeses, and he was hastily stuffing big chunks of cheese into his mouth. When he caught my eye he gave me a guilty look.

'You want a piece cheese?' he asked.

'No, thank you,' I replied as he returned to his chair with his mouth very full, munching hungrily. 'Incidentally, these figures are wrong.'

'Balls,' he said, wiping his mouth.

'That is certainly the right word for these figures,' I said.

Even though the atmosphere was boorishly hostile I had guessed that he was not likely to fire me on the spot because I had a contract with a period still to run, and Maxwell was not the sort of man to waste money on buying out his employees' contracts: after an encounter such as this a chap might find his life such a misery that he would resign without compensation but I had no intention of giving him that satisfaction, either. All the same it was clear that our revels were now ended. The party was over. The cabaret had finished and the band had gone to join the ghosts down Archer Street. I was sitting in a nightclub in the morning.

Looking back, it had all started farcically, too. As a child I had bright hopes of a career in the theatre, writing plays, possibly acting in them, maybe directing them; there seemed *nothing* – absolutely nothing – half so much worth doing as simply messing about in theatres. Whether I could have made a living in the theatre is a question that is now impossible to answer, but one sure thing is that there was always a theatrical air hanging over my association with newspapers, sometimes drama, more often comedy. For example, it was a dog that brought me a job as a columnist. I was a young reporter on the *Daily Mirror* at the time.

One sweltering afternoon in the summer of 1946 I was sitting in the reporters' room, idly scanning the *Sporting Life* and wondering whether the time was ripe for me to leave the paper and try my hand at something else. Everything was quiet; the world was on holiday; it was the silly season. One of the telephones rang and I picked it up. It was the news editor.

'I have a yarn for you,' he said. 'Come on down.'

When I went into the newsroom he handed me a slip of paper. It was a message from a local stringer. It simply said that in Royston, Herts, there was a dog that talked, and added the dog's address.

I looked at the news editor and he looked at me. We both had the same thought in mind. It was a waste of time.

Today it is not uncommon for dogs to be seen on television, usually in Miss Esther Rantzen's programme, making some strangulated sound that is half bark and half grunt, and receiving loud applause for a brave shot at simulating the human voice: they are described as talking dogs; but although in those post-war years we lived in a world full of uncertainties, both the news editor and I knew that one thing was certain. Dogs do not talk.

'I'm sorry, old boy,' he said, shaking his head. 'I know it's not the outbreak of World War Three but I just have nothing else to offer you. Not a sausage. Give it a whirl, eh? You might make a funny out of it.'

So off I went to Royston. I found the cottage, knocked at the door, and was invited in by Mr Alf Brissenden. The man from the *Mirror* was always welcome in those days. He was a friend.

'Come into the kitchen and have a cup of tea,' said Mr Brissenden.

We chatted while he made the tea, but I avoided mentioning the dog; I wanted to see it first. Then we sat at the table and Mr Brissenden put some biscuits on a plate and pushed the plate over to me: 'Have a biscuit,' he said.

Into the kitchen at that moment hurried a little Jack Russell terrier, clearly galvanized into action by the word 'biscuit'. He put his paws up on my knee and, with a melting look in his eyes, remarked: 'I WANT ONE.' He said it clearly in a deep and sonorous tone.

My heart warmed to this little white dog with the black patches. I said to Alf Brissenden: 'Your dog says he wants a biscuit.'

'Well, tell him he can't have one,' said Alf. 'He's getting fat. Tell him to wait for his dinner.'

The dog jumped over to his master's knee and looked up at him with urgent appeal. 'Oh, Alf,' he said, wheedlingly, 'I *want* one. Alf – one! *I* want one.'

'How long has he been doing this?' I asked.

'Oh, a long time,' said Alf. 'But he's getting much more fluent. And he understands everything you say. Sometimes I find it uncanny.'

I spent the rest of the afternoon interviewing the neighbours, talking to the vicar, getting quotes that confirmed the strange ability of the dog to talk, sewing up the story. Then I went back to Alf Brissenden's house and, with the little dog, Ben, sitting on my knee, I wrote it.

4

Years later I saw with amusement that the first sentence I jotted down then, the lead to my story, was cited in a textbook for teaching young people the craft of journalism, as an example of how to arrest the reader's attention at the start. In my case it was simply a matter of beginning the story with a statement of fact. My first sentence was: 'I have just had a short conversation with a dog.'

Alf Brissenden had no telephone in the house, and the nearest telephone box was a fair distance off, so Alf advised me to go down to the local pub and telephone from there. With the scribbled copy in my hand, ready to dictate, I went through first to the night news editor, a former regimental sergeant-major called Bill Ryder-Ryder, a ramrod man with a parade-ground voice who was noted for his scepticism and his deep distrust of all reporters.

'Oh, Bill,' I said, 'put me over to copy, would you, I've got a smashing little yarn here. I've just been having a chat with a dog.'

There was a silence. Then Bill said, 'Where are you speaking from?'

'From the local pub,' I said. 'Put me over, would you.'

'You go and have a lie down,' roared Ryder-Ryder in a menacing tone. 'Ring me back in an hour's time. Drink plenty of black coffee. Try to get something to eat.'

'But Bill,' I pleaded, 'honest to God I am as sober as a judge. This dog definitely talks. I'll tell you what – I will go and get the local vicar to come to the telephone and confirm it to you.'

'Do that thing,' barked Bill. 'And let me warn you, if you are trying to have me on, you're for it, lad. Understand?'

So I went and asked the vicar, who did not really want to have anything to do with the *Daily Mirror*, but he was a kindly soul so he agreed to our ringing Ryder-Ryder from the vicarage. He spoke to Ryder-Ryder, confirmed everything I had said, and handed the telephone to me.

'Bill?' I said. 'All right now? Can I go over to copy?'

'How do I know that was the bloody vicar?' he roared. 'It could have been anyone. There is something fishy about this. Bring the story in tomorrow – I am not running it tonight.'

'Look here, Bill,' I said, playing my last trump card. 'I am now going to get the dog and bring him to the telephone, so that you can talk to the dog yourself. If we don't run this tonight we'll lose it – everyone's talking about it down here since I turned up.'

I went and collected Ben. I put him on the telephone to Bill Ryder-Ryder and he did his stuff magnificently.

Bill's last suspicious parting shot was: 'Why does the bloody dog keep

5

calling me Alf – didn't you tell him my name?' But he put me over to copy just the same. And he sent a photographer down hotfoot. Next morning the story was on the front page.

I stayed down overnight, of course. All the major newspapers sent reporters and photographers to Royston next day, and they were far from gruntled when, one by one, they burst into the bar of the local pub and found me there. I heard one of them say: 'That bloody Whitcomb – I can hardly bring myself to buy him a drink.' But they all tried to buy me a drink. Because they had all been to Mr Alf Brissenden's house first and found that neither he nor Ben was at home.

Early that morning I had driven Alf Brissenden and the dog to the Royal Veterinary College Field Station where veterinary specialists were examining Ben in strict secrecy.

The evening papers ran the story on their front pages, and every national newspaper except *The Times* carried a follow-up next day; but all their stories were based on quotes from local people who knew the dog. Nobody found Ben. He was mine. My pal, Ben, the Jack Russell who changed my life.

Our own story in the *Daily Mirror* next day, which took up most of the front page and a large part of the back page as well, came as a severe blow to rival papers which, unable to get exclusives for themselves, were already using spoilers mocking Ben. We ran interviews with two of Britain's leading veterinary surgeons, Professor W.C. Miller, professor of animal husbandary at the Royal Veterinary College, and Dr W.R. Wooldridge, scientific director of the Veterinary Educational Trust. Neither of the experts minced their words. They both spoke unequivocally.

Professor Miller said: 'In all my experience I have never heard a dog so nearly simulate the human voice. It is remarkable.'

Dr Wooldridge said: 'Ben does actually use his mouth, and to some extent his tongue and lips, to formulate and control words. He cuts his words clearly and appears to use his tongue to change from one word to another. I have never known anything like it before.'

So that was that. Official. No argument. Ben was no longer just a silly-season story. He was world news. During the ensuing few weeks his picture, together with feature articles of different kinds from the scientific to the folksy, appeared in newspapers and magazines all over Europe and America; *Paris Match* ran a big feature on him; *Oggi*, the Italian magazine, did likewise; *Esquire* ran an amusing piece about him, as a rival to Rin Tin Tin and Lassie. Ben was famous.

Every publication that used a Ben picture, or an interview with Mr

Brissenden, had to pay Alf Brissenden a fee for it; Alf had asked me in the beginning if I would handle it for him, and I willingly did so. Alf worked as a storeman at a Ministry of Supply depot, so he was by no means well off, but unusually – uniquely, in fact, among the many people with a hot story to sell that I have since met – he was not greedy. I came to respect him considerably. He had a natural dignity.

To squash the sceptics for good and all, we arranged for Ben to be interviewed on BBC radio, on the then equivalent of the *Today* programme. Ben was not merely articulate, he was loquacious. Ben's fan-mail was prodigious. I started a fan club for him, and thousands of children all over the world joined; every one of them received a photograph of Ben, signed with a personal paw-mark, and Ben took great delight in his signing sessions; the *Daily Mirror* paid for all the photographs and postage: next-generation circulation.

Alf Brissenden turned down a big offer to take Ben to America because he did not want his little dog to become a fairground exhibit; but he took him to Filey for a week, as the star attraction at Butlin's Holiday Camp, and at Christmas Alf allowed Ben to make guest appearances in Bertram Mills' Circus at Olympia. The fees were not enormous, but Alf was satisfied. Ben remained the family pet.

As for me, hardly a dog-show took place in Britain that year to which I was not invited as guest of honour; and owners of dogs that displayed some grotesque talent – one of them a toothless Pekinese who kept a set of false teeth by his bowl with which to eat his dinner – were offering me inducements to become the official chronicler of their canine phenomena, the Boswell of their Bonzos. But, as it happened, I was otherwise engaged. My own dog-days were beginning.

During the talking-dog episode my pay had been raised to twenty-four guineas a week. High pay. On my first day back in London I received a telephone call from a secretary at the *Daily Express*, telling me that Mr Arthur Christiansen, the editor, would like to see me at six-thirty that evening, in his office, if it was convenient. It was convenient.

Clearly Chris was going to offer me a job. The *Daily Express* was the top-selling national daily at the time, with a circulation of four million, well ahead of the *Daily Mirror*. Although the public perception of the two newspapers was that they were completely different, one a working-class rag and the other a middle-class paper, from the viewpoint of a working journalist they were much of a muchness; both were sensational papers of frequently dubious accuracy; both were dominated by men with political axes to grind and, in the case of Lord Beaverbrook who owned the *Express*, vicious vendettas to conduct.

Today, as I write, it is widely accepted that standards in British mass-circulation newspapers deteriorated consistently throughout the 1980s and that their present standard is at its lowest for more than half a century. Part of the reason for this is that the more serious newspapers have captured the upper echelons of what used to be the 'pop' circulations, by moving steadily down-market to accommodate the tastes of a readership for more serious newspapers that, socially and educationally, did not exist previously. Proprietors at the upper end of the business have appointed editors who understand this rougher trade: for example, Charles Wilson, who edited *The Times* during the early years of the Wapping period, and Max Hastings who was appointed editor of the *Daily Telegraph* in 1986, were both experienced in popular journalism – Wilson had worked on the *Daily Mail* and Hastings learnt his craft on the *Evening Standard*. Both men are highly skilled news-papermen of proven quality but there is no getting away from the fact that because of their provenance they naturally pushed their papers towards the more popular end of the market. Which is what they were engaged to do.

Once it was only the 'pop' Sundays – sometimes called 'the dirty Sundays' – that boasted mass circulations, but now the *Sunday Times* sells in millions and caters for the slightly educated but generally undis-criminating middle class whose tastes have developed largely from what used to call itself the working class when I was writing for it. Newspapers of all kinds have merely moved in the direction that society itself is moving. The *Daily Mail* and the *Daily Express* – re-dressed in the jeans and T-shirts of the tabloid form but both still redolent of arsenic and old lace – have been saved from the knacker's yard only by the fact that Britain has become a nation of geriatrics, and old reading habits die hard.

So the scorned mass-circulation popular dailies have been impelled by *force majeure* to dig deeper down the social scale to find their readers, or else give up the ghost. The *Daily Star*, never the flavour of the month among our learned friends, had its burning chestnuts pulled out of the fire when my old colleague Brian Hitchen was appointed editor; the *Sun*, that *enfant terrible* which everyone loves to hate, remains streets ahead of its rivals in understanding the name of the wicked game; and the poor old *Daily Mirror* has wearily slithered down the tubes, utterly crestfallen, a spent force. The fault, dear Brutus, is not in our stars, but in our dismally poor post-war state education service which produced three generations of tabloid-fodder during forty-five years of inferior and frequently politicized teaching. Mass-circulation popular tabloids, manufacturing their product in a way that fulfilled the requirements of their market, ceased to be newspapers at all. It was no longer necessary. Their readers could obtain whatever news they might want about current affairs from television. So they turned themselves into comics and scandal-sheets. Simple as that.

There was no televison in 1946 when I received my command to attend upon Arthur Christiansen, editor of the *Daily Express*. The *Express* was a broadsheet newspaper, with longer and wider columns than a tabloid, and this was attractive to journalists such as myself who wanted more elbow-room for words; the paper was a fine showcase for popular writers such as Chapman Pincher and Bernard Wicksteed, and that was the sort of display I wanted. But I also wanted something else as well. I wanted my own column, with my name on it, and the freedom to choose my own subjects.

This type of column, the name column, although it had been used sparingly in the past, was soon to become Fleet Street's great new selling-point, the newspaper version of the old Hollywood star system; but in 1946 we were still in the days of mostly *nom-de-plume* columns, outstanding among which had been the *Daily Express* William Hickey column written by Tom Driberg.

Driberg, a product of Lancing and Oxford, was a communist and a homosexual, and although this did not bother Lord Beaverbrook, who would not have cared much if the man had been a dangerous anarchist so long as he wrote a good column and pulled in the readers, it was an irritation to the less liberal-minded and more family-oriented Arthur Christiansen, who privately regarded Driberg with contempt. So when Driberg moved into party politics as a Labour candidate (a new career in which he went to the top and ultimately was ennobled as Lord Bradwell), Chris did not immediately attempt to replace him with a journalist of similar quality. The William Hickey column in the *Express* was an ailing feature when I received my summons from Chris, and I felt it must be possible that he was going to offer me this job.

As I waited in front of the lifts that evening in the Black Lubianka, as the new black vitrolite-and-glass *Express* building was known, a lift door opened and out came a number of *Daily Express* reporters, all of whom I knew. As if on a command, all their eyebrows raised.

'Hallo, old boy,' said one. 'Slumming?'

Going up in the lift to the editor's office I knew for sure that my visit would not go unmentioned in the Fleet Street pubs that night.

Chris poured me a gin and tonic and came straight down to business. It was not well looked upon for one newspaper openly to poach the staff of another, and such raids were usually conducted discreetly by news editors or features editors in the Press Club; but Chris was the sort of man who did not bother with subterfuge, and if he wanted a man to work for him he made the approach in person.

'You have been doing some smashing stuff recently, Noel,' he said, 'and although I know that you are a loyal *Mirror* man I think you would be even happier here on the *Daily Express*. My guess is that our way of going about things is possibly more in tune with the way you think.'

He went on to offer me twenty-eight guineas a week to join the *Express* as a special-writer. For about two seconds I hesitated. He had not offered me the column that I had hoped for. Observing my momentary hesitation, Chris gave me no chance to reply.

'I don't want you to answer now, Noel,' he said. 'What I want you to do is to think it over tonight. Think it over carefully. Then give me a ring tomorrow.'

Realizing that I had made myself look an indecisive idiot, I walked slowly back to the *Mirror*. On the noticeboard in the reporters' room was an envelope addressed to me. My mind elsewhere, I opened it without much interest. It contained a note from the managing editor:

Dear Noel, I am pleased to tell you that your salary has been raised to thirty-three guineas a week. Also I have just received a call from the chairman's secretary saying that Mr Bartholomew wants to see you in his office at midday tomorrow.

The ink of the signature was hardly dry. Fleet Street's bush telegraph was working as well as ever.

I put the letter in my pocket and went home early for a change.

Harry Guy Bartholomew, a self-made tyrant who affected a passion for the common man, was chairman of the *Daily Mirror*; commonly known as Bart, he was greatly feared.

By the time I walked along the corridor to Bart's office, just before noon on the following day, my mind was made up. I was leaving the *Daily Mirror*.

Doubtless, I said to myself, it would come as a shock to old Bart when he discovered that one of his reporters, a man whom he had just promoted to the princely wealth of thirty-three guineas a week, had merely dropped in to bid him goodbye.

It was probably a thing that had never happened to him before. A new

10

experience for him. But there is a first time for everything. I would be polite, of course, even generous in my approach to him, but I would be firm. I would not be swayed by his importunity. I would merely shake my head, with just a touch of sadness, and I would give him my inscrutable Clark Gable smile.

How sharper than a serpent's tooth, he would say, it is to have an ungrateful reporter.

Bart was standing behind his desk when I walked in, monarch of all he surveyed, scowling at me through his horn-rimmed spectacles. A casual observer might have hazarded a guess that he was about to fire me. But I divined what the trouble was. In appearance I represented so many of the characteristics he disliked. I guessed that he would have preferred it if I had marched in wearing a red tie and giving the clenched-fist salute. Poor old Bart. No longer young, a grandfatherly figure of sixty-eight years. No point in upsetting him. Best to show the friendly spirit, even if I was about to spoil his day. I switched on my Clark Gable smile.

I had perfected my Clark Gable smile during my time in Wardour Street when I had helped to prepare a campaign sheet for *Gone with the Wind*. I had even toyed with the idea of growing a Clark Gable toothbrush moustache to go with it. It was a world-wise smile. It necessitated keeping the right side of the face immobile while the left side of the face rose up to a point at which the lips were twisted to an angle of forty-five degrees and the left eye was nearly closed.

Bart had turned his back on me to pour himself a large Scotch, and when he turned again and stared at me he took a big swig at the Scotch and looked alarmed.

'What's the matter, Noel?' he asked, anxiously. 'You all right? Toothache?'

'No, no,' I said, straightening the face hurriedly. 'Absolutely first rate. Teeth in perfect working order.'

'Good,' said Bart, clearly relieved. 'Glad to hear that you are not in pain because the editor and I have decided to give you your own column in the *Daily Mirror*.'

I gulped. This changed everything. Then suddenly a horrifying thought occurred to me.

'*Not* gossip,' I said.

'Hot gossip?' said Bart, mishearing me. 'Well, I suppose you could use hot gossip if you wanted to. But I don't want a social gossip column. I don't like gossip.'

'Nor do I,' I said. 'Dislike it very much. Wouldn't write it.'

'Well that's all right then,' said Bart. 'Can't see why you suggested it in that case. What we want from you is light-hearted comment on the world in which we live today. It is a hard world for most of our readers, full of rationing and shortages, poor housing and not much to laugh about. Your job will be to cheer them up. Give them something to make them smile.

'Satire,' I said, musing happily.

'Don't try to be too bloody clever,' said Bart, tersely. 'Have a go at bureaucrats if you like, but keep it light. No party politics – we have experts to do that. Just look at a lousy world and see the funny side. You can spend money. Go and do the things that our readers would like to do if they could afford it. Got the idea?'

'Got it,' I said.

'Right then,' said Bart, pouring himself another large Scotch but still not offering me one. 'Hop off and see the editor about the technical details.'

As I walked back down the corridor I passed the open door of the managing editor's office, and he waved to me. 'Good morning, Noel,' he called. 'Good luck with the new column. Oh, and by the way – give my regards to Chris.'

So that – for the benefit of any youngster who is misguided enough to want to become a columnist – is how to do it. How to get into newpapers in the first place is a more difficult question. There are several ways of doing it. Mine is by no means the only one – in fact, there are some people who would say that mine is not even the ideal way to go about it.

I started as head printer of the *Economist*.

I am aware that if, having stated this simple fact, I were to move straight on to other matters, the reader might feel that I had left what is called a credibility gap. Probably the same applies to the fact that my second job in newspapers carried the description of staff poet. So I will hasten to furnish what the lawyers call fuller and better particulars.

I was a schoolboy at the time, a very young schoolboy. I had been sent to boarding school early because my brother Jimmy had been born when I was six years old, and my mother, who was unwell, could not cope with two young children in the house. A nanny was brought in, Nanny West, who was efficient, but who regarded me as a limb of Satan. I was an obnoxious little boy – an important qualification for a career in newspapers – and I made Nanny West's life such unadulterated hell that she delivered an ultimatum: either she went or I went – either I was packed off to boarding school double quick or she handed in her notice.

It had to be a Catholic school because my mother was a Catholic – Irish, née O'Donnell – and my father insisted that it had to be near enough for him to drive over on Saturday mornings and bring me home for every weekend. So off I went with my trunk and tuckbox, vowing revenge on Nanny West.

I settled in fairly well, hating it of course, and my first term was enlivened by a wonderful happening. They say you never forget your first girl, but without wishing to elaborate on that I can certainly vouch for the fact that you never forget your first job – especially if you happened to be about seven years old at the time.

One weekday morning in the spring of 1926 I was called out of class and told to go to the headmaster's study. I knew what it was about. I had been caught smoking in the lavatory the previous night. However, when I knocked on the rector's door and was summoned into his study the first sight that met my eyes was my father. For one awful moment I thought that I was being sacked for smoking. Then I noticed that although both my father and the rector were smiling, there was something more serious in the wind. Somebody was dead. Please God it was not my mother. Please God it was Nanny West.

'With the permission of the rector,' said my father, 'I am taking you to London for a while to help me. I have some work for you to do.' And so he had.

It was the year of the General Strike. Attempts by private coal owners to cut miners' wages had brought industry to a halt. The entire working class was out. Of course, I didn't know anything about all that, but if it meant that I was going to London I was all for it. The managerial middle class were trying to break the strike by turning their hands to unfamiliar skills, driving buses and manning machines, and they were bringing in their wives and children to help by performing any useful task of which they were capable.

I was capable of turning the handle of a Roneo duplicating machine, so that is how I became head printer of the *Economist* for the duration of the strike.

In fact, I was the only printer. The first issue of the Emergency Number, price 3d, dated 8 May 1926, was headed with the words: 'For the first time in eighty-four years "The Economist" is unable to publish its normal weekly issue.' The first copy of that issue that I rolled off was handed to me as a souvenir by Walter Layton, later Lord Layton but at that time editor of the *Economist*. I still have it, although it is crumpled from being stuffed into the back pocket of my short trousers. After all, in its way it is more than a mere souvenir – it is a sort of first edition.

Even though I was only a child I soon discovered what was going on. Apparently it was the *Daily Mail* that had caused the shut-down in Fleet Street, and I have always been grateful to the *Mail* for that. The editor of the *Mail* had sent down for typesetting a leading article that urged workers to defy their union officials and keep the wheels turning for King and Country. The article was set in type, but when the compositor who was handling the leader page – a print-union official – took a dab of the leader and read the words on a soggy galley, he blew the whistle. Everybody out. Except young Whitcomb – he was in.

Of the national dailies, only *The Times* continued to appear regularly throughout the emergency – our only serious competitor. Lord Astor brought in his chauffeur and eight gardeners from Hever Castle, and they rolled off copies of a single-sheet typewritten newspaper on a thing called a Multigraph machine; it was more sophisticated than our Roneo but we didn't need a chauffeur and eight gardeners to work our duplicator – all we needed was one dedicated head printer. We were equally feudal in our fashion, though; my great-great-great-grandfather worked briefly for the *Economist* when it was founded as a newspaper in the early 1840s, and my grandfather worked there for a time – and my father was working for the paper while I was doing the printing, so even at the age of seven I felt like an old retainer.

I loved the smell of the place. It was my first experience of the unmistakable smell of a newspaper office. In those days the *Economist* was produced editorially in Arundel Street, off the Strand, and printed – when I wasn't doing it – by St Clement's Press in Portugal Street, off Lincoln's Inn.

We were a tight little staff. There was Walter Layton, the boss, a dry, donnish academic; his brother, Gilbert Layton, tall, scholarly and withdrawn; Mr Flood, the advertising manager, a shambling Scot with a soup-strainer moustache and an amazing capacity for Scotch whisky (Mr Flood had no work to do during the strike because there was no advertising in the emergency editions but he could not bear to tear himself away from the field of battle); then there was Henry Bernard, my father's assistant and long-time friend – my second Christian name is Bernard, after him; and, of course, my father.

All the copy for the emergency issue was obtained on the telephone, news from industrial, banking, commercial and parliamentary sources; it was discussed and its importance analysed at morning conference, for which I made the tea; then it was written in précis form by individuals in the team; after which it was retyped on a sheet of special paper which was attached as a master-copy to the rotary drum of my Roneo. When all was ready I stood on a box beside the machine and turned the handle – and the mighty presses roared.

It was an old machine, stiff and creaky, heavy for a child to turn, but if necessary I would have gone on turning that handle until either the handle or my arm fell off – I was acutely aware of the importance of my job.

At lunchtime everybody went out for a drink and a snack and the offices were locked; this was necessary because in parts of London there was fighting in the streets, and striking workers were attacking buildings where they thought blacklegs were carrying on. They couldn't leave me alone in a locked office, so they had to take me with them, to a pub called the Devereux nearby. It was the first pub I had ever been in – another unforgettable smell – and I sat down in the corner with my sandwiches and lemonade, watching the scene with deep interest. From time to time people would come over and talk to me, to find out what I was doing there, and I would tell them proudly that I was working as printer for the *Economist*.

That was how I met several friends who were more important than I realized, including G.K. Chesterton; I can still hear old G.K.'s fruity voice calling over to my father, 'I say, Harold, may I ask your Head Printer to join me in a glass of . . . ah . . . lemonade?'

It was a few years later when G.K., remembering our time as comrades in arms, gave me my first so-called editorial job. I was still at school, so it was a holiday fill-in. Mr Chesterton was at that time publishing and editing a literary magazine called *G.K.'s Weekly*, and what he really needed was an office boy, due to the sudden and unexpected departure of the previous holder of this portfolio; but old G.K. was a kindly man, and he knew I had writing ambitions because we had discussed my future in the Devereux during the General Strike, so he solemnly described my temporary appointment as that of Staff Poet. Staff Lunatic would have been closer to the mark.

Walking down Rolls passage, off Fetter Lane, where the offices of *G.K.'s Weekly* were situated, G.K. – striding along in his flowing cloak and his wide-brimmed black hat, with his pince-nez perched on his nose – briefed me on my new duties: 'Apart from writing the occasional short verse, a villanelle perhaps or possibly a sonnet, which I shall consider for publication if it is suitable, you will look after the post, stamp the envelopes, make the tea, and ensure that our visitors are courteously welcomed.'

Among the visitors whom I welcomed were Mr George Bernard Shaw, who told me that he had once written music criticism for a

15

publication edited by my grandfather; the squeaky-voiced Mr H.G. Wells; and, of course, Mr Hilaire Belloc. So even though I later became involved with journalists of a lower brow, at least I started among the right sort of people.

Going back to the General Strike, it was during this period that I decided not to go into newspapers when I grew up, but to make a career in the theatre instead – and this was because, for the duration of the industrial crisis, I lived in what you might call high-class theatrical digs.

My father was staying round the corner from the office at the Savoy Hotel, in the Strand, which was always a favourite resort of Fleet Street journalists and which became my own home-from-home for many years. He was using his bedroom at the hotel as an office at night, and his sitting room was in similar use by Henry Bernard, so it was no place in which a child could sleep undisturbed because the telephone was ringing all the time. Hotels in central London were full to capacity because of the transport stoppage. So when my father was looking round for somewhere nearby for me to stay, he chanced to mention this problem to two of his friends, the Melville brothers, who were theatrical impresarios of the period and who owned the Lyceum Theatre just across the road in Wellington Street, off the Strand.

They were like the brothers Cheerible, Nicholas Nickleby's bene-factors, so when my father was talking about this difficulty they beamed in unison and said, 'My dear Harold, that is no problem at all. Send the boy across the road to stay with us at night, at the Lyceum. He will be well looked after. Florrie, in the circle bar, is a motherly soul with children of her own. She will look after the lad.'

So every night during the General Strike, after supper in the Savoy Grill or at Gatti's in the Strand – one of London's early Italian *trattorie* – my father would take me across the road and leave me at the stage door of the Lyceum in the care of my new guardians.

On the first night this happened, Florrie was sitting waiting for me in the little office of the stage-door keeper, Ginger. I took an immediate liking to both of them. Many of the regular staff of the theatre were living in, marooned by the strike, sleeping in their offices or work-rooms. As I sat sipping a cup of hot cocoa in Ginger's stage-door box, talking to some of my new good companions who had come down to make me feel welcome, I was wondering where my bedroom would be.

I soon found out. My bedroom was the stage. I can still remember the sensation of heavenly bliss I had when I was led by Florrie and Ginger on to that great stage and shown my bed. It was a single four-poster, trimmed with French draperies. It had been used in some recent

16

production set in the great days of Versailles, and it was known as 'the Dauphin's bed'.

The Lyceum stage was enormous, and the curtains were kept drawn back so that I looked out into the vast auditorium, black except for the dim lights over the exit doors; but it was not frightening – it was exciting. Florrie slept in her circle bar and, looking down, could keep an eye on me. I felt completely safe and so full of joy that I had difficulty in behaving in a dignified fashion suitable to my new rôle as a working lad and not jumping up and down with delight. The stage itself was another unmistakable smell, too. Proust wrote about the powerful way in which certain smells could summon up the past for him, and even today I cannot walk on to a theatre stage without glimpsing suddenly in my mind's eye the stage at the Lyceum with the Dauphin's bed in the middle.

With the connivance of my friend Ginger I quickly came to know every nook and cranny of that vast theatre, from the gods to the warren of passages and stone staircases that lay behind the pass-door to the stage. I loved the place. I hoped the General Strike would go on for ever.

In fact the strike lasted for only nine days and ended on a Wednesday. In normal times Thursday is press night for the *Economist*, but it was decided that a special 'Strike Ends' edition should be printed on that Wednesday night, although I think only a few copies were distributed; so I was kept busy at my organ-grinding act until late that night. Sandwiches and snacks for supper were sent over to Arundel Street by Mr Alan Barber, then landlord of the Devereux, and I was tired but happy when, at last, my father delivered me for the last time into the care of my friend Ginger at the Lyceum stage door.

I scampered straight up to the stage and was about to prepare for bed when Tommy Rees, the theatre's chief carpenter, entered from the wings. Tommy was a very tall man with pebble spectacles and a lugubrious expression, always gruff and laconic. (His son, young Tom, later became box-office manager at Drury Lane, and during his time there I saw every production at the Lane but never paid for a seat – I was family.)

'I want you to come along with me for a minute, boy,' growled Mr Rees. 'We have a surprise for you.'

He led me across the stage, past the stacked scenery and piled-up props and stage furniture, down to the world below where all the stage machinery was kept – including my favourite, the trap-door mechanism which enabled the demon king to appear on stage in a cloud of green smoke – and on down to the carpenters' shop, an enormous vault.

All my new friends were in there: the stage carpenters, the scenery painters, the electricians, the stage manager, the props man, and, of course, Florrie and Ginger. They all had smiles on their faces.

On the floor in the centre of the workshop stood a perfect reproduction in miniature of the Lyceum stage. It was five feet square and it was exact in every detail: at the front, the gilded proscenium, flanked by the rococo stage boxes with golden angels on their curves; the rich red velvet curtains with the royal coat of arms embroidered in gold; the orchestra pit; the footlights; everything, exactly as I knew it so well, all exquisitely craftsman-made.

One of the electricians pressed a switch at the side and the curtains opened to reveal the familiar room with three walls, the stage. It was set, with hand-painted scenery and lighting all in miniature, for the transformation scene in *Cinderella*: except that, in the very centre, was the Dauphin's bed.

'It's for you, son,' said Tommy Rees.

The expression on my face must have been so bewildered that they all burst out laughing.

One of the carpenters said, 'We didn't have anything else to do, you see, what with the strike and the theatre being dark, so we made it for you as a present – so that you'll remember.'

Remember! Oh, yes, I remember.

2

The origins of almost every book lie
hidden somewhere in the writer's past.

Peter Quennell, *The Pursuit of Happiness*

It seems strange to me that the stage-struck little lad who trotted around
in school cap and blazer was myself, the chrysalis version; although the
past comes ever sharper into focus as we grow older, it is the song that
becomes more familiar, not the singer: ourselves when young are always
strangers.

Away from school, which is now a blur of cricket and Virgil, my
childhood world centred round the attic at home where I kept my
theatre; here I lived in the holidays, planning and mounting stage
productions, even turning out programmes for them on an Adana
printing set that had been given to me for my birthday by Brendan
Bracken, another of my General Strike acquaintances.

My birthday is Christmas Day, hence my first name, and the
Christmas holidays were the most exciting because my father always
took us all to London for a week for shopping and shows and exhibitions.
We stayed at the usual canteen across the road from the Lyceum, and I
spent every permitted moment in the theatre. Ginger would wave me
through the stage door with a wink, but I had to watch my step because
the pantomime rehearsals were in progress and small boys are not
welcome in theatres at such times. Occasionally the producer, whom I
did not know, would spot me and shout, 'What's that boy doing here?
Get the little bugger out.' But by the time he looked round again I would
have vanished. I knew my way around. I was the phantom of the opera.

On the night of the dress rehearsal my father and mother and my
brother and I would take our places grandly in the red plush luxury of
Box A. The sound of a pit orchestra still makes my pulse beat faster. And
at the end, after the Harlequinade, came my big moment of the year.
George Jackley, a great panto comic of the time, would stage a tug-o'-
war with a giant Tom Smith's Christmas cracker, which would be
pulled apart with a thunderous explosion, sending a shower of ordinary-

sized Christmas crackers cascading over the stage. George would dive to pick up the first one and, as the limes swung round to illuminate Box A, he would toss it up into my eagerly waiting hands, shouting, 'One for Noel.'

It was heady stuff for a stage-struck child. After the final curtain we went backstage for drinks in George Jackley's dressing room, and my dear friends, Florrie and Ginger, would find a reason to slip in for a moment and say hallo. But it was Charlie Naughton, little Charlie of Naughton and Gold, who tried to put it into perspective for me. He brought me over a lemonade and, with the sad seriousness that is natural to all comedians, said: 'I'm going to tell you something, son. You're getting the wrong idea about all this. You think it's a life of wonderful fun, don't you? All glamorous nights and music and applause. Well, it bloody isn't. It's dingy digs in Manchester and trains on cold Sunday mornings and wondering where the next job is coming from when this show closes. You need to be the sort of man who likes a drop of stout and a plate of jellied eels and an afternoon's racing at Alexandra Park when there's no matinée. That's not the life for you, boy. Your dad is getting you educated, Latin and algebra and all that, so that you'll end up a newspaperman like him. I know that Florrie and Ginger think you'll be the next Sir Henry Irving, but it's not on the cards, son. Enjoy it for a lark but don't take it serious.'

Often in later years, when I was a newspaperman, I used to see Charlie Naughton and the other members of the comic team that became the Crazy Gang, but he never remembered me as the schoolboy to whom he had made this prophecy, and I never reminded him.

That night when Charlie gave me the lecture was also the last time I ever saw Florrie, whom I loved so dearly. I have no idea what happened to her. Yet, oddly enough, I can still see her again any time I wish, as she was then. There is a picture in the Courtauld Institute in London of a girl standing, as Florrie did, behind a bar: the big brown eyes, the fair hair in a fringe, the full, pale lips; the black velvet jacket, tight-waisted, with buttons down the front; the low-cut dress with a locket on a black velvet ribbon round her neck; the strong arms, the bangle, the bottles ranged in reach of her reddened hands along the bar: that is my Florrie to the life. Edouard Manet had painted a portrait of Florrie more than twenty years before she was born, behind a bar at the *Folies-Bergère*.

Home in those idyllic days was the Surrey village of Pirbright, truly rural then, where my father was captain of the village cricket team, chairman of the football club, a man of sporting tastes; he was a good shot, a fair horseman, a *bon viveur* whose friends were mostly bohemians, and his passion was horse racing. Among the colourful miscellany of journalists, struggling artists, hard-up writers and resting actors who came to stay with us at weekends, I liked the racing people best, and of these my favourite was Mr Edgar Wallace, formerly a racing writer on the London evening *Star* but by that time a well-known novelist. I liked Mr Wallace best because he was instrumental in my going racing for the first time.

'Let the boy learn a few bad habits, Harold,' he said to my father. 'Take him to Ascot with us.'

We saw a horse called Brown Jack win that afternoon, a horse that became famous; but I assume that neither my father nor Edgar Wallace backed it, because it was a couple of silent and gloomy sporting men who brought the boy home with them. I now know the feeling well.

Mr Wallace – who bet heavily and had been known to lose £50,000 at a meeting – said he would have to knock out a book quickly to get some of his money back; my mother provided a service of hot, weak, sweet tea to his room, and within a couple of days he had written a novel. I never knew which of his novels that was – he wrote about 150 – but a few days later he sent me a copy of one of his earlier racing books, *Grey Timothy*, and I put it in pride of place on the long bookshelf in my attic, ahead of William Blake, John Donne, Pepys, Milton and Montaigne, Hazlitt and Swift, Descartes and Plato, Lamb, Victor Hugo, Dickens, Conrad and Surtees, Defoe, Steele and Addison.

This selection of books was not there because I had chosen them, indeed it took me many years to read them later, but they were my prized possessions because they had belonged to my grandfather, Horace Whitcomb, and my father had given them to me. Horace was my boyhood hero, more admirable even than Jack Hobbs or Herbert Sutcliffe; he had died three years before I was born, but I knew him intimately and felt a deep affinity. The debris of his life was in my attic.

He was a journalist, of course, and life had not always treated him gently or even justly, but he was a man of principle; a Victorian eccentric of scholarly bent, as was the fashion among serious news-papermen of his time, he scorned hypocrisy and stood for no nonsense from anyone; that was what I loved about Horace, he was upright and pig-headed. When Horace saw a villain he went for him in print, publish and be damned, and to hell with the disasters that followed.

His first villain was Frank Harris, who was his editor at the time. Harris owned and edited the *Saturday Review*, at the period when its contributors – apart from Horace Whitcomb, who wrote a weekly City article – included George Bernard Shaw, H.G. Wells, Max Beerbohm,

Aubrey Beardsley, Arnold Bennett and Oscar Wilde; but although Frank Harris was a talented man he lived a life of such feckless extravagance that he was always in money difficulties. This led him into an arcane association with a wheeler-dealer called Ernest Terah Hooley, who dealt flamboyantly in millions and entertained with astounding lavishness.

Companies promoted by Hooley, some of them obvious duds, began to receive favourable mention in the *Saturday Review*. Horace bristled. He went to see Frank Harris and called him a crook.

'Put that in writing if you dare,' said Harris, with menace.

So that was what old Horace did. He went to the trouble of starting a new publication specifically for the purpose of putting it in writing. He took offices at Burleigh Street, Strand, and on 12 September 1896 the first issue of the *New Saturday* was published from that address. The first printing sold out on the day of publication, and not only because it contained a blistering article by old Horace in which he tore the seven veils of villainy one by one from Frank Harris: it was an exceptionally good literary and arts magazine as well; even Bernard Shaw, typically, wrote and asked Horace for a free copy.

Horace had a triumph on his hands. A flawed triumph. Because in his leading article, signed, he fulfilled a dangerous promise. 'A few months ago,' wrote Horace, 'I should have thought Mr Frank Harris the last person in the world to put himself in the pay of notorious company-promoters.' He went on to give chapter and verse of instances in which Frank Harris and his malign paymaster, Ernest Terah Hooley, had attempted to defraud the public.

It was a celebrated libel case. Against the evidence, the jury awarded ferocious damages against Horace. A short time later Frank Harris was unmasked as a swindler and a blackmailer, and Ernest Terah Hooley was sent to gaol for fraud; too late for Horace, because both men were bankrupt by that time. And it did not teach him the lesson that all journalists should learn, that truth is beautiful but seldom a safe defence.

When Ernest Terah Hooley came out of prison he went straight to see Horatio Bottomley, visiting that colourful man in the blue and gold drawing room of his opulently furnished private suite above his London offices. Together they cooked up a clever publishing scheme. They registered a company called John Bull Ltd. Armed with a prospectus that he himself had written, Bottomley called on the Odhams bothers, then small printers in Covent Garden, and persuaded them to print *John Bull* and to back it with £50,000 of their own money.

It was a gold mine. With Horatio Bottomley's picture regularly on the front page, together with tempting details of competitions with gigantic cash prizes, the John Bull magazine was an instant money-spinner. The trouble was that it was rooted in fraud. Not only were the competitions rigged, but Bottomley used the publication in many other smart but bogus ways to milk the public of stupendous sums in small savings.

Horace Whitcomb could not bear to watch it. So he used another of his literary weeklies to expose Bottomley as a charlatan, a mountebank, a confidence trickster and a criminal. In which public-spirited enterprise his motives were faultless, his facts accurate, and his intentions beyond reproach; but his timing, which is the essence of all journalism, was slightly awry. Bottomley was the public hero of the hour. When he sued Horace, conducting his own case with spellbinding oratory, and won exemplary damages, the crowds outside the court cheered their conquering hero.

There was little compensation for the cheering crowds when, soon afterwards, they found that they had lost their savings and Bottomley was sent to gaol for fraud, having become known as 'the greatest crook in England': no compensation for Horace, either, because Bottomley, like Frank Harris and Ernest Terah Hooley before him, was bankrupt. It is morally satisfying to be proved right, but in the case of poor old Horace it was always cripplingly expensive.

His family loved him. He had ten children and the family home was in Hertfordshire. All his seven daughters were christened with the name of one of his publications as a second given name. Most of my seven aunts were diffident about revealing this fact, especially Aunt Madeleine whose middle name was *Hawk*; the exception was my aunt Connie – Constance Londoner Whitcomb – who was born in 1892, the year in which Horace launched *The Londoner*. He published it from offices at 1 Norfolk Street, Strand, and it carried a front-page banner that was typical of its editor's indomitable optimism: NOT OF AN AGE, BUT FOR ALL TIME. Ben Jonson's tribute was true of the Sweet Swan of Avon, but inappropriate for *The Londoner*, even though it was Horace's favourite among the many titles he invented. Several magazines have been launched with the same title during the near-century since Horace first sent it into the London streets in 1892. One of them was published by Michael Heseltine's Haymarket publishing house, and more recently I read with wry amusement that Robert Maxwell, following the spectacular failure of his *London Daily News*, had announced his intention to publish an evening paper called *The Londoner*. I am glad that Horace was not alive to read that. It would only have caused a lot more trouble.

Maxwell is not the sort of man who would have been admired by Horace. Horace would surely have written about him.

Horace died as he had lived, engaging in controversy. He had been knocked down in the Strand by a motor car. Quite apart from his dislike of motor cars as alternatives to his beloved horses, he saw them as a potential danger which, unless brought under strict control by law, would kill and maim thousands of citizens in years to come. So, lying in bed in his London flat in Doughty Street – just a few doors away from the house that had been the home of his father's old parliamentary reporter friend, Charles Dickens – Horace was preparing an article attacking the Horseless Carriage Company. He was very ill, but would not give in.

'Harold,' he called to my father one day. 'Harold! Go and bring me up a bottle of Bass, there's a dear fellow, and bring my typewriter and the file on those blasted horseless people.'

All of which errands my father hastened to perform. But when he returned to the bedroom with the bottle of Bass and the typewriter and the file, the old knight in shining armour was dead.

One of my aunts, Lydia, realizing that there would be little money left to distribute among the family, tried to persuade my father to take legal action for damages against the Horseless Carriage Company, one of whose vehicles had brought the old man low. But my father was not a litigious man. He had seen too much of it. 'Death settles all bets,' he said, leaving what money there was to be shared among his sisters, and taking for himself only Horace's Yost typewriter, a few dozen books from the old man's library, and a Gladstone bag that Horace had commended to his especial care.

These, then, were the treasures that my father passed on to me, to furnish the green-room of my attic theatre.

The Gladstone bag had probably not been opened for more than a decade when I first sorted through its puzzling contents: a dozen bunches of keys, some enormous and very old; handwritten letters from Bernard Shaw, opposing Horace's decision never to accept free first-night theatre tickets for his reviewers; a gold cigarette-case engraved inside with a message of gratitude from Ellen Terry; a soft leather purse with a drawstring top containing Roman coins; a packet of correspondence concerning the disputed ownership of a racehorse; a copy, signed affectionately to my father, of a translation Horace had made of the odes of his namesake, Horace, the Roman poet and satirist; and a long cylinder made of tin containing a scroll that was part vellum and part parchment.

24

It was this last item that captured my particular attention. It must have been Horace's secret, the reason why the old satirist saw himself as a natural protector of the interests of the common man, the source of his oddly autocratic *noblesse oblige* approach to his craft as writer and publisher: it was his family tree.

In the tin with the scroll was a sheaf of notes, handwritten in black in Horace's small, neat, square monkish script, reminiscent of a mediaeval psalter, mostly about his recent kinsmen. But it was not the details of these latter forbears, mostly writers, soldiers and lawyers in the county of Hertfordshire, and, earlier, wine merchants in Gloucestershire, that I found interesting; it was the provenance indicated in more distant times that captivated me.

At the head of his tree was Pharamus de Wydecombe, Lord of Wydecombe and Ashe in the parish of Martock. According to the Domesday survey, the township of Martock, in what later became the county of Somerset, was held in chief of William the Conqueror by Eustace, Count of Bolonia (Boulogne); Eustace, having married Adela, William the Conqueror's daughter, was therefore King William's son-in-law; when Eustace died, his widow Adela conveyed the Martock inheritance to their son, Stephen, Count of Blois, who later became king of England. Upon Stephen's death, the inheritance went to his son, William, Count of Bolonia, and when this William died it passed to his son, Pharamus, who became known as Pharamus de Wydecombe.

A note in an earlier hand, not Horace's, claimed that the un-differenced arms of the Wydecombes of Wydecombe in Martock had been proved by John Whitcomb at the Visitation of Salop in 1623, and later by Richard Whitcomb, barrister at law, in 1818.

Whether this shaky evidence of noble descent was merely the secret solace of a beleaguered Victorian journalist, savoured as a consolation when he was licking the financial wounds inflicted by shysters of common blood, I do not know. All I know is that, as a boy playing in my attic, I saw my ancestors as crusaders in the age of chivalry, accoutred in chainmail, their horses caparisoned with plumes, some wearing spiky crowns perched above their thin, Plantagenet faces, and all those faces looking like the daguerreotype portrait of Horace that I had drawing-pinned to the bare wooden rafter above the books.

There is no doubt that this slightly ludicrous secret, which I shared with Horace and with nobody else until this moment, coloured my early attitude towards the world and all the people in it: in a chastened manner I felt seigneurial. Vestiges of this subliminal air of natural superiority have irritated, sometimes infuriated, people around me throughout my life, including all my employers; they have seen so little apparent reason for it; even my wife and daughter have from time to time rebuked me sternly, sometimes in scathing terms similar to those used by the children of Mrs Wentworth-Brewster in Noël Coward's Piccola Marina lyric: 'Who d'you think you are? Nobody can afford to be so lahdy-bloody-da.' But then, of course, they never knew about Pharamus. Nobody knew but me.

The very fact that I can remember those details would make a telling revelation for a psychologist, because I have few of Horace's documents to consult; most of them, including nearly all the bound volumes of the publications he edited, were given by my mother to the Red Cross during the war for paper salvage: much good they must have been, but I can recall my mother's answer to my horrified remonstration. She made it quietly clear that by her gesture of selfless patriotism and generosity she had gone far towards winning the war single-handed; a brand of reasoning that must have sounded puzzling in our Surrey village, but would have been instantly recognizable in Dublin.

In the slanting sunlight of one hot August evening when I was rising seventeen, I was playing tennis with my father, knocking him all over the court because I was good at the game and very fast, when he dropped dead.

That scene, that dreadful scene, is still before my eyes, and I try not to remember it because, even after all these years, it still hurts. The world of my childhood died that evening, too.

After the funeral, my uncle Ernest took me aside. He was senior partner of his own firm of solicitors in the City, and he looked a dry old stick, but he must have been something of a Lothario in his time because he had eloped with my aunt Ethel when she was ostensibly happily married to a senior civil servant, a sort of Sir Humphrey type, and this was a juicy morsel of gossip in its day.

'I must tell you,' said Ernest, coldly, 'that your father's estate will not amount to much. I understand from documents in my keeping that it was his intention that you and your brother would go up to Oxford in due course of time. This will not now be possible.'

'Never mind,' I said, too downcast in misery to care.

Ernest went on: 'You were often in your father's company in London, so I wondered if you knew whether he had any . . . er . . . particular extravagance.'

I knew what he meant. My anger stung me to a rude reply. 'If you mean was he thinking of eloping with anyone, the answer is no,' I said. 'No fast women – only slow horses.'

26

As things turned out we were by no means badly off financially. My mother was able to manage easily, and my brother and I received small legacies, probably enough to buy a house apiece had we been so minded; which neither of us was.

I went looking for a job, but was too proud to ask my father's friends for help. The average pay on offer for a lad with no qualifications apart from first-class honours in matriculation was thirty shillings a week: this I regarded as frivolous. However, luck came my way and I was soon taken on by an encyclopaedia company with offices in the Strand. They paid me the sensational sum of £7 a week, so I should have known that there was a catch in it. The encyclopaedias contained a great deal of out-of-date information, and were sold in sets of twelve for a high price by door-to-door salesman, mostly natural con-men. The main sales-pitch was that every lucky buyer would receive not only a lifetime's reading entertainment but also a passport to a new and highly educated style of life, because every purchaser had the right to use our research bureau, free, for life; from the moment the purchaser signed the contract, he or she could send for expert information on any subject, no matter how abstruse, and our research bureau would supply that information in simple words of dazzling scholarship.

I was the research bureau. That was why I was getting £7 a week. Some of the questions were a delight to me, and I spread myself in answers to such questions as 'What did Leonardo da Vinci do apart from painting?' or 'What is the meaning of T.S. Eliot's poem *The Waste Land*?' But when Uncle Ernest heard what I was doing he put his foot down. 'You must leave immediately,' he said. 'Do not go back to that office. I shall seek alternative employment for you. Perhaps,' he went on gloomily, 'I may even decide to offer you a post in my office.'

'Most kind,' I said, viewing the prospect with equal gloom, 'but I do not think I am cut out for the law.'

His face brightened. 'Doubtless you are right,' he said. 'It is a profession that demands qualities for which you show little aptitude. I shall speak to some friends of mine and see what can be done.'

One of his friends was a director of Lloyds Bank, and as a result of a discussion between the two men I was summoned to Lombard Street for an interview. Predictably I was told that I was a suitable applicant and that I would hear from the bank in due course about my new appointment.

Before returning home I went to my father's tailor in Savile Row and ordered a blue pinstripe suit with a double-breasted waistcoat on which I could hang a slim gold chain; then I went to Lobb to order a pair of black shoes; then to Lock for a brown soft felt hat with a curled brim, at that time known as 'The Newmarket'; finally to Swaine and Adeney in Piccadilly where I selected a snakewood walking stick with a gold top. My reasoning was that if I was going to settle for a career as something in the City, I might as well dress for the part; it did not cross my mind that the part I was dressing for was closer to Shaftesbury Avenue than Lombard Street.

However, when my papers came through from the bank I discovered that I was not being called upon to start my career in the City; to my chagrin, I was being posted to the Woking branch, the nearest branch to where we lived. I suspected that this was my uncle Ernest's doing, probably on the grounds that although the City is a full square mile it was too small an area to contain both him and me.

I had a fortnight to spare before I was due to report for duty, and my mother suggested that I should have my eyes tested because I spent so much time reading. So I went to an eye-man in Wimpole Street and he told me that although I had perfect vision in my right eye, there was a slight astigmatism in my left eye which needed correction, and for this purpose he gave me a prescription for an eyeglass.

I was pleased about that because my favourite character in fiction at the time was P.G. Wodehouse's Psmith – *Psmith Journalist, Psmith in the City* – my *alter ego*, an elegant young *flâneur* who sported an eyeglass and had the engaging habit of always calling his boss 'comrade'. I was still practising wearing my eyeglass when I reported to the manager on my first morning at the bank.

The manager was a Mr Nicholls – a tall, thin man with a mournful expression who, if he had been wearing a black top hat, would have looked the very picture of an undertaker; he was bald on top, with sidepieces of hair above his ears, and his solemn expression gave him a disapproving air.

Breezing into his office with the amiable intention of putting him at his ease from the start, I placed my hat and walking stick on a side table and beamed at him warmly through my eyeglass. 'Comrade Nicholls,' I said, 'what a delight it is for me to find myself joining the happy team of toilers under your enlightened command.' This was, I think, a direct quote from Psmith. I had rehearsed it.

The manager showed no sign of reciprocating the warmth of my greeting. 'Sit down, Whitcomb,' he said, coldly.

He began with a lecture on the deportment and conduct required of every member of the bank's staff: both on and off duty the attitude towards all customers should lean towards the deferential, and familiarity of any kind was to be deplored; then he outlined my duties, which sounded simple enough, and finally he added a codicil. 'There is one further matter to which I must refer,' he said, 'and it is most important because it is a question affecting the discipline of the bank. You must listen to me carefully.'

Fixing my eyeglass more firmly in my eye and attempting an expression of rooted attention, I gave him the stage: 'Say on, Comrade Nicholls,' I said. 'You have our most attentive ear.'

'You must remember, Whitcomb, and I insist on this, that we are not in Soviet Russia. We are in Woking. The word "comrade" as a greeting is not in common use here. I shall not bring up the question of your politics because they are, to some extent, a matter for your own conscience.'

'Very right and proper,' I nodded. 'Secret ballot and all that. All the same I do not mind telling you, as my new colleague and superior, that I am chairman of our village branch of the Junior Imperial League. True blue, you know, true blue – up the Conservatives, what?'

'I am relieved to hear it,' he said, drily. 'That is an even greater reason why you should understand that you must address my rank with appropriate respect. I shall not tolerate your calling me comrade, do you understand that? You will call me either Mr Nicholls or sir.'

'Your wish is my command, dear old Sir Nicholls,' I agreed, far too cheekily but still apeing Psmith.

To my surprise, I enjoyed working at the bank; I learnt about hitherto obscure subjects such as money management, investment, how to read a balance sheet and how to add up figures at a glance, all of which were useful to me in later life. The rest of the staff were kindly and helpful to the new junior, regarding me as a sort of mascot rather than a colleague, because my habit of arriving for work wearing a clove carnation and carrying a copy of the *Sporting Life* was considered perilously provocative. Nobody thought I would last. The manager watched me like a hawk, never losing a faint suspicion that, in spite of the eyeglass and the gold-topped cane, I might be a tool of the Kremlin in disguise.

Life marked time pleasantly enough, and although I accepted the probability that I was never likely to become one of the world's banking moguls, I had no idea what else might happen to me; apart from the fact that, sure as hell, we would all soon be required to take part in a war.

Most journalists' children grow up politically aware and reasonably well primed in current affairs, if only because of the torrent of newspapers and periodicals that constantly floods the house, and for several years past there had been no doubt in the mind of anyone in our family that another war with Germany was inevitable: the only question was when.

I had done some token OTC training at school, and had learned rifle and revolver shooting with my father at Bisley, but I realized that this was not enough to keep me out of the cookhouse when the whistle blew, so I decided to join the territorials.

Having a vague fancy for a cavalry regiment, but knowing nothing about the army, I consulted a neighbour with whom my father had been friendly. Colonel Reggie Crosse-Kelly was an old China hand. He had been there during the Boxer Rising but had returned to serve out his days as a desk-bound Whitehall Warrior at the War Office. He put me straight briskly. No point in trying for a cavalry regiment, he said, because there would be no horses in the coming war, only tanks, aircraft and guns. Being an old artilleryman he offered to recommend me for acceptance into the HAC, the Honourable Artillery Company.

Gratefully I accepted, and within a few weeks I was inducted into the regiment at Armoury House in London. It was ironic that this favour turned out to have such a completely unexpected effect. On the evening of the day that I had been for the first time to Armoury House, I called on Colonel Crosse-Kelly to thank him for his kindness. It was a summer's evening, and we walked round his garden, chatting about my future as a soldier.

In Reggie's garden was an enormous wooden hut, probably a hundred feet long and thirty feet wide, and he led me towards it with a happy smile on his face. He intended to give me a surprise and this, indeed, he did. Inside the hut I looked round with astonishment. It was a theatre. I had heard in the way of gossip that old Reggie regarded himself as a theatrical impresario *manqué*, and that he ran some sort of amateur theatricals, but this was a revelation. It was a beautiful little theatre.

I was not the only one taken by surprise that evening. The colonel was amazed to find that this young lad from a neighbouring house knew exactly how his theatre worked, technically. When he quizzed me about how I had come by this unexpected knowledge, I told him diffidently about the Lyceum and about my theatre in the attic, and he laughed out loud with pleasure. He had found a candidate for the job that nobody else among his company of amateurs was skilled to do: a ready-made technical assistant.

From that evening on I re-entered the world I loved best, the world with three walls. Reggie's company of amateur strolling players was known as The White Rabbits, and the theatre was called The Hutch. That became my new home. I swept the auditorium, emptied the

30

ashtrays, advised on dialogue rewrites, made changes in the lighting, printed programmes, checked the props, assisted the stage manager, stood in as prompter, wrote a play and at last became an actor. I was back among the dressing rooms, sniffing the familiar Leichner Nine and Five, peering through a crack in the tabs to watch the audience stream in, calling out 'Act One – beginners, please!', changing hastily into white ducks and striped blazer before bounding on through the French windows in the backdrop.

The HAC parades at Armoury House came and went, but the newest recruit was always absent. He was busy with rehearsals of a more frivolous type. Sometimes I imagine that somebody in the regiment must have remarked, 'Didn't we sign up a lad called Whitcomb? I wonder what happened to him.' What happened to him was that he was having the time of his life.

The White Rabbits, all friends of the colonel, became my beloved friends. They could hardly have been more different from my father's sporting and bohemian circle. They were members of the upright middle class, professional consultants or company directors, and their sons, fledgling barristers and trainee stockbrokers, together with their débutante daughters, with all of whom I fell in love, individually and collectively. I had moved into the world of Betjeman's Joan Hunter-Dunne.

We all went everywhere together, inseparable friends, theatricals all. We went to Ascot and to Lord's. We went dancing at Bramley Golf Club and night-clubbing at the Ace of Spades on the Kingston by-pass or the Pantiles in Bagshot. We went to Sandhurst for the June ball, where Reggie's son, Dick, was being made ready to join the Royal Inniskilling Dragoons. We went to Maidenhead and Henley for elegant evening parties at houses that had lawns running down to the river (one of which I later owned). 'By roads "not adopted", by woodlanded ways, we drove to the club in the late summer haze, into nine-o'clock Camberley, heavy with bells and mushroomy, pinewoody, evergreen smells.' In Rover and Bentley, Lagonda and Alvis, we crunched over a lot of private gravel. And the war was coming closer every sunset.

Hitler had marched on Vienna. Neville Chamberlain had returned from Munich with his umbrella and his piece of paper. Young men of my age were leaving their jobs and joining up. I saw that my career in banking was drawing peacefully towards its close. But it was an odd incident that precipitated my departure.

Throughout my life I have been accustomed to have an occasional bet on a horse, ever since the afternoon at Ascot when I had a shilling on

Brown Jack. One of our customers at the bank was a Mr Wally Enticknap, a prosperous, hail-fellow-well-met type of man who was the local bookmaker. Before joining the bank I had patronized the famous Douglas Stewart ('Duggie Never Owes'), but as Mr Enticknap always gave me a jolly wave when he came in, I transferred my custom to him.

Of course I never made out a cheque to him for my losings at the end of the month, because that would have been asking for trouble; backing horses was, for obvious reasons, strongly discouraged among his staff by Mr Nicholls, the manager. So, when I received my bill from Wally Enticknap, I would wait until I saw him in the bar of the nearby Albion Hotel in Woking, and then quietly pay him in cash. Usually he would cheerily ask me what I was going to have to drink; I was a relatively small client, but of the sort that no sensible bookmaker wishes to offend.

One evening Wally and I were sitting at a table in the bar with a couple of local racehorse owners, one of whom had put up a bottle of champagne. In walked Mr Nicholls, the manager. When he saw me sitting there drinking champagne with three well-to-do members of the local racing crowd, all customers of the bank, I knew the game was up: I was shooting down almost every one of the bank's most sacred rules with one barrel.

That night I wrote a courteous note of resignation from the bank, explaining that I had decided to join the army. I had the note in my pocket next morning when, as expected, I heard a thunderous call from Mr Nicholls commanding me to attend upon him in his office.

Collecting my hat and walking stick in readiness, I strolled through the open door into the manager's office. Mr Nicholls sat at his desk, glaring at me balefully. I handed him the envelope. Impatiently he tore it open and read the note. Then he looked up at me with a new expression on his face.

It was the first time I had ever seen him smile.

3

Everybody has two businesses –
their own business and film business.

Sam Goldwyn

Casting aside my eyeglass for ever, and putting on a pair of grey flannels and an old tweed coat, I took a taxi to the recruiting office in Guildford and joined up. I had expected that they might ask questions about why I had skipped training with the HAC, but they were too busy. They just gave me a medical, passed me Al, and accepted me for the Royal Artillery: Gunner Whitcomb, N, 941075. I was posted to the 3rd Field Training Regiment at Fort Gomer, Gosport, and assigned to a squad called the POs, Potential Officers.

Lads of my age used to do an imitation of Charles Laughton as Captain Bligh of the Bounty: 'Mr Christian, Mr Christian, a captain is a captain and a seaman is a seaman but a midshipman is the lowest form of life in the British navy.' We POs were the lowest form of life in the British army. We did the usual month of square-bashing in denim overalls, and the disciplined life with few comforts came as a hardship to some of the working-class boys, but it was no shock to those of us who had been at boarding schools. I was put on to specialist courses such as ballistics and map-reading, and began to enjoy the simple life of a soldier.

We were a mixed bag of all-sorts. One of the lads in our battery kept a room permanently at the Queen's Hotel in Portsmouth, just across the water on the ferry, for the use of his family when they came to see him; he allowed a few of us to keep our dinner-jacket suits in his wardrobe, and on Saturday evenings when we had a pass we would make our way there and change into black ties, and dine in the restaurant. It was against the rules, because Other Ranks were supposed to wear battle-dress at all times outside the fort, but we took the risk because it cheered us up. Another youngster in our circle was a member of the Costain family, who built Dolphin Square and other London landmarks, and he had an SS Jaguar car in which he used to drive us to the Gosport ferry.

It was on one of these jaunts, sitting back after dinner with a cigar and a glass of claret, that I had my idea. 'What we ought to do,' I said, 'is start a regimental magazine. We could prepare it in the evenings in the hut. Whiteaway could write about his travels in Europe. Jimmy Mutton could do illustrations. We would have a theatre column and a film feature, an arts page and a letters section. The general features about army life at the fort would be mostly satirical, of course. It would give us an added interest. It might even cause a stir.'

The plan was accepted with enthusiasm. I was elected as editor because they assumed that I knew how to do that job. We decided to call it *The Rangefinder*, a title which carried satirical implications because the rangefinders we were using in training were notoriously out of date, some said Crimean issue.

It was a clandestine operation; everyone in the hut was sworn to secrecy; we wanted it to come as a surprise. In that objective, if in nothing else, we were explosively successful.

On the evening of the day when the first issue of *The Rangefinder* came hot off the presses, Sergeant Frost came striding into our hut and marched me off to the guardroom. I was under arrest.

'Shades of old Horace,' I said to myself as I stood there, waiting to be charged.

Sergeant Frost was an old sweat who was in charge of our training, and he had little time for literary soldiers: 'Fuckin' editors,' he said, scornfully. 'I'm not 'aving 'orrible men like that in my mob.'

Most of the articles in the magazine were light, with an arts and literary flavour, but one was a satirical survey of the way in which the Army General Staff in Whitehall were conducting what was then being called 'the phoney war'.

'Fuckin' near 'igh treason,' said Sergeant Frost, moodily. 'You're for the 'igh jump, son. Court martial, I shouldn't wonder.'

There have been several moments in my life when the famous words from old film serials, 'With one mighty leap, Jack was free', have been apposite. This was one.

For several nights we had been doing exercises on Portsdown Hill in sub-zero temperatures, and I had what I thought was a bad cold. But next morning it was clear that I was ill. I was shifted to the hospital hut with a soaring temperature and a diagnosis of pneumonia. I felt awful, but relieved. They could not, I argued to myself, shoot a sick editor at dawn.

The officer on hospital-hut inspection duty was a young subaltern called John Wills, reputed to be a member of the tobacco family, and when he came round visiting the beds I lay doggo, pretending to be asleep: the last thing I wanted was discussion. He stood at the end of my bed, examining my temperature chart.

'Pretty high temperature, this one,' he said to the gunner medical orderly.

'Yessir. Very 'ot man, this.'

'Isn't this the magazine chap?'

'Yessir.'

'Chap who wrote that bloody article?'

'Yessir. He may not live, sir.'

I nearly sat up on hearing that, but the young officer cheered up considerably: 'What bad luck,' he said. 'Still, probably all for the best. God alone knows what would happen to him otherwise. Probably jankers for life.'

My brain was sluggish but one thing was clear. I had to get away from the fort. What would Beau Geste have done?

When the orderly came round taking temperatures that evening, I was still pretending to be asleep; he stuck the thermometer under my tongue and moved on to the next bed.

I had a cigarette lighter under the bedclothes. Surreptitiously I took the thermometer out of my mouth, played the lighter-flame over it for a few seconds, then stuck it back in my mouth. The orderly wandered back and removed it, holding it up to the light to get a reading.

'Christ almighty!' he shouted. 'Get an ambulance!'

They took me to Haslar, a nearby naval hospital, and from the moment I arrived there I became, for technical reasons, the responsibility of the Royal Navy. After taking X-rays they discovered that I had a tubercular spot on my left lung: so I spent the next year in sanatoria until I was finally invalided out of the army with a hundred-per-cent disability pension. An ignominious end.

As a parting gift the army gave me a silver-coloured metal badge to wear in the lapel of my civilian suit, to show that I had served, however ineffectively. One of these badges, which were circular and about the size of a blazer-button, was issued to all men of call-up age who had been in the services, to protect them from being scorned as cowards who were dodging the column; it was a talisman to ward off old ladies brandishing umbrellas, and prevent the scenes that had occurred during the previous war when young men in civilian clothes had been attacked in the streets and jingoists thrust white feathers into their hands. I wore my badge as a wordless explanation, but felt shamefaced about it – embarrassed to be sidelined from the war. However, there was nothing I could do about it. Despite my long illness I felt reasonably well, and obviously had to find some work to do. In London there was an appointments board, set up to help ex-servicemen find useful employment, so off I went. The office was in Whitehall, and a crowd was waiting when I arrived: they gave me a chit to come back for an interview at four o'clock; it looked a dismal place.

It was only mid-morning, so I strolled towards the Strand, and met by chance a man of about my own age with whom I used to play tennis at Stoney Castle, the summer camp of the Blues. He was now in uniform and was on his way to Buck's Club in Clifford Street, so he asked me along for a drink.

Most of the men at the bar were in uniform, but a few were in civilian clothes like myself, and nearly everyone was talking about getting jobs. I said that this was what I was up to, and mentioned the appointments board, which produced a chorus of groans.

'Absolutely hopeless, my dear fellow,' said one of the civilians. 'Waste of time. What you do is write to individual chaps who are in a position to hand out jobs – brasshats, that sort of chap. Remind them that you met them somewhere – not that you ever did, but they won't remember – and ask if there is anything going. Some of them will see you, and pass you on to somebody else. That's the way to start.'

In the club cloakroom, where I went to collect my hat and stick, I noticed that all the other pegs held either service caps with swagger canes or bowler hats and umbrellas. Realizing that I needed to make a subtle readjustment to my image, I walked round the corner to Bond Street and went into Herbert Johnson, the hatters.

'You want a hard hat, sir,' said Mr Warburton, who later served me with hats for many years. 'What we call a Coke.'

I left the shop wearing the bowler hat that Mr Warburton had perched at a forward angle over my eyes, insisting that I must always wear it like that; as I walked round the corner from Bond Street to Piccadilly I was practically groping my way along, and was thinking that what I needed with this hat was a white stick and a dog rather than an umbrella; but I found my way to Swaine and Adeney and purchased the regulation silk brolly, tightly rolled, with a gold band below the handle.

My problem now was that I was carrying a large hatbox containing my brown felt, plus an umbrella and a walking stick, and I needed somewhere to park this excess baggage. So I walked briskly up Piccadilly to the Ritz and was depositing my impedimenta with the cloakroom attendant when a hand clapped me on the shoulder.

'Noel, dear old boy,' said a familiar voice. 'Come and have a drink.'

Evelyn Waugh said that most of the useful information he had discovered when he was a journalist came casually from conversation in a hotel bar; he said that so much of one's help comes in this way that he wondered how teetotallers ever get about at all. That was certainly my experience.

The man who had clapped me on the shoulder was Jimmy Hutchison, a friend from my Betjeman period of party-going on the river. His father-in-law was a man called George Peake, whose family had been founders of the Prudential Assurance Company, and I used occasionally to play gin rummy with old George at his house near Weybridge. Just the sort of man who might now be in a position to hand out jobs. So, over a glass of champagne, I outlined my mission to Jimmy.

He shook his head, dubiously. 'I don't want to put a damper on the idea, old son,' he said, 'but I wouldn't have thought that the Whitehall desk-wallah sort of job was your cup of tea. Why don't you try for something more creative?'

'All very well,' I said, 'but where? I've tried. They won't have me.'

Jimmy looked thoughtful. 'Look here,' he said, 'I was playing poker last night with an important man in film business who was talking about the difficulty he was having in finding a first-class press man for his publicity department. You could do a job like that, couldn't you?'

'Tailor made,' I nodded, although I was not at all sure what such a job entailed.

'Right,' said Jimmy. 'I lost a tenner to Maxie at cards last night, so he owes me a good turn. I'll scribble a note to him on the back of one of my cards. Drop in and see him – it's worth a try.'

So I took a taxi to the offices of Columbia Pictures in Wardour Street and handed Jimmy's card to the commissionaire with a request that it should be taken to Mr Maxie Thorpe, the managing director. It looked a lush sort of world compared to the bleak trestle tables of Whitehall. I seated myself comfortably in one of the expensive armchairs in the lobby, and began to study a copy of the *Daily Film Renter*, a publication I had not seen before.

Along came a vividly pretty girl wearing a tight skirt, low-cut silk blouse and high heels. 'Mr Thorpe will see you right away, Mr Whitcomb,' she said. 'Please follow me.' Going up in the lift she asked, 'Are you a movie actor?'

'Not yet,' I replied. 'But I'm working on it.'

'So am I,' she whispered with a seductive smile. 'Maybe we should work on it together.'

I made a mental note to buy Jimmy Hutchison a bottle of champagne next time I saw him. The idea of a job in movies was growing on me.

Maxie Thorpe's office was enormous and was furnished like the grand hall of a Tudor castle – panelled in oak, hung with chandeliers; all it lacked was suits of armour.

'Come in, my dear boy, come in,' said Maxie, advancing the length of a cricket pitch over a reproduction Aubusson carpet towards me. He was a well-built man, running to fat, and he wore a beautifully tailored pearl-grey suit with a flamboyant silk tie; his greying hair, elegantly cut, was wavy at the sides, and he extended to me a plump, white, manicured hand.

'Sit down, my dear boy, sit down,' he said smiling warmly and waving me towards a tall oak throne. 'Let me take your hat.'

How was I to know that this was the man who was feared throughout Wardour Street as a cross between the Emperor Caligula and Sultan Haroun-al-Raschid, a man whose name sent shivers down people's spines as the London equivalent of great Hollywood magnates such as Cecil B. de Mille or Darryl Zanuck? To me he looked a pussycat.

'I have here this note from our dear Jimmy Hutchison,' he said, waving Jimmy's card, 'and I want you to know that I regard Jimmy not only as a dear friend but as a genius. A genius,' he repeated, nodding. 'If he has a fault it is that he tends to over-value a hand containing only two queens.' Maxie smiled indulgently and added, 'I took a thousand pound off him at poker last night.'

Jimmy had said that Maxie had won a tenner. I was to learn that this was the measure of exaggeration that Maxie applied to everything. All Maxie's sparrows were peacocks. He was looking me over, and with a wave of his hand at his own lapel he indicated the silver ex-service badge I was wearing. 'I see that you have been one of our gallant fighting lads,' he beamed.

'Up to a point, Mr Thorpe,' I nodded.

'No chance of being called up again?'

'I am receiving a one-hundred-per-cent disability pension,' I said.

'One hundred per cent,' he repeated, appreciatively, enjoying the words. 'One hundred per cent! With so much as a one-hundred-per-cent pension, thank God you are not dead.'

I smiled and shrugged. 'It was nothing,' I said. 'Really nothing. Honestly.'

Maxie rose from his throne and walked over, patting me on the shoulder. 'I love modesty,' he said. 'And I know that Jimmy would not have sent you to see me unless he knew that you were a brilliant writer with a deep knowledge of newspapers and friends in high places in Fleet

Street, because Jimmy knows that this is the only thing I will settle for. He told you that, did he?'

'Jimmy told me you were looking for a press officer,' I replied, guardedly. I was beginning to add up Maxie.

'Good,' he said. 'Very good. So let us waste no time.' He pressed a button on his desk and called into an intercom: 'Miss Hayward, ask Mr Denis Lyons to come up. Right away. This minute. No – wait a minute. Don't tell him anything. Don't call him at all. We will go down to his office. I want to see what he's doing.'

Motioning me to bring my hat and umbrella, Maxie Thorpe led the way out of his office and down some stairs to a door marked: PUBLICITY DIRECTOR – DENIS LYONS. Bursting in with the air of a police inspector heading a raiding party, Maxie looked from side to side with a sweeping glare as though he expected to find roulette wheels, dancing girls and bottles garlanded with balloons and streamers. But all he saw was a middle-aged man with a red-veined, harassed face, sitting at a desk in his shirtsleeves and poring over some proofs of colour advertisements.

'Ah, Denis,' said Maxie. 'I knew I would find you busy, hard at work as usual. Lucky I caught you in. I want you to meet Mr Winslow, who is one of the great young writers of our time. A Fleet Street man of quality.'

Denis Lyons looked me up and down with a thoughtful eye. He observed the bowler hat and the umbrella and his eyes narrowed. His expression said clearly, 'Oh, my God!'

'Yes, Mr Thorpe,' he said. 'Thank you, Mr Thorpe.'

In all my time in Wardour Street I never heard anyone say, 'No, Mr Thorpe.'

'I am going to leave Mr Whittaker with you, Denis,' went on Maxie, 'so that you can discuss with him the job that you have vacant. Test him, Denis. Put him through the mangle. He is one of our gallant fighting lads who sustained terrible injuries in battle – one-hundred-per-cent injuries – and I have a feeling in my heart that he will come through with one-hundred-per-cent flying colours.'

I could hear the bugles calling as Maxie spoke, and the brave music of a distant drum. I could almost smell the cordite. If he had produced a Union Jack from under his pearl-grey jacket and waved it, I would not have been surprised.

'Yes, Mr Thorpe,' said Denis, as Maxie swept triumphantly out of the room.

Denis sat there for a few moments, looking at me with a puzzled frown, and at last he said, 'You're not Jewish.'

39

'No,' I said. 'Not Jewish.'

'That's odd,' said Denis. 'I mean, Maxie has relations in offices all over the building. He has nephews and cousins and his wife's nephews and cousins working for him. Some have names such as McTavish, Maxwell or Campbell – Maxie's own real name is something unpronounceable – but they all have one thing in common. They are all Jewish. How come he decided to hire you?'

'I was recommended by a pal of his.'

'Well, son,' went on Denis, 'I'll be frank with you. I don't think for a moment you are likely to be any good at anything we do here. It's not a bowler-hat-and-umbrella job. It's specialized work, son. But I'll tell you what I'll do. I'll give you a chance.'

Picking up the telephone he dialled a number. There was a pause. Then he said, 'Plaza cinema box office? Good. Denis Lyons here. What time does the next showing of our film start. Three o'clock. Right. Reserve a seat in the front row of the circle for somebody I'm sending down. I'll give him a note to you. 'Bye.'

He scribbled a note on Columbia paper, handed it to me and said, 'Go and see this film. Then come back here and write five hundred words about it. I want it on my desk before six o'clock. Right? Off you go.'

The film was *You Were Never Lovelier*, starring Fred Astaire and Rita Hayworth. It certainly never crossed my mind that in later years these two people would become friends of mine. I thought she was gorgeous and he was brilliant, but the film itself was mainstream corn. So I took a taxi back to the Columbia building soon after five, knocked out the review on a typewriter in the general office, and took it in to Denis Lyons well before six.

He was wearing his hat and overcoat, ready to leave, and his secretary was standing beside him as he signed letters. He looked up with surprise when I came in. He had forgotten all about me. But he sat back and read my copy. Then he looked up at me and said, 'Holy cow!'

My heart sank. 'Not any good?' I asked.

'Any *good*?' he echoed. 'By Christ, boy, if Maxie Thorpe read this he'd have you banned the bloody building. Don't you realize that this is *our* motion picture? Nobody here is allowed to be satirical about *our* pictures. Motion pictures are big money, and money is what it is all about, so any picture we make is the best that has ever been seen on any screen. Don't you forget that.'

He leaned forward and examined me more closely, taking in the blue pinstripe suit with the slim gold watch-chain, the bowler hat and the umbrella. 'You're in heavy disguise, aren't you?' he said. 'Where did you learn to write like this?'

'I edited a magazine in the army,' I replied, hoping he would not ask for further details.

'There's more to it than that,' he said, thoughtfully, still examining me closely. 'This is professional stuff. Still, that's your affair. I don't want to know. All I know is that most of the people Maxie sends me write like trained chimpanzees. Anyone who can turn out stuff like this can start here tomorrow, provided they remember the rules of the game. Twelve guineas a week, take it or leave it.'

'I'll start tomorrow,' I said.

In those wartime days of the London blitz, Wardour Street was dreamland with bombs. Most people went to the cinema at least once a week because there was little else to do with leisure time. Hollywood was at the height of its glory and Wardour Street was flanked on both sides by fine buildings that housed the great, mega-rich film corporations. All the surrounding streets of Soho, later to become so down-at-heel and sleazy, were full of excitement, cosmopolitan, vivid, a marvellous mix of rich and poor. The rest of the country was rationed and hard-pressed, but in Soho you could get anything you wanted. The restaurant proprietors went to gaol on almost a rota basis for serving fine food illegally, but they came out again and continued to offer their favoured customers succulent meals of rich ingredients, finely cooked: it was a matter of pride; Soho was a clandestine club.

Nights in the London blackout had the throbbing quality of darkness artificially imposed for reasons of danger. Air raids came and went, leaving destruction; but so long as you were not killed or maimed, so long as yours was not one of those muffled voices that sobbed and keened among the rubble in the dusty and stinking light of dawn, it was thrillingly enjoyable. That is a guilty secret we keep shrouded from those too young to have known it. No film has ever captured that reality: it was grisly, hysterical fun. I loved it.

The pubs at night were full of people talking excitedly in loud voices above the jangle of the piano at which some heavy-handed student of Charlie Kunz was belting out *We'll Meet Again* or *Roll Out the Barrel*; the sirens wailed and the adrenalin ran fast in an atmosphere that was more euphoric than fearful. Those who were young and therefore revelled in the night did not go home; those who were older and wiser preferred to return to their safer firesides outside central London before the sirens sounded. Maxie Thorpe was one of these. Maxie was particularly allergic to any explosive noise.

Maxie, knowing that I was always around at night, sometimes asked me to do his fire-watching duty for him. Everyone was on the fire-watching rota, from the boss to the office-boy, and the duty carried an honorarium of five shillings, to cover the cost of a late meal. As you could get a delicious dinner of Hungarian goulash with a glass of wine for five bob at the Café Bleu in Old Compton Street, I was always happy to oblige.

One night during a lull in the blitz, I was doing Maxie's duty but he was still upstairs playing poker with friends. The sirens sounded and the raid started almost immediately. Fire-bombs began scattering down, so I jammed on my tin hat and raced up to the roof with my stirrup pump and bucket, ready to put out any incendiaries that might have dropped on our building. We were lucky that night, the roof was clear, so I worked my way down, floor by floor, to the cellar. All was well.

I was just about to leave the cellar when I heard a noise in the far corner. There was an old table in the corner, up-ended and jammed at an angle to the wall. With my hatchet at the ready, I tiptoed over, Chinkajook fashion, and kicked the table aside. There, in the corner, cowering down, was Maxie Thorpe.

'Good evening, Mr Thorpe,' I said, hastily lowering the hatchet and struggling to keep a straight face. 'Everything all right?'

'Fuck off,' he said, 'if you will excuse the phrase.'

After that night there was always a wary look in Maxie's eye when he caught sight of me. But I never told anyone. It would have been a cheap laugh.

One task common to all the press officers employed by the big film companies was to write a long article for the trade papers to go with the advertising when a collection of new film releases was being announced. There were three trade papers, the *Daily Film Renter*, the *Cinema* (also a daily) and the *Kinematograph Weekly*; all of them flourished because they carried so much advertising. When a film company was launching a fleet of forthcoming attractions, all three papers would carry a dozen or more pages of colour advertising, one whole page to a film, and every page a lurid example of Hollywood poster art. Some of these advertisements were brilliant in their eye-dazzling way, but the words that went with them were traditionally tawdry, strings of flowery adjectives spattered with exclamation marks. Nobody read the words.

I did not like the idea of nobody reading my words, so I tried a new approach. Kicking out the adjectives and banishing the frighteners I tried to produce a shock effect with simple words bitten off into short sentences and fired at the reader like machine-gun bursts, to match the vivid colour-ads. This caused some talk. Three companies sacked their press officers. Maxie gave me a two-guinea rise.

One morning I had a telephone call from a man whose name I knew but whom I had never met – Arthur Allighan, publicity director of the British Lion Film Corporation.

'Come to lunch,' he said.

'Delighted,' I agreed. 'When?'

'Today,' said Arthur. 'See you at one o'clock in De Hem's.'

De Hem's is a pub in Macclesfield Street off Shaftesbury Avenue, and I had intended to go to the bank and get some money on the way, but I was late and had to run. Arthur was standing at the bar.

Decades later when I first saw George Cole playing the part of Arthur Daley in the *Minder* television series, I nearly jumped out of my seat. Arthur Daley was Arthur Allighan: the camel-hair overcoat, worn open; the slow, warm, beguiling but utterly untrustworthy smile; the naïvely bogus air of the prosperous businessman, transparent as plate glass; the capacity for quick thinking and fast talking to get himself out of trouble and leave his pal wallowing in the sweet violets; that was my Arthur, separated from his identical twin on television by more than thirty years.

Arthur ordered us a dozen oysters each and a bottle of hock, and came straight to the point. His boss, Sam Smith, managing director of British Lion, had told him to get hold of me and take me on as press manager.

'I found out on the grapevine that Maxie is paying you fourteen guineas a week,' said Arthur, 'so I told Sam he would have to offer you eighteen to make sure you couldn't refuse. I could have said sixteen and you would probably have come, but I wanted to make sure you would be on my side. Are we in business?'

'We're in business,' I nodded, shaking the proffered hand.

We followed the oysters with fresh baby lobster and champagne while Arthur told me about my new boss, Sam Smith, who produced his own films in England. When it was time to go, Arthur put his hand in his pocket and his face fell. 'Oh, good lor',' he said. 'I meant to go to the bank and I forgot. I'm skint.'

I was already beginning to form an opinion about Arthur so I said, 'I haven't any money on me, either.'

The situation was clearly not unfamiliar to him. 'Right,' he said, 'this is what we do. You stay here and order another drink. I'll go and find some money.'

After ten minutes, when it was close to closing time, I began to feel anxious, but Arthur bustled back with two fivers in his hand, kissed both notes before he put them on the counter and called loudly for the bill.

'Stills,' he said, grinning. 'See what I mean about being on my side?'

Film fans used to write to the big companies enclosing postal orders and requesting black-and-white photographs, known as stills, of their favourite stars. It was customary for the publicity director's secretary to send off the stills and pay in the postal orders to the bank. But that was not Arthur's custom. His secretary sent off the stills but Arthur put the postal orders in his drawer against a rainy day.

I laughed, but I did not like it. Petty pilfering seemed so incongruous for a man with his job and his pay. He sensed my uneasiness immediately and told me not to be a bloody hypocrite. In Arthur's philosophy everything to do with money was a joke. He was one of those well-paid people who spend their lives almost permanently broke. Every day Arthur had money; every night he spent it. When Arthur had money in his pocket it drained away like bath water; sometimes it was dog-racing, sometimes girls, but whatever Arthur did at night he invariably ended up broke next morning. He had been bombed out several times and felt he was living on borrowed time.

Another of Arthur's sources of income was playing snooker in the afternoon at the Empire Billiards Hall in Dean Street. That was where we went after our first lunch.

'Five bob a frame,' said Arthur, chalking his cue. 'You can owe it to me.'

When I was a boy at home we had a billiards table and my brother and I played often, so we became quite good at the game. Arthur observed this fact with mounting astonishment. I was just about to pot the black to win the first game when Arthur knocked over a glass of beer and I missed the shot.

'Sorry, mate,' he said. 'Just an accident. But from now on you and me play together. There's always people down here looking for a game. We ought to do all right as a team.'

Arthur rigged the fire-watching rota so that we were always on duty together, and we did all Sam Smith's duties too. We would start in the Old Ship pub in Wardour Street, go on to the Gargoyle Club round the corner in Meard Street (where we would sometimes drink with Dylan Thomas and his friends) and the night would usually end with Arthur taking some film-struck blonde back to our offices to show her how the beating heart of the British film industry worked. These conducted tours would invariably end in Sam Smith's office, where there was an enormous leather sofa known as 'Sam's casting couch', and Arthur would emerge from Sam's office with the blonde next morning before the cleaners arrived.

One night he bought a racing greyhound for £100, and I watched him write a cheque for it. I knew that would mean trouble, because Arthur never had a hundred pence in the bank.

Next morning he said, 'Fly me a kite for a century, would you? I just need it for a couple of days.' Flying a kite was a slang term for giving somebody a good cheque after he had issued a bad one, so that his account would appear to be in credit when his own cheque was paid in, and therefore would not bounce.

'I won't fly you a kite,' I said, 'but I can lend you fifty.'

'I'll get the other two ponies from that moneylender in Regent Street who advertises loans by note-of-hand alone,' said Arthur. And so he did.

'You'll be sorry you didn't have half of this dog, mate,' said Arthur, when the deal was done. 'It's the fastest thing on four legs since Mick the Miller. It catches pigeons. It's been smuggled in from Ireland and nobody knows anything about it. Not yet. But they will on Saturday night.'

On Saturday night we went to see the dog run, and Arthur strode around the club enclosure in his camel-hair coat, telling everyone to get on his dog for their maximum because it was a stone-cold certainty.

I said to him, 'Take it easy, Arthur, you're spoiling the market for yourself.'

Arthur beamed patronizingly. 'When you have the astonishing good fortune to own dog as brilliant as this,' he said, 'you should share your luck.'

Arthur's dog opened in the market at 100-8 against, started even-money favourite and came fourth.

It was very consistent dog. It ran several times after that and always came fourth.

One morning I had a letter from a moneylender with a Scottish name in Regent Street, saying that I was responsible as guarantor for a loan of £50 he had made to Mr Alfred Arlegon, and that unless he received from me the sum of £197, which was the sum now owing including agreed interest, he would take action against me.

Furiously I marched into Arthur's office and threw the letter on his desk. He looked up in astonishment and then read the letter. 'Ah, yes,' he nodded. 'Surely I didn't forget to tell you that I put you down as a reference? But there is nothing to worry about. He's just trying it on. You can't be a guarantor because you didn't sign anything.'

I was angry. 'You had better pay this nasty little crook right away or else there is going to be trouble,' I said.

'Not so fast,' said Arthur. 'Let me tell you what happened. You call this man a nasty little crook and that is what he is. The interest rates he charges are nothing short of extortion. He is a snare for mugs. So when I went to see him I showed him my identity card and other documents right away, and while we were talking I put them back in my pocket. He had an accent of some sort and he was calling me Mister Arlegon, so when he pushed the form over to me I filled it out as Alfred Arlegon, with an address in Putney. That's why I've never heard from him since. But it serves him right for being careless. If he catches up with me, which I expect he will soon, I shall be furious about having been impersonated by somebody who didn't even know how to spell my name.'

'Look here, Arthur,' I said. 'What you are going to do is give him back the fifty he lent you and tell him to go to hell for the interest. Otherwise I'm not on your side.'

'I'll talk to him lunchtime,' said Arthur. 'I knew you'd see it my way.'

Next morning the following conversation took place in Arthur's office.

'Did you see the moneylender?'

'No, but I rang him.'

'Offer to pay?'

'No. I told him my brother Garry is a big shot on the *Daily Mirror*.'

'Is he?'

'Yes. Sure he is.'

'So what?'

'So my brother could have this feller crucified in the paper for charging illegal interest rates. Expose him. Close him down.'

'You told him that?'

'Not half. I shan't have any more trouble from him.'

I couldn't help liking Arthur, but I had a feeling of relief when I received an offer from Mr Ernie Fredman, proprietor of the *Daily Film Renter*, to write a daily column for his paper at a salary of twenty-two guineas a week.

Arthur took it as a personal affront when I told him I was leaving. 'If you have no value for friendship,' he said, solemnly, 'if your conscience does not trouble you about giving no thought to loyalty, then you had better go. I won't stop you, my son. All I will say is that you should learn that money is not everything.'

'Coming from you, Arthur,' I said, 'that is a very moving speech. You never wanted a press manager here, you wanted an accomplice. And don't forget you still owe me fifty.'

To obtain material for my daily full-page column in the *Renter* I had to make frequent visits to the studios at Pinewood and Denham where all the British pictures of any consequence were being made. Both studios belonged to J. Arthur Rank, the multi-millionaire flour miller, who had virtually created the British film industry and owned more or less everything and everybody on the production side; a man with a dream of making the British film industry rival Hollywood, he was known to everyone as 'Uncle Arthur'.

In the 'commissariat', the canteen at the studios, I lunched with and came to know all Uncle Arthur's employees: David Niven, Dirk Bogarde (Bogarde was Rank's biggest star for over ten years), John Gielgud, Larry Olivier, Dickie Attenborough, Margaret Lockwood, Stewart Granger, James Mason, Moira Shearer, Roger Moore, Alec Guinness, Deborah Kerr, Ann Todd, Oliver Reed, Joan Collins ('Britain's Bad Girl') and a sweet kid called Jean Simmons who was still at school in Golders Green: all promising youngsters and worth a few paragraphs in Ernie Fredman's paper.

Ronald Neame was working as a cameraman, and he showed me the secret, under pain of death if I revealed it, of Uncle Arthur's screen trademark, The Man with the Gong: the gong was made of wood and plaster and it made a squashy sound if you hit it; the sound on the screen came from a small musical instrument called a tam-tam.

Everyone wanted publicity in the trade press, so I was always welcome: Michael Powell and Emeric Pressburger were among the directors with whom I became friendly, Earl St John and John Davis among the executives, and Cyril Howard who was the boss of Pinewood. They were all princes of considerable importance, but Uncle Arhur was the king, and I came to know him quite well because Ernie Fredman would often call upon him by appointment at the Rank offices in South Street, Mayfair, to do an in-depth interview on the state of the industry, and while Ernie asked the questions I took down the answers for the long article I would write.

Michael Caine was office boy at South Street until Uncle Arthur, a passionate anti-smoker, caught Michael smoking in the men's lavatory and sacked him on the spot.

It was a good job and I was enjoying it. I seldom saw Arthur Allighan, but one morning he telephoned me. 'Listen, mate,' he said, 'we are in trouble with this moneylender.'

'*We* are?' I echoed. 'You mean *you* are. I'm not. It's nothing to do with me.'

'Don't be difficult, mate,' he said in a mollifying tone. 'We must have a talk. I'll see you in the Annexe at one o'clock.'

The Annexe was a drinking club in Brewer Street, run by a Frenchman called Louis and much used by theatricals and film people. I was there early and fell in with Jessie Matthews and her brother Billy, a boxer who had been European featherweight champion; they had both been born in a flat above a butcher's shop round the corner in Berwick Market. I thought at the time that Jessie was the most beautiful girl in the world, and I still think with affection of that talented and later tragic star.

A man of about my age was standing beside me at the bar, talking to friends, and I heard him say, 'I can't stay long because there is a job for a reporter going at the *Daily Mirror*, and I am on my way to Fleet Street to see the news editor about it.'

On impulse, I leaned over and kissed Jessie goodbye, left my drink on the counter, walked out into the street and hailed a taxi. '*Daily Mirror*, Fetter Lane,' I told the driver.

I sent up a chit from the main door requesting an interview with the news editor, and was shown into a waiting room. As I sat there, straightening my tie, adjusting the clove carnation in my buttonhole, balancing my Newmarket hat on the gold top of my walking stick, I began to wonder whether I was doing something foolish. I was earning twenty-two guineas a week and good expenses. I had written a screenplay and a treatment, and in the back of my mind was the thought that after the war I might have a crack at Hollywood. I thought of Cyril Connolly's stern advice that the only purpose of writing is to write a masterpiece. No masterpieces in the *Daily Mirror*. And yet . . . and yet . . . this might be my only chance to find out what it was like to work in Fleet Street, the land of my fathers.

Into the room bustled the news editor, and as soon as he grinned at me I knew who he was. I sat staring at him, transfixed like a rabbit dazzled by the headlights of a car. There was no mistaking who he was. He was Arthur Allighan's brother.

4

Garry Allighan, news editor of the *Daily Mirror*, sat himself down in a chair on the other side of the table in the waiting room and looked me over with an appraising eye.

Then he said, 'The only person I've told that we have a vacancy here is a chap on the *Daily Express* who is coming to see me today. How did you know?'

'Heard about it in a club,' I replied. 'These things get around.'

'Funny,' mused Garry. 'Very odd. Anyway, you're here now. I see from the badge that you've been in the services.'

'Army,' I nodded. 'Briefly. Never saw a shot fired in anger.'

Garry pointed at the walking stick and asked, 'Gammy leg?'

'No. Both legs in working order, thanks.'

'What's the red carnation for?' he asked. 'Been to a wedding?'

'No. I usually wear one.'

Garry's face again broke into the familiar Allighan grin. 'Well, a chap like you would be a change round here, anyway. We don't have a high sartorial standard. I've got one reporter who hasn't changed his shirt for months, and if he took his socks off he could stand 'em up in the corner. Irish, of course,' he added, 'but he's a top-class ferret. You don't look to me like a reporter,' he went on. 'Any experience?'

I gave him a brief run-down on my past, ending with the *Daily Film Renter* column in Wardour Street.

'Wardour Street, eh?' said Garry. 'Do you know my brother Arthur?'

'He was my previous boss,' I said.

Garry laughed out loud. 'I know who you are,' he chuckled. 'You're the lad Arthur was telling me about. He said he had a feller working for him who went around disguised as Lord Peter Wimsey but who was a right tearaway behind the mask. Never goes home, he said. Blondes, brunettes, redheads, no reasonable offer refused. The Casanova Kid, he said.'

'Arthur told you that?' I asked.

'He sure did,' nodded Garry. 'In glorious Technicolor.'

'He should talk,' I said. 'Arthur is known throughout the length and breadth of Soho as The Man with the Golden Whatsit. Families supplied daily. Tonight and every night. A prize every time.'

'You can have the job if you want it,' said Garry, still laughing. 'On a month's trial. Ten guineas a week. Start Monday evening, six o'clock. Get in about half-past five and I'll introduce you to the night news editor, because I finish at six. OK?'

'OK,' I said.

The *Daily Mirror* was housed in a building that looked like an early Bauhaus design for a seaside cinema; situated at the end of an alley off Fetter Lane it was called Geraldine House, after Lord Northcliffe's mother. A man with a flavour of Oedipus as well as the Midas touch, Lord Northcliffe loved his mother. He founded the *Daily Mirror* in 1903 as a votive offering to 'my darling mother who is in my thoughts a thousand times a day', and announced it as 'the First Daily Newspaper for Gentlewomen.'

To ensure that no crudeness would offend the morning eye of the old lady of Totteridge, as Northcliffe's mother was known, he engaged an all-woman staff, from the editor down. Women journalists were rare birds in 1903, and far from streetwise. The features editor commissioned a column from Paris and titled it 'Your Own French Letter'; the fashion editor ran a piece headlined 'Knit Your Own Dutch Cap'; the gossip columnist wrote lyrically about the wedding of a well-known actor and actress who were appearing together in the West End, and ended her report with the words: 'Later that evening, the usual performance took place.'

The ribald laughter that rocked Fleet Street from Temple Bar to Ludgate Circus did not amuse Lord Northcliffe, who was accustomed to obsequious respect. Furthermore the paper had cost him £100,000. So he took a hatchet to the female staff, who left in floods of tears, and replaced them with a straggle of the usual hacks, just in time to save the *Daily Mirror* from becoming merely another notch in the statistics of infant mortality among newspapers. Then he sold it to his accountant brother, Harold, the first Lord Rothermere, who turned it into a public company, and by the time I arrived on the paper none of the gentlewomen for whom it had been originally designed would have picked it up with a pair of tongs.

The *Mirror* had recently emerged from the most turbulent period of its maverick life: the wartime cabinet had threatened to close it down for spreading class dissension, Churchill had described the paper as 'vicious and malignant' and Attlee had said it was 'subversive'. All of this was over-reaction because the *Daily Mirror* had never been deliberately destructive of the nation's interest; it had simply been born a bastard and had grown up truculently, a delinquent with two fingers permanently in the air.

When I walked into the reporters' room for the first time, only two other men were on duty, both about my own age. One was Arthur La Bern, a wandily thin man with a mocking smile and a stutter that he concealed by talking in brief shafts of derisive wit; I liked him on sight. The other was Harry Proctor, a sturdy Yorkshire lad with a guileful smile; I mistrusted him instinctively. Throwing my hat and walking stick on the table, I introduced myself.

La Bern picked up my stick and lunged with it like a fencer with a foil. 'T-tell me,' he said, 'do you have a sword concealed in this stick? B-because if not I would advise you to get one fitted right away. I have a f-feeling you are going to need it.'

Proctor said, 'Welcome, lad. You are just in time to take part in the little gamble we usually have to brighten up the evening. We have a sweepstake, a fiver a head, on who gets the biggest story in the paper next day. Are you game for a bit of fun?'

I did not know that an untried, new reporter hardly ever gets a story in the paper on his first day, but I did know that men such as Proctor do not make bets of that sort unless they have inside information. All the same I took a fiver from my wallet and handed it over: it was nearly half a week's wages in my newly reduced circumstances.

In the next morning's paper Proctor had two small stories on the middle spread, La Bern had a single-column piece on the front page, and I had the back-page lead with a story about some new radio programmes that were in preparation.

When I arrived for work on that second night, Garry Allighan called me in. 'Where did you get that BBC story?' he asked. 'It was a beat, you know.'

'Just luck,' I admitted. 'Recently a chap called Huw Wheldon in the Royal Welch Fusiliers introduced me to a man called Kenneth Adam, because he knew I was sniffing round for a writing job, and Adam is information director at the BBC. So when the night desk asked me to check a query with the BBC, I rang Kenneth Adam at home. He was furious.'

'I can guess,' said Garry. 'He sits on God's right hand.'

'Anyway, he told me that all press queries must go through John Hytch, chief press officer at Broadcasting House. Hytch anwered the query, and then as a long shot I asked him if he had any other news. He read over to me the new radio schedules that had just been prepared for mailing. That was all. Just luck. Anybody could have had it if they had asked.'

'Just as I thought,' mused Garry. 'We are missing a lot of good radio stories because, like all the other dailies, we wait for the press releases before we take any interest.'

I did not know it but Garry, in typical Allighan fashion, was helping C.O. Stanley of Pye and other big radio manufacturers to promote the Radiolympia Exhibition, as a sideline, so he had a special interest in getting stories about radio into the paper.

'Look here, young feller-me-lad,' he said, 'I've got a plan for you and I think you'll like it. Instead of coming in here every evening at six, I want you to go first to Broadcasting House and talk to the people in the press office, see what you can pick up. Then go round the corner to a pub called the George in Mortimer Street. That's where all the creative people drink. Find out what they are doing. You can buy the odd round of drinks and put it on expenses, but don't try anything fancy. Got it?'

Next night I went to the George, 'the Gluepot' as it was known to BBC people, and the first man I saw at the bar was Dylan Thomas, my pal from the Gargoyle Club. He bought me a drink and introduced me to a BBC producer called Douglas Cleverdon, with whom he was having an argument. Cleverdon had commissioned Dylan to write a radio play under the working title of *The Town That Went Mad*. Dylan did not like the title and he was also arguing about his fee for the job, five guineas a thousand words. Should be six guineas, he said.

I thought it was a handy little story so I wrote it, but it was not used. The *Mirror* had precious little time for poets. Furthermore, like old Horace before me, my timing was awry; ten years were to elapse before the play was broadcast on the Third Programme as *Under Milk Wood*.

But I found plenty of other stories in the Gluepot. It was the haunt of many talented topers whom I came to know: Augustus John, Aleister Crowley, Louis MacNeice, Constantine Fitzgibbon, Cyril Connolly, Constant Lambert, some of them diabolists but all of them good companions. Often I was late back at the office to start my evening turn, but never empty-handed: always there were at least a couple of stories in the paper next day to account for the time I had spent.

Garry was pleased but the night news editor objected because he said he was always short of reporters to cover the news stories that came in at night. Garry solved this problem in the familiar Allighan way. He called me in.

'The radio stuff you are turning in is not bad,' he said, 'so I am going to give you a big chance. I am going to put you on the rota for the ten o'clock morning shift, which means that you will get a crack at the bigger stories that usually happen in the daytime. You will finish about six in the evening so you can always nip in for a drink with your pals at the George on the way home.'

I immediately saw through Garry's devious plan – two shifts a day for one pay envelope – but it never occurred to me to object. In later years a scheme like that would have resulted in the calling of a mandatory union meeting, but we did not go much on unions. Competition was the name of the game. Every reporter in the street knew every other reporter, and every friend was an enemy. We all met in the pubs, which were hedged in by tribal protocol. Every newspaper had its own particular pub, which was generally a no-go area for staff of other papers, and inside these pubs there was always one specific area that was ringed round with invisible rope, reserved by common acceptance for executives; any foolish or tipsy reporter who trespassed in this area was frozen out; if he did it a second time he was sacked.

Most formalized of all was El Vino, the wine bar. It was run by a man called Frank Bower, who looked like Billy Bunter grown up. A Free Vintner and a Freeman of the City of London as well as a Knight of Malta, he was portly, white-haired and red-faced with owlish spectacles and he always wore a black coat and striped trousers with a cravat and a fancy waistcoat of heavy silk embroidered with flowers. Frank was a tyrant. He set rigid rules, and anyone who stepped out of line was immediately barred – 'Out of my house this minute, sir, and do not let me see you in here again.' Queasily obsequious to his more important customers such as editors, Frank treated nearly all others as intruders, and kept them under constant surveillance.

The most heinous crime you could commit under Frank's regime was to take a woman in to stand at the bar. Regulars would not have dreamed of doing so because they knew it would mean being barred from El Vino for life; but occasionally some poor sap who thought it was an ordinary wine bar would wander in with a girl on his arm, only to find that he had unwittingly stepped on a landmine. Frank would come striding through the crowded bar, pushing people aside and spilling their drinks, charging like a rogue elephant towards the offender, his face purple with indignation. 'Do you not know the rules of my house, sir?' he would cry.

'No ladies may stand in this bar! The lady may sit at one of the tables in the back room, provided she is accompanied by a gentleman, but she may not walk through my bar. She must come in through the back door, which is in the passage alongside the house.'

In later years, after Frank had brought in his young kinsman Christopher Mitchell to help run El Vino, the rule was relaxed to permit women to sit at the side tables in the bar as well as in the back room, where Philip Hope Wallace, drama critic of the *Guardian*, held court. Later still a horde of feminists from the NUJ stormed El Vino demanding for women the same rights as men. They were evicted by the staff using soda syphons as fire-hoses; the case went to court under the sex equality act and eventually the women won their right to stand at the bar, although few subsequently exercised that right. I think Frank would have barred them anyway, which he had a right to do. Frank sometimes barred people simply because he did not like them. At one time or another he barred Hugh Cudlipp, Bill Connor (Cassandra) and Peter Wilson; he barred Vicki the cartoonist for life because Vicki took Frank's bowler hat off the coat-rack and tried it on.

Occasionally a stranger who was not wearing a tie would wander in for a drink, and would find himself back on the pavement before he understood what had happened.

On the dot of 3 p.m., closing time, Frank would bellow imperiously, 'May I have *my* glasses back, please, gentlemen. *My* glasses, please!'

Once, shortly before 3 p.m., somebody broke into song. The whole bar froze. Frank, behind the bar, stood speechless, quivering. In the sudden silence that had fallen, the miscreant's voice died away like a protracted fart after the consecration bell. In an atmosphere throbbing with anticipation, his friends rushed him out of the bar in the nick of time before Frank reached the door. Frank stood there, staring out, disbelieving, breathing fire.

Another capital crime in El Vino was to walk in from Fleet Street and stand at the corner of the bar nearest to the door. Any man who did this might call or wave to one of Frank's barmaids for as long as his patience lasted, but he would not be noticed. Frank's barmaids, pretty and demure-looking girls who were always interviewed for the job by Frank in his office in the cellar, and who were subsequently on oddly intimate terms with him, would always ignore any would-be customer who was rash enough to stand in Bart's corner, even when Bart was not there.

Bart, Harry Guy Bartholomew, chairman of the *Daily Mirror*, was the first of many top bosses of popular newspapers I came to know, and he was an excellent beginner's guide for students of that ward of crypto-psychopaths. A stout man with sleek white hair and horn-rimmed spectacles, he walked with a Napoleonic strut and exuded an air of menace; because of a facial resemblance to the Harmsworths, who stamped their progeny with a similar cast of feature, he was rumoured to be one of Northcliffe's bastards (of whom there were several in Fleet Street) but in fact he was the son of a Bob Cratchit-type City clerk and could barely read and write when he joined the *Daily Mirror* as an office boy in 1904.

Bart never did learn to write properly, and the notes of congratulation I occasionally received from him looked like the scrawl of a housemaid, but he had a natural talent that amounted almost to genius for visual display. In the 1930s, when the *Mirror* was still an insignificant little right-wing paper with an ominously diminishing circulation among the elderly middle class, Bart had worked his way up through the job of assistant to the picture editor, Hannen Swaffer, and was appointed editorial director. He took the weary newspaper by the throat and gashed its front page with screaming black headlines, splashing big, arresting pictures over it. He founded the tabloid revolution, not only in Britain but throughout the world; the New York *Daily News*, first of the American tabloids, copied its format from Bart's London *Daily Mirror*. Bart galvanized the *Mirror* circulation from a few hundred thousand into ultimately the millions; in the history of the world's newspapers, Bart is a cardinal figure.

He turned the *Daily Mirror* into the strident, hectoring voice of the common man, but whether he liked the common man is a question open to doubt; what is certain is that he disliked uncommon men, and reserved his bitterest venom for the educated élite: hatred was his most powerful motivating force. In later years the *Mirror* had a political editor called Joe Haines who was said to suffer from the Bermondsey Dockers' Syndrome, a loathing of everyone who had started life in better circumstances than himself; Bart was the *Mirror's* prototype exhibitor of that outlook. He was a misfit, a loner, and even the bosses of other newspapers gave him a wide berth. On the *Mirror* his only close friend was the mild and complaisant Bill Jennings, a small-time accountant who had been promoted by Bart to the position of company secretary, and the two men drank together in El Vino on most days; Jennings's only hobby was backing horses, and they were an oddly matched pair.

Most of the *Mirror* staff were scared of Bart, seeing him as Genghis Khan with a telephone, and not without reason because he delighted in cruelty: a white envelope on the notice-board usually signified a dismissal, and the board was always festively decked with white envelopes in the week before Christmas. Arthur La Bern used to warn new reporters, 'K-keep away from his office at night. He c-conducts human sacrifices in there.'

Bart's sense of humour never rose above the level of the custard pie in the face. The editor of the *Mirror* in my earliest days was a nice old man called Cecil Thomas, son of a country parson. Sometimes when Cecil was sitting in his office talking to friends, Bart would creep up behind him and hit him on the head with a flat piece of board; this would produce such a reverberating bang that all present would go pale, thinking they had witnessed a murder; but the board was only a piece of plywood that made a noise like a pantomime slapstick, and the editor was never much hurt apart from the damage to his dignity.

One night when I was having a drink in the editor's office after Bart had played this silly trick, Cecil told me a secret that he would not otherwise have revealed to a reporter: he told me that Bart wore corsets. I spread this news discreetly among the staff and it had a salutary effect, because it is difficult for people to feel reverential towards a plump little dictator when they know that he secretly wears stays.

I was getting plenty of stories in the paper, finding myself in demand; the *Mirror* was bouncy, iconoclastic, vivid and skilfully produced, and although it had not reached the period of years during which it was to contain good writing, it was not a bad vehicle for a young man with his hat on the side of his head. To say that I was popular among my colleagues would be an exaggeration because none of us was in the mutual admiration business, and some of the staff who were card-carrying members of the Communist Party eyed me with active opposition: so there was an air of cheered expectancy in the newsroom when the rumour went round that I was about to be fired.

It was touch and go. Some of the *Daily Mirror* editorial staff did a Saturday turn for the *Sunday Pictorial*, the *Mirror*'s sister paper, later renamed the *Sunday Mirror*; it was optional, and people did it if they wanted to earn a couple of extra guineas, but I did not volunteer because I thought the *Pic* was nothing but a rabble-rousing scandal sheet and I made no secret of my opinion.

However, one Friday evening I had a call from Stuart Campbell, known to his friends as Sam, the wartime stand-in editor of the *Sunday Pic*. He said that one of his reporters was ill, and asked if I would do a turn for him next day. Sam was a stocky man who usually wore a ferocious grin, notorious for his savage temper, a man not lightly to be crossed. I knew him only by sight, but he knew about me because I had become regarded as a good reporter, willing, sober, fast, and usually to be relied on to bring back a decent story. So I replied: 'Of course, Mr Campbell. I shall be delighted.'

On the Saturday morning I sat in the reporters' room, doing *The Times* crossword. It was a dull day for news. Nobody called me, so at midday I went early to lunch, and strolled towards Soho to have a drink in one of my old haunts, a little dive called Smokey Joe's; Smokey was a Negro who dressed like a cabinet minister, and his club was a haven for the more *louche* sector of London's literati.

I had been in there only five minutes when Ernest Hemingway came in, sat beside me at the bar and began chatting away as though we were old friends. I was impressed. Hemingway was the Picasso of the typewriter, a man whose prose-style we all tried to imitate from time to time. He talked about the old days in Paris with Gertrude Stein, James Joyce and Ezra Pound, and told me he was in London because the *Sunday Graphic* had commissioned him at an enormous fee to write a series of reminiscenses of his days as a reporter. When I told him that I, too, was a reporter, and he discovered that I knew some of his books almost by heart, we became bosom buddies. He was regaling me with lurid details of stories he had covered when the telephone on the bar rang. Smokey Joe answered it and pushed it over to me. 'For you, baby,' he beamed. 'Your office.'

It was a colleague in the reporters' room and he said, 'You're supposed to be in Brighton. If I were you I should get down to Brighton right away and ring the desk from there. Sam Campbell has been raising hell about where's-that-bloody-Whitcomb. He wants you to cover some yarn about vigilantes.'

I had only a sketchy idea of what vigilantes do, and I admitted as much to Papa Hemingway after I put the telephone down.

'In that case,' growled Papa, 'what you need is an expert on vigilantes as your leg-man. Drink up and we will go to Brighton and crack this story together.'

Hemingway had a car and driver waiting outside, and on the way to Sussex we picked up his girlfriend, a blonde called Mary who worked for the *Daily Express*. As soon as we had all checked in at the Bedford Hotel in Hove, Papa and Mary made for the bar and I rang the office.

'Get over to Kemptown right away,' said the man on the desk. 'It's a slum area and the whole population is rioting because their houses are not fit for habitation. Sam Campbell had a tip-off about it from a special informant of his own in Brighton, and he is calling the rioters vigilantes. He wants you to put over colour stuff on the freedom fighters as quickly as possible.'

I took a cab to Kemptown and began interviewing everything that moved. There was a germ of truth in the story but it was no big deal. A man who had a grudge against the council had managed to rally a small amount of half-hearted support among his neighbours for a campaign to organize some bad publicity for the council, and he had telephoned the editor of the *Pic*; but there was no mass insurrection, and the streets were somnolently quiet. So I wrote a few paragraphs putting the matter into perspective, telephoned it over, and asked to speak to the editor. Sam Campbell was out, so I explained the situation to a man on the news desk, and gave him the telephone number of the Bedford Hotel in case there were queries.

'Sam is not going to like this,' said the man on the desk. 'He is planning to lead the paper with your story of the Brighton vigilante riots in the last edition.'

'Well, he can't do that if it isn't true, can he?' I said, and went off back to the Bedford.

Hemingway was holding court in the bar when I arrived and he greeted me as a long-lost friend whom he had not seen for many years. He had forgotten all about the vigilante story and, indeed, I suspected he had even forgotten why he was in Hove instead of Smokey Joe's. He was teaching the hotel barman how to make vodka daiquiris, using a secret formula that had been entrusted to him by a (not surprisingly) dying barman in Manila.

These vodka daiquiris needed to have their ingredients measured with the care you would expect of a hospital pharmacist; when mixed, they had to be poured with sacramental care into a glass jug that was exactly half-filled with ice cubes; the mixture was then slowly stirred and a fragment of lemon peel squeezed over it; it was then decanted very gently into a fresh jug which had to be snatched out of the fridge while the frost was still on it: the drink was then served in a cocktail glass with a cherry on a stick.

It looked innocuous enough, almost girlish. But Hemingway claimed that by using this secret method the drink retained the innocently fragrant rum bouquet of the classic daiquiri while taking on a whole new philosophy that gave it the additional fire-power of a Sherman tank. He kept the barman working at it like a slave on an old Southern cotton plantation, urging him on to greater efforts in producing jugfuls. The drinks kept popping up with the speed of clay pigeons, and we kept shooting them down as fast as they came into our sights. The barman was doing his best but Hemingway kept shouting, 'Come on Joe – hit me again.'

I did not like the first one I tasted. I did not think much of the second one, either. But by the time the telephone rang I was on about my thirteenth and had found they grow on you.

The barman himself was looking flushed. Due to his selfless devotion to the stern code of the United Kingdom Barmen's Guild, whose pennant he proudly flaunted behind his bar, he had been tasting every jugful to ensure that he had got the formula exactly right and when the telephone rang his concentration was so deep that he had to look all round the bar to find where the ringing noise was coming from. At last his eye alighted on the raucous instrument, which was in its usual place at the end of the bar, and he made a little dive at it, just managing to grasp it before it flew away.

With solemn deliberation the barman picked up the receiver, placed the mouthpiece to his ear and hiccupped loudly. Realizing that the sound of a human voice was coming from far away at the other end of the handset, he gravely reversed it so that the earpiece was at last against his ear. He listened attentively for some moments. Judging by the expression on his face it seemed probable that somebody was talking to him in a foreign language. Then he announced judicially, 'Ish for Mishter Wishcomb. Mishter Sham Campbell on the line.'

I made a move to stand up and walk to the telephone. Nothing happened. My blood froze. I saw the whole picture in a flash. My legs were paralysed. I had been cut off by cruel fate at the outset of a promising career.

The barman was watching me, and with the eye of experience he understood my predicament better than I did. So he picked up the telephone and tossed it over to me.

There have been moments, fielding in the slips or at square leg, when I would have caught it easily; but this was not one of those moments. The telephone slipped out of my fingers and crashed to the floor with an unholy clatter. I slid off my stool and sat on the floor beside the instrument, picking up the receiver.

'Christ almighty!' the voice was saying. 'Have you got an air raid going on down there? Is it the riots? Are you all right? Who is that? Whitcomb? Is that Whitcomb?' Sam Campbell was on the boil. 'Whitcomb? Why don't you speak to me? What's the matter with you?'

'Sham,' I said, sentimentally, 'my *dear* Sham. How *very* good to hear you again. How *kind* of you to telephone. How *are* you?'

'What's it got to do with you how I fuckin' am?' he yelled. 'Where's the rest of the copy? I want the colour stuff on the riots and protest marches – NOW!'

'No,' I said. 'You can't print it.'

'Can't print it? Who says so? Who's editing this bleeding paper, you or me?'

'You are, dear old Sham,' I said, blandly. 'I would not edit your dishgushting paper if I were lured with cargoes of apes, peacocks and ivories. The riots story does not stand up. All quiet on the Brighton front. No mass disquiet among the Brighton proletariat. Your informant has handed you a canard – to use your own sort of phrase it's all balls.'

There was a pregnant pause. I could hear Sam Campbell breathing heavily. Then at last he said, 'Whitcomb, you're fired. Do you hear that? Fired.'

'Too late, dear boy,' I cried. 'I have already resigned. I decided to hand in my portfolio at least an hour ago. I was just about to ask my friend here, Ernest Hemingway, to telephone you and break the bad news.'

There was a strangled cry, as of a fox caught in a steel trap, followed by a crash as Sam Campbell slammed down the telephone.

When I went into the office next morning, with a splitting headache, I expected to find a white envelope awaiting me on the noticeboard. Not that getting tight after the day's work was done could be considered a firing offence, because if that had been the rule there would have been a daily mass exodus from Fleet Street; nor that refusing to write a story that was untrue could be offered as a reason for dismissal; but considerations of fairness never entered into matters of this sort: I had impugned an editor's *amour propre* and the only question was whether the editor of the *Daily Mirror* would agree to dismiss me because I had refused to write a story for the editor of the *Sunday Pic.*

I was in a high-security dog-house from which there appeared to be little hope of escape. Yet once again the phrase from the old silent-film serials came into play: 'With one mighty leap Jack was free.'

The *Daily Mirror* film critic, Reg Whitley, had fallen ill that very morning, and the only man on the staff who was qualified by experience to take over at short notice was me. We had small staffs at that time, just a handful of people to produce the paper instead of the hundreds of journalists upon which the union insisted in later years, and if a specialist fell ill the editor was in a spot. Garry Allighan told me to act as stand-in film critic and continue doing my other work as well. 'And think yourself lucky, lad,' he added. 'Sam Campbell was demanding your head on a charger.'

Reg Whitley was an ideal film reviewer for the *Daily Mirror*. He was a tipster rather than a critic. He did not bother much about whether a film was good or bad, but concentrated on the question of whether *Mirror* readers would enjoy it. A pot-boiler starring Norman Wisdom would always receive the Whitley accolade: 'Rip-roaring laugh-a-second funathon, a whizzo romp for our Norm and just the job to tickle the fancy of all the family'. *Hamlet*, starring Lawrence Olivier, would receive a sterner notice: 'Top actor in a classic yarn about a foreign prince who goes potty. All right for some.' The word 'classic' as used by Reg was not a description but a warning.

I had no wish to appear smart, but I took a different approach to the task. I was dismissive of rubbish (and a great deal of rubbish was being churned out by the studios because the public appetite for films was so voracious). Without going so far as to treat films as an art form, I did at least differentiate between entertainment and trash. This came as a nasty shock to Wardour Street. Top film executives began threatening the editor that they would withdraw all advertising unless I were replaced. The editor managed to keep the wolves at bay, but even he was nearly forced to admit defeat when I did not fall over backwards with admiration for Alexander Korda's production of Tolstoy's *Anna Karenina*. It was a vast-budget production with a publicity campaign that was extravagant even in the heyday of Hollywood hype; hordes of journalists were invited to champagne breakfasts before the press showing and the scene was set for an orgy of adulation.

Scenes set in old St Petersberg had been shot in Park Lane, London, and I found it distracting to see the Dorchester Hotel appearing in Mother Russia. I said it looked like Hyde Park Korda. There was a row, of course, but most critics on more serious papers took the same line as the *Daily Mirror*, and, more to the point, the readers split their sides with laughter at the spectacle of a millionaire film producer being forced to bite the dust, especially as he was a foreigner. I was given an extra job as temporary theatre critic, in the footsteps of a scholarly old leader-writer called Bernard Buckham, who was on the point of retirement. Two tickets for all West End theatre first nights became a privilege that I enjoyed for many years. And Garry even went so far as to give me a two-guinea rise.

'Don't spend it all at once,' he said with the usual grin. 'Invest it – buy yourself a chorus line.'

Oddly enough it was my preoccupation with matters theatrical that sent my life as a reporter lurching down a side alley, leading me into a brief life of crime. I was sent to Aberdeen on what sounded to be a fairly routine story: a local councillor who was also managing director of

Aberdeen crematorium had been charged with the theft of coffin lids, and a local undertaker with receiving them. It was a story that would create some interest in any age, but in those days towards the end of the war when public sensitivity on all matters concerning respect for the dead was at high tide, it had a special significance.

Having entered newspapers by an unconventional route, I had never been into a courtroom before. All the other reporters in court were old hands at the game and sat back with notebooks at the ready, chatting in whispers about football; but I was electrified by the scene before my eyes. It was not merely the solemnity of the setting, the wigs and gowns and robes; it was the stage furniture and props that I found so compelling: in a rack in the forecourt coffins were stacked, *used* coffins, with red tickets hanging from them like drapers' price-tags; the smell of death arose from them. It was Grand Guignol. I asked myself what Edgar Allan Poe would have done with this.

There was no television, and the era of filmed courtroom dramas had scarcely started, so the public sense of the dramatic in such matters had not been blunted by familiarity; certainly mine had not; my pulse raced.

Into the dock came the defendant, tall, pallid, red-eyed. Six babies' coffins, tiny white caskets, purple lined, no bigger than dolls' cradles, were thrust under his nose. Had he, counsel for the prosecution asked, removed the bodies of dead babies from these coffins and placed them at the feet of unnamed adult corpses to be burnt in the crematorium furnace? Even the judge shuddered when counsel held up a white shroud that had a withered spray of wild flowers pinned to its breast, its sleeves turned tellingly inside out. When counsel sat down after his examination I had difficulty in restraining myself from applause.

That night I dictated a report that ran to some fifteen hundred words. In those days of thin newspapers a news story that ran to six hundred words was considered to be of epic length, so I expected a call from the night news editor asking me if I had gone mad. No call came.

Next day the story was all over the front page. You could almost smell the stench of the charnel house rising from the paper, but reading it over in the morning light I realized with a touch of sadness that I was no Edgar Allan Poe, merely the fat boy of Peckham: I had made their flesh creep. But this was good enough for the editor, who sent me a telegram of congratulation, so I continued writing reports in the same vein throughout the four days of the trial and on the fifth day my background story occupied the two pages of the middle spread with a byline in seventy-two point type. After the first day of the trial all other national newspapers had sent up top men from London; but they were proper crime correspondents who knew the accepted way of reporting a trial, which I did not; I treated it as a well-produced play, and the *Mirror* led the rest from start to finish.

They were so cock-a-hoop about this that they gave me a further rise of five guineas, although I did not know the real reason for this munificence at the time. Arthur Christiansen, the talented editor of the *Daily Express*, used to put a bulletin on his noticeboard every day, analysing that morning's *Express*, praising work well done and criticizing faults, and sometimes paying brief tribute to a writer on another paper who had handled a story in a noteworthy way: during my absence in Aberdeen I had twice been handed a bouquet by Chris in his bulletin, and that was the reason I was given my rise; the *Mirror* had discovered a new crime reporter and did not want to lose him.

Crime, together with sex, money, the wicked misuse of power and the endless depravity of the rich have always been the main ingredients in the circulation figures of popular newspapers, and no sane newspaper would chance losing a discovery in the sphere of crime reporting for the sake of a mere fiver. Bylined as 'Your Crime Correspondent', I was given my five minutes of fame. No major murder trial was complete without my presence in court, and there was a spate of sensational murders during the dying days of the war when life had become so cheap. Hannen Swaffer, the Dean of Fleet Street, pontificated in his weekly column in *World's Press News* that this new style of court reporting could be dangerous if it were copied by reporters who had less experience of court reporting than young Whitcomb obviously had. Other older journalists, who knew me, were cynically amused and talked of the *Mirror* 'sending young Whitcomb to review another murder'; one night when I went into the office in evening dress on my way to dinner, the night news editor called over mockingly, 'Off to another first night at the Bailey?'

In those days before the abolition of capital punishment in Britain, when the shadow of the noose hung over every murder trial, the working classes still smacked their lips over murder cases with the relish with which their forefathers had savoured tales of Jack the Ripper or Sweeny Todd; reports concerning murder most foul still sent a *frisson* of excitement down every street, and all the gory details were eagerly snatched from the street-corner newspaper sellers – a good murder meant big business for the popular papers. Consequently top crime correspondents such as Percy Hoskins of the *Express* and Norman Rae of the *News of the World* were big stars in their newsrooms – princes of Fleet Street. That changed dramatically once judges were no longer required to go through the chilling ritual of putting on the black cap before sentencing the prisoner to be hanged by the neck until he – or she – was dead: the public's interest in murder trials diminished, and crime reporting became a job of far less importance.

I hated it. A dilettante by nature, I shrank from being pushed into specialization. Furthermore I have never been interested in crime as a subject and I found it tedious. But journalists are like actors in the matter of typecasting: one needs only to write a couple of good reports on the Chelsea Flower Show, making it sound like a fresh event, to become in grave danger of being appointed gardening correspondent. I could see my life stretching out ahead in constant conversation with beer-swilling, hollow-legged detectives from Scotland Yard, standing in the downstairs bar of St Stephen's Tavern beside the Houses of Parliament and chatting about 'chummy', which was the friendly name they used for their prey in the underworld because good policemen need to think with the same mental mechanism as crooks.

However, I was saved from this fate by the bells that rang out from churches all over the land for the first time in five years, joyfully signalling the end of the war in Europe: immediately I was switched from tales of crime to paeans of celebration of the victory of the allies.

The streets were thronged with euphoric multitudes, singing and cheering, kissing one another in elation. It is easy to recreate a recognizable picture of that period, so familiar now from old film clips which show all the clichés that we smilingly recognize, the strange fashions in clothes, the seeming simplicity, the naïvety of a bygone age before the atom bomb, the camaraderie, the Vera Lynnishness of it all: every television-watcher knows it well. Less easy to recreate and less recognizable is the feeling of desperate disquiet that rose from those mafficking crowds almost as visibly as a mist over a meadow on an autumn evening.

That feeling crystallized into one insistent question: What now? Everyone knew that Britain was broke, all her assets spent. Rationing was tightened; shortages of food, clothing, petrol and everything that people longed for became more severe than ever, and so much more irksome now that the reason for them had ended. All around was chaos and, worse still, the excitement was over: no more danger in the night, no more high-pitched laughter in the factory, no more of the brave and simple hatred that had so contributed to love. What now? Suddenly it all seemed empty, like awakening from a dangerous but wonderful and silly dream. Mixed with relief was the psychological hangover, the post-coital sadness. Into this vacuum seeped the 1945 General Election.

Everyone of any consequence knew that Churchill would win. He was the hero, the incomparable warrior, the great Englishman who had led Britain out of her darkest hour to victory. Everyone of any consequence knew that it would be unthinkable, even if only from simple gratitude, to dislodge Churchill from his seat of political power at the zenith of his achievement. The trouble was that people of no consequence did not see it that way: the one thing that they knew they deeply wanted was change; no going back; a fresh start. They had become different people; and one important reason for this difference was that during the six years of war the semi-educated masses had become regular newspaper readers for the first time.

Most of them read the *Daily Mirror*, and the *Mirror* was their friend. Men in the forces, at home and abroad, turned eagerly every day to have a look at Jane, the cartoon stripper, and whistle over what clothes she had taken off; even the men submerged in submarines had received a newspaper, loaded in bulk but distributed daily, produced as a gift for them by the *Mirror*. They trusted the little paper; and the little paper now turned round and told them to vote Labour.

Few people in the middle class or in what was left of the upper class either knew or cared about this. The *Mirror* was a comic. Ever since its faltering start in pursuit of gentlewomen, the paper had been politically a reed in the wind: under the proprietorship of Lord Rothermere in the pre-war years the *Mirror* had supported Oswald Mosley's blackshirt hooligans, and indeed Rothermere's last two signed articles in the paper had been headlined GIVE THE BLACKSHIRTS A HELPING HAND! and HURRAH FOR THE BLACKSHIRTS! Serious labour politicians disliked the paper as much as the conservatives, but all agreed that it held no serious political clout. Just a rag.

As were many other journalists in Fleet Street, I was in a seat in the stalls to observe the speciousness of this reasoning. Harry Guy Bartholomew could see from the flood of letters to the *Mirror*, mostly disgruntled, that he had his hated enemies, the aristos, on the run. He was their Robespierre; Churchill was Lafayette; Bart's fangs dripped blood in print. There were no opinion polls then, no busy fingers on the public pulse, only the crystal ball.

Garry Allighan had stepped down as news editor and entered the fray as Labour candidate for Gravesend, a seat he was to win; but often in those pre-election days I used to walk down to El Vino with him for a drink, and chat with his friends, Nye Bevan, Michael Foot and other hot-head hopefuls; not surprisingly, they did not like me, and I would have been unwelcome but for Garry. It was Garry Allighan, an unimportant name now scarcely traceable in the annals of his time, who turned the final trick for Labour in that election, and he had the vital idea one lunchtime when we were chatting with Nye Bevan in El Vino.

'It's the wives we ought to be wooing, not the servicemen,' said Garry. 'Sod the servicemen – most of 'em will vote for us anyway. But their poor bloody wives don't know whether they're on their arses or their elbows as far as the election is concerned. Most of 'em will vote on Churchill's side because he's the only name they know and he won the bloody war. If we could get the wives on our side we'd be home and bloody dry.'

'Go and tell that to Bart,' said Nye. 'Explain it to him.'

So Garry did. And next morning the *Daily Mirror* appeared with the three-word headline: VOTE FOR HIM!

Any woman who had a husband or son serving overseas had a proxy vote to cast for him. The use of those proxy votes for Labour decided the election outcome in a landslide that shocked the world.

I have read a number of accounts of the prelude to that uniquely untypical general election, some well informed and some by historians of note, but none completely fits with the facts as I saw them from where I was sitting at the time; and I was sitting on the news desk at the *Mirror* as an assistant with no influence over anything, because everyone agreed that it would not be prudent to allow me to write anything for the paper until the battle was won. Even subliminal influence could be dangerous, and they knew that I – alone among the staff – would root for the Grand Old Man.

The job on the news desk as 'an inside man' was considered to be promotion, because this was the path that led to the editor's chair; but although I had nothing against the idea of becoming an editor, the accepted route up the mountain to that eminence was unattractive. 'Inside men' were shift-workers, tied to a desk like clerks, slaves to routine, going out for their 'breaks' in the pub and forever talking shop, jealous of their senior colleagues, guarding every tiny privilege as they struggled up the ladder of promotion. It struck me as a dog's life.

In fact it was a dog's life – the life of Ben, the talking dog – that shortly afterwards thrust me into my career as a *Daily Mirror* columnist, as I have described earlier in this narrative, and although I have always had an affection for that little Jack Russell terrier I have equally wondered at times whether he really did me a favour. Whether or no, that first brief encounter with the breed seems to have established a bond between my family and the Jack Russell family. They have cropped up in my life ever since. Currently I am taken out for my morning exercise by a sprightly little Jack Russell bitch whose name is Portia, but whom I call Porkie because we are on very familiar terms, and she came into my life in almost as unconventional a way as my earlier Jack Russell friend, Ben.

Years ago, when she was a puppy and we had not met, Porkie had a terrible accident. She was run over by a hit-and-run car on the road and, badly smashed up with many bones broken, she was left to die in the gutter. It was late at night. A passing police car picked her up and took her to the nearest veterinary surgery so that she could be put of her misery. The vet on duty at the time happened to be my daughter Kate, who is now our local veterinary surgeon in Kensington. Instead of putting her down Kate took her into the operating theatre and worked throughout the rest of the night to save the little dog's life. Successfully. My wife later brought the little invalid back to our house to convalesce, and we all became very fond of her. The police said that if, after three months, nobody claimed her, the usual thing was for a stray to be sent to Battersea Dogs' Home. But by that time she was getting so fit that she would have objected to leaving her new family, so she is still with us. She is such a happy and intelligent little dog that sometimes she reminds me of Ben – she almost talks to you. Almost.

However, there is one thing that I must say. If she ever did talk – if, during one of our morning walks in Holland Park she stopped sniffing the trees and started to recite the soliloquy from *Hamlet* – I would tell nobody: even if she started singing Puccini's *O Mio Babbino Caro* in fluent Italian – I would take no notice. It would remain our secret. Once bitten twice shy. I don't want to start another column.

5

Language is like a cracked kettle on which
we beat out tunes for bears to dance to, while
all the time we long to move the stars to pity.

Gustave Flaubert

On the morning when Harry Guy Bartholomew called me in and, out of
the blue, gave me a column of my own to write in the *Daily Mirror*, I left
his office with my mind whirling round and showering off sparks like a
Catherine wheel. I was delighted, of course. This was what I had
wanted. But . . . but . . . the thing to do was to go for a walk and find out
why a small voice in the back of my mind kept saying 'but'.

Leaving the office I turned away from Fleet Street and began walking
slowly through streets where I was unlikely to meet anyone I knew. Out
of the attic of my mind I took some of the old ambitions that I had
stowed away there years before, and blew the dust off them.

There was this old icon labelled WRITER. Well, what about it? I had
become a writer, hadn't I? I was earning a living by putting words on
paper and arranging them in an order that persuaded one small number
of people that they were worth buying, and another, far larger, number
of people that they were worth reading. Admittedly that is not what I
meant, not what I meant at all. But, surely it would do? It was well paid,
probably better paid than the other way. So all that had happened was
that a few old dreams had decayed. I had learned my limitations. Like a
tailor who riffles through a swatch of materials and feels the different
qualities from cashmere to fustian, I could recognize different qualities
of writing at a glance, and knew the grade into which my own fitted: I
was a journalist. I had wandered into the literary rag trade and taken to
it. So what was all the fuss about?

Well, perhaps all this soul-searching was about whether I should be
content to stay in the mass-production sector of the rag trade, or try to
move into the *haute couture*. Was that the problem? Because, if so, this
was a silly time to be thinking about it. I had just been given a big

opportunity. All this pompous maundering was nothing but a whiff of smelling salts for a conscience that had been in a dead faint for years. Wake up and face the facts. Money was the name of the game. Admit it and follow old Omar's advice – take the cash in hand and waive the rest.

Yes, true enough, but wait a minute. That's only half the battle. The serious fact to face is that I do not really like the *Daily Mirror*. The readers were all right but the people who ran it were all wrong: most of the older executives were frauds posing as reformers, and the younger ones were all like Mr Hooper in *Brideshead*. They tolerated me because I was useful. Yet if I went ahead with this new column in the *Mirror* it was likely, on the formbook, that it would be successful, and that might mean that I would become married to the *Mirror*, forsaking all others for as long as I may live. That was the real problem, and this was the moment to face it. This minute. Now. Before it was too late.

I looked at my watch. Oh, my God – two o'clock! What a time of day to be conducting a wake round the coffin of dead aspirations. I had a column to find. The bird was on the wing. What a fool to spend all this time in gloomy soliloquy. Serve me right if my first column was a stinker.

I had drifted into Smithfield meat market during my reverie and, looking up, I saw that I was outside what appeared to be a butcher's shop; but not an ordinary butcher's shop because it had only tripe on display in the window. The fascia board above proclaimed: HENSON'S – TRIPE SPECIALISTS.

I laughed out loud. The perfect analogy. Mr Henson and I were kindred spirits. He in his fashion, I in mine. Here was a gift from the sardonic gods for my new column. I pushed open the door and walked in.

In the next day's issue of the *Daily Mirror* my first column began with a few paragraphs that ostensibly concerned a success story. They traced the career of Mr Henson, tripe specialist. He had set out when young to become a butcher in the classic mould but had discovered early in his career that there was more money in tripe. After a certain amount of soul-searching, because butchery of the skilled and proper kind had long been in his family, Linc Henson decided to grasp the substance rather than seek the shadow. He specialized in tripe. Soon he had fifteen shops, all built from the proceeds of tripe. He educated two sons, one to become Leslie Henson, the great comedian, the other, Bertram, to become a notable barrister-at-law. The name of Henson became famous, a glittering symbol of success, not only in Smithfield where it was a byword but also in the theatre and the law courts: the arts and the judiciary were enriched, and all because old Mr Henson had one day made the fateful decision to sell tripe.

Hoisting a banner over my new career, I ended this homily with the four words that affirmed my new philosophy: 'There's money in tripe.'

I have that old cutting of my first-ever column before me now, evidence in yellowing black and white that I was a bumptious young idiot who should have been fired for making a monkey out of the newspaper that was paying him. But nobody noticed. They even thought it was rather good. Over the years that followed I wrote thousands of columns for the *Daily Mirror*, but that first column was the only one in which I ever cocked a snook at the newspaper in its own pages: after that I grew up. Having expelled that first cryptic sneer from my system, I came to terms with the job. I made my bed and lay on it. In Lucullan comfort, which is always the most efficacious medicine to settle a rumbling conscience.

The world today is knee-deep in columnists; peer behind any curtain, remove any dustbin lid, and you find a columnist lurking; they come in all shapes and sizes, and it is unusual to walk through any restaurant with gourmet pretensions without tripping over one; but in my fledgling days this was not the case. We were far more rare, and those of us with our own name and picture on the column were as seldom seen as badgers. One reason for this was that paper was still rationed; newspapers were thin, and a week's magazines could have been displayed on one shelf of a newsagent's shop: paradoxically, at a time when television was almost unknown and the general public relied largely upon reading for its information and entertainment, there was far less on offer to be read.

As a consequence of this, we columnists found ourselves in disproportionate demand; everybody loved us, or, to be more exact, everybody who had something to sell, something to publicize or somebody to promote; we were fawned on, invited, fêted, treated with that profound respect and loving friendship due to the indispensable but evanescent stratum of society known as celebrities. Without ever taking it seriously, because it always seemed to me a splendid joke, I enjoyed it hugely. The *Daily Mirror* was advancing towards a readership not far short of one in three of the entire population, and was already a rich enterprise, so it was not neccessary for its columnists to accept hospitality, as became the norm in later years; indeed, it was frowned upon, and blatant publicity of the sort that later became customary in newspapers and on television was rigorously excluded from the paper; general columnists of my sort had a virtual *carte blanche* in the matter of expenses, which enabled us to repel the blandishments of publicity people offering hospitality, and we lived the life of Reilly because popular newspapers of the period spent money with the prodigality of nineteenth-century dukes.

My own work for the paper was, as it continued to be throughout my life, based on the pursuit of my own hobbies, foremost among which were the theatre and thoroughbred horse racing. Such subjects filled my column. It was the heyday of one of the most remarkable generations of talent that the English theatre has ever known, and on a stroll down Shaftesbury Avenue you would see a lustrous galaxy of names on the marquees, Gielgud, Coward, Richardson, Thorndike, Evans, Ashcroft. At times when I had seen every play in London I would turn my attention to the opera, always one of my delights; once I devoted a whole column to a new production of Donizetti's *Don Pasquale*, which evoked a stern telephone call from the editor on the morning it appeared: 'Watch it, son,' he warned. 'Don't push your luck.' But a dozen readers wrote in to say that this was a welcome step in the right direction, and as readers' letters were always watched with care I was appointed opera critic. On the *Daily Mirror* this was a task that required almost as infrequent work as that of a coronation programme seller, but as it resulted in my receiving a pair of tickets for every new production at Covent Garden for many years, I was well content.

In later years, when I was once again mildly rebuked for writing a column that apparently had too little sales value for a mass readership, the editor asked me into his office for a drink to discuss the matter, and the editorial director and managing editor were also present.

The managing editor remarked truculently, 'I must say that I don't think Noel pays sufficient regard to the fact that the *Daily Mirror* is his employer.'

The editor of the time, Lee Howard, an enormous man with a blandly debonair style, who called everyone 'doll' or 'duckie', drawled, 'If you want my opinion, duckie, Noel never has regarded the *Daily Mirror* in the customary way as an employer, but rather as an indulgent rich uncle who is a bit of a swine.'

One thing that saved my bacon time and again was that I always got on so well with the readers. They were on my side. We had an excellent rapport. Postage was cheap and they wrote to the editor on every conceivable subject, in vast quantity. Sometimes the letters were scrawled on the back of a used envelope or on a paper bag, but they still had a point to make, an opinion to voice. Life for them was hard and serious at the time, and I think they liked me because I did not take life seriously, but laughed with them at the grotesque absurdity of it all. The old-fashioned British working classes lacked the advantage of education

71

but they were by no means the idiots that some newspapers privately considered them to be.

Furthermore, we had a number of tastes in common, one of them being horse racing; there is an old saying that all men are equal on and under the turf, and although this is as untrue as most old sayings it is a fiction sturdily maintained by most Silver Ring punters, who are Conservative voters almost to a man; as Eliza Doolittle's father pointed out so eloquently, they are the undeserving poor, and they observe the rich not with resentment but with envy, staunchly believing that with a little bit of luck they could find themselves on the other side of those far rails with a top hat and big cigar and a bird and a magnum of champagne. The fact that the little bit of luck is perennially elusive does not damp their optimism. For some reason that would be pointless to examine without a psychologist present, a mutual affinity has always existed between them and me; one Derby day at Epsom when I was walking with some acquaintances from the members' enclosure to the paddock, people kept waving to me from the crowd on the other side of the fence and calling out, ''Ullo, Nole – good luck, mate!'

One of my acquaintances, looking most uncomfortable, asked, 'I say, Noel, do you know these people?'

'Oh, yes,' I replied, 'they are my friends.' Which was true.

The matter of the little bit of luck that *nearly* happened, but not quite, is a topic of unfailing interest among racing people, and as this was almost my consistent experience it provided me with some popular columns. I originally discovered this on my first visit to the Grand National. Although I have been to Aintree for that great occasion more than forty times since, that first visit stays in my memory. Most of the keen racing crowd, trainers and owners, stayed at the Adelphi Hotel in Liverpool, where at night we had a series of parties of the sort that would today elicit an outcry of simulated shock and grave censure in the Sunday papers.

Among the many friends I made on this particular enjoyable occasion were the connections of an Irish horse called Lovely Cottage. At first light on the day of the big race I went with them to watch him have his early morning gallop on the course; I took a few cubes of sugar in my pocket, which Lovely Cottage accepted with relish after his work, and I came to the unreasoning conclusion that he would surely win the National: he was not fancied in the ante-post betting but he was a grand, kindly, brave animal, and my heart rode with him.

The Grand National was run on a Wednesday in those days, and the *Daily Mirror* needed to have copy about the event immediately the race was over in order to get it into the northern editions, because at that time we printed only in London. So I laid my plans with care. I arranged with the landlord of the Sefton Arms, a big pub beside the racecourse, to have sole use of the telephone in his office for an hour after three o'clock on the big day; then I arranged with a taxi-driver to pick me up outside the pub at 4.15 p.m. so that I could catch the five o'clock train from Lime Street back to London. This fixed, I walked round the Grand National course – some two and a quarter miles, which the horses cover twice – to familiarize myself with the formidable obstacles that I had never seen before.

On the far side of the course, distant from the stands, some bookies were offering fifty to one against Lovely Cottage; most of them were rumoured to have spiked running shoes in their satchels as a precaution against loss, so I was not tempted; in any case I would have had no time to collect after the race, so, taking five £10 notes out of my wallet, I approached the Tote and had them all on Lovely Cottage, on the nose.

A vast crowd was gathered at Aintree, because British horse racing was enjoying a boom period; the throng that poured through the turnstiles was largely composed of ex-servicemen who were cheerfully spending their gratuities before facing up to the realities of life in a near-bankrupt land that had little to offer its heroes.

Reporters were not allowed on the course for the start of the race, but photographers were, so I slung a Leica round my neck in order to get close up to the nerve-strung excitement that tingles in the air as the horses circle and cavort in preparation for getting into line and then erupting into a cavalry charge to the first fence: those minutes before the start of the National, when all the crowds become hushed and the stands gradually go quiet as a church have never ceased to make my heart beat faster.

As soon as the horses were off I ran back in front of the stands and waited to watch the horses jump the Chair on their first circuit of the course, and then I ran back to the winning post in plenty of time to see the finish.

It was a misty March day. I could not pick out the colours as the horses still in the race approached the elbow, the point at which many a tired horse has used the rails to keep him straight for a final effort. The horses were nearly upon me before I could pick out the green and silver colours of Lovely Cottage. He was in front – right bang in front. When Lovely Cottage passed the post to win by four lengths I let out a whoop of joy and turned to leg it back to the Sefton Arms, singing at the top of my voice. What a beauty!

The copy-takers at the *Daily Mirror* were ready for me, and I put my story over quickly; as I recall, it may have run slightly to hyperbole.

Outside the pub my taxi was duly waiting but the driver, standing beside it, was swaying in the breeze. Always on Grand National day there were coachloads of people who arrived from all over the North and were set down at the Sefton Arms, where many of them stayed throughout the rest of the day, without ever setting eyes on a horse, until the coaches returned to take them home again. My taxi-driver had joined one such party. He was in no state to drive. So I found a local man who was sober and gave him a couple of pounds to walk the taxi-driver home, and then set off on my own long walk back to Liverpool. Every bus was full to overflowing and the chance of finding another taxi free was zero, but my heart was light and I was happy. I had enjoyed a superb day and, as a little bit of luck, Lovely Cottage had been returned at 25-1 on the book, so I must have won something in the region of twelve hundred and fifty quid, which was the price of a lovely cottage in the country. I felt the Tote tickets in my wallet to make sure they were still there. I would put them in the post to Tote headquarters when I returned home, and they would send me a cheque.

I had walked no more than a few hundred yards when a Rolls Royce purred in towards the kerb and stopped beside me. The window rolled down and out beamed the face of Major Cyril Dennis.

'Jump in, old boy,' he called. 'Looks as though I can be of some small service to you. We all go the same way home, what?'

I climbed in, gratefully. Cyril Dennis was fairly typical of my acquaintances at the time. After a flamboyant career as a soldier he had retired with little more than his pension, but among the souvenirs of his colourful past was a certificate for a large number of oil shares, which he had bought for the price of a bottle of rum from an alcoholic prospector in Venezuela. Soon after Cyril had settled himself into a cottage in the Cotswolds, philosophically accepting the probability that the rest of his life would contain little more exciting than a bit of hunting and an occasional day's racing, the oil well in Venezuela started gushing. At a stroke, or perhaps it would be more accurate to say at a squirt, Cyril became mega-rich.

He was not the sort of man to take his good fortune shyly; unlike Paul Getty, who always looked so miserable about his oil, Cyril was never subsequently seen without a 500-watt smile on his face: when the sea of oil began to lap round his shore, he pushed the boat out. He bought a grouse moor in Scotland and a house in Mayfair and in the matter of joyous ostentation he could have given Mr Toad of Toad Hall fifty yards start in a hundred yards race and passed him in under five seconds.

'Old boy,' he said to me with his Lord Scamperdale smile when I was settled in the car, 'I have to tell you that giving you a lift is not a charitable act but a piece of enlightened self-interest. Fact is, old son, we need a fourth for a game of poker on the train.'

He gestured towards the other two men in the car. One was a cabinet minister in the Labour government who was known for his taste for the high life, the other a racehorse owner who was celebrated in the gossip columns as a *bon viveur* and a high-roller, known to his friends as Bones. I had met both before.

'If one does not take precautions,' went on Cyril, beaming, 'a journey by train these days can be a wearisome affair, so I have arranged a simple repast to brighten our lives on the way down. A salmon that I hooked on my bit of fishing on the Tay has been sent to the chef on the train, together with some fresh *foie gras* that I had flown in from Strasbourg. Then we shall have some young chickens from my farm in Hampshire, with a few fresh peaches and a bit of Stilton to round it off.'

'Thank God I missed my lunch,' I said, devoutly. It was the period when five shillings was, by law, the maximum that any restaurant was allowed to charge for a meal.

The cabinet minister, whose gloomy expression suggested that he had not backed Lovely Cottage at the races, said, 'I could do with a beer.'

'That may be possible,' said Cyril, 'but if there is no beer on the train we shall not go thirsty. I have arranged for a few bottles of vintage Dom Perignon to be sent to the *sommelier* in the dining car, and also the odd few bottles of an unpretentious but delicious white wine from my little vineyard in Burgundy. If you find that boring I have also provided him with a few bottles of Mouton Rothschild 1927.'

At Lime Street station Cyril instructed his chauffeur to drive the Rolls back to Berkeley Square and we walked along the platform, past coaches with corridors jammed to capacity, until we came to Cyril's reserved compartment where we sat back in comfort after our tiring day. The wine waiter arrived bearing ice-buckets containing the Dom Perignon, and behind him came another waiter with a mahogany cabinet of Havana cigars.

'Right,' said Cyril, unwrapping a pack of cards that had arrived with the cigars and shuffling them. 'Now to the serious business of the evening.'

I imagine that Cyril and Bones and I all had the same thought in mind: we hoped that the Labour cabinet minister had brought his cheque book with him. But by the time we went in to dinner, the old politician, still looking gloomy, had taken the best part of £1,000 off each of us. By the time we got to the Stilton, which came with some Taylor's '38 port that Cyril had forgotten to mention, I was consoling myself with the thought that, thanks to Lovely Cottage, I was still about £250 in hand on the day. We played again after dinner, and I managed to claw back another £250, so when we steamed into Euston I reckoned that I had had a narrow escape.

Thanking Cyril for his hospitality, I marched to the taxi rank, buying a final edition of the *Evening Standard* on the way. 'Lovely Cottage Wins National at 25–1,' said the headline. I smiled, figuring that I must still be about £500 ahead on the day. Then I turned to the small print that showed the Tote odds. Lovely Cottage had paid 11-1 on the Tote. I climbed into a taxi and gave the driver my address. The end of a perfect day. I had exactly broken even.

Looking back at those days of wine and roses I find a temptation to reflect that Britain was so different then, such a foreign land by comparison with today: no television; no widespread house-ownership; no new-style middle class, with two-car families commonplace among the folk who used to go by bike; no mass exodus by air for summer holidays abroad; no football hooligans or lager louts; no credit cards, no wine bars, no customary mortgage, no computers. Yet, looking closer, one can see that the fundamental similarities between then and now are more striking than the superficial differences: the rich are still extremely rich and the poor we still have with us; we have redefined the word poverty, time and again, adjusting it to quantitative expectations; but, as old Mr Crouchback pointed out to Guy, quantitative judgements don't apply.

All the *Mirror*'s half-dozen senior writers were caged in a row of offices on the fourth floor of Geraldine House. My next-door neighbour on one side was Barbara Betts, a young woman with flaming red hair and politics to match who had been brought in by Garry Allighan to take over his Question Time in the Mess column; the ostensible purpose of the column was to explain to members of the armed forces what their rights were, but Barbara did this in such a provocative way that it was always a wonder to me that she did not start a mutiny. Garry Allighan, soon to be member of parliament for Gravesend, took me along to her wedding when she married Ted Castle, a former picture editor on the *Mirror*; as Barbara Castle, she herself became a Labour member of parliament in 1945, and later a cabinet minister. Ted Castle remained a colleague of mine until he retired, when he became Lord Castle.

In the office on my other flank was Giles Romilly, brother of Esmond

Romilly who was married to Jessica Mitford. Giles and Esmond had been *enfants terribles* during the immediate pre-war years, having been expelled from school only to become notorious for writing 'subversive' Communist pamphlets and later to join the International Brigade in Spain; it was during that period that I first met Giles, at a party to which I went with Philip Toynbee and Peter Nevile at Esmond's house in a slum area somewhere eastwards along the Thames. I saw him only infrequently for a few years after that, until one day after the war I ran into him in El Vino. He told me he was looking for a job.

'I suppose there is no chance they would have me on that frightful rag you work for?' he asked.

'I could get you an interview with the editor,' I said, 'but I think that even the *Mirror* might regard you as a bit too hot to handle.' Then I had an idea, and went on, 'Winston Churchill is your uncle, isn't he?'

'Oh, yes,' said Giles, 'but we're not on speakers. If old Winston had his way I would be languishing in the Bloody Tower.'

'Never you mind,' I said, thoughtfully. 'The *Mirror* people may not know that. If you were to see the editor and give the impression that in spite of past differences you are still Uncle Winston's favourite nephew, they might be interested.'

The *Mirror* was in cahoots with all the senior members of the socialist administration, but, not surprisingly, the paper was short of contacts inside the Tory party; so when Giles went in asking for a job and told them that Winston was his favourite uncle, they hired him on the spot: they saw him as a mole who could sit in Uncle Winston's drawing room at Chartwell and listen to all the secrets, and then pass them on.

Giles, like his sister-in-law, Jessica, was still a revolutionary Communist, so although the *Mirror* never achieved the objective of having a mole in the Conservative party, they found some of the left-wing articles he wrote highly acceptable. He and I usually went to El Vino for a drink in the evening, often in the company of Claud Cockburn, another Communist, who was at that time editor of *The Week*, a probing and satirical magazine which was the precursor of *Private Eye*. Giles regaled us with extraordinary stories of the Mitford girls, particularly Unity, who had become a friend of Adolf Hitler in 1935 and had taken her parents, the Redesdales, to meet him, which was a move loudly applauded by Lord Rothermere and the *Daily Mirror*. Unity remained Hitler's starry-eyed disciple right up to the outbreak of war when she shot herself with a revolver that the Führer had given her as a present. I have since read David Pryce-Jones's biography of Unity, but although it is a fascinating document it does not include some of the wilder anecdotes that Giles used to tell.

On the face of it Giles and I were, in different ways, odd goldfish in the *Mirror* tank of piranhas; but, despite appearances, the *Mirror* people – farouche and devious as they were – never had much of a chance against Giles; or against me, either, for that matter: when hitting back after attack, neither of us bothered much about the precise location of the belt. Giles's constant need for self-protection in a predatory world had turned him into an upper-class Arthur Allighan, typical of many amoral young drifters from decent families. I have always had a proclivity towards attracting such people as friends, which may reveal more about me than it does about them: we shared a desperate sense of humour, an awareness that all human comedy is rooted in anguish.

One service for which I remember Giles with gratitude was that he introduced me to Nancy Mitford, who remained a beloved friend until she died of cancer many years later. Every time I was in Paris during those years, which was often, I used to visit Nancy at her house in the Rue Monsieur, just along from Cardinal de Retz's house. Loving France so passionately, she came to visit England increasingly seldom, pretending that the reason she disliked London was that it had become full of such bogus people; there were, of course, more cogent reasons.

When Nancy wanted something done in London she would ask her friends. One such task that she set me, much to my anxiety, was to straighten out Dominic Elwes, who called her Aunt Nancy because of a kinship through her marriage to Peter Rodd. Nancy was fond of Dominic, in the same exasperated and disapproving way that she was kindly towards her other recalcitrant cousins, Giles and Esmond, but when she asked me to use my uneasy friendship with Dominic to help him become *un homme sérieux* I realized immediately that this was a commission that St Jude would have turned down flat; delightful and amusing companion that he was, there was no hope for Dominic: product of an old Catholic family, educated at Downside, endowed with enough talent to make a reasonably successful life, he was nevertheless born among the damned.

He was claiming to be a Communist at the time, a fashionable flag for young misfits who wished to infuriate their families, but in fact he never was a political animal; all he really wanted was to become rich and happy, in both of which objectives life constantly thwarted him because he had no natural talent for achieving either of those desirable but elusive conditions. In his search for the end of the rainbow he devised a number of hair-brained schemes that would have caused even Ukridge to pause for reflection, and in most of these he sought to enlist the help of my column because he had an ineradicable belief that all publicity was a good thing, whereas in his case it was such a bad thing that it ultimately led to his suicide in despair and remorse.

I do not believe I ever wrote about Dominic in the newspaper, much to his irritation, because he kept asking me to help him with his outrageous plans and he considered my lack of co-operation an oddly unfriendly act. Once, in the wake of a series of sensational elopements, he invited me for a drink at the Ritz and, in conspiratorial fashion, asked me if I would handle his own elopement, on a commercial basis, if he could find a sufficiently rich heiress: he was genuinely astonished when I became so angry that I nearly hit him.

In fact he later engaged a publicity man, Freddie Mullally, to perform this service for him, with inevitably dismal results. Poor Dominic, poor Sebastian Flyte.

When Nancy Mitford knew that she was mortally ill, but before she moved to Versailles to die, I dropped in for coffee one morning. She was in a *grande dame* humour and she poured me a large Scotch.

'But Nancy dear,' I objected, 'it's only ten o'clock in the morning.'

'With friends of Dominic's,' she said accusingly, 'one never knows.'

She had been reading a letter from her sister, the Duchess of Devonshire, and she waved the letter in the air with a despairing sigh. 'Now I shall never visit London again,' she said.

'Why not?' I asked.

'Because Debo tells me they are closing down Woollands.'

'Woollands?' I echoed. 'Is that important?'

'It is the only place left in London where one can conceivably shop,' she said, 'and since everything else in London has already gone there can be no possible purpose in returning there.'

I must have looked so dubious about this eccentric idea that she laughed out loud and made me a cup of coffee, knowing that she had the wrong audience for play-acting of that sort.

Every newspaper column worth its salt develops a personality of its own, which is not necessarily that of the writer, and I found that mine quickly became the focal point for eccentrics who wrote to me or telephoned from all over the country; they swarmed around the column like wasps at a picnic. One such was John Gawsworth, the poet, who was also King of Redonda. Redonda was an island in the Caribbean of which his family had, during the eighteenth century, become kings, and although John himself lived an artist's life in Chelsea he maintained a court there, issuing decrees and appointing his own aristocracy; the Foreign and Colonial Office regarded him with a mildly disapproving eye, but there was little it could do because there was some substance to his claim.

Hoping to use my column as a sort of court circular for the Kingdom of Redonda, His Majesty conveyed to me the dukedom of Bonafides; after the investiture his letters to me always began, 'My dear Bonafides,' and were signed, 'Juan I'. When I reported it, this esoteric honour caused some hilarity among the readers and they continued to refer to me as 'ole Nole'; it cut a little ice in Chelsea, however, because on occasions when I visited the Markham Arms in the Old King's Road for a half-pint with the king I would always be greeted as Your Grace. Life was a good joke.

Another long-lasting friend who drifted my way during those early column days was Zoë, Lady Hart-Dyke, who was hot in pursuit of publicity for silkworms. At Lullingstone Castle in Kent she had founded the biggest silkworm farm in England and made silk for great ceremonial occasions. The culmination of her efforts was the production of silk for the Queen's coronation dress, which was designed by Norman Hartnell. Zoë was the incarnation of Bertie Wooster's Aunt Dahlia; she stood for no nonsense, brooked no argument, issued commands in lengthy telegrams, talked on the telephone in a voice that could be heard across several fields, and was at heart the kindliest soul that you could wish to meet.

After sending me a formal invitation to attend the first Blessing of the Silkworms ceremony at St Michael's Abbey in Farnborough, Hampshire, she telephoned, presumably to make sure that I could read and had got the message. 'Do try to totter down, dear boy,' she said, 'and bring a photographer – I assume you keep one in a kennel in your office. It's going to be very dignified, you know, so I want no jiggery-pokery in the paper. Are you receiving me loud and clear?'

Holding the telephone at least a foot from my ear, I said I was.

'I'm not a Catholic,' she went on, 'and I don't suppose you are, what? – but I'm having the ceremony at St Michael's because I think the Catholics always do these showy things so well. Our chaps are first class for a country wedding or a harvest festival but I always say that if you want a theatrical production you've got to go to the Catholics, what?'

She was tall and she dressed in the Edwardian style of a duchess in an Ealing film comedy. When I arrived at St Michael's Abbey she already had the assembled monks, mild men wearing cowls over their heads, well under the whip.

'All you chaps line up over here,' she trumpeted. Obediently they shuffled into a wavy line.

The ceremony of blessing the silkworms, all of whom were present, was simple and elegant with just a touch of the feudal. The workers from Lullingstone sang their hearts out. After it was over I was standing in the abbey porch when Zoë came striding up.

'Dear boy,' she said, 'while I talk to the abbot will you do something for me? Go and fetch that willowy monk, the very tall thin one who looks as though he hasn't had a square meal since the third Sunday after Pentecost, and bring him over here. I have just heard that he is one of the world's premier experts on the eating habits of silkworms, and as we give the little darlings nothing but the old-fashioned mulberry leaves diet I would like to have words with him and pick his mighty brain.'

Feeling that I had by chance strayed into a plot at Blandings, I marched off to find the willowy monk, whose name was Dom Edmund; he eagerly agreed to come and talk silkworms with Lady Zoë.

For several years after that I went back to Farnborough for the annual blessing and always had a long chat with Dom Edmund – until a year came when he ceased to be there. I often wondered what had happened to him but it was twenty years before I found out.

I was writing some columns in the north of Scotland and, passing an ancient monastery outside Elgin, I turned and drove in on impulse. The abbot received me gravely and when I told him who I was and what I was doing he said that if I wished to stay for a few days and use the monastery as my base I would be welcome. I accepted gratefully and was shown to a simple cell with a bed and a table; it was soothing to fall into the quiet and ordered routine in which everyone was summoned by bells, like being back at school during a retreat.

The monks were Benedictines who had previously occupied a monastery at Prinknash in Gloucestershire, at which time they were Anglican Benedictines; but after a collective *crise de conscience* on the matter of whether it was correct to deny the doctrine of transubstantiation, they all converted to the Church of Rome, which meant leaving Prinknash because it belonged to the Church of England.

Two of the monks set off on foot to seek a new home, and some weeks later they found themselves looking at the ancient ruins of Pluscarden Abbey in Scotland. It was a thirteenth-century ruin, its roof open to the sky, but the monks from Prinknash moved there and set about the formidable task of repairing it. To provide money for the materials they needed, they set up a market garden in the grounds, and also kept chickens, pigs, sheep and beef cattle; they soon had a thriving enterprise on their hands.

It was happy place in which to stay; I found it easy to work there and, as a matter of courtesy, took to attending plainsong in the crypt after midnight: those Gregorian chants, sung in the echoing vaults whose pillars had been carved by St Bernard's followers more than six centuries before, were movingly beautiful.

On the day before I was due to move on I was strolling through the garden, admiring the vegetables, when I saw a tall, thin monk hoeing potatoes: unmistakably Dom Edmund, the willowy monk. I called to him and waved, but although he looked up and smiled he went on with his work; the order had an austere discipline, similar to that of the Trappists. However, that afternoon there was a knock on my cell door, and it was Dom Edmund; he had obtained permission from the abbot to speak to me.

I was delighted, as he was, and he told me that it was the first time he had met anyone from outside since he joined the monastery from Farnborough, many years before. We chatted about the old days, the silkworms and Lady Zoë, and he was eager for news.

'Yours must be an interesting life,' he said. 'So many people to meet, so much to write about. I myself once decided to write a book, when I was on the stage. I promised Noël Coward that I would. But I never kept my promise. It came to me that I must dedicate my life to God's work. So here I am at Pluscarden, promoted to head gardener and loving every moment of it.'

Then it came out in conversation that he had worked in the theatre with many names that had been famous in their day. We chatted about Cocky and The Guv'nor, the Master and darling Gertie, Jack and Cis, Dorothy and Phyllis, Mis, Jack and Elsie, Larry and Viv, Totie and Toni, Gladys and Bee, Bobby and Binney – all faces from the past that were fresh as that morning's dawn in the mind of the kindly old monk who sat so happily reminiscing in the incongruous setting of my cell. I asked him if he often thought about those days when he was working in the garden.

'Not often,' he replied. 'We have little time. There is one recreation I permit myself,' he added with a smile, 'and I expect you will think it awfully silly, but every year I make time to re-read all of dear Nancy Mitford's books. If ever in my mind I go outside the walls, that is the world I prefer to visit. Sometimes, dear boy, when I remember you in my prayers, I see you living in that world.'

I laughed with embarrassment as he rose to leave, but realized that the courteous old man had paid me the gentlest compliment in his vocabulary; not only did he remember me, but, brushing aside the rough world of newspapers, he preferred to think of me in a world no more real than Alconleigh, Hetton or Manderley: untrue as it was, it was the best that he could wish for me, the nearest to the angels.

Back in the cradle days of the column, my pay was still rising and I began to toy with an old ambition to own a racehorse. Already I knew many people in racing and among them was Peter Thrale, a veterinary surgeon who had become a trainer and who was an exceptional judge of yearlings. So I arranged to meet Peter at the Newmarket sales, the intention being that he would try to sort me out a promising individual that would come under the hammer for less than a monkey – £500. I stayed with friends in Newmarket the night before and early next morning went out walking on the Heath, watching the horses from the different stables at work.

It was a beautiful morning of cool sunshine and high, wispy clouds, and in the distance I could see a lone figure seated before an easel, sketching; I sauntered in that direction, thinking to pass close enough to get a glimpse of the work he was doing. Soon I recognized the figure. The old jacket, the battered hat, the unmistakable Sir Alfred Munnings, president of the Royal Academy. I was a few yards behind him, craning my neck, when he turned and shouted, 'I say – whose horses are those?'

He was pointing to a string of horses on the skyline so I put up my binocular and replied, 'The Captain's. Probably second lot.' Everyone in racing referred to Cecil Boyd-Rochfort, the royal trainer, as The Captain.

'Thought so,' said Sir Alfred, and began folding his easel and gathering his things together ready for departure. 'Do you have any horses?'

'Oh, no,' I said. 'Not yet, anyway. I am a journalist.'

It was always my habit to tell people like Sir Alfred that I was a journalist, right at the start, because some of them hated journalists, often with good reason, and it gave them the chance to make a quick escape. But the old artist was a man who judged men and horses on the evidence of his own two eyes, not by hearsay, and he fell into step beside me as we walked back towards the town. Even when I told him that I wrote a column for the *Daily Mirror* he did not appear to regard this as a form of terrorist activity; the *Mirror* was, after all, still regarded by people who did not read it as a ticking bomb under the canopy of respectable society, dedicated to piling the middle classes into the tumbrils.

Before we parted Sir Alfred gave me his London address and invited me to come in for drinks on the following Thursday evening, an invitation that I accepted with pleasure because not only did I like the old gentleman but I had an enormous respect for his work, bracketing him in my mind with Stubbs.

The drinks party was fun. Some of the guests were artists and most were familiar faces from the café-society circuit. Lady Munnings, who had the reputation of being a dragon, was particularly nice to me, which was a pleasant surprise because she was noted for protecting her less worldly husband from intrusive newspapermen.

It was some weeks later, in November, before I came across the Munningses again, this time at the Lord Mayor's Banquet at Guildhall, an occasion that I covered for many years because I was the only man on the *Mirror* who had his own white tie and tails, and it saved them sending somebody else to Moss Bros. The usual splendiferous scene was in evidence as I walked under the floodlit canopies that decked the outside of the historic building, bombed in the war; bankers, ambassadors, tycoons, worshipful fishmongers, cabinet ministers, all jostled together in the foyer, a star cast of players in Britain's power and money dramas.

I was talking to some people I knew when I heard my name being called and looking round saw Lady Munnings weaving her way towards me through the crowd. She was dressed in the appropriate finery, but she had an unusually big black handbag.

'Noel, dear,' she said, 'I wonder if you would do me a tiny favour?'

'Delighted, Lady Munnings,' I replied.

'Fact is,' she went on, 'Alfred and I have got to line up to shake old George by the hand' – Sir George Aylwen was the new Lord Mayor – 'and I always find these reception things difficult with my handbag, so I wondered if you might be kind enough to take it into the banqueting hall for me – I notice on the seating plan that we are sitting close together.'

Cold horror gripped my spine. This was the late 1940s and the sight of a man in full evening dress with a handbag was not only rarer that it would be today, it was unthinkable. But I took the handbag and forced an unconvincing smile. There was no chance of concealing it because it was so big. I tried tucking it under my arm but it only made me look like a burglar making off with the silver. There was only one thing to do. Brazen it out. Walk on with the head held high, a quizzical smile on the face, handbag hanging from the arm.

As I marched up the stately staircase I saw several people I knew, but after one glance they all looked hurriedly away. The staircase was flanked by a guard of honour from the Honourable Artillery Company, my once and nearly regiment, wearing plumed helmets and breastplates;

one of them nearly dropped his halberd when he spotted me with my handbag. I heard a hoarse whisper in the distance: 'That's Godfrey fuckin' Winn, y'know.' I could cheerfully have murdered Lady Munnings.

Halfway up the stairs something happened that made my blood run cold. The handbag was moving. There was something alive in it. Resisting the impulse to turn round and run for it, I strode on. At the top of the stairs were two Special Branch men, watching with keen eyes as the guests passed. One of them recognized me and gave me an almost imperceptible nod. For one ghastly moment I thought he was going to ask me what I had in the handbag and only sheer terror restrained me from breaking into a trot. In the galleried reception hall a small orchestra was playing and people were standing around in clusters, chatting; but I did not hang about; like an arrow from a bow I made straight for the banqueting hall, found my place, stuck the handbag under the table, and stood there mopping my brow. I would have given half my kingdom for a large Scotch.

Examining the place-cards I discovered that the Munningses were next to me, but it seemed like several weeks before the rest of the guests streamed in and at last Lady Munnings bustled up. 'Dear Noel,' she beamed, 'it was sweet of you to bring Blackie in for me. He never lets me down by barking in public, but I did not want to take a chance of creating a rumpus right in front of the Lord Mayor.'

She had brought her dog to the banquet, in the bag.

The dog, whose full name was Black Knight, was a Pekinese, and when Lady Munnings sat down she opened the bag, which was between us, so that he could poke his nose out and see what was going on. He had a disdainful expression on his face, but after I had slipped him a few morsels of roast partridge he cheered up. When the speeches started he quietly climbed out and sat on my lap, panting, with his tongue hanging out.

'He's thirsty,' I said to Lady Munnings. 'Do you think he would care for a saucer of this Bollinger '37? It's awfully good.'

'No, dear,' she replied. 'He doesn't drink. Unlike Alfred,' she added, darkly, casting a glance at her husband who was putting the liquor away in style to take the edge off his boredom.

In the middle of the Archbishop of Canterbury's speech, Blackie looked up and barked. He was on my lap under the tablecloth and nobody could see him, so I began to cough loudly as though I had swallowed something that had gone down the wrong way. Dis-approving eyes were turned on me and a few people hissed 'Ssh!' But the day was saved. Blackie went back to sleep and Lady Munnings smuggled him back into the bag before we left the table.

As we walked down to the foyer to wait for our cars to be called, Sir Alfred said to me, 'That was damned quick-witted of you, Noel. About Violet's dog, I mean. Could have been nasty, what? Specially when the old Archbish was sounding off. Very decent of you, I thought. Come in for drinks tomorrow evening, eh? Any time after eight.'

I was late getting away from the office on the following evening and the party was in full swing by the time I arrived. A good deal of drink was being taken and everyone was in high spirits. I knew several people in the crowded studio, but in the corner I saw a painting on an easel, and went to look. It was the Newmarket scene, the finished picture. Beautiful. That pale blue East Anglian sky with smoky white clouds, never done better even by that other miller's son, John Constable; and in the distance the horses on the heath. Looking at it I could feel again the cool of the morning air. It was exquisite.

I had been gazing at it for several minutes when Sir Alfred came over. He had been just behind me, talking to friends, and I had heard his voice above the chatter. He had been telling them how extremely hard up he was and how he feared for the future. It did not seem likely to me that he could have much to fear, but some men, when they become old, get a fixation about becoming poor: I had not long previously visited Bernard Shaw at his house in Ayot St Lawrence, and had noticed that he was obsessed by the spectre of poverty, though with little enough reason.

'I can see you like the picture, Noel,' said Sir Alfred, laughing.

'It is one of the loveliest paintings I have ever seen,' I replied, sincerely.

Sir Alfred had obviously had plenty to drink, and suddenly he said, 'It's yours, my boy. Take it with you. A present. You were so bloody decent about Vi's dog. Apart from which, we like you. Go on – take it before I change my mind.'

I couldn't. I wanted to, but I couldn't. I thanked him, of course, and tried to make a joke about what Lady Munnings would say if he started giving all his paintings away. Then I went back to the office.

Next morning Sir Alfred telephoned. 'We were all a bit tiddley last night,' he said, 'but I want you to know that I meant what I said.'

Once more I declined.

The Munningses continued to invite me to their parties, and even set up a lunch for me to meet Pietro Annigoni, who became a lifelong friend; a few years later Sir Alfred painted a picture of Black Knight sitting among a tumble of racecards in his studio, and sent me a signed photograph of it. The dog had just died. Violet Munnings wrote on the back of the photograph, 'This is probably the best small picture Alfred has ever painted.'

The year before he died, the old man sent me another signed photograph, this time with their new dog, a black retriever, taken when the dog was jumping up at him in his studio at Castle House, Dedham. Violet wrote on the back, 'Munnings sends you his best wishes and I – just lovely memories of my little dog.'

Recently I saw again the painting that Sir Alfred had wanted to give me. It still gave me that *frisson* that I get from the work of a few masters. And I saw in my mind's eye that morning on Newmarket Heath. Somebody remarked that the picture would now fetch about half a million if it came under hammer in the saleroom.

For reasons that I would find hard to explain, and which would probably sound unconvincing if I did try, I have never for one single moment felt sorry that I did not accept the gift. Probably something to do with Horace.

6

If ever any beauty I did see,
Which I desir'd, and got, t'was but a dreame of thee.

John Donne, *The Good-Morrow*

One day I walked into the news room and saw a girl talking to the news editor. I had never seen her before. She was wearing a black two-piece with a cream silk blouse. Although I had for years been careful to guide all conversations with girls away from the serious subject of marriage, this idea now came clamouring into my mind with a peal of bells. It was the best idea I had ever had in the whole of my life. Within thirty seconds of seeing her for the first time I had decided to ask her to marry me.

One difficulty, as I soon found out, was that she did not rate me highly in the charts. She told one of her girl friends, in confidence, that she considered me to be a Champagne Charlie, a playboy, a lounge-lizard, a rake, all top hat and no breakfast: in which opinion there was some evident truth. Whether, over the ensuing forty years, I ever completely convinced her that this was an exaggerated view which failed to take account of my sturdier qualities is open to question, because Yorkshire-women do not change their opinions hastily, but the important fact is that I persuaded her to marry me; which, looking back, was the only really clever thing I ever did. That day when I first set eyes on her in the news room of the *Daily Mirror* was unquestionably the luckiest day in all my lucky life.

She came from a Yorkshire family of local squires who had farmed in the North Riding village of Barton-le-Street since before the Vikings came, the roots that perennially produce crop after crop of people who are kind and true. These were qualities that were lacking in my life, working as I did among the *jeunesse dorée* of café society who seldom strayed far from the racecourse or the Ritz, and I valued them far above rubies. Having decided to become a journalist she had set about learning the craft with typical thoroughness; starting as a trainee on the *Western Morning News*, she had quickly graduated to woman's page editor with a column of her own, and had then moved to the evening paper in

Norwich as splash-sub, a rare job for a woman in those days; then to London as features editor of Lord Kemsley's *Sunday Graphic* where she had a flaming row with the editor, a mercurial old boozer called Reggie Simpson, chucked in the job and moved to the *Daily Mirror* as a reporter, seeing the job as a stop-gap while she looked round for something more suitable. Fortunately for me. Through all the good and bad times since, not a day has passed on which I did not reflect that there was one aspect of my unruly life upon which fate had smiled.

We were married by the registrar in Paddington, secretly because the *Daily Mirror* was publicizing me as the archetypal bachelor-round-town and they would have frowned upon the liaison; but my wife, scorning subterfuge, soon gave up her job on the paper so that she could set about organizing our life. An affordable place to live was hard to find in bomb-scarred London because property racketeers were demanding high premiums, but my wife found an ideal mansion flat in Bloomsbury, with spacious rooms, reasonable rent – I think it was £6 a week or less – and only ten minutes from the office.

We went everywhere together, and she found so many stories of interest to women that I could have filled my column with them, and sometimes did. Some of the stories were so obviously seen with a woman's eye that I created a new character for the column, attributing ideas to my girlfriend Liz, and this delighted the newspaper because Liz started getting an enormous fanmail of her own, and invitations avalanched in for 'Noel Whitcomb and Liz'. Liz became a celebrity in her own right, which was fine for the newspaper and caused me to receive another rise in pay, although my wife was not too happy about it; she disliked the limelight and furthermore she did not care much for the *Daily Mirror*.

Furnishing a flat in those days was a task requiring ingenuity and an expert eye, because nearly everything was either unobtainable or on coupons; fortunately my wife possessed both those attributes. She had just about completed the flat to her satisfaction and my delight when the editor of one of the better Sunday newspapers telephoned and asked her to write a weekly column; this she agreed to do. The first of her columns appeared on the following Sunday under the byline Sally Whitcomb. It was a good column.

When I went into my office on the Monday morning all hell had broken loose. Bart wanted to see me immediately or sooner; the editor wanted to see me right away; the managing editor wanted to see me urgently. I chose the managing editor first.

'Ah, Noel,' he said, as I walked into his office, 'what the hell do you think you're up to, allowing your wife to write for another newspaper?'

I was very angry. 'What the hell do you mean by talking to me like that?' I said. 'Damned impudence. My wife does not work here. You have no right whatever to dictate what she may or may not do. Blasted impertinence.'

'Calm down, old boy,' he said in a more soothing tone. 'I understand how you feel about it, but the fact is that Bart and the editor and I are all of the same opinion – the name Whitcomb belongs to this newspaper.'

'Rubbish,' I said. 'Suppose my name was Smith?'

'That's the whole point,' he said, 'it isn't. There is no other Whitcomb writing on national newspapers at the moment. When a column appears under the name of Sally Whitcomb, everybody is going to know that it is Liz. And Liz belongs to us.'

'Liz,' I said, fighting to keep my fury under control, 'belongs to me. Or, more to the point, in this case she belongs to herself. If she decides to write a column for another newspaper that is her business. Not yours. Not mine. Hers.'

The managing editor sighed. 'You had better make it your business, old son,' he said, 'because otherwise you will be generally considered – not only here but up and down Fleet Street – to be cashing in on your name to publicize another newspaper that has nowhere near a quarter of our circulation. And before you explode again, do me a favour. Go and have a chat with Sally. You see, old boy, she has more commonsense then you have. She will see the point. She can go on writing the column, of course, but under another name.'

'Go to hell,' I said, 'and take my resignation with you. You will have it in writing by this afternoon.'

I went straight home. My wife was putting up the last of the curtains. To my astonishment, instead of taking off like a rocket, she smiled. 'I wondered about that,' she said. 'I thought it might bring the pains on. I think they are being a bit pompous but I can see that in their way of looking at it they have a point.'

'Nonsense,' I said. 'It's monstrous. In any case, I've resigned.'

'They won't take any notice of that,' she said. 'You ought to know them by now. What they are looking for is a way out that does not damage their investment. Think on. You are now earning nearly three thousand a year from the *Mirror* plus another three thousand in expenses. Would it make sense to toss that away out of pique?'

'It's not pique,' I said, 'it's a matter of principle.'

My wife has always been a staunch supporter of women's rights, and I have no doubt that she privately felt the wrongness of it as keenly as I did, but what she said was, 'The simplest way round it to save a lot of fuss is for me to arrange to write my column under another name.' Which she did. But not without a certain amount of argument. The Sunday paper wanted her to go on writing under the name of Sally Whitcomb, because, they pointed out, it was a good circulation name. And that, she emphasized to me as a salve for my bristling sense of outrage, showed that there had been some substance in the *Mirror's* objection; but all the same it did little to diminish my growing sense of disillusionment with popular newspapers, and once again I began to think longingly of leaving the River Bank and exploring the Wild Wood.

The dying years of the 1940s in a Britain that was exhausted after six years of war were notable for a frothy suface of frivolous pleasure-seeking which concealed deep hopelessness and anxiety for the future: the streets were bedraggled, still pitted with rubble-strewn bomb-sites; most people were racked by austerity because as a nation we had no money left; the atom bombs that had ended the war in the Far East had started a cold west wind of fear; the taut nervous excitement of war had drooped to the daily misery of peace; on top of that the British Empire was crumbling, Indian independence had been followed by a bloodbath, and at home we had a Labour government that revelled in the philosophy of the hair-shirt but gave little indication of having the skill to solve the problems.

The entry of a Labour government at such a time of social disquiet is always a relief to the more discerning Tories who have already made their financial dispositions in preparation for it: the blame lies squarely on the shoulders of the representatives of the working class, so it is their fault and the masses can hardly complain. It brings a breathing space, and so long as it does not last too long it is traditionally good for the equity market, providing a shake-out in shares that catches the unwary on the hop – and serve them right – and there is a clear-out of old money, a mass slaughter of the dinosaurs pilloried by Nye Bevan as Tory vermin, leaving the financial soil ready and prepared for the planting out of seedling Jimmy Goldsmiths. In the lusher pastures of the rich, it is a matter of *plus ça change*. As Hilaire Belloc remarked:

The accursed power which stands on privilege
(And goes with Women and Champagne and Bridge)
Broke – and Democracy pursued her reign
(Which goes with Bridge and Women and Champagne).

91

Social and political circumstances of this kind historically provide a breeding ground for petty crooks and fiddlers, and in London we had a vintage crop of these. Everyone knew a 'spiv' who could, at a price, get the things that were unobtainable legally, and the black market flourished, leading to the formation of gangs modelled on the lines of the old Chicago mobs in prohibition days.

My own 'fixer', who could produce out of his pocket at any given time a large quantity of petrol coupons and clothes coupons, was a former professional boxer called Frankie Blake; he was a good-humoured, amusing man who lived in Soho, and although he came from a respectable family – his brother was a priest, a Monsignor in Liverpool – Frankie preferred to live the razzle-dazzle life on the fringe of the underworld.

I met him through Felix Fenston, who was the son of a Jewish theatrical impresario who had put on *Chu Chin Chow* and taken it on tour sometime after the First World War, and made a reasonable fortune out of that successful musical, but who had never done much after that except enjoy spending the money. So young Felix started life with nothing but a bright brain in money matters. He joined the army, was quickly promoted to corporal, then had a motor-bicycle accident which resulted in the amputation of a leg, after which he returned to civilian life in wartime London.

When bombs were falling, property became extremely cheap. But Felix was one of a handful of subsequent multi-millionaires who realized that a time would come when the fighting had to stop, and after that property would be the thing to own. So, having no money, he bought property on tick. It was the period of the old joke about one property dealer saying to his partner, 'We could buy that building for £10,000 if we could only raise a £10 deposit.' That was how Felix worked, buying and selling buildings on the turn, and he quickly became rich. His one extravagance was that he always kept his father in the luxury style to which the old man had become accustomed, but in his own life Felix was a frugal man; once, when he invited a few of us to a house-warming party at his new offices in Upper Brook Street, Mayfair, he sent Frankie Blake out for a half-bottle of Gordon's gin. That was the first time I met Frankie. The last I heard of him was some forty years later when Jeffrey Bernard used his *Low Life* column in the *Spectator* to write Frankie's sole obituary.

As well as working for Fenston, Frankie did some useful contact jobs for me; he was, surprisingly enough, on intimately friendly terms with several of the rich old Anglo-Irish families who kept racing studs and stables on their estates in Ireland, and I used to take him to Liverpool for the Grand National meeting and to Cheltenham because we would immediately find ourselves welcomed into the inner circle of the *crème de la crème*. How they stood for Frankie I shall never know, because he was always broke and on the make, but they loved him, and he introduced me to many people who became my good friends from that time on.

Frankie also took over the role of minder to my earliest Fleet Street colleague, Arthur La Bern, who, like myself, was upwardly mobile. He had done well as a journalist and was writing a novel.

A previous occupant of the flat my wife had found was James Agate, the literary and theatre critic, and I went to see him about some queries concerning the lease. He and I shared a passion for horses, and although his interest was mainly in harness horses rather than thoroughbreds, he spent most of his money on horses and we got on famously. We also talked about books, and I told him that a colleague of mine, Arthur La Bern, was just finishing a first novel.

'Tell your young friend to make sure I receive a copy of his book,' said Jimmy Agate as we parted. 'Don't forget – tell him to send it direct to me.'

I passed on the message. Whether or not Arthur did send him a copy I do not know. The novel was called *It Always Rains On Sunday* and was set in the East End of London where Arthur had grown up. When it was published, James Agate, who was at that time the most widely read critic in Britain, devoted the whole of his column in the *Daily Express* to it, praising it highly and describing it as the best first novel since Somerset Maugham's *Liza of Lambeth*.

The book became an immediate best seller, bringing instant success to Arthur who became a celebrity overnight. The film rights alone were sold for £20,000, an enormous sum at the time, and Arthur found himself transported into the glamorous world of studios and famous names when the Rank Organization made a big film of his book starring Diana Dors, Jean Kent, John McCullum and Googie Withers and many other top box-office names of the booming British film industry. The film also was an outstanding success. Arthur bought a big Armstrong Siddeley car and engaged as his chauffeur and gentleman's-personal-gentleman an amiable cockney called Bill Bailey, who in later years became head porter at Claridge's.

Arthur and I used to meet often at lunchtime in the American bar at the Savoy or at the Café Royal in the evenings or, later still, at Ciro's or the 400, and sometimes we used to go racing together. I was on the verge of getting married, and numbers of our friends were getting married, so wedding bells were in the wind all round and Arthur proposed to a pretty nurse called Sylvia.

The wedding was to take place at Caxton Hall, with a reception afterwards at Arthur's new flat, and Frankie Blake was put in charge of arrangements, which included getting hold of a vast quantity of bootleg liquor and normally unobtainable foods such as caviare and *foie gras*.

On the morning of the wedding Arthur changed his mind, and decided to set off forthwith on safari to some far-distant foreign clime beyond the reach of all modern forms of communication; but Frankie Blake was receiving wages to ensure that his boss arrived unscathed and in good shape at Caxton Hall, and Frankie was a conscientious man, so he locked Arthur in the bathroom until Bill Bailey brought the limousine round, and then the two of them bundled Arthur into the car by main force.

After the wedding we all went back to Arthur's flat, where a big crowd had already assembled. As Arthur's book had centred around life in the East End, it had given him considerable *cachet* in Whitechapel among the gangland bosses such as the notorious Jack Spot and the equally dreaded Billy Hill, and they all turned up, a few with invitations but most of them without. Some of them were at daggers drawn with each other, but had decided to sink their differences momentarily in celebration of Arthur's great day. As well as most of the senior figures in the criminal world, the reception was also attended by almost everyone who was anyone in the British film business. It was a glittering array.

Frankie Blake had entered with enthusiasm into his task of procuring hard-to-get supplies, particularly in terms of many dozens of cases of champagne, and a very large amount of drink was swiftly taken to toast the bride and groom. In consequence of which fighting broke out and a Wild-West-saloon type of mêlée was soon in progress, with furniture and crockery being smashed everywhere around the apartment, some of it over other people's heads. Frankie, the ex-boxer, was in the middle of it, knocking out people right and left and leaving numbers of recumbent bodies on the floor.

When things had quietened down, and a couple of ambulances had helped to speed the wedding guests upon their way, Sylvia came to me in great anxiety and said that she could not find Arthur. I told her not to worry. I took a taxi down to El Vino and there he was, at the bar, chatting with a group of our old colleagues. So I took him home.

The marriage did not last long, but the pressures of sudden wealth and fame are seldom conducive to long-lasting marriages.

After I had been writing the column for a few months, William Connor returned from his service on army newspapers and restarted his Cassandra column with the opening line: 'As I was saying before I was so rudely interrupted . . .' Bill Connor's Cassandra column had been, from its beginning, a controversial feature in the *Daily Mirror*, bitterly hated by many people who saw it as naked subversion, and words written by Connor had been at the vortex of the early wartime political whirlwind that had nearly blown the *Daily Mirror* to extinction. During those earlier years he had been the undisputed king of the castle as a writer on the *Mirror*, but when he returned after the war his column and mine occupied the same position in the newspaper on alternate days. Both columns had an enormous following among the readers, who were by then counted in millions. This understandably led to a coolness in his attitude towards me. I was an upstart. Bill and I were friendly but we were not friends, a concealed gulf that was widened not so much by jealousy on either side as by the physical fact that we preferred to drink in different places. Bill loved pubs, almost all pubs, and I cared for them less than he did, so when he wished in his mild way to offer a reason why we saw little of each other he would say, sadly, 'Noel is not a *tap-room* man.' Coming from Bill, that was a severe rebuke.

Connor was, with the possible exception of my old friend Ian Mackay of the *News Chronicle*, the best essayist-type columnist that any British daily newspaper employed this century until the arrival of Bernard Levin on *The Times*. He was also one of a small coterie of journalists who turned the *Daily Mirror* into a squalling, bawling, blistering newspaper of consequence for two decades, and his death in 1968 coincided with the beginning of that newspaper's gradual decline. Yet his background, as in the case of nearly all the rest of us, gave little indication of the measure of success he was to achieve, culminating in a knighthood in Harold Wilson's 1967 New Year's Honours List.

His father was an Ulsterman and his mother a Scot, and they lived in the London suburbs where Bill and his twin brother received a humdrum education at local schools. When he left school, Bill had a series of jobs as a clerk, living a larky life among the terraces of Victorian villas that still had a lingering flavour of the curly bowler and the bicycle. It was not until he drifted into a job with an advertising agency that his talent for using words as hand-grenades became apparent. From the pen of this apparently meek and mild man came explosive phrases and short paragraphs that blew up in people's faces.

When this valuable quality brought him to the notice of the *Mirror*, and he was hired to write a column, Bart gave him the pseudonym

'Cassandra', unaware that Cassandra the soothsayer was a woman. Connor himself had to look it up before he discovered that Bart had accidentally changed his sex.

He was a heavily-built man with spectacles that gave him a grave and judicial appearance, but his voice was high-pitched and parsonical and his general air was one of diffidence, almost timidity. In conversation he customarily called me 'Boss', which was by no means intended as a reflection of the way in which he saw our working relationship but more as a form of greeting with an undertone of warning in it: it was a conversational gift of the sort that made the Greeks so feared. At home he lived a quiet, family life in an old rectory in the Buckinghamshire village of Fingest, and his hobbies were cooking and cats.

But although domestic cats were the love of his life, when he sat in front of a typewriter he became a raging tiger, attacking his prey with bare-toothed savagery. He used the typewriter like a machine gun, firing off words in lethal bursts. He was a man with the distant smile of a bishop on his face and a bludgeon in his fingertips. He wrote his column in the office or at home, frequently rising in the early hours of the morning to do it, and he spent most of the rest of his time in pubs, so he seldom had occasion to meet the people whose reputations he crucified; sometimes when he later met his victims in the flesh he found that he liked them.

An example of this was P.G. Wodehouse, at whom Connor sprayed verbal vitriol with such damaging effect that it is no exaggeration to say that Connor's attack was primarily instrumental in wrecking the happiness of Plum Wodehouse's later life. As the incident occurred some half a century ago, during the early days of the war, it may seem difficult for some younger readers to understand how such a con-flagration could be lit by such a little spark, but it was vividly comprehensible in the circumstances prevailing at the time.

Wodehouse, one of the least political men who ever lived, had stayed on with his wife at their house in Le Touquet after war broke out in 1939, believing that the French Maginot Line would surely prevent the Germans from invading France. When the swift invasion came, Wodehouse was one of several British nationals who were rounded up by the Germans and sent to internment camps.

While he was imprisoned in Upper Silesia ('If this is Upper Silesia what must Lower Silesia be like?'), Wodehouse wrote five intendedly amusing pieces which he read as talks to his fellow prisoners – talks that were designed to bring a humorist's eye to their predicament. But his German captors, hearing these talks, immediately understood what powerful propaganda value they could have – a fact which Wodehouse himself did not realize, because he thought they were merely funny – so they put him on German radio to read them again. He agreed to do it because he thought they were to be broadcast to America, which had not yet entered the war and where he had many friends who he thought would be cheered by hearing his voice and learning that he was alive and well and still seeing life as a comedy.

However, Dr Goebbels' shrewd propaganda machine put the talks out on a wavelength that was beamed to radio listeners in Britain, and there was an immediate outcry of anger and disbelief. Was it a trick? Or had P.G. Wodehouse of all people – the quintessential Englishman who had invented Mike and Psmith and Bertie Wooster – been suborned by the enemy?

The British government was furious. The matter was discussed in cabinet. Duff Cooper was assigned to find some journalist who would hit Wodehouse where it hurt. He gave the job to Bill Connor because Bill was notorious for having a devilish gift for spewing bile in words.

Connor was directed to read his piece after the nine o'clock news on BBC radio, prime listening time for all the nation. He did his hatchet job with such outraged ferocity that he left poor old Plum Wodehouse bleeding from more wounds than Diocletian inflicted on the unfortunate St Sebastian: it was not merely a *tour de force* – it was an *auto-da-fé*. Bill scourged Wodehouse as a contemptible traitor, an unspeakable turncoat, and he left the writer whom Evelyn Waugh had described as 'the head of my profession' with his life in tatters.

Although Plum Wodehouse, in later years, received a knighthood from the Queen, he never felt that his reputation in Britain recovered from that diatribe; while admitting that what he had done was foolish and naïve, he always believed that in the public mind in Britain there remained the detritus of suspicion – 'there's no smoke without fire' – the unkindest cut of all; so he continued his writing in America after the war and never returned to live in his homeland.

The BBC's lawyers later admitted that Connor's vilification of Wodehouse had been inaccurate and libellous. But the old man never ceased to feel the twinges of the injustice that had been done.

When the war was over Bill Connor went to the United States to meet P.G. Wodehouse, and after their meeting he became one of the old genius's most vociferous admirers.

Too late.

Although Connor wrote many a column that read like the score of a concerto orchestrated for sledgehammer and pneumatic drill, he could also at times be extremely funny and occasionally even lyrical. He was a master of the journalistic technique known as 'the delayed drop', and one of his most effective tricks was to take the reader gently by the hand and lead him down an idyllic country lane of words, until the last sentence when he turned and shot the reader in the kneecap.

Here is a sample of his columns in that vein. It was headlined HERRINGS FOR BREAKFAST.

I always say there's nothing like a herring for breakfast. Some people despise 'em. Not me. Crisp and smoking hot so that the white juicy flesh comes clean away from the bone – that's the way to eat them. You can have your bacon and eggs. You can have your grilled tomatoes. But give me a herring. And they're cheap – dirt cheap. I suppose that's why some folks despise them . . .

There are some very high cliffs on the Yorkshire coast near Bridlington called Speeton Cliffs. Yesterday the trawler *Skegness* went ashore there. It wasn't very rough when they first went aground, so the crew waited to see if they could refloat on the rising tide. Soon it began to blow hard.

High on the cliff, exhausted coastguards peered to where the *Skegness* was last seen. Yes, she was still there. But now she had rolled on her side. Her crew gathered in a huddled little bunch in the wheelhouse; you could just see them crouching there. Up on the cliffs they tried to fire rockets.

Seven times they shot but the line was flung back by the tearing gale. Someone signalled from the wheelhouse with a flashlamp. At 4 a.m. the flickering light stopped.

There was no more wheelhouse and no more crew. Eleven men died in the thundering surf. Six widows are left.

Yes, there's nothing like herrings for breakfast – they're cheap, too. Dirt cheap.

Most of Bill Connor's Cassandra columns contained a political ingredient, even though it was often concealed.

Both Bill Connor and I were encouraged to travel abroad in search of columns and I recall my first sortie for this purpose because at one point I thought I might be lynched. It was my first visit to Ireland, which, although so close, is the most foreign country of all to the English. It was my own fault because, although I was accustomed to writing frivolous and satirical material, I was unaware that this approach holds hidden dangers in Ireland; fighting is a divine right and guns can be fun in John Bull's other island, but gentle mockery is always a terrorist activity.

One disastrous trap I fell into was that I thought I knew so much about the place. I had listened at my mother's knee to stories about her family's homeland, picking up a smattering of random information about Ireland's history in the superficial way that some children of my generation misguidedly believed themselves to be familiar with Shakespeare's plays because they had read *Lamb's Tales*. I was aware that my mother's colourful version of past events was always highly partisan, but was unaware of the explosive potential of such views of history when discussed in their country of origin. My mother had told me tales of the Brian Boru, first great chief king of all Ireland, whom she claimed as an ancestor of her O'Donnell family. (Nearly all old Irish families claim Brian Boru as an ancestor, and as there was such a tiny population in Ireland a thousand years ago they may well all be right.) I had been weaned on harrowing stories of the last century's famine years and of Queen Victoria's scornful gift of £50; of Parnell and Kitty; of the Easter Rising, the Four Courts and the General Post Office; of the murder of Michael Collins by his own people; of the unspeakable 'Tans' and the devious Dev; I even knew some Irish rebel songs. So as I was going down Sackville Street I felt entirely at home; I was the buckeen who knew it all.

I was surprised to find Dublin so poor, but it exercised upon me its old and very special charm. I had hardly been there a day before I had a dozen new friends, all delightful; but one vital fact that my mother had neglected to tell me was that although it is the right and privilege of every Irishman to attack his country with flowing eloquence, and laugh uproariously at its nonsensical shortcomings, this privilege is not extended to visitors from across the St George's Channel. My mother should have told me that in any bar in Ireland, on any night you choose, you can fall in with entertaining companions who will talk beguilingly of the sad misfortune it is to live in the most distressful country that you have ever seen; you begin by parrying the criticisms and pointing out how much you like the place, but towards the end of the evening you eventually capitulate, out of politeness, and agree that Ireland must be a lousy country to live in: after which you pick yourself up off the floor and brush the sawdust off your suit; criticism of Ireland is a national pastime but it is strictly for the natives.

Leaning on the parapet of O'Connell Bridge one night, looking at the moon reflected in the Liffey, I composed a column about the moonshine through which so many romanticists see Ireland: beneath all the dancing gaiety of the fiddlers and the pipers lay a sad temperament; behind the Georgian façades of the fine houses lay crumbling cornices and threadbare carpets; after the lively conversation in the pubs lay the rows at home and the black eyes; below the good Catholic acceptance of large families as a gift of God lay the devilish poverty of children without shoes; beyond the blessing of the rosary lay the repressive arrogance of the cassock.

In writing the column I lightened it up, of course, pouring these thoughts obliquely on to the page with a froth of comedy: but that did not fool anyone. It was even more outrageous because I was using their own technique of wrapping up a serious thought in a confection of marzipan words. There was an outcry. Local newspapers throughout the twenty-six counties reprinted extracts from the column together with trenchant leading articles that not only rejected with indignation every line I had written but also asked what better could you expect of an ignoramus who made a living by writing lies for a disgraceful example of the British gutter-press that lured its monstrous circulation by printing photographs of half-nude women. I was denounced from pulpits up and down the country.

Thinking that perhaps it might be wise to curtail my visit and start a war somewhere else instead, I was sitting in the bar of the Shelbourne Hotel and sipping a valedictory half-pint of Arthur Guinness's draught stout when a party of the most widely read columnists from the Dublin newspapers descended on me and began to slap me on the back with congratulations and much hilarity. 'Well done, old fellow,' they cried. 'Drink up, dear man. Don't think of leaving us. Hold your hour and have another.'

They treated me as their dearest friend. Apart from having a happy and convivial time, they were in fact interviewing me for quotes which, in their self-consciously literary style sprinkled with classical allusions, they could use to lambast me from hell to breakfast in their own columns. Unwittingly I had engaged us all in Ireland's favourite indoor sport.

A few of the Irish columnists I met that morning remained my friends for many years. On the whole they regarded themselves less as journalists than as poets *manqués*. True or not – and often not – I found it an endearing approach to the work. Even the titles of their columns and the pseudonyms under which they wrote gave notice that they were, in their fashion, newspapermen of higher quality than their clockwork counterparts in Fleet Street. No English national newspaper at that time would have allowed its popular columnist to sign himself Quidnunc, as did Patrick Campbell (later Lord Glenavy) and some of his successors who also became friends of mine; or Brian O Nolan who wrote his column in the *Irish Times* under the title *Cruiskeen Lawn* and signed it Myles na Gopaleen after the horse-coper and poteen-distiller in Boucicault's *The Colleen Bawn*. The William Hickeys and John Evelyns of the British press were prosaic by comparison.

One curious fact that I discovered then about Irish writers of all kinds is that most of them avoid writing at night. Cyril Connolly, observing this idiosyncrasy in himself, put it down to a fear of the Celtic Twilight which, he said, consists of an addiction to melancholy. In *Enemies of Promise*, Connolly remarked that he always tried to write in the afternoon because he had just enough Irish blood to be afraid of the Irish temperament: 'When I write after dark,' he said, 'the shades of evening scatter their purple through my prose.' I have a feeling that he must have written that sentence after dark.

Musing on the mystery that this night-time addiction to melancholy does not appear to have affected the writing habits of Irish teetotallers such as Bernard Shaw, I once asked Brendan Behan if he wrote at night.

'I do,' said he. 'But as I am usually out and about at night, I write the notes of my thoughts on any scrap of paper that comes to hand. In the morning I am seldom able to read what I have written. Do you see? It is not the thoughts that deteriorate during the hours of darkness, it is the handwriting. This is a great sadness in my life because I am convinced that some of those scribbles which I cannot read contain the finest thoughts I ever had.'

He called for another drink, and I told him that I was in the habit of writing in the mornings.

'Ah, God,' he sighed, 'it's your mother's fault. The only Irishman who ever got away with writing at night was James Joyce. Every single bloody word of *Finnegan's Wake* was written after closing time. And wouldn't you know?'

Although I returned to Ireland time and again over a period of thirty years, the columns I wrote from there never ceased to get me into hot water. Ten years after my first visit, following talks I had in Belfast and Dublin with Irish politicians including a young lawyer called Charlie Haughey, I wrote a column detailing instances of the ways in which the IRA was secretly regrouping after years of inertia. Angry Irish nationalists burnt copies of that issue of the *Daily Mirror* in the streets of London, and paraded a coffin with my name on it through Hyde Park. Priests walked in my funeral cortège.

Ten years later still, when I was in Londonderry and Belfast to write about the long-anticipated recrudescence of the old troubles, I was attacked by Paisleyites for outlining the facts behind the grievances of the Catholic minority in Ulster. I was given some sort of minor award in London for that reporting, but like most journalists I have never been much impressed by Oscars, and the aspect of the affair that gave me most satisfaction was that I continued to receive death-threats from extremists on both sides of the conflict, which fostered my illusion that I was at last beginning to understand Ireland. Nobody understands Ireland, least of all the Irish.

Every time a man sneezes in Ireland it is a political sneeze, but it was certainly not politics that lured me back so frequently; more often it was the horses and the theatre. I went for visits to the races at Punchestown or the Curragh and the plays at the Abbey Theatre or the Gate, with sometimes the added treat after the performance of sitting down to supper with Micheál Mac Liammóir and Hilton Edwards and listening, over a few glasses of wine, to their captivatingly baroque theatrical conversation. Ireland is a country where they keep the memory green, and even during that post-war period the long-gone years when the Irish theatre was world-famous seemed like yesterday in the minds of Dubliners; the names of Yeats and Lady Gregory, Synge, O'Casey and Lennox Robinson were bandied about in bars as though they were friends who had just left the room; in drinking haunts of journalists and sporting men, pubs such as the Pearl or Davy Byrne's, matters concerning the plays of Shaw, Wilde and Boucicault would crop up nightly in conversation, and as the night progressed voices would rise in an increasingly self-conscious display of histrionics, as if to make sure that the gallery could hear. All the city was a stage.

Everybody in Dublin was an actor playing a part and even the beggars sounded like the Shaughraun: they learned their lines, not always sticking to the script but changing their act according to the audience; in those days before the mass influx of visitors, when Dublin was a capital but still a village, the professional beggars were able to take time to research their likely prey, to find out on the grapevine who was fresh in town with money in his pocket and then to apply what Jeeves would have called the psychology of the individual. They had their art to consider, even as small-part players. There was no sidling up and whining, no pleading for the price of a cup of coffee. It was always a theatrical production in its small way. At night when I left Jammet's restaurant after dinner or the Red Bank, the Dolphin or the Bailey, a shabby figure would emerge from the shadows and then turn, as if meeting me by happy coincidence. The soft touch.

'Well, Sir Noel – what an unexpected pleasure! What brings yer honour to these uneventful shores? Ah, good luck to yez and nice to see you again – still a bright ornament in the Street of Adventure across the water, so I hear.'

Without waiting for the intricate account of the sad circumstance that had led this old acquaintance to be inexplicably short of five bob till Friday, I would hand over two of the *Daily Mirror*'s half-crowns: there, but for the grace of God, went we all.

One of my occasional companions to the races at the time was another Irishman, John Godley, later Lord Kilbracken, who was also perennially short of five bob till Friday. In a roundabout way I was among the people who were responsible for John's misfortune in being offered a job as a racing correspondent on the *Daily Mirror*; it would have been more to the advantage of this former Fleet Air Arm pilot if the *Mirror* had engaged him as a sailing correspondent or a flying correspondent or even a cookery correspondent, because as a racing correspondent he unfailingly lost his wages every week.

John Godley had been school bookmaker at Eton, an unofficial task that was later undertaken by my old friend Clive Graham; but although John's passion for the sport of kings was unquestionable, he did not possess that spirit of detachment which enables most racing writers to see race after race go by without striking a blow at the ring; before every race John could be seen either pushing his way through the crowd in Tattersalls towards the bookmakers or striding purposefully up and down the line of bookies on the rails: which is, as every racing man soon learns, the best way to avoid making a fortune.

At Oxford on an ex-service grant after the war, still in his mid-twenties, John was doing well at Balliol when a singularly Irish calamity befell him: he dreamed one night that he had bought a copy of the London *Evening Standard* and turning immediately, of course, to the fudge – the stop press column on the back page – he cast his eye down the winners at Newmarket. Then he glanced at the front page and noticed the date. IT WAS TOMORROW'S PAPER.

John awakened with a start and began to rack his brain for the names of the winners he had read, because they were the names of horses that were due to run on that very day. He rushed out for a newspaper and ran his finger down the list of runners at Newmarket. Two names leapt out at him. Bindal and Jaludin. They were names that he had read as winners in his dream.

Godley rang his bookmaker. He also told his undergraduate friends, who were naturally sceptical, but who had a little bet just for fun.

Both horses won. John collected £30 from his surprised bookmaker, who was not accustomed to paying out on the Godley account, and he became the toast of Balliol. Nearly everyone had had a small touch. The whole college was eager for more of this inspired information. Even dons would say to him, 'Why don't you get an early night, Godley? Have a good sleep, eh? And don't forget to put a pencil and paper on the table beside your bed. Remember Freud's advice. Try to remember all the winners next time, not just two.'

Despite the urging and encouragement of pullulating doctors of philosophy and suchlike studious punters, John failed during the ensuing weeks of term to come up with the goods; he dreamed all right, he even dreamed at times that he was reading a newspaper, but either he never reached the racing pages or else, when he did, he could not read the small print. His friends advised him to take a magnifying glass to bed; they were disillusioned with him, a mere morning glory.

It was during the vacation, back at Killegar his home in Ireland, that the gift returned. As I heard it described by John Godley on a journey to Newbury all those years ago, the household at Killegar sounded not dissimilar to that at Boot Magna, home of that other journalistic celebrity, John Boot, who also became briefly a name on Fleet Street's roll of fame in circumstances that were unorthodox. Killegar was deep in the drowsy Irish countryside, cut off from the urgency of the modern world; the postman would bring the family's letters at some time during the day and deliver the newspapers as well, the London papers always being two days old. Life passed agreeably, little touched by turmoil.

On the morning when John Godley awakened to find that he had once again been reading the racing winners in his dream, he rushed downstairs in high excitement.

'I've done it again,' he shouted. 'I've dreamed today's winners.'

'I am so glad, dear,' said his mother, pouring coffee.

The problem was that, in his excitement, John forgot the names of the horses he had read, with the exception of one that he remembered not too clearly. It was Tuber-something, Tubermore or Tubermost, a name like that. He telephoned Mrs McGuinness, postmistress in the neighbouring village of Carrigallen, and asked her to look in the *Irish Times* to see whether there was a horse called Tubermore engaged to run that day.

'There's a thing called Tuberose running in the first race,' she said. 'Would that be the one you are after?'

Tuberose won at 100-6.

Realizing that no sane bookmaker would allow him to go on winning, and would close his account if he started to back winners only, he decided to jettison his plan to join the diplomatic service and seek

104

instead a job as a racing tipster on a London newspaper, offering a regular service of sure-fire winners gleaned from his dreams; the more serious newspapers turned him down flat, because newspapers receive offers of that nature from eccentric readers almost every week. In desperation John rang the *Daily Mirror*. The reporter who took the call (and it happened to be my future wife) asked him to leave his name and address and also to name two horses that would win at Lingfield that afternoon. Godley gaver her two names, Baroda Squadron and The Brogue; we all had a good laugh and we all had a little punt.

Both horses won.

Our *Mirror* tipsters, Newsboy and Bouverie, were having a run of misfortune at the time, and I was among the people consulted about what we should do. 'Why don't we give this Gypsy Petulengro Godley a chance?' I suggested. 'He can't dream more losers than Bouverie is coming up with.'

So we plastered the story of John's two-winner dream across the centre spread, headlined THE STRANGE DREAMS OF MR JOHN GODLEY, and the managing editor sent him a cheque for £25 for the story and offered him a job on trial. It is a matter of record that John's flair for dreaming the future deserted him as soon as he set foot in our racing department; but at least he started a career as a writer which later brought him adventure and success.

In Geraldine House we were feeling the first eddying gusts of a wind of change that was ultimately to blow us all out of the building and into a custom-built headquarters at Holborn Circus. Hugh Cudlipp returned from the army, where he had been editing *Union Jack* for the troops in North Africa and Italy, and resumed his pre-war job as editor of the *Sunday Pictorial*; Sam Campbell, who had been keeping the chair warm for him, moved to Odhams as managing editor of *The People*: this made no difference at all in my life, because after my brush with Sam following the Hemingway episode I had refused to work for the *Sunday Pic*. I had met Cudlipp a few times in the company of Warwick Charlton, wartime editor of *Eighth Army News*, Monty's clever house-magazine, but I knew him only as an acquaintance.

Hugh Cudlipp, later Sir Hugh and later still Baron Cudlipp of Aldingbourne, was one of three sons of a Welsh commercial traveller based in Cardiff. From this unpromising start the three boys brought off the longest-odds treble chance in the history of Fleet Street, because they all became editors of national newspapers: Percy was editor of the *Evening Standard* and later of the *Daily Herald*; Reginald was editor of the *News of the World*; and Hugh's only national newspaper editorship was of the *Sunday Pictorial*, although he was, in time, to become far more important than an editor. The three Cudlipps were young men in a hurry, tough as rhinoceros hide and sharp as *kukris*, bandits in silk shirts, all talented journalists; but Hugh was the toughest of them all, the archetypal go-getter who became the virtuoso of the tabloid orchestra. He left school at fourteen to become a junior reporter on the *Penarth News*, fought his way up through jobs of increasing seniority in the provinces, landed in London at the age of nineteen as features editor of Lord Kemsley's *Sunday Chronicle*, and then, by answering an advertisement in the jobs-vacant column of the *Daily Telegraph*, he joined the *Daily Mirror* as assistant features editor, quickly rising to features editor when the holder of that office, a brilliant maverick called Basil Nicholson, was fired by Bart.

When Cudlipp achieved this position of authority there was a man on his staff who wrote a regular column under the headline THE MAN WITH A THOUSAND SECRETS. This column was the writer's pride and joy, but Cudlipp thought it was dull. So one of Hugh's first actions was to pick up the telephone and ring the Man with a Thousand Secrets.

'Cudlipp here,' he said. 'Do you want to know a secret?'

'Oh, yes, please, Mr Cudlipp,' said the man, eagerly.

'You've been fired,' said Hugh, and put down the phone.

That was vintage Cudlipp. He was abrasive, sardonic, rough. Success mellowed him somewhat, but his instinct stalked always in the jungle.

His ally and supporter was Cecil King, who in those days was a director of the *Mirror* but a man of no particular importance. On the face of it, this was a strange alliance. Cudlipp was the thrusting iconoclast from the working class, King the lofty highbrow, product of Winchester and the House: most observers saw it as an attraction of opposites, but in fact neither man was what he appeared to be on the surface.

King was a man whose talents, though not inconsiderable, never matched his own opinion of them: he was half Irish, his father being Sir Lucas White King of the Indian Civil Service, and he was brought up in Ireland; but his mother was a Harmsworth, sister of Lord Northcliffe, and it was the Harmsworth gene of precarious mental balance that influenced his life.

I met him first in Scotland in the late summer of 1947. My wife and I – we had been married earlier that summer – were on holiday, visiting the Braemar games, and he came up and introduced himself, inviting us to a shooting party at a house he then kept at Cushnie, in Aberdeenshire. We were not keen to go, and I had no guns with me, but he swept aside our excuses.

The austerity of his family lifestyle came as a surprise to us because he was clearly living above his means, struggling to maintain a landed-gentry image that his funds did not justify. He had expected to receive a big legacy from his Uncle Northcliffe, but when Northcliffe died, leaving a fortune of more than five million pounds, he bequeathed only a scornful £500 to Cecil. With little more than his income from the *Mirror*, and four children to educate at public school and university, Cecil and his family were living on short commons, and indeed it was not until he was well into middle age that he became reasonably well off.

In the dining room at Milton Cushnie, where we would gather for a frugal evening repast after a day's shooting, one wall was dominated by a large oil painting of Lord Northcliffe, Cecil's family lar; the facial resemblance was uncanny, and when I first saw the picture I thought it was a portrait of Cecil. Cecil himself always believed that the mantle of the great press emperor would one day fall upon him, and he treated the portrait with gravity and respect. If, during our chatter as we sat round the table at the evening meal, one of his sons said something that sounded even the slightest bit uppish, Cecil would silence him and, pointing an imperious finger at the portrait of Northcliffe, would say icily, 'Never forget that your ancestor once pushed a barrow of secondhand books for sale down Farringdon Street.' Whether that was true or not I do not know, because I have never read it in any biography of Northcliffe; what I do know is that Cecil himself consistently forgot his own advice – studied arrogance was his favourite pose.

His three sons, Michael, Francis and Colin, were all likeable young men, and Colin, who was at Eton at the time, later became a friend of mine until his early death. They were all good shots, and Cecil himself was a first-class shot, which was just as well because grouse were few and far between on his moor, and anyone who missed a bird with the first barrel would receive a sharp reminder from Cecil that cartridges were expensive. Cecil's first wife, whom he called Birdie, and whose mind later cracked under the strain, was a sweet woman; she would drive out to an appointed place on the moor with our luncheon, which consisted of thick sandwiches spread either with Gentleman's Relish or with dates and which we all ate ravenously. We were always hungry. I do not know whether Cecil's three sons, all burly chaps, managed to find private supplies, but I took to slipping out secretly in the evenings and running to the local post office to buy bars of chocolate which I would smuggle back into our bedroom.

Cecil was a Victorian-style paterfamilias, strict and stern, discouraging levity. After the early evening meal we would all retire to the

107

drawing room, composing ourselves into a Winterhalter scene, Cecil reading, Birdie sewing, Priscilla embroidering, the rest of us playing beggar-my-neighbour. At nine o'clock Priscilla, Cecil's only daughter, would go to the kitchen to make herself a milk drink from her personal tin of Ovaltine that she kept there; this eccentricity always provoked discussion, and it was clear that Cecil regarded it not only as wanton self-indulgence but also as a sign of an extravagant nature.

Cecil himself retired to bed at precisely half-past nine, a habit he seldom broke throughout his life; even when he became a mandarin, chairman of the largest publishing company in the world and chairman of the newspaper with the largest daily sale in the Western world, and was much sought after as a guest of honour at dinner parties and banquets, his chauffeur invariably brought the Rolls round in time for Cecil to be between the sheets by 9.30 p.m. This habit – which played havoc with London's public dinner timescale – arose partly from a lack of physical stamina, which caused Cecil to need a lot of sleep, but also partly from boredom: being a loner by nature, there was a limited amount of human company that he could tolerate after the day's work was done; he preferred books to people.

Occasionally in Scotland a telegram would arrive from Hugh Cudlipp in London, telling Cecil about some story that Hugh proposed to use in the *Sunday Pictorial*, or seeking his advice, and this would please Cecil greatly, because he always liked to feel that he was a press baron deciding great issues. In fact at that time he had little power in the *Mirror* organization; he had risen to the position of advertisement director, and although he exercised some influence over the *Sunday Pictorial* his nose was kept firmly out of the *Daily Mirror* by Harry Guy Bartholomew, his boss, who did not like him. Cecil was an unusually tall man of patrician appearance and condescending manner, which made him an automatic *bête noir* for the upper-class-hating Bart. However, Bart had to put up with him because during the *Mirror*'s period of peril in the early days of the war, when the cabinet came within an ace of closing the paper down, it was Cecil who had saved the day; although only a junior member of the board, he had been deputed to deal with Winston Churchill because Bart realized that if he himself had confronted the old statesman the *Daily Mirror* would have been swept into the national dustbin forthwith. Cecil negotiated with the *sang froid* and good manners that Churchill understood, and pulled the *Mirror*'s chestnuts out of the fire.

After that, although Bart continued to do his best to keep Cecil's fingers out of the pie of the *Daily Mirror*, he had little option but to show some recognition of Cecil's achievement, so Cecil was allowed to take an increasing hand in the editorial affairs of the *Sunday Pictorial*. Cecil, for his part, kept his sword polished and watched for the moment when he might lunge at the old bull in the chairman's office and deliver the *coup de grace*.

Bart was well aware of the danger. He knew that Cecil was breathing down his neck. This caused him to view Hugh Cudlipp with a beady eye, because Hugh was briskly pushing up the circulation of the *Sunday Pictorial* and thereby advancing Cecil's importance; so Bart decided to get rid of Cudlipp, and waited his moment. He did not hurry: he knifed his victim at our Christmas lunch.

Always at the *Daily Mirror* the annual pre-Christmas luncheon for senior editorial staff was something of a Roman orgy; in 1948 it was held at Emil's, then one of the smarter eating places in Fleet Street. It was Christmas Eve, when no newspaper was produced and nobody had to work, so everybody present was looking upon the wine when it was red, or white, or any other colour that came up. There was a festive atmosphere of goodwill to some, if not all, men, and most daggers had been left in office drawers: except for Bart's; Bart had his dagger ready.

There were some Olympic-standard drinkers in Fleet Street, but Hugh Cudlipp, like myself, was not among them; he drank an enormous amount but after two or three bottles of claret he tended to turn ugly. Bart himself was a heavy drinker but at that luncheon he was unusually abstemious. Towards the middle of the afternoon, in the midst of the flow of self-congratulatory speeches that always drear on at such festivities, Bart introduced a controversial subject. Cecil King had been travelling in Africa and had sent a cable to the *Sunday Pictorial* containing news of a riot that had led to the death of several people at the Enugo coalfield. It was the sort of story that would have made the front page of a serious newspaper, but the *Pic* was a paper that concerned itself more with society scandals and naughty vicars (its front-page headline advice to one such errant clergyman was GO – UNFROCK YOURSELF!)

At all events, for whatever reason, the *Pic* had spiked the story. Cecil King was furious because his scoop had been ignored and he fancied himself as a journalist; the editor, Hugh Cudlipp, had been called on to explain. It was the sort of relatively minor lapse that usually blew over. But Bart brought it up at the Christmas lunch. Making it clear that he was protecting the good name of his friend and fellow-director Cecil King, who had been disgracefully treated, Bart prodded and provoked Cudlipp with scathingly scornful words until Cudlipp's wine-inflamed temper erupted into a torrent of fiery rudeness to Bart.

The whole room went silent. Then Bart said, quietly, with a look of triumph in his eyes, 'Get out of here, Cudlipp. You are dismissed.'

Bart had a merry Christmas.

My mother, née Ethel O'Donnell

My father, Harold Whitcomb

Where did you get that hat? The author aged about four, with his aunts Dora and Kiffy, two of Horace Whitcomb's seven daughters

Who called that rookie an editor? Gunner Whitcomb, 1939

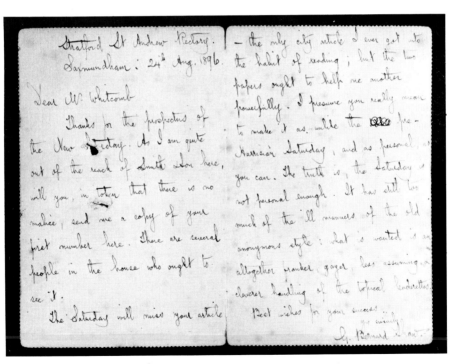

George Bernard Shaw had a public row with Horace Whitcomb about Horace's
policy of forbidding his reviewers to accept free first-night tickets; but, typically,
he asked Horace to send him a free copy of the *New Saturaday* 'in token that there
is no malice'

My pal Ben, the talking dog, broadcasting to the United States a message that went straight to the heart of every all-American consumer – 'I WANT ONE!' Interviewers Merrill Mueller of NBC and Bob Musel of United Press are on the left, and on the right is Ben's owner Mr Alfred Brissenden. Big-money offers to buy Ben flooded in, including a bid of fifty thousand dollars from Hollywood impresario Jack Sparks – a sum that in 1946 would have made Alf rich – but Alf turned down all offers because Ben was the family pet. There was some argument about whether Ben should be described as a Jack Russell or as a smooth-haired fox terrier, but there was never any argument about the fact that this clever little dog talked Bart into offering me a job as a columnist

The Caligula of Fetter Lane, Harry Guy Bartholomew, 'Bart', the semi-literate genius of the tabloid press (© Syndication International Ltd)

Cecil King: there, but for the grace of God, went God. Tall, shy, aloof, arrogant, he was a mixed-up man but in retrospect was more far-sighted than some of the men who brought about his downfall

Hugh Cudlipp – tabloid virtuoso. One of the most able tabloid journalists of the twentieth century – possibly the cleverest – Hugh was the man who made it possible for Cecil King to realize his dreams of grandeur; but, ironically, he was also the man born to be King's undoing

(Left) Bill Connor (Cassandra), the brilliant columnist, outside the Law Courts during the Liberace libel case (recognized as the most entertaining law case of its decade – *Time* called it 'The Liberace Show'). In colourful phrases, Connor had accused Liberace of being a homosexual, which cost the *Mirror* £35,000 in damages and costs (© Hulton Pictures)

(Right) Rooftop reporter working at the Khrushchev summit meeting in Paris, 1960. After Khrushchev stormed out of the meeting, the *Daily Mirror* sent him a front-page message: 'DON'T BE SO BLOODY RUDE MR K!'

With 'Young Max', Sir Max Aitken, Lord Beaverbrook's air-ace son, at a party in the old *Daily Express* building in Fleet Street

With Jimmy Goldsmith and Isabel Patino at Blair Adam in Scotland at the height of the elopement drama, when the pursuing pack of pressmen were in full cry at their heels (© Syndication International Ltd)

'It won't be a stylish marriage, 'cos I can't afford a carriage' – with Roddy Oliver in the rusty old pig-van that took Jimmy Goldsmith and Isabel Patino to Kelso for their wedding

Prose can paint evening and moonlight, but poets are needed to sing the dawn; at 5 a.m. in the old Covent Garden flower market with Yevgeny Yevtushenko

The poet and the lunatic and all that jazz: with Yevtushenko and Satchmo (Louis Armstrong)

7

The Holy Bible says that the race is not to
the swift, nor the battle to the strong – but
that's the way to bet.

Damon Runyon

Fleet Street during those post-war years was not so much a street of
adventure as a street full of adventurers. Most journalists lived by their
wits: if George McDonald Fraser's books about the post-school life of
Harry Flashman had been published at the time, Flashman would have
been our patron saint.

Most editorial staff, certainly on popular papers, had come up the
hard way from poor circumstances and although some were bright few
were sufficiently educated to have found equally well-paid jobs
elsewhere, except possibly as salesmen or politicians. Qualifications or
references were less important than quick thinking and an instinctive
talent for outflanking rivals: we took no prisoners.

Several of my early colleagues had been married young, some to
waitresses or factory girls from their home surroundings, but nearly all
of them soon jettisoned these wives in favour of secretaries or nurses as
they moved up the ladder. One who experienced more trouble than he
had bargained for in getting rid of his first wife was a lad who had fallen
in love with a tart in Germany; he had given her British citizenship by
marrying her, only to find that when he brought her home to London she
immediately took up her old trade again, plying for hire among his pals
in Fleet Street. An unusually heavy crop of black eyes was to be seen
around the pubs during the months that it took him to sort his problem
out.

The possession of capital in any sizeable quantity was unusual. Few
journalists owned possessions of any value – a gold cigarette lighter was
a trophy to be used with pride – and fewer still owned the houses in
which they lived. Indeed, the accumulation of money, apart from
day-to-day spending money, was looked on as an indication that the

possessor was a mean skinflint who dodged buying his round of drinks or a dreary clerk more suited to an accountant's office. Reporters saw themselves in the image of Raymond Chandler's Philip Marlowe, private eyes who took their pay and got their man, or as artists living in a garret in the romantic style of Henri Murger's *Scènes de la Vie de Bohème*. John Gordon, editor of the *Sunday Express*, used to drive round in his own Rolls Royce, and this ostentatious show of wealth was the subject of scornful hilarity, especially when it became known that the Rolls was a secondhand car that had been given to him as a tip by his employer, Lord Beaverbrook.

Most journalists claimed to be socialists; in some cases this was the result of an intellectual decision, but in far more instances it arose from being outsiders who did not fit into the social pattern: few news-papermen of that era were completely at home anywhere except in Fleet Street. It was a life based on empiricism and none of us, as I recall, was ever faced with Yeats's choice between perfection of the life or of the work.

My own life bowled along happily enough and although most of the columns I was writing were as shallow as a puddle occasionally I chanced my arm by straying into deeper waters. In 1947, when the Edinburgh Festival was first launched, I went there to write a few columns, and this was a daring thing to do because it was essentially a highbrow festival of the arts and therefore the sort of occasion that the *Daily Mirror* at that time would normally either have ignored or attacked. On the overnight train to Scotland I fell into conversation with a man who talked interestingly about the concerts that were about to take place in Edinburgh; he had a bowler hat and an umbrella, which made him look like a City gent, but in odd contrast he also had a Viennese accent. I assumed he was a musician. We dined together on the train, and chatted for an hour afterwards, but it was not until we exchanged visiting cards that either of us knew who the other was: he was Rudolf Bing, artistic director of the festival.

During the following couple of years we met from time to time, either in London or Edinburgh, and occasionally lunched together. It was Mr Bing who had planned the Edinburgh Festival, and made it an international event, although the original idea had come from Audrey Mildmay, who had been a singer with the Carl Rosa Company and had then married John Christie who, before the war, had spent a fortune on turning his Sussex home at Glyndebourne into an opera house.

Mr Bing – almost everyone called him Mr Bing, except Maria Callas who called him Rudi – had worked with John Christie at Glyndebourne during those early days, and when the plan arose to light a beacon in art-starved post-war Britain the Christies asked Bing to go to Edinburgh and see what could be done. Against all the odds he not only collected tens of thousands of pounds in sponsorship – a method of financing the arts by commercial patronage that was then in its infancy – but he also assembled a glittering array of names in the world of art and music to perform, and in consequence he pre-sold a quarter of a million seats for opera, ballet, symphony and drama before a note had been played or a word spoken on stage: an astounding feat.

The festival became not only a *succès d'estime* but also, even more surprisingly, big business. To the astonishment of most people in Britain, apart from the Christies and Rudolf Bing, culture became a tourist attraction and attracted large quantities of much-needed foreign currency. By 1949 the Edinburgh Festival had become an established event of interest even to the popular newspapers; the *Daily Mirror*'s old editor, Cecil Thomas, had recently retired, and the new editor, Silvester Bolam, was an economics graduate from Durham University who was passionately keen on providing the masses with opportunities to improve their lives; so I no longer courted reproach by writing about an arts festival because I had Bolam's active encouragement.

Rudolf Bing was by that time travelling the world to engage artists, but he telephoned me during the week before the 1949 festival and we agreed to meet on the night train to Scotland. We were joined at dinner on the train by Malcolm Sargent the conductor, another man who saw it as his mission in life to bring good music to a wider audience; an immensely likeable companion, Malcolm had a sincere faith that the common man would appreciate the finer things if only they were presented without pomposity, and although he was later to prove his point with outstanding success, he earned himself the nickname of Flash Harry in the process, though only among snobs.

There was nothing at all snobbish about Rudolf Bing, although his patron, John Christie, a former usher at Eton, was intolerant of any standard below excellence, which earned him a deserved reputation for arrogance. I had not met Christie at the time, nor had I sought to do so because he was the sort of man who would have loathed the *Daily Mirror* and would have suspected everyone connected with such a newspaper of having base motives. However, on the train to Edinburgh that night Rudolf Bing and Malcolm Sargent hatched a plan to set up a small private dinner party at which both John Christie and I would be guests, and the purpose of the meeting would be to soften John Christie's disdain for the popular press and bring him to realize that mass-circulation newspapers were a necessary ally if he wished to make a reality of his dream to bring good music and fine art within the appreciative reach of all the population.

I was not keen about this plan to make me a go-between because I did not think it would work; I knew from experience that men like Christie and the popular press were oil and water, and that even if the tabloids encouraged his ideas Christie would be irritated and depressed by the way in which they did it: later I was proved to be correct about that, but my objections to the experiment were overruled when Rudi Bing told us that time was short to try it because he had been offered, and had accepted, the job of general manager of the New York Metropolitan Opera, and this was to be his last Edinburgh Festival. (He told us in confidence that his pay was to be £7,500 a year, which both Malcolm and I found impressive.)

John Christie's dream, as he outlined it at dinner later that week, was that 'bright spots', meaning small festivals of music and the arts, would be lighted all over Britain. Dozens of young composers, hundreds of young musicians, singers, actors and artists of all kinds would have a string of local showplaces for their talents, extending through the English summer. Christie was realistic about the difficulties, but typically he saw local mayors as the army of philistines that would be hardest to defeat. 'All mayors are vulgar people,' he said, gloomily, 'but it would be necessary to deal with them. Rather like your newspaper, dear boy,' he added without enthusiasm.

That week in Edinburgh twelve hundred performers and assorted artists were displaying their wares before the eyes of the world. 'Now that we have made it possible for this to happen here,' said Christie, 'why should we suppose that it is impossible to light the Edinburgh flame in places such as Bath and Bristol, Leeds, Manchester, Nottingham, Brighton, Liverpool, Plymouth or even Birmingham?'

It was a brave concept, although I doubt whether any of us at the dinner table apart from Mr Christie believed it possible. Yet if John Christie were alive today he would see that his dream has all come true, and even mayors and tabloid newspapers bask in its reflected glory.

One of my tasks in Edinburgh, apart from writing the column, was to review new plays, and in 1949 I was particularly looking forward to the world première of *The Cocktail Party* by T.S. Eliot, with a cast headed by Alec Guinness and Irene Joyce; but, as it happened, that first-ever performance of the play did not end until well after midnight, far too late for me to file a notice. When I returned to my hotel that night I wrote a review but knew that it would have little chance of getting into the paper, so the following morning I telephoned Mr Eliot, who was staying in digs in Edinburgh, thinking that I might get an interview which would enable me to discuss the play in the column. He invited me to lunch.

I had supposed that this prince among poets would have literary lions swarming in prides around him after his triumph of the night before but he told me later that I was the only person who had telephoned him that morning because he had forgotten to give anyone his Edinburgh telephone number, except Alec Guinness, from whom I had obtained it. He came to the door in shirtsleeves and wearing carpet slippers, unshaven, a weary-looking man of just turned sixty.

'Do you chance to have any cigarettes?' he asked as he showed me into his untidy room. 'I seem to have run out and I'm dying for a smoke.'

I produced a pack of Camels.

'I say, you were lucky to get these,' he said. 'Very difficult to find in Scotland.'

I had some others so I gave him the packet. I knew he was American born but I did not know he always smoked American cigarettes for preference. It was a good start.

During my column years I met thousands of famous people and was impressed by few, but T.S. Eliot was among the few. I knew large chunks of *Prufrock*, *The Waste Land* and *Four Quartets* off by heart, and my visit to interview him was not so much a journalistic job as a pilgrimage: in my personal pantheon Eliot was ranged alongside G.B.S., G.K. and Munnings.

He was an intensely private man, but friendly and kindly, and during that first lunch he talked about philosophy, about his time as a schoolmaster when he taught the schoolboy Betjeman at Highgate, about his 'journalistic years' as editor of *The Criterion*, about Bertrand Russell and Virginia Woolf, about his years as a bank clerk from which Ezra Pound had rescued him by raising a subscription among writers including the impoverished Hemingway and the rich Gertrude Stein in Paris, scarcely mentioning his own poetry. He had the schoolmaster's gift of treating an eager student as an equal, even if the student happened to be a reporter. I did not write a column about our conversation because, for the *Daily Mirror*, it would have needed to be written in a jazzy fashion that he would have disliked, and I had no reason to upset him. I saw Tom Eliot often in later years, and although I know little about his private life it seems to me that some of the memoirs written about him by his *soi-disant* friends after his death owe more to the fiction-writer's art than the biographer's.

There is an old joke about the schoolboy who was asked in class what his father did for a living, and replied that his father played the piano in a brothel; when scolded by his mother for telling a lie, the boy said, 'Yes, but I didn't want to admit that my dad is the editor of the *Daily Mirror*.' I worked with eight successive editors of the *Mirror*, and although all were competent journalists and decent enough men in their fashion the one I liked best was the one who was most disliked by his peers and whose career ended in ruins: Silvester Bolam, Bish to his friends.

Bish Bolam, although a dedicated socialist, did not have the rancorous class hatred that motivated so many of the other *Mirror* top executives, and this fact, plus the fact that he was an intellectual by nature, caused him to be treated with suspicion in Geraldine House. Harry Guy Bartholomew, who had appointed Bish to the editorial chair, liked him because he was a member of the working class, but that was not enough for most of his other senior colleagues, nearly all of whom were jealous of him for having been appointed over their heads.

During his five years as editor Bish Bolam drove the *Daily Mirror*'s circulation up to the pinnacle at which the paper proudly claimed, 'The World's Biggest Daily Sale' (Hugh Cudlipp used to say in private, 'How about *Pravda*?'), but Bolam did not achieve this solely by the customary mass-circulation formula of sex and sensation: he took important social and political issues of the day, such as the Beveridge Report which was the foundation document of the welfare state, and gave them extensive coverage in the paper, using experts to explain them in simple terms that everyone could understand; he also used graphs, which was tantamount to sacrilege in a tabloid.

I may be accused of prejudice in his favour because Bolam and I share one odd distinction: on the day he finally left the *Daily Mirror*, only one of his colleagues said goodbye to him. But I also shared his belief that one rôle of a newspaper such as the *Mirror* was to guide the tabloid-reading public towards an appreciation of a fuller life; and, like Bish but unlike some of our other colleagues, I did not believe that the gutters must run with aristo blood before this could be achieved. Bish, a keen supporter of Christian Action, was an educator; coming from the deprived area of Newcastle, he had a dream of the British working class of the future, opening their bottle of Pomerol to let it breathe, lighting the candles on the dinner table and putting a Rubenstein recording of Chopin nocturnes on the radiogram. Earnestly pursuing the *ignis fatuus* of egalitarianism, Bish looked forward to the distant day when all the Durham miners would be living graciously; at least he foresaw the affluent society, if nothing else.

I was a willing bricklayer in helping Bish to build his brave new world, believing that newspapermen like us should, in Winston Churchill's words, condemn tyranny in whatever guise and from whatever quarter it may present itself and seek to defend the privileged and underprivileged alike. Not that this entailed becoming pompous, boring or patronizing; Bish and I also shared T.S. Eliot's view that fish and chips and greyhound racing were as integral a part of the British way of life as the *Book of Common Prayer*. There were, however, differences of degree in our approach: for example I agreed with Bish that it would be a noble sight if all the proletariat were wearing grey top hats at Royal Ascot, my only reservation being that they should remain in Tattersalls and not be allowed into the Enclosure. In fact, in later years many of them were.

Bish, that kindly and uncomplicated man, saw me as an ally in his campaign, and among the tasty morsels that he tossed into my cage during this period of social awareness was a task that caused all my colleagues to turn green with envy: I was appointed *Daily Mirror* vintage correspondent. Now, the fact is, and always was, that the *Daily Mirror* needs a vintage correspondent about as much as it needs a Greek philosophy editor; although today there are thousands of *Mirror* readers who enjoy a drop of the old vino, at the time of which I write they all drank beer. So I must explain the circumstances in which this esoteric function came my way.

At the end of the war the French wine-growers faced a serious problem. During the conflict in Europe their only foreign customers had been the occupying Germans, who were more inclined to commandeer their wine than buy it. So the French viticulturists were short of cash with which to revivify their industry. England was still a customer for champagne, Burgundy and Bordeaux, but the old traditional export trade to Britain was not big enough to provide the wine-growers with the wherewithal to repair the ravages of war; they needed to expand the market in Britain, and to do this they needed to popularize wine-drinking among the British pub-going classes. They did not have the money for a big advertising campaign, so what they really needed was a Trojan Horse in every British pub: the *Daily Mirror*.

The editor began to receive letters inviting him to send his vintage correspondent on small and elegant conducted tours of the vineyards and the châteaux: all former editors would have tossed such invitiations

117

in the bin as blatant attempts to use the newspaper for free advertising; but Bish Bolam saw them as an opportunity to instruct the readers in matters of discrimination such as the difference between a first growth and a bumptious little wine with amusing pretensions. Bish was in some ways a dreamer but in matters concerning his staff he was realist enough to know that to send almost any of his reporters on a roving mission to the wine country would be like handing the man a one-way ticket to the White Man's Grave; to assign the average *Mirror* man of that era to a tour of the *caves* and châteaux where unlimited wine was free would have been like sending him to that undiscover'd country from which no traveller returns: sure as hell the happy chap would have ended up as the Ginger Ted of the Côtes du Rhône.

All that was needed technically for the job was a presentably dressed fellow who could speak a little French, who was interested in wine without being in the habit of shaving in it, and who could be relied upon not to end the day singing *Knees Up Mother Brown* or being sick on Baron Philippe de Rothschild's Aubusson carpet. For two or three newspapers the choice would have been easy. *The Times* could have fielded a cricket team of reporters like that; they would probably have had frayed trousers-bottoms and leather-patched elbows, because *Times* staff were notoriously badly paid, but they would have sported old boys' ties from minor public schools. However, even in those days when the editorial staffs of popular papers such as the *Express*, the *Mail* and the *Mirror* were largely interchangeable, the *Mirror* was sorely short of what might now be termed a touch of class; when it came to the appointment of a court correspondent or, as in this case, a vintage correspondent, the editor was not faced with an *embarras de choix*. It was a spin of a coin between me and a reporter called Clifford Davis, but as Davis had already been earmarked to take over as the *Mirror's* Paris correspondent, I was handed the portfolio.

Celebrating this appointment, I walked down to El Vino for a glass of my new work and fell into conversation with James Wentworth Day and Macdonald Hastings, the latter having recently sired a boy who was later to become editor of the *Daily Telegraph*. We were joined by Rupert Denny, a tall, white-haired, genially garrulous Yorkshireman who gloried in the title of vintage correspondent for the *Daily Telegraph*; Rupert was a man who never stopped talking, usually about wine, and was widely regarded in Fleet Street as a stupendous bore.

'I mustn't stop long,' beamed Rupert, appreciatively sniffing a glass of Bâtard Montrachet, 'because I'm just off to Bordeaux.'

'To bore who?' inquired Hastings, coldly. This story later became a Fleet Street *conte*, and I have since heard it in several versions.

I listened attentively to Rupert's chatter, seeking to pick up some of the wine jargon that he trotted out so fluently. After he had left, I picked up my glass by the round base at the bottom of the stem, nonchalently swirled its contents, waved the red wine reflectively under my nose and then peered at it through the flame of the candle that was stuck in a bottle on the bar. While I was doing this I was joined by Frank Bower, the proprietor of El Vino, who was a master vintner; he was watching me with puzzled interest.

'This is a big, ambitious wine, Frank,' I said, thoughtfully. 'Robust and full-bodied, don't you know. One might even call it complex and voluptuous, what? Even so, I would say that it is slightly intense and tends towards the exotic, and although it is undoubtedly starting to drink it will be even more powerful and massive for another five years of cellaring – wouldn't you say?'

Frank gave me a searching look. 'That's our house plonk,' he said.

At that time I had not much travelled in the realms of gold, as Jeeves would have put it, so when I first set eyes on Château Monbousquet in St Émilion I knew how stout Cortez must have felt when with eagle eye he stared at the Pacific. The château stood, white and shuttered, beside a lake in pastoral countryside. Exquisite. This was my introduction to my new task. We had been invited by Monsieur Daniel Querre, owner of the château and the vinyard, who was in charge of publicity for the area. He was a man with a heart as big as his smile, who took pleasure in educating his guests on the subject of wine, and he was as generous a host as he was a teacher. As soon as we arrived he gave us a glass of cool champagne to soothe away the fatigue of the journey, and then he sat us down to dinner.

I shall never forget that dinner. Bertie Wooster, acknowledged by Jeeves as a connoozer in such matters, described with lyrical appreciation the culinary work of that great master, Anatole, when in mid-season form, citing particularly Anatole's *Timbale de ris de veau Toulousaine*, his *Selles d'agneau aux laitues à la Grècque* and his *Sylphides à la crème d'écrevisses*. By the time we reached the cheese that night I had come to the conclusion that Anatole must have been a mere snack-bar operator by comparison with Madame Querre: her cooking was celestial.

Our small group of guests from England included John Murray, son of the publisher, and his young wife, who were as much interested in the literary associations of the area as the wine because Montaigne had lived nearby and had at one time been mayor of Bordeaux; also John Arlott, already well known as a BBC cricket commentator and just beginning a parallel career as a wine writer; only two of us were journalists, the other being Stanley Baron of the *News Chronicle*, whose wife, Betty Franks, a former ballet dancer, also wrote for the *Chronicle*; Betty had been invited but had been unable to come, so Stanley had brought his teenaged daughter in her place, a sweetly pretty girl who was starry-eyed with enchantment. She was the object of devoted attention from Monsieur Querre's teenaged son, Alain, who seldom took his eyes off her; Alain had previously spoken little English, but his efforts to learn the language took a quantum leap forward that weekend.

The sunny days sped past in a dreamlike sequence of continuous new delights to the eye and to the palate. On our last afternoon we had a picnic, the scene of which remains in my mind's eye like a Pissarro or a Morisot; returning towards the château we stopped on a hillside and sat, blissfully happy, on a terrace that looked down on the small town of St Émilion. It was a perfect evening. The air was warm and fragrant with the scent of jasmin. As twilight gave way to a starry sky, the lights in the valley below flicked on. On such a night as this it was as clear as the moon to all except one of us that young Alain wished to be talking to the pretty English girl.

The odd man out who did not notice this was John Arlott, and the reason he did not notice it was that he was preoccupied by the extraordinary discovery that young Alain had never heard of the game of cricket: John, speaking uninhibitedly in franglais with a rich Hampshire burr, was determined, if only out of gratitude to his hosts, to put right this lacuna in the education of Daniel Querre's son.

'Dans le jeu de cricket il y a deux équipes, you see,' said Arlott, his voice rising alone above the gentle chatter of the cicadas, 'et dans chaque équipe il y a onze hommes. L'équipe qui sont fielding – vous comprenez "fielding", Alain? – sont dirigé par leur capitaine aux leurs places dans le champs – probablement mid-on, mid-off, possiblement silly mid-off, slips, gulley, square leg . . .'

'Square legs, m'sieu?' inquired Alain, disbelieving.

'Oui, square leg. C'est le nom d'un position dans le champs. Ils sont tous sur le qui vive pour attraper le bal dans les mains après il a été frappé par le batsman.'

'Par le quoi, m'sieu?' asked Alain, bemused and mystified and longing to get away and sit with Stanley Baron's daughter, who was by herself at the end of the terrace, gazing at the moon.

'Par le *batsman*,' repeated John. 'Je ne sais pas le mot en français – peut-être il n'existe pas parce que le jeu de cricket est obviously pas bien connu ici, not yet anyway. Alors, revenons à nos moutons, un des hommes in the fielding side est dirigé par le capitaine à prendre le bal. Il est le bowler. Cet homme marche pour un considerable distance behind le wicket, et puis il commence a courir à grande vitesse en direction des stumps. Vous me suivez, Alain?'

'Oui, m'sieu,' nodded the unhappy but perfectly mannered boy.

'Voilà,' continued John. 'Cet homme, le bowler, jete le bal aussi vite que possible at the batsman.'

Alain sat up, shocked. 'To *hit* heem?' he inquired.

'Non, non, non, non, non, non, non – to get him au dehors. Si le bal frappe les stumps, le batsman is au dehors – he's out.'

At this point the kindly Daniel Querre came over to talk to Arlott, and thereby to rescue his bewildered son, who moved swiftly over to sit beside Stanley Baron's daughter.

Never again did I return to Monbousquet, but the memory of that idyllic weekend came back into my mind some thirty-five years later when I chanced to find myself in the town of Bordeaux; with nothing to do for an hour while I waited for a car to arrive to take me on to Arcachon, I began strolling past the shops and stopped outside an information centre for inquiries concerning the local wine-growing region: on impulse I walked in and asked the girl behind the counter whether Château Monbousquet was still flourishing.

'Bien sûr,' she smiled. 'It is a very lovely place, well worth a visit for the English tourist. It is run by Monsieur Alain Querre, who is also the head of publicity for all the wine-growers in this district. And as an English tourist you would have no language difficulty there, because Monsieur Querre's wife is an Englishwoman.'

Stanley Baron's daughter.

The small flight of swallows from Fleet Street who worked as vintage correspondents during those post-war years were treated as ambassadors and were showered with distinctions that in normal times are reserved for serious experts. We few, we happy breed, not only ate and drank like emperors but also we solemnly paraded and processed in borrowed robes at traditional wine ceremonies and were installed as members of honour or chevaliers of ancient orders; we had medallions hung around our necks, were kissed on both cheeks and fêted at innumerable *vins d'honneur*. In later years wealthy tycoons from California and other centres of culture were able to buy, at an astronomical price, specially designed trips to the wine region where they were welcomed as honoured guests and stayed at the châteaux; but they never had it so good as we had it – and we were paid to go. Looking round in England today and observing the proliferation of wine shops and wine bars I think that we must have fulfilled our function as the *avant-garde*.

Hand in hand with the top end of the wine industry goes the promotion of *haute cuisine*, so during those years I found myself often at banquets of surpassing luxury prepared by the world's greatest chefs, and at one such banquet I was presented with a diploma which certifies that 'Mr Noel Whitcomb has been awarded the distinction of Member of Honour by the International Academy of Chefs de Cuisine.' After accepting the diploma from the hands of that great expert on food and wine, André Simon, I made a short speech of thanks and then sat down, feeling slightly foolish. The guest sitting on my other side was Charles Forte, at that time a restaurateur without a hotel to his name, and I whispered to him, 'To tell you the truth, Charles, I feel a bit silly because I must be the only man around this table who cannot scramble an egg.'

'You seem to be missing the point, old boy,' said Charles. 'The whole room is stuffed with culinary geniuses who can cook eggs in any way you like, but until tonight they never had a blood-brother with fourteen million readers.'

Although I was sufficiently happy in my work during that period to have suspended all thought of leaving the *Daily Mirror*, the reverse was the case with my colleague Bill Connor (Cassandra). Bill had been senior among *Mirror* writers before the war, and he resented the fact that my column was now given equal prominence with his; he missed the patronage of his old buddy Hugh Cudlipp, who had moved to the *Sunday Express* as managing editor after being fired by Bart, and he bitterly disliked the new editor, my friend Bish Bolam. So Connor was far less upset than I was when Bolam's career in newspapers was wrecked after the *Daily Mirror* committed a flagrant contempt of court.

A woman had been murdered in Notting Hill, and a man called John Haigh was arrested and charged with the murder. A Scotland Yard contact tipped off the *Mirror*'s crime correspondent that this man Haigh had committed several other ghastly murders, and had sucked the blood of his victims through a straw before finally dissolving their bodies in an acid bath. Greatly excited by this scoop, the *Mirror* splashed these gruesome details all over the front page, under the headline VAMPIRE HORROR IN NOTTING HILL. The story itself did not mention John Haigh but merely concerned itself with sensational details of this appalling series of crimes; however, with almost unbelievable foolishness, the paper printed a picture of John Haigh in handcuffs, alongside the story. This juxtaposition carried the clear inference that Haigh was the vampire who had committed all these murders. It was judgement before trial, and as such it was flagrant contempt of court. For this heinous journalistic *faux pas* the *Daily Mirror* was rightly fined £10,000 and the editor, Bish Bolam, was sent to gaol where he remained for three months.

How such an extraordinary folly could be committed by experienced journalists is difficult to understand. What actually did happen inside the *Mirror* on that fateful night is even more extraordinary and would make a chilling short story if written as fiction. However, there is little point in going over those details now, forty years later; all that needs to be said now is that although Bolam, as editor, was the man who bore the responsibility and paid the price, he was not in the office at moments when crucial decisions about the matter were taken.

There are some men who can serve a prison sentence and come out relatively unscathed. Bolam was not one of them. When he came out of Brixton prison he had aged twenty years. He did not complain, because in the eyes of the world he had nothing to complain about – he had committed a monstrous offence and had been punished for it – but his face told the story of his anguish. While he had been in prison his children had been ostracized at school, and he never forgave himself for the effects his disgrace had upon his family. A few years later, in his mid-forties, he died of shame.

However, when Bolam came out of Brixton prison he was reinstalled as editor of the *Daily Mirror*, which was a great surprise to many people; but Bart, the ageing chairman, was by that time well aware of everything that had occurred in the run-up to the case against the *Mirror*, and he wanted to make sure that it would not become public knowledge. There was also another reason for Bart's apparent and uncharacteristic magnanimity. He himself was under siege from his fellow directors, who wanted to winkle him out, and Bolam, as an ex-officio member of the board of directors, was the only ally upon whose support Bart could rely. Bolam had originally been Bart's protégé, and now after his reinstatement as editor Bolam owed him another favour. At a vital time. Nemesis in the guise of Cecil King was catching up on Bart, and Bart knew it only too well.

Bart was in his early seventies: the *Mirror* had been his life for just short of half a century; the days of his genius were past; he was drinking more than a bottle of Scotch a day, he was almost friendless and he was making mistakes. He was old and ill and terrified and tight. Even so, his fellow directors were still scared of the now toothless tiger who had terrorized their jungle for so long; they wanted to oust him but they were by no means sure what they would do if he refused to go. To depose the chairman, a unanimous vote of his fellow-directors was needed, and there was one odd man out: Bolam was reluctant to turn against his former benefactor, and demurred. But the time came when the company's business was getting into such a mess that even Bolam agreed that the old man had to go.

It was Philip Zec, the cartoonist who had been at the centre of the wartime trouble that had nearly closed down the *Daily Mirror* and who was the most junior director on the board, who was given the task of marching into the chairman's office and telling Bart that he had been fired. As Zec told me soon afterwards, it was a bizarre scenario. Bart's first reaction to Zec's announcement of the board's decision was predictable. 'Fuck off,' he said.

'Please be reasonable, Bart,' said Zec. 'The whole board is unanimous.'

'Bollocks,' said Bart. 'You will never get Bolam to agree.'

'Bolam has already agreed,' said Zec.

'He's agreed!' cried Bart, horrified. 'The Judas fucking Iscariot!'

It was probably the nearest Bart ever came to a classical allusion. In his hour of agony he identified himself with Jesus Christ. He then broke down in a flood of tears and sobbed for half an hour, from time to time reaching for the whisky bottle to refill his glass. Then he lurched down the corridor and took a taxi home. The old tyrant had been assassinated and Cecil King seized the throne.

One of Cecil's first actions as chairman was to bring his old ally, Hugh Cudlipp, back into the building, first in his former job as editor of the *Sunday Pictorial* and then as editorial director of both the *Mirror* and the *Pic*: which proved to be an excellent move to the advantage of the newspapers, but which left the Sword of Damocles dangling over the head of Bish Bolam; Cudlipp did not like Bish any more than his pal Bill Connor did.

Bolam, the intellectual radical who believed in using the paper to educate the underprivileged, was not the sort of editor who fitted into King's grandiose dreams – 'My readers are virtually the country,' said King on television – or into Cudlipp's plans for serious frivolity: so a formal announcement was made that Bolam had 'resigned due to a disagreement with the management'. This occurred suddenly, and on the night Bolam was kicked out he came into my office waving a cheque for his payoff that he had just collected from the cashiers.

'Come and have a drink, Noel,' he said, trying to sound cheerful. 'Although I have just been given the push I have also been given riches beyond the dreams of avarice. Let's celebrate.'

We went to a pub that was known as the Falcon in the Ruins, and Bish called for champagne. In walked Bill Connor with a friend called Bob Balmforth, a features sub-editor on the *Mirror*. Bolam hailed them heartily. 'Come and join the wake,' he called. 'I've just been paid off and we're celebrating.'

Connor said, 'I don't drink with jailbirds,' and, turning on his heel, walked out.

Sometime later Bill Connor used one of his Cassandra columns to deliver a thunderous attack upon another newspaper that had printed an article contemptuously critical of Bolam, but as the article in question was an obituary, Connor's olive branch was no consolation to poor old Bish who had died of a broken heart.

Bill and I remained colleagues and met often until the morning in 1967 when I attended the memorial service for Sir William Connor in St Paul's Cathedral; but neither of us ever forgot that night in the Falcon in the Ruins and there was always a coolness between us: some things are difficult to forgive.

8

Oh, we don't want to lose you, but we think you ought to go,
For your king and your country, they both need you so . . .

from a Great War recruiting song

As midnight struck at the climax of New Year's Eve celebrations in 1949, heralding the new year of 1950 and the second half of the twentieth century, I was in Bricktop's nightclub in Rome singing *Auld Lang Syne* with the Shah of Persia.

This improbable-sounding episode, well worth a few paragraphs in a newspaper column, would not normally be worth recalling in a book except for the odd circumstances that led up to it and the even odder circumstances that arose from it.

I had spent the Christmas of 1949 at home with my wife and our new baby daughter and had then decided to write a series of columns from the capitals of Europe, starting in Rome because on a stroll round Rome you can always see more stories than Bernini fountains.

No sooner had I checked in at the Excelsior Hotel in the Via Veneto than a page-boy began walking round the lobby bearing a banner with my name chalked on it, and calling, 'Signor Whitecow . . . Signor Whitecow . . . telephono.'

It was my office. If a big news story broke in a foreign country where I was on a visit, the *Mirror* always telephoned and asked me to handle it. Although, to avoid argument, I agreed to look into the story in this instance, I had no intention of doing so because it was a gossip story of the kind I have always loathed.

Ingrid Bergman, the actress, then married to a Swedish brain surgeon, had been making a film on the island of Stromboli, directed by Roberto Rossellini, and they had fallen in love. They decided to marry as soon as Ingrid could get a divorce, and Rossellini asked a Vatican correspondent, Signor Cianferra, to issue a statement to this effect. His idea in doing this was to formalize the affair and cool the gossip, but naturally it had the opposite effect, and a thundering herd of reporters and photographers from newspapers all over the world came charging into Rome on the trail of Miss Bergman. She went to ground, distracted, unwell, ashamed and pregnant.

Press persecution of a celebrity in trouble is always an ugly sight; but in this case, as so often happens, they had no idea where to look for their prey so the only effect of their presence in the Italian capital was a steep increase in liquor sales in Rome's most expensive hotels. I knew Miss Bergman slightly, through film work, so my colleagues from other papers in Fleet Street kept a sharp eye on me, sometimes shadowing me to museums and other places of interest on the suspicion that I might be going to some secret assignation; in fact I was merely doing the tourist sights and collecting material for columns; Ben Hur's chariot horses would not have dragged me into the search for Miss Bergman.

One of the people I met in the hotel was an amiable Iranian who said he was an inventor; when he discovered that I wrote a column for a British newspaper with an enormous circulation he tried hard to persuade me to write about one of his inventions that he wanted to market. He did not tell me at the start that his work as an inventor was merely a hobby, and that his main job was as a diplomatic adviser to the Shah of Persia. I discovered this only when he brought me an address scribbled on a sheet of hotel writing paper. It was the secret address at which Ingrid Bergman was staying.

'How on earth did you get it?' I asked him.

'Diplomatic,' he replied, smiling broadly, and then he explained about his job as a courtier to the King Emperor.

It was not tender-heartedness nor was it mere scruple that caused me to put a match to the piece of paper and watch it burn in an ashtray: if the *Mirror* had discovered that I knew where Ingrid Bergman was hiding, my life would have become intolerable as well as hers; the story would quickly have turned into a mass siege outside the house, and I had no intention of getting mixed up in that sort of public execution.

So I did a deal with my new Iranian friend. I promised him that sometime in the future I would write about his invention, provided he promised me to forget about the address and give it to nobody else. He agreed happily to that, and invited me for drinks to his suite in the hotel that evening. It was there that I met the three sisters of the Shah of Persia; Princess Achraf, his twin, and the Princesses Fatimeh and Chams. They were staying at the Excelsior in Rome to await the arrival of their brother, who was on his way back from an official visit to the United States. Officially His Imperial Majesty had been seeking a loan from America to underwrite his seven-year plan for the industrialization of Iran, at that time a poor country; in fact, in his discussion with

President Truman, the Shah had shrewdly laid great stress on the vulnerability of his long frontier with the Soviet Union and, in consequence, had come away with a loan of 250 million dollars provided he used most of it to buy armaments.

This was a matter for celebration, so when the Shah arrived in Rome to stop off for a few days' rest on his way home he instructed his entourage to arrange a big dinner party, to take place on New Year's Eve; everyone of social importance in Rome was invited (though politicians were left out), the emphasis being on ambassadors, members of Italy's black aristocracy and *emigré* royalty from European countries that had dispensed with crowned heads. I received an invitation, presumably because my name had been put on the list by Princess Achraf, who was in those days described as 'the power behind the Peacock Throne'.

We all gathered in what was normally the nightclub in the basement of the Excelsior, but which had been taken over for this special occasion, and we lined up in the usual way to be presented to His Majesty. After I had been formally received by the Shah I moved on, but he called me back and chatted for a few moments, presumably because his sisters had mentioned me to him. The only single thing that he and I had in common was that we were both about the same age, both about thirty.

The dinner was predictably luxurious but, as is frequently the case on such evenings, the occasion itself was boring. I was sitting with an aged Italian princess on one side and an ancient Austrian countess on the other, and as they talked about nothing but their own grandeur in the past, time passed slowly. I noticed that the guests of honour surrounding His Majesty were also long in the tooth, and he was not looking too happy.

When the speeches and formalities were over, my friend the courtier came quietly up behind me, tapped me on the shoulder and whispered, 'Do you chance to know any nightclubs in this city?'

'All the good ones,' I whispered back.

'Please come with me,' he said.

We walked into an ante-room where he explained that the Shah had become bored with being surrounded by greybeards and ladies of advanced age because he had expected to be having some fun after his long and successful journey on behalf of his country. 'His Imperial Majesty wishes to go and look at the nightlife of Rome,' said the courtier, 'and I told him that you would know the best places to go.'

So off we went. Nightclubs are much of a muchness all over the world, the only difference being that some are dingier than others;

128

Rome boasted a few of the world's smartest of these upholstered sewers at the time, and we made brief visits to a couple of these before ending up at Bricktop's shortly before midnight. Bricktop, so called because she had brick-red hair, was an American woman who had become famous in the *demi-monde* as a caterer to the late-night whims and fancies of the rich, and her membership included more kings than you would find in a baccarat shoe, so she immediately recognized the Shah when we walked in, even though I signed him in as 'Mr M. Pahlavi'.

'I'm giving you the best table, darling,' she murmured to me as the headwaiter led us through the darkness, 'although there will probably be a rumpus about it when old fatso Farouk arrives.' King Farouk of Egypt was a regular, and although he, like the Shah, did not drink alcohol, he bought large quantities of champagne for the nubile Italian girls who decked his table.

Bricktop brought over a hand-picked covey of her best-looking girls to sit at our table; they realized that my companion must be somebody important but they did not know who he was so they called him 'Johnny-boy'. However, although the selection of one or two of these girls to take back to the hotel with him had been among the prime reasons for his visit, His Imperial Majesty's eye was far more taken by a young English girl who was in Rome with her new husband on her honeymoon: he sent a waiter to invite them to our table. Before we left, he said to his aide, 'Arrange for that English girl to be brought to me at the hotel at midday.'

I was quite shocked. I said to him, 'Even money to a hundred dollars she won't play. She's on her honeymoon.'

The Shah did not understand my racing slang, which was lucky for me because as it turned out I would have lost the bet. Human nature has never ceased to surprise me.

Monarchs seldom carry money so I paid all the bills. As we strolled back at dawn through the streets of Rome to the hotel, the Shah said, 'My dear Noel, you have been a most kindly host tonight and one day I shall repay you.'

One becomes accustomed to such amiable remarks, spoken in the early morning light after a night out, so apart from some polite reply such as, 'Not at all, it has been an immense pleasure,' I forgot all about it.

But I was to remember it in later years. The Shah was not a man who made promises lightly, not even in a Rome dawn after a night out on the tiles.

During the ensuing years in which Iran became oil-rich and the Shah an important figure in international affairs, he sometimes invited me to parties that he gave while on holiday in St Moritz, and when he decided that his country had become rich and influential enough for him to be formally crowned as its monarch – which had not happened before because such a conspicuous display of wealth would have been politically unwise – an invitation to the coronation in Teheran arrived from the palace.

As a result of accepting that invitation I became embroiled in a very odd series of events, and although that story belongs, chronologically, to a later period of my life, I will recount it now because it all happened as a result of the Shah's remembering my insignificant hospitality to him in that first dawn of the year 1950.

By the time of his coronation the Shah had become one of the three richest men in the world. He was revered throughout Islam as a descendant of the Prophet, and in his own country as the Shahanshah, King of Kings, King Emperor, Shadow of the Almighty, Centre of the Universe, Light of the Arians, Lion of the Peacock Throne. Yet he was not the scion of a long line of royal blood; in fact he had been born in a poor suburb of Teheran. His father, an illiterate, had risen by the power of his personality to seize the throne and become the brutal and greedy monarch whose brilliance as an administrator enabled his country to begin the long march out of the dark ages into the modern world. After the old king's death, his son, Mahomet Pahlavi, the new Shah, who had been educated in the West, continued the modernization of Iran with passionate energy, thereby incurring the implacable opposition of the mullahs, including Ayatollah Khomeini, who was forced into exile in Paris. The mullahs, Islamic fundamentalists, sought to undermine the Shah because he introduced Western thinking into Iran, so it was ironic that the American CIA ultimately became their instrument in deposing him.

Teheran during the Shah's coronation week was a wonderfully pretty sight, a confection of scenes from the Bible and the *Arabian Nights* all in the setting of a Hollywood musical – Flecker's *Hassan* with neon signs and traffic jams.

Mazda is the ancient Persian god of light, and fifteen million coloured lights had been strung above the streets, all reflected by myriads of silver and gold discs that danced and glittered among a forest of flags, red, white and green, the colours of Iran. The Shah had allocated twenty million pounds for the party, a substantial sum in the early 1960s, but he had designed it as a 'private, domestic occasion', and no other royals or heads of state had been invited; apart from diplomatic representatives in Iran, the guest-list of 500 people was made up of people the Shah knew personally, including friends he had made at school in Switzerland and – in my case – an acquaintance who had shown him round the nightspots of Rome.

Not much over a decade previously Teheran had been little more than a shantytown with starving people dying in the gutter, but since the oil boom an educated middle class had grown and flourished, intelligent and friendly people, most of whom later either fled the country or stayed on only to be murdered by Khomeini's savage rabble. It was an affluent city bustling with swarms of private cars and taxis, all hooting like mad amidst the crowds of nomadic tribesmen who were streaming in from the hills with their donkeys and mules laden with pots and pans and carpets, accompanied by retinues of warrior sons, veiled daughters and wives swathed to the eyes, wearing the *chadur* and carrying swaddled babies, all arriving to pay homage to their Shahanshah on his great day of celebration.

Although during my life I have observed the contrast between great riches and desperate poverty in many countries, and there has never been anything unusual about it, Teheran staged a particularly ominous example of it during that week. The rial was a strong currency against the American dollar, and even stronger against the wilting pound sterling, so there was evidence on all sides of consumer prosperity alongside the tented encampments with their tethered camels and disgusting smells that fringed the city; but it was the jewels that one was allowed to see in the vaults that made even the dormant conscience pause and wonder – two-foot-high heaps of uncut emeralds, diamonds by the basketful, rubies and sapphires by the hundredweight; in the Hall of Mirrors five crystal chandeliers lighted the way to the Naderi Throne, made of gold encrusted with 26,733 precious stones, emeralds as big as golf balls shining green from a sea of diamonds, with rubies making patterns of lions and salamanders. Most of it, including the Peacock Throne itself which had been plundered from India, represented spoils of wars going back to Assyrian times, but it was an eye-opener that gave one food for thought: technically it was national treasure to be used as collateral security in foreign deals, but in effect it all belonged to one rich man.

After that rich man had been formally crowned with the pomp and ceremony that surrounds such occasions, bands and cavalry and crowds lining the streets, my wife and I decided that we would take a holiday and travel south to Shiraz, the city of great Persian poets where Hafiz and Saadi lived, and then on to Isfahan: I had already booked a suite at the Shah Abbas Hotel in Isfahan, the centuries-old caravanserai that the

Shah had tranformed into his country's showplace hotel for rich foreign visitors, furnishing it with priceless antiques and old Persian carpets of exquisite design; I had even drawn the money for this holiday in cash from the bank, because those were the days before credit cards, and cheques on English banks were unacceptable in Iran.

We had arranged to set off as quickly as would seem polite after saying goodbye to all the new friends we had made in Teheran, and we were in the midst of packing when a chasseur arrived bearing on a silver salver a large envelope addressed to me; the envelope contained a handwritten note from the minister of the interior inviting me to join a small group of Iranian dignitaries, headed by the Shah, who were flying to Mashhad on the following morning. Mashhad is a place of pilgrimage, holy to the Shia moslems of Iran, similar to Mecca; my wife was not invited, because that would not have been customary on such an occasion in a Moslem country, but even though it delayed our arrangements she insisted that I must accept because to decline such an invitation at that particular time would have looked gratuitously rude. So I went.

It was a small group that gathered on the airfield early next morning, comprising most of the Iranian cabinet ministers plus a few senior government officials, including the chief of police, and myself – the odd man out; it was odd because if it had been decided to have a representative of the British press at this royal pilgrimage they would surely have invited the man from *The Times*, certainly not the *Daily Mirror*; apart from which, I was the only foreigner present.

The Shah, wearing Iranian Air Force uniform, piloted the aircraft. During the flight several of the other passengers, most of whom I had met during the preceding week, came to chat with me in a friendly way, probably realizing that I must be a little puzzled – as indeed I was. Mr Hovedah, the prime minister, was particularly kind: he arranged for me to sit next to him and explained all that I should know about Mashhad; he also made it clear that this was not a trip that I was expected to write about, but purely a private expedition. Without needing to be told, I realized that it all stemmed from the night at Bricktop's in Rome, all those years before.

The contrast between Teheran and Mashhad was striking: during the flight we had moved a thousand years back in time; Mashhad, near the USSR–Turkestan border, was dusty and poor, jumbled with old and crumbling buildings, its quiet streets thronged with pilgrims, many in rags. After I had been shown to the simple room in a monastery where I was to stay, the minister for the interior came to collect me. 'We are

132

going to the mosque for the ceremony,' he said. 'It is an important pilgrimage for us.'

We left our shoes outside the entrance. All the official party from Teheran, plus the governor of the province and local people of importance, lined up in two ranks, one on either side of the ante-room, and I was shown to my place at the end of one rank. Then in came the Shah. He walked slowly through, stopping here and there for a brief word; as he came to me he tapped me lightly on the shoulder and nodded in the direction he was taking, indicating that I should follow him. We walked together to a flight of steps, which we descended, just the two of us.

At the bottom of the steps we entered a small room, like a crypt, bare of furnishings or decoration; the whole of the far wall was taken up by a gigantic tomb, made of massive silver, engraved and embossed. The Shah knelt before the tomb and I knelt beside him. Then we leaned forward until our heads touched the stone floor, and remained for a while in this attitude of prayer. Then, together, we walked back upstairs without exchanging a word, and the Shah went straight into another room to hold a *divan* among the governors of nearby provinces.

The minister of the interior came over to me and said, 'You have been most extraordinarily honoured, Noel. You are the only European ever to pray with His Imperial Majesty before the tomb of Shah Reza.'

It was arranged that I should meet my friend the minister at the monastery that evening, because we were flying back to Teheran at dawn next morning, and I was offered conducted tours to places of interest in the meantime, but I asked if I might simply walk around the town on my own for a few hours; this was agreed with slight reluctance, and the police chief made out a special pass for me in case any of his men might stop me to find out what I was up to – there were always spies along the Russian border.

It was a fascinating afternoon; I wandered through the narrow streets and alleyways among the swarms of pilgrims, many of whom had trekked for weeks or months across the mountains; I walked for hours and was tired when I returned to my room in the monastery. I began to undress for a bath and took everything out of my pockets: everything – except my wallet. That was no longer there. It had gone. Stolen.

I sat on the bed and pondered. This was a bad business. The wallet had contained all the money that I had drawn for our holiday, a large sum in high-denomination notes; but, even worse, it had also contained all the identification documents that I needed for getting around in Iran, including the *laissez-passer* from the police chief.

133

My first inclination was to say nothing about it until after I had returned to Teheran, to avoid embarrassing my hosts; but I quickly realized that this was not a practical idea because I would at some time have to explain how I had lost all my documents, in order to obtain replacements, and it would look odd if I had not reported the matter as soon as I had discovered the loss.

So I told the chief of police. I asked him not to make a fuss about it and to tell as few people as possible, preferably not the Shah; it was due to my own carelessness and it could have happened anywhere in the world. He was anxious because I was a newspaperman, and feared that I might write about it in my column, but I assured him that I had no intention of doing any such thing, and that as far as I was concerned it was a secret between the two of us.

On the flight back to Teheran Mr Hovedah, the prime minister, told me how distressed he was that such a misfortune should have occurred and asked me to allow him to arrange for the amount of money I had lost to be restored, quietly and unofficially, through a payment from the national bank; this I declined with thanks, explaining again that it was all the result of my own stupidity and that my own bank in London would arrange further credit for me to cover the rest of my private holiday in Iran; he was clearly very relieved that I did not propose to let anyone else know about it except my wife.

My wife, after listening to an account of my adventures in Mashhad, told me that I was a careless idiot, which I knew already, but I explained to her that I had become a Mashhadi, which was a distinction cheap at the price, and after waiting for some more money to arrive from London we set off on our holiday.

It was one of the most memorable holidays we ever had. Although I had written to reserve only a small suite at the Shah Abbas Hotel in Isfahan we found that they had allocated to us the royal suite, which was furnished in the costliest way imaginable and was a bower of exotic flowers when we arrived; I was mildly anxious about this unintentional extravagance after my expensive experience in Mashhad, but money is only money and we were having a marvellous time.

During our week in Teheran we had been taken to visit a caviare factory on the Caspian, where, kitted out in borrowed furs, we had been shown into a vast freezer-room that contained five hundred tons of caviare; caviare was so plentiful in Iran that there was a small specialist restaurant in Teheran which invited customers to eat as many caviare blinis as they wished for the equivalent of £1. I have always been partial to the delicacy, and at the Shah Abbas in Isfahan our room-waiter used to place a big bowl of it, containing about a kilo, together with a bottle of iced vodka in our sitting room every evening, as an *aperitif* before we went down to dinner. The cooking at the hotel was so superb that we ate there mostly during our stay.

Naturally I was expecting a hefty bill, because the Shah Abbas was one of the most expensive hotels in the world at the time, so I went to the bank on the morning of our departure and drew out a big sum. At the hotel reception desk I called for my bill, and after a brief wait the hotel manager came out and said, 'Mr Whitcomb, there is no bill. I hope you have enjoyed your stay.'

This irritated me because I assumed that he, like so many people in England, was offering me free hospitality in exchange for writing about his hotel. So I said to him, 'Go and get my bill. This is a private visit. My wife and I are on holiday, and I am not writing about it. Please hurry because the taxi is waiting for us.'

'I cannot do it, sir,' he said. 'It is more than my job is worth.'

Then a light dawned on me. 'You don't mean to say,' I asked incredulously, 'that you have received instructions about this?'

The hotel manager nodded. Then a seraphic smile spread over his face. 'His Majesty,' he whispered. 'On the telephone. To me. To me personally.'

About a year later, when I had forgotten all about the whole affair, I had a telephone call from the Foreign Office in London asking me to pick up a wallet which contained documents that showed it belonged to me. The caller said he had no other information about it, so, being curious, I telephoned Dennis Wright, then our ambassador in Teheran, whom I knew from having met him during our coronation visit.

'Don't ask any questions, old boy,' he said, 'because if I knew the answers I would not tell you. All I can say is that the wallet was sent to me by the police chief here. Obviously yours, although I have no idea how you came to lose it. Was there any money in it?'

'Yes,' I said.

'Well, there isn't now,' he said. 'Only your personal papers. When you pick it up, think yourself lucky that there is not a severed hand clutching it.'

I never used the wallet after that, and I wished that they had not found it. The idea of a pilgrim walking round without his right hand on account of my carelessness was unattractive. But Iran is a cruel country. That savage cruelty made me feel even more sad when, at the end, I saw television pictures of the Shah, gaunt and terminally ill with cancer, being forced to leave his country as a fugitive while rampaging mobs in

Teheran went wild with religious ecstasy in welcoming the return from exile of the sinister Ayatollah Khomeini. In his final years the Shah had shown increasing signs of megalomania, but that is not unusual among kings or even newspaper proprietors; and when, while driving to the office one day, I heard on the car radio a newsflash announcing the brutal murder in Teheran of Mr Hovedah and some other ministers who had been kind to me, I was half ashamed to find that involuntary tears of anger were rolling down my cheeks.

The development of *folie de grandeur* is an occupational hazard for a newspaper columnist, partly because he mixes so frequently with people who suffer from the same malaise; during my earliest column years I had the opportunity of studying several examples of this affliction at close range, particularly among the ministers of the new Labour government, some of whom had risen to the seats of power from lowly circumstances. Major Clement Attlee, the prime minister, who was described at the time as a modest man with a great deal to be modest about, was a stern disciplinarian with his feet firmly on the ground, but some of his cabinet colleagues soon had heads the size of barrage-balloons, and although they were all sincere enough in their belief that they could build Jerusalem in England's green and pleasant land, few of them showed much talent in the way they went about it. It was a depressing era of unavoidable austerity made worse by the Gradgrind policies of men and women who thought they were freeing the country from the oppression of the rich but succeeded only in inculcating mental attitudes that started the spread of the British Disease, which resulted in industrial anarchy that hampered the country for the next forty years.

It was generally accepted, though never completely true, that the *Daily Mirror*, like the TUC-controlled *Daily Herald*, would never rock the boat but could always be relied upon to support the Labour Party; this made sense because it was the British working class who had put the Labour Party into power, and nearly all the British working class at that time were readers of the *Daily Mirror*, so the thinking was that if the *Mirror* opposed the wishes of its readers the paper would lose circulation: which was the worst conceivable scenario.

However, from time to time the *Mirror* reflected its readers' discontent by having a dig at some of the government's more penitential policies, notably the fiscal restraints introduced by the ascetic chancellor, Sir Stafford Cripps, and during one of these periods I wrote a tongue-in-cheek column launching an Association for the Abolition of Austerity. It was all in fun but it touched a nerve in the populace and readers wrote in by the tens of thousands to support the campaign, asking how to join. Though there was nothing overtly political about the column itself, any article of that kind is bound to have subliminal undertones, so although the *Daily Mirror* itself was delighted with the idea because it was good for circulation, the government saw it as an insidious piece of treachery, and I was called in to see the prime minister.

Mr Attlee, shrewdly, received me with uncharacteristic *bonhomie* and set about giving me an interview that he knew the *Mirror* would publish; he pointed out that the abolition of austerity was the government's constant aim, and therefore he fully agreed with our compaign in principle; but in practice, he said – off the record – it was not helpful for a great newspaper to incite discontent at a time of such financial complexity, and he added that he had already been in touch with the editor to assure him that the *Daily Mirror* would receive full credit for its campaign when the chancellor's policies had succeeded in bringing prosperity back again.

So that was the end of the game for my Association for the Abolition of Austerity; when the whistle blew, the final score was: Major Attlee 10 – Association nil. It was never heard of again. But it resulted in my being given another odd and entirely unofficial job. Herbert Morrison, then deputy prime minister, invited me to supper in a basement flat in Lambeth to discuss plans for the Festival of Britain. This invitation came as a surprise because Morrison did not trust me an inch further than he could see out of his one good eye, but I soon discovered the reason for it: the volcanic eruption of response from *Mirror* readers to the column I had written about the need for injecting more brightness into people's lives had made him realize that I might be a useful ally in publicizing the government's forthcoming set-piece of national jollification.

Herbert Morrison, 'Our 'Erb', was a Lambeth-born cockney who had started life as an errand boy, but he was a clever man. He had helped to form the London Labour Party and had learned the art of government in Winston Churchill's wartime cabinet; as a former leader of the London County Council he longed to see the crestfallen capital rise out of its ashes and once more take its rightful place among the world's great centres of art, science and innovation. He did not know how to do it but he felt in his heart that it could be done, and furthermore that he was the man to do it.

The opening fanfare in the pageant of revitalization was to be sounded by the Festival South Bank Exhibition, due to open in London in the spring of 1951, and conceived by Morrison as a modern mixture of the old Cremorne, the Tivoli Gardens and Prince Albert's Great Exhibition of a century before. He talked of it proudly as 'my festival', and had a vision of going down in history as the creator of a London version of Kubla Khan's stately pleasure dome. But as plans proliferated in detail he became suspicious of what he called 'the fancy-pants brigade' of pseudo-artists who swarmed over the twenty-seven previously derelict acres on the south bank of the Thames that were to be transformed into the festival site; he needed advisers who could help him to relate artistic dreams to the demands of a rapidly-changing working class. That was where the practical experience of the *Daily Mirror* came in.

Morrison the politician longed to become Morrison the world-famous impresario – a whiff of show-business is a powerful hallucinogen; but a big production of that sort inevitably relies upon the work of many different experts, and to have a producer who tinkers with every specialized department is a recipe for disaster; so my only function was to persuade Morrison to be the ringmaster but not try to train the elephants as well, and when he saw the sense of this we came to like each other. The cabal in the Lambeth basement did little apart from dreaming the dreams of Goldwyn over bottles of light ale, and although the festival itself did not turn out to be a work of art, largely because it was a period of third-rate architectural design in Britain, it certainly was what *Variety* would have called SOCKO BOXOFFICE; and in that aspect the *Daily Mirror* helped, because that is what the *Mirror* was good at: if you could translate SOCKO BOXOFFICE into Latin it would have made the perfect motto to go in a scroll under the *Daily Mirror*'s coat of arms. Books have been written about the political influence of the *Daily Mirror* in its day and about its social significance, but although both themes contain a measure of truth, SOCKO BOXOFFICE was what it was really all about.

Inside Geraldine House a great *risorgimento* was in progress: Cecil King described his ousting of Guy Bartholmew from the chairmanship as 'a palace *coup*', a phrase that delighted him because he saw himself as Prince Machiavelli, but in truth it was more in the nature of what the Sunday papers call a Mercy Killing. Bart's unsteady hand on the tiller had guided the *Mirror's* business affairs into turbulent waters, and the old man knew it; on Bart's last Christmas card to me, only months before he was fired, was a scribbled message: 'It looks a mess – but for you (and me) it means a very happy New Year.' Alas for Bart, he was right about me but wrong about himself.

Cecil King was the ablest administrator of all the nine chairmen of the

Daily Mirror during my time, but he was also by far the most tortuously complex character among them all; even by the standards of Fleet Street, where psychosis was more prevalent than the common cold, Cecil was an exceptionally mixed-up man; if Sigmund Freud had met Cecil it would have been like a Klondike prospector striking a rich vein of gold; Cecil had more hang-ups than a clothes line.

Those whom the gods wish to destroy they first make mad, and the gods had marked down Cecil for a spectacular destruction which was to occur nearly twenty years later when Hugh Cudlipp, Cecil's *protégé*, turned on his protector as Bolam had turned on Bart. King's dismissal was a comic opera of punctured dignity that made the public chortle because the libretto was vintage Whitehall farce; but to those of us who were watching the rehearsals, the plot was closer in style to a melodrama of the *East Lynne* period, and in the Wagnerian crescendo of blaring brass and crashing cymbals that preceded the final curtain of that particular twilight of the gods, some of us heard also the death-knell of Fleet Street: but that first step on the road to Wapping was far in the distance.

Among the problems that Cecil King inherited when he became chairman of the *Mirror* was the company's commercial involvement in Australia. This had started during the early post-war years when the outlook for economic growth in Britain was at its bleakest; Britain was on the rocks and prudent investors were looking for safer havens for their money. The *Mirror*, as a Labour paper, paid lip-service to the restrictive measures on the movement of capital that had been introduced by the Attlee government, but at the same time it was clear to the directors that safety lay in deploying part of the shareholders' capital outside the European danger area. So when they heard that an Australian newspaper proprietor called Ezra Norton was thinking of selling out, Bart was despatched to make the the 13,000-mile journey and talk to Norton.

The two men did not get on. Both were bandits, and neither trusted the other. During a hilarious sequence of secret negotiations Norton changed his mind about selling, because, in the style of a P.G. Wodehouse plot, he had discovered a way of curing his indigestion, and this enabled him to continue grappling with the worries of a newspaper tycoon provided he avoided eating lobster and stuck to nut cutlets. So Bart was stymied. But not for long. He had the bit between his teeth and he bought an Australian newspaper called the Melbourne *Argus*, a daily publication that was, had Bart but realized it, so much less attractive as a commercial proposition than the Norton newspaper empire that old

Ezra Norton was heard to laugh out loud for the first time in years when he heard about Bart's big deal.

The *Argus* proved to be an albatross. As fast as the *Mirror* made profits in Britain, the *Argus* swallowed them up in Australia. So Cecil King, as the new chairman, was faced with alternatives, both fraught with danger: either he could close down the *Argus* and write off a serious capital loss which would have looked grim on the *Mirror* balance sheet during the earliest years of his stewardship; or, by injecting more capital, he could try to turn the *Argus* into a success. He chose the latter, not enthusiastically but *faute de mieux*.

One morning he walked into my office and slumped his enormous frame into the chair on the other side of my desk. I was surprised. Cecil was not the kind of boss who goes round the office calling in on members of the staff; his system was to summon people to his presence, like the man in the Bible who sayeth come and they cometh, and go and they goeth; not the sort of chairman who hobnobbed with the *canaille*. Off parade, outside the office, we called each other by Christian names, but on parade, inside the office, it was strictly mister on both sides, and that went for everyone including Cudlipp.

Cecil usually cultivated a lugubrious expression, but on this particular morning he looked downcast; sores had broken out on his forehead and on his scalp beneath his thinning hair, and he looked the picture of a man who should hastily consult a good neurologist. I offered him coffee, which I knew he would refuse because he despised the time-wasting habit of coffee-drinking among the staff. He sat there, silent, for a while, and then he said, 'Noel, I find it necessary to take a journey round the world and I wondered whether you would care to accompany me.'

'I cannot think of anything that would delight me more,' I replied, and meant it, with reservations: the idea of a jaunt round the world was attractive although the thought of having Cecil as a constant companion had a more limited appeal.

We drove to Heathrow airport in Cecil's new Rolls Royce, of which he was as proud as a schoolboy with a new bicycle; he had always owned an old car before, like me. In those early years of civil aviation at Heathrow, flying was a far more gentlemanly affair than it was soon to become; first-class passengers were met at the entrance by a butler who dealt with the chauffeur about the luggage while the passengers themselves were conducted by a secretary to a small drawing room where a senior airline official was waiting to greet them.

Since those days I have flown more than a million miles, and have always turned sharp left into the first-class cabin after boarding the aircraft, but although the arrangements today are reasonably luxurious they do not match the elegance of civil aviation's early years: on BOAC Constellations crossing the Atlantic one had a sleeper, similar to the arrangement on a train, and after a good dinner cooked in the galley by the chef one would climb a few steps to the sleeping compartment above, where one would put on one's pyjamas and sleep until the steward arrived next morning with the bacon and eggs and coffee. This was how Cecil and I travelled on the final homeward leg of our Odyssey, but outward from Heathrow we flew in one of BOAC's new and fast but ultimately ill-fated Comet IV jets.

In the VIP lounge we were offered glasses of champagne, and I took one. Cecil looked at me disapprovingly and said to the waiter, 'I shall have a glass of water.'

'Ice?' asked the waiter.

'What?' barked Cecil.

'Would you like ice with your water?'

'Good heavens, no,' said Cecil, sternly. As the waiter walked away Cecil muttered, 'Ice! What an extraordinary idea.'

On the aircraft we settled down, side by side in silence. I was reading a Raymond Chandler and sipping a gin and tonic; Cecil was sitting bolt upright and reading *Le Père Goriot* in the Tauchnitz edition. Cecil always gave the impression that he spoke French fluently, but I noticed that he was making heavy weather of the book because it took him about twenty minutes to read the first page. In case I had not noticed what he was reading, he eventually turned and showed me the cover of the book, asking, 'Have you read this?'

'Oh, yes,' I nodded.

He was not pleased. His system of one-upmanship, always carefully designed, was not firing on all cylinders. So he added, 'You read it in translation, of course?'

'No,' I said, shaking my head and adding – with a touch more top-spin than was strictly necessary for the shot – 'I have never thought that Balzac was well served by his translators into English.'

Cecil looked as though he had been stung by a wasp and he sulked for the next half hour.

During a refuelling stop at Rome we had lunch on the airport, and Cecil took an occasional sip from his glass of water while he watched me drink my glass of wine: there was something odd, something almost envious about the way in which he observed me going about my life in a normal way, as if he expected that I ought to be intimidated by his ostentatious abstinence.

It was not until we sat at table together for our first dinner in the South Australian Hotel in Sydney that I discovered the answer to this puzzle. We had ordered our food – Cecil, who ate sparingly at home, had ordered a particularly large quantity – and the waiter handed me the wine list. I picked a bottle of vintage claret and said to the waiter. 'One bottle of number 23.'

'*Four* bottles,' said Cecil.

He was a sailor on leave at last.

We were a day late arriving in Sydney, due to a delay that occurred after we left Bahrain. In the seat across the aisle from me was a tall man with a wing-tip moustache, obviously an ex-RAF man because he looked so like a popular cartoon character of the day called Flying Officer Kite; he was closely studying the big route-map that BOAC gave to passengers, when the captain of the aircraft came walking through, chatting to people here and there and explaining that there would be a delay.

'Hullo, Skip,' said my neigbour when the captain arrived beside him. 'Aren't we going in to Karachi, then?'

'No,' said the captain.

'Aha – I thought we were off-course for Karachi – the old eye hasn't lost all its cunning, eh? What's happened at Karachi – some crate pranged on the runway?'

'Yes,' said the captain.

'Oh, good lor', bad luck. Not one of these?'

'Yes,' said the captain.

'Crikey! Where are we going to land, then?'

'Mirpur,' said the captain.

'Mirpur! Good old Mirpur. I wish I had a quid for every game of cricket I've played at Mirpur. Of course, when I was there it didn't have a runway long enough for one of these to land on.'

'It still hasn't,' said the captain.

Cecil and I had both been listening to this conversation, and when the captain moved on Cecil said to me, 'What do you suppose that means?'

'My guess is that it means our next landfall will end in a crash landing,' I replied.

'Oh, I see,' he said, and went back to reading his book.

Both he and I pretended to go on reading as we were bucketed about in the bumpy crash-landing at Mirpur; when the aircraft finally came to a stop in the middle of a ploughed field, most of the passengers were white-faced and trembling. Cecil was still reading. Eventually we disembarked and were told that we would be continuing our journey on a different aircraft, but that there would be a further delay because we would be heading for Delhi instead of Calcutta, this deviation being due to bad weather. Cecil said to me, 'Do you suppose that means we shall have to crash-land at Delhi as well?'

'If it does,' I replied as I gulped down a brandy and soda, 'I am going to walk the rest of the way.'

Our peregrinations in Australia occasionally took on undertones of the Pickwick Club, with Cecil in the unlikely rôle of Mr Pickwick; sometimes he cast me in the part of Mr Tracey Tupman, sometimes as Alfred Jingle, and once as Sam Weller; when we dined with prime minister Robert Menzies in Canberra Cecil introduced me as 'my friend and colleague'; but when we dined in Sydney with Frank Packer – Kerry Packer's father – Cecil waved a lordly hand towards me and said, 'This is Noel Whitcomb, one of my columnists.'

He said these words with such a swagger that it was almost possible to see him changing visibly into Ernest Shepard's illustration of Mr Toad, with goggles, cap, gaiters and voluminous overcoat. Frank Packer, a former amateur heavyweight boxing champion of Australia and a swashbuckling buccaneer who had fought his way to the top as one of Australia's great newspaper tycoons, had a keen sense of humour and he could see that Cecil was trying to impress him: so, with a sideways wink at me, he mischievously lured Cecil on by asking, 'Do you have a helluva lot of columnists, Cecil?'

'Oh, yes, a lot,' nodded Cecil, loftily. 'But only two that matter. Noel is unquestionably one of my best two.'

Frank was trying not to laugh, and I kept a straight face, merely remarking, 'Cecil will probably leave me to somebody in his will, like Mr Shakespeare's second best bed.'

'Ah, Shakespeare,' said Frank. 'Now there's a writer who would have suited you, Cecil,'

Cecil took the wisecrack in his stride, nodding as if he thought that there was something in what Frank Packer had suggested. He frequently told people that he did not actually read the *Daily Mirror* himself, and once I heard him remark, 'If my editor of the *Daily Mirror* were to produce a paper that would interest his chairman, he would immediately reduce our circulation to one copy per day.'

Although Cecil assumed the air of an ivory-tower intellectual, the truth was that he was not a naturally gifted man; at school and at Oxford he had not been one of the high flyers, and all his later scholarly prowess was garnered the hard way, by unremitting application: his whole life was dedicated to self-improvement and to conquering the shallowness of thought that ultimately became so apparent in his published diaries.

One thing that gave him great delight was to shock people who bored him. In Adelaide we were dining with Sir Lloyd 'Roly Poly' Dumas, boss of the Adelaide *Advertiser* and a pillar of local society. Lady Dumas, a nice little body, was a terrible snob, and was getting a vicarious kick out of asking Cecil about important people that she supposed he knew in England. Cecil became more and more irritated as he parried her questions about the royal family and a number of aristocrats whose names appeared frequently in the gossip columns, and he could stand it no more when she began to quiz him about a well-known lady of title whose family were associated with newspapers.

'What happened to that nice second son of hers?' she asked.

'He was cashiered from the cavalry,' replied Cecil, tartly, 'after a particularly ugly incident involving a love affair with his horse.'

That settled the hash of Lady Dumas. She spilt her coffee.

On our way back to the hotel I said to Cecil, 'You were a bit hard on the old girl.'

'The only indoor sport available in a cultural hell-hole like this,' he said, 'is *épater les bourgeois.*'

It was on the tip of my tongue to remind him that it would have been difficult to find a family more bourgeois than his, or mine either, for that matter, but I restrained myself in the interests of peace. However, he sensed the implication of my silence, and returned to the subject over a number of large brandies back at the hotel.

'We will teach all those idle and stupid people a lesson in the *Daily Mirror*, won't we, Noel?' he said, with sudden bitterness.

'Which idle and stupid people?' I asked, although I knew he was referring to all the high-born people in England whose rejection of him as an equal rankled.

'You know who I mean,' he muttered, angrily. He was touchily conscious of the streak of coarseness that ran through the Harmsworth family, and made so many of its members unacceptable in rarified social circles despite their wealth and influence.

'Do you know my cousin Rothermere?' he asked.

I shook my head, not wishing to tell him that the only contact I had had with that branch of the family had occurred when I had been provoked into punching young Vere Harmsworth, Esmond Rothermere's son, on the jaw and stretching him out on the floor in the Cock Tavern in Fleet Street; I was not a belligerent young man, and it was not a drunken brawl, but it had happened soon after I came to Fleet Street from Wardour Street, when I had a girlfriend called Rosemary. Rosemary was a well-brought-up girl, a descendant of the Dean Farrar who wrote *Eric, or Little by Little*, and she was much embarrassed by the fact that wherever we went she was followed by the vulgar Vere who kept trying to pinch her bottom. I warned him several times to clear off, but that particular night in the Cock Tavern his behaviour became so outrageous that I could no longer ignore it, so I laid him flat on his back.

Cecil was envious of the Rothermeres, who were immensely rich, and contemptuous of their commonness which generations of education had failed to breed out. He began to talk about his mother's family, but we had both had a fair amount of drink, and I knew that he would subsequently suffer agonies of remorse at the memory of having been so personally frank, so I switched the subject to a matter that I knew would grip his interest.

Among Cecil's reasons for our being in Australia was to prepare the ground for what he hoped would be a controlling interest that he would gain for the *Daily Mirror* in Australian commercial television, which was due to start in the following year; this was a secret, and very few people were supposed to know it; the *Mirror* already had a controlling interest in the most profitable radio station in Sydney, and the expansion into television was a natural move for the company. However, when we had been chatting in different groups before dinner that evening, Roly-Poly Dumas had tried to sound me out on the subject, and although I pretended to know nothing about any such plans I had been very surprised that Dumas seemed to know about them. So I told Cecil, and he switched in a split second from the maudlin to the razor-sharp.

'How does Dumas know?' he asked. 'Did you find out?'

'I doubt if he does know,' I said. 'I think he's guessing. There was apparently a function recently that was attended by most of the big publishers – the Fairfaxes, Norton, Packer and others – and there was some speculation about whether you were fattening up the *Argus* before taking it to market or whether you were empire-building here. The subject of who will get television franchises obviously cropped up. It seems that young Rupert Murdoch suggested that lobbying should be done in Canberra to abort the chances of any non-Australian getting such potentially valuable rights.'

Cecil mulled this over in silence. He was a man with exceptional commercial foresight, and even in those early days he had clearly laid plans for making the *Daily Mirror* the cornerstone of a vast edifice of world-wide publishing; capturing the Australian commercial television rights was the ace up his sleeve that would take the first trick.

'Are you sure it was young Rupert Murdoch who put this idea up to them?' he asked.

'No. It was just an impression that I got from something that Dumas said.'

Sir Keith Murdoch had been a journalist of world quality, and when his reporting days were over he had returned to his native Australia and taken control of a group of newspapers that included the Melbourne *Herald* and the Adelaide *News*. He had died only recently, and his son Rupert, having been educated at Oxford and trained on the *Daily Express* in Fleet Street, had returned to Adelaide to run the family publishing business at a time when it was vulnerable to take-over.

'Of course,' mused Cecil, 'Dumas tried unsuccessfully to buy young Murdoch out, so there is no love lost there. All the same, it is my information from a number of sources that this young Rupert Murdoch will come to no good.'

That remark must still rank as one of the twentieth century's most inaccurate forecasts.

We travelled for over a thousand miles through the Australian outback, being driven in an enormous custom-built Ford Lincoln. Sometimes we passed the time by trying to identify the beautiful birds and unfamiliar creatures and plants we saw. Neither of us was a naturalist or a botanist but Cecil, with his usual thoroughness, had brought with him a couple of books about Australian wildlife. Once we were walking past the sweet scent of frangipani blossom and Cecil stopped, his nose high in the air, sniffing like a foxhound.

'What tree is that – do you know?' he asked.

'I think it's frangipani,' I said, pronouncing the word in church-Latin as 'franjipahni', to rhyme with Frankie-Marnie and with a soft *g* (which, incidentally, is the pronunciation given in the OED).

'FranGIPPanny!' he yelled. 'The word has a hard *g* and should be pronounced franGIPPanny. Obviously, dear boy, you learnt your Latin from an Italian waiter.'

He would have made an excellent schoolmaster and when he made his donnish little jokes to score a point it put him in high good humour.

One constant uncertainty was whether Cecil was in one of his gormandizing moods, when he would eat with the voracious appetite of Henry VIII and drink in Rabelaisian abundance, or whether he had reverted to his home image when he assumed the monkish asceticism of St Francis of Assisi. In the wild outback we stopped at a sort of pull-up for swagmen where such delicacies as eggs and beans or spaghetti on toast were scrawled on a blackboard outside the shanty. I ordered eggs on toast and Cecil went for eggs and beans and sausages.

'Anything to drink?' asked the serving girl.

'Yes,' I said. 'I will have a can of Foster's and my friend here will have four bottles of Château Mouton-Rothschild.'

'Water,' said Cecil, icily, to the puzzled girl. Then he turned to me and growled, 'One of these days you will go too far.'

The central purpose of our visit to Australia was for Cecil to make one final attempt to salvage the sinking *Argus* in Melbourne. The customary panacea for all ailing newspapers – colour printing to attract more advertising – had been decided, and offset colour presses had been installed at heavy cost to print colour on the run. But there was one more secret weapon in Cecil's armoury – cheap newsprint. Newsprint, the paper on which newspapers are printed, is always one of the most expensive production items, and in Australia at that time it was exceptionally costly. So we flew to Tasmania to see the secret weapon that was designed to win the battle against rising costs and mounting losses.

This weapon was an extraordinary mechanical process, most modern of its kind, that had been bought for a quarter of a million pounds. Without becoming technical, the essence of the machine was that you fed in eucalyptus trees at one end and reels of newsprint came rolling out at the other end. Eucalyptus trees had not been, up to that time, considered particularly good for making paper, but this new process solved that problem.

In Tasmania we drove to the Florentine Forest to see the 350,000 acres of trees that were being felled to feed our hungry presses. For Cecil it was an exhilarating sight but for me it was a sad occasion. As we walked in the ageless, cathedral-like quiet of the undergrowth beneath the towering eucalyptus trees, 300 feet high, we saw gaudy parrots in the tree-ferns, cockatoos in the sassafras, wombats and possums and rat-kangaroos, all of which were to be dispossessed of their homes in the interests of printing profitable rubbish.

'Do you know that every one of these great trees turns into fifty tons of newsprint?' asked Cecil, with a smile. A laughing kookaburra sitting on a nearby bush guffawed. That bird knew something that Cecil did not know.

Back in Melbourne, preparations for the relaunch of the *Argus* were busily in progress. What surprised me most was the quality of the staff; many of the senior men appeared to be better at their jobs than their counterparts on our staff in Fetter Lane. Men such as Jack Patience, who was chairman of the *Argus*, and Alex McKay, the advertising director, were executives of obvious quality; their columnists, including Clive Turnbull, a sociologist, and Peter Russo, an orientologist who spoke both Mandarin Chinese and Japanese, were streets ahead of our people in talent: in fact, several of them later became top executives in Fleet Street. I had simply been suffering from the delusion that affects most pommies on their first visit down under, which is to expect that nothing there except the weather will be better than it is in England.

I took Cecil to the races at Flemington, home of the Melbourne Cup, and the *Argus* tipster gave us five winners out of six.

'He was wrong about that last race,' commented Cecil, censoriously. Cecil had never been to the races before, and was wondering whether the *Argus* tipster was really good enough.

While we were in Melbourne I went to visit my aunt Mildred, one of the seven daughters of my grandfather Horace Whitcomb. Back home in England Mildred had married a well-to-do widower, Jack Vickers-Willis, who already had two sons and for whom she bore three more children. She had a difficult time with Jack in the early days of their marriage, because Jack had an eye for the girls. He was a fine-art expert and antique dealer who had spent some of his early life living in India and later in France, and he was a sophisticated type of man with intellectual tastes and also a fancy for high living.

After Jack's first wife died he returned to London where he married my aunt Mildred, but his business was becoming shaky because he was spending so much money having a good time, and this good time did not always include my aunt Mildred. She put up with it for a while but when he started flashing around Mayfair in an open touring car with an enormous Great Dane sitting in the front with him and an attractive young actress called Gertrude Lawrence sitting on the other side of the dog, Mildred put her foot down. She told Jack that he had to make his mind up, either Gertrude Lawrence or her, and when she won that battle she decided to take Jack as far away as possible from Gertie Lawrence: so they emigrated to Australia.

Jack took a load of antique furniture with him from the house in England, intending to set up in Melbourne as an expert in fine art matters, but he soon found that there was not a lot of call for fine art in the land of Oz. Sheep was the name of the game at that time in Australia, and poor old Jack did not know one end of a sheep from the other unless it was made of porcelain. They lived in an attractive house in the Melbourne suburb of Brighton, but as time went by, with five children to feed and educate, money became an increasing problem.

Saddened by the lack of interest among Australians in art, and beset by a mounting pile of bills, Jack turned to spending his time upon a hobby that had once been his passion in India, the study of the stars and of astrology. When he came to the conclusion that he could even fortell weather by studying the stars, some of his friends thought unhappily that the old boy was going off his rocker with worry. However, Jack pressed on with his esoteric studies, and one year in June he forecast from his study of the stars that the whole of South Australia would be hit by a violent and serious thunderstorm at five o'clock on the following Christmas Day. Jack felt that a warning about this should be issued to the people of South Australia, so he issued a detailed forecast of the coming disaster to the local papers.

This seemed such a jolly joke to the local journalists that the newspapers published it, in tongue-in-cheek fashion, as an example of how cranky some apparently intellectual people can become. But when the mighty storm broke loose in South Australia dead on the dot of five o'clock on the following Christmas Day, they remembered Jack's forecast and went back to him in a more serious fashion to ask him to prepare a forecast of weather for the forthcoming series of test matches against the English cricket team. Jack brought off a spectacular double by getting this right in day-to-day detail, all from studying the stars.

It was no longer a joke. If you are a farmer or a racehorse trainer in Australia, to be able to pinpoint what the weather is going to be like on a particular day in the future can be worth a lot of money, so big farmers and wealthy racehorse owners and trainers began beating a path to Jack's door to commission weather forecasts for particular occasions. He soon became famous and reasonably rich again, and when I went to call on him he was working out horoscopes for 109 racehorses.

This was an especial pleasure for him because he was a keen racing man and mad about horses, as most of the men in our family have been for many generations, and it brought him into contact with some very useful information about the chances of individual horses, from which he profited even further by shrewd investment with the bookies. It struck me forcibly once again that our family motto should have been *There's One Born Every Minute*.

Jack and Mildred's eldest son, my cousin Jim Vickers-Willis, having been brought up as I was on tales about our grandfather Horace, the brilliant but eccentric newspaperman, decided himself to become a journalist and went to work for Sir Keith Murdoch, Rupert Murdoch's father. Sir Keith was very kind to him and saw considerable prospects ahead for the lad, but in the days before 1939 when the menace of a forthcoming war in Europe became apparent throughout the world, Jim took ship for the first time to the land of his parents and joined the RAF in England. He learnt to fly fighter aircraft, became a Spitfire pilot, and ended the war as a survivor of that small band of skilful and brave young men of whom Churchill said that never in the history of human conflict had so many owed so much to so few.

It was Jim's intention then to return to Australia and resume his job as a newspaperman with Sir Keith Murdoch; but in the tradition of a family prone to sudden divergences that resulted in a change of plan, something happened to Jim that enabled him to hit the jackpot in a fashion as unconventional as his father's method of earning a good living. Just before he left England on his way home Jim saw a new-fangled craze called square-dancing, a form of country dancing in which a 'caller' acts as master of ceremonies and calls out the steps to the dancers. Jim took careful note of how this was done, and when he returned to Melbourne he set himself up as a square-dance caller. The new dancing craze took off in a big way in Australia, as it had done in England and America, and by the time I met Jim in Melbourne he was the square-dance king, earning £1,000 a week at it, which was a decent wage in 1953. Jim had 30,000 regular fans, he broadcast three nights a week, his records were selling by the ton and he was a celebrity throughout the Australian continent.

I did not envy Jim his good fortune, and in any case I was doing pretty well myself, but I noticed that he had a nostalgia for his original career as a writing journalist, and I could not help reflecting upon the strange quirk inside our family that guided so many of us to set off in pursuit of a career that lurched suddenly down an unexpected path, leaving us as popular people in the public eye and reasonably well off financially but still at times uneasily regretful about what might have been. A gene of dissatisfaction with the wrong sort of success.

Jim stayed in Australia and is living there still, as I write, with a fine and successful family, but my aunt Mildred, his mother, decided to return to England, and before she left she sold all the contents of the house. The family silver was bought by Rupert Murdoch's mother, so it is not improbable that when Rupert returns to his old home today his mother, Dame Elizabeth, pours his tea from a Georgian silver teapot with the Whitcomb coat of arms on it.

During this happy trip that was my introduction to Australia, while Cecil King was waiting in Melbourne for the relaunch of the *Argus* and I was waiting with him in the wings, I persuaded Cecil to come on a tour round some of the wine-growing areas, then in their early stages of production. With us came an expert, Sir Philip McBride, at that time Australian minister of defence.

With my tiny fragment of experience as a pullulating wine buff in the vineyards of Europe, I was expecting to taste some rough old plonk and to see some primitive viticulture methods; so I was – much to Cecil King's delight – taken by surprise to find that some of the wine was first class by any standards, and also that the ingenuity of the wine-growers was impressive.

Philip McBride, for example, owned 10,000 acres on a barren patch of offshore land called Kangaroo Island. Nothing would grow there. So he called in an agronomist who discovered that the land was lacking in molybdenum. It needed only a minuscule addition, just a few ounces to the acre, but when that tiny additive was applied the desert bloomed and crops grew luxuriantly.

On the night of the *Argus* relaunch we had a big celebration party. The giant reels of newsprint from the tall eucalypts in the Florentine Forest were in place, the colour presses were ready to roll, the journalists on the back bench were working on the late material to be sent down, the atmosphere was tense with the controlled excitement that every journalist will understand.

The colour picture that was to occupy the top half of the front page was a photograph of the all-conquering Melbourne football team. By arrangement with the distributors and retailers, a special army of delivery boys had been assembled, and their job was to place a copy of the *Argus* outside every front door in the area, folded in half so that the colour picture would be the first thing to greet the eye of the householder when he opened his door.

The weather in Melbourne was hot and the sun was strong.

When Melbourne woke up that following morning, householders opened their doors to find what looked like a large brown paper bag outside. The paper made from eucalypt trees in the Florentine Forest had turned brown in hot sunlight.

There was, of course, a great deal of hilarity among rival newspaper owners; but above their chuckles I could hear the raucous laugh of the kookaburra bird in the forest.

Cecil was a resilient man. With little further ado he decided to pull out the plug on the *Mirror's* Australian interests and start again in Africa.

Cecil had some cousins in San Francisco whom he had arranged to visit, so we travelled back through the South Pacific, stopping a couple of nights in Fiji and then going on to Honolulu. It was in Honolulu that he sacked me – the first and only time I have ever been fired, apart from Sam Campbell's abortive attempt.

We had been booked into the Royal Hawaaian Hotel on Waikiki Beach, at that time the only big and swagger hotel on the island. It was full of rich and elderly Americans who wore mink bow-ties in the evening, and we must have looked like Basil Radford and Naunton Wayne when we walked into the dining room for dinner, talking seriously about cricket.

It had been a tiring journey, and Cecil was back on frugal meals; towards the end of dinner he said, 'Noel, I thought it might be fun if we were to take a look round the island tomorrow. Do you agree?'

'First-rate plan,' I nodded. 'I will tell the hall porter to arrange a car.'

'No,' said Cecil. 'What I had in mind was a boat trip. Would that suit you all right?'

'Perfectly,' I said. I knew he wanted to get to bed, so I added, 'Leave it all to me – I'll lay it on.'

'How kind of you, dear boy,' he said, gravely. 'And now I expect you will be wanting to go out and observe the Hawaaian nightlife, what?'

Cecil was under the permanent impression that after he retired to bed at 9.30, I went out whooping it up round the nightspots; I think he had a vision of me in the wee small hours with a bottle of bubbly in one hand and a can-can girl in the other; it was probably my fault, because I did not bother to disillusion him, although I sometimes wondered when he supposed I wrote the column and telephoned it to London if I did not do it after he had gone to bed.

At any rate, on this particular night, after Cecil had departed, I wandered back towards my own suite, telling the bell captain on the way that we wanted to do a boat trip round the island on the following day.

'Yes, sir,' he said, efficiently. 'If you are returning to your suite I will ring you there with the details as soon as it is arranged.'

In fact, somewhat to my surprise, it was the general manager of the hotel who rang me about half an hour later. 'Everything is arranged, Mr Whitcomb,' he said. 'Please be good enough to report to Pier 5 at nine o'clock in the morning.'

Cecil arrived down for breakfast in his holiday attire. In urban surroundings, when we were working, he always wore his blue suit. But now he was arrayed in the off-white lightweight cotton suit that had obviously been packed in his suitcase throughout the trip; it was all crumpled like a pair of pyjamas, but Cecil was sublimely unaware that he looked rather like Sidney Greenstreet in a Humphrey Bogart movie set in Havana; it would never have crossed his mind to call the valet and have his suit pressed; Cecil was forever the honourable schoolboy. His panama hat had also been packed in his case, and when he put it on it had none of the air of Glorious Goodwood about it – it made him look more like Robert Morley in a sinister rôle. People in the hotel, mostly wearing Bermuda shorts with flowery Hawaiian shirts, watched us with puzzled suspicion as we walked through the foyer and out to the taxi that was taking us to Pier 5. Walking along beside this six-foot-four giant who was dressed as a tatterdemalion remittance man, I must have looked like Peter Lorre; no wonder they stared.

It was precisely nine o'clock when we arrived at Pier 5, but there were no small boats to be seen. We walked slowly along the pier, looking down over the side in case our little craft was bobbing up and down out of sight from the pier, but we saw nothing.

'I hope you made it clear about the time,' said Cecil, edgily, because he hated to be kept waiting.

At that moment I saw a crew of sailors approaching us from the far end of the pier, all dressed resplendently in white and led by an officer who looked like an admiral because he had gold rings on his sleeves almost up to the elbows. He was making straight towards us, and my blood froze.

The sailors had trooped down the gangplank from an enormous yacht that was moored at the end of the pier. It was like Aristotle Onassis's yacht, *Christina*, all gleaming and beautiful, ostentatiously luxurious. As the procession reached us, the admiral stopped, saluted, and said, 'Mr Whitcomb?'

'Yes,' I said. 'That's me.'

'Sir,' said the admiral, 'your ship.'

Cecil turned and looked at me and his face was a picture. 'Is this what you ordered?' he asked.

'It appears so,' I replied, swallowing hard.

'Kindly follow me, gentlemen,' said the admiral.

Cecil strode after him first, his face set in a cold fury. We were piped aboard and conducted to the stern, where two large chairs like thrones were placed side by side, with ice-buckets beside them containing bottles of vintage champagne. In front of each of the chairs was a fine and sturdy fishing rod, suitable for big game fishing, attached firmly to the deck.

Cecil, whose expression was becoming more thunderous with every passing moment, did not say a word until the admiral and the stewards had departed. Then he said, 'You realize, I suppose, that when I suggested a boat trip I had in mind that we would hire something with oars.'

'Oh, that would have been unwise in these waters,' I said. 'In a little cockleshell like that we would both have been drowned, for sure.'

'Poppycock!' barked Cecil. 'I most assuredly did not request you to charter the *Queen Mary*, or whatever the name of this liner may be. This is . . . preposterous. This is a floating palace for a maharajah, not a boat for taking two people on a trip round the island.'

'Little boats like that are notoriously unsafe when we get out to sea,' I said. 'Would you care for a glass of champagne?'

That was the last straw.

'Look here, Whitcomb,' he said, with ten degrees of frost in his voice, 'I have been meaning for some time to point out to you the flagrantly extravagant abandon with which you spend my shareholders' money. I have observed you on this trip and previously spending the company's money with a profligacy that would have seemed grossly excessive in an eighteenth-century duke. I am not a hard man, as you know, but a time must come when it is my clear duty to stem such a torrential drain on the company's resources. That time has now arrived. Enough is enough. The company will not pay for chartering this luxury yacht. You ordered it and you shall pay for it. And furthermore you are dismissed.'

At that moment there was a whirring noise from the fishing rod on my side. The reel was running. I leapt towards it. The line was running out fast. I have never been interested in fishing and know nothing about the sport except that the object is to catch a fish. This object seemed to have been achieved in a pretty big way, because as I tried to reel in the line I could see, threshing about at the other end, a fish that looked to me to be about the size of Captain Ahab's great white whale. I was struggling to hold this monster at bay when I realized that Cecil was jumping up and down beside me and trying to grab the rod.

'No, no, no,' he was shouting, 'not like that, you silly ass, you'll lose it. Here – give it to me. Let me do it.'

Still struggling with the line I turned and gave Cecil a cold look. 'I am not a hard man, as you know,' I said, 'but if I am paying for this bloody boat I am going to do the bloody fishing. Apart from which, it's on my side.'

'Oh, please,' said Cecil, urgently. 'You are doing it all wrong. I know how to do it. Look here – I say – the company will pay for the boat.'

'That's different,' I said, stepping aside and leaving him to take over.

Cecil was a passionately keen fisherman. For what must have been nearly an hour he battled with the fish, which was enormous. The

154

captain of the yacht – the officer who looked like an admiral – came running, and offered to help Cecil, explaining that he was a big game fishing expert.

Cecil, red as a ripe tomato in the face and sweating profusely, waved him aside. 'This one is mine,' he cried as he fought the fish. It was like a scene out of a Hemingway novel. Cecil had torn off his coat, tossed his hat aside, and was waging war on the big fish as though it were a personal grudge: his eyes were shining with the light of battle, and his tight-lipped excitement reminded me very strongly of Melville's Cap'n Ahab. It was a fight to the death.

I left him to it, and wandered below, seeking the radio officer.

When I returned, Cecil, who must have sweated off half a stone in weight, was on the point of victory. The big fish was being hauled aboard by four members of the crew, still lashing madly with its tail until a seaman gaffed it. It lay on the deck, blue and green and gold, iridescent and gleaming in the bright sunshine, a beautiful creature. It was some sort of dolphin. I wished it had got away.

Cecil was deliriously happy, mopping his brow, his shirt soaking wet, striding round in triumph. 'That was magnificent,' he beamed. 'Absolutely superb. D'you know, dear boy, this is the best day I've had for years.'

He called the steward to open the champagne, and we sat back in our throne-like chairs, Cecil gulping down his first glass and refilling it, still radiantly happy. 'By the way, Noel,' he said, sipping his second glass, 'will you be writing about this in your column tomorrow?'

'Of course,' I said. 'There is not much else for me to write about today.'

'I only wanted to mention,' he went on, 'that I would prefer not to be named as the person who caught the fish. Perhaps you could say that a friend of yours caught it. Put it your own way, of course.'

'But Cecil,' I said, 'you appear to have forgotten that I have been fired. I shall go on sending columns until we get back, of course, but you no longer have any right to tell me what the hell I am going to do.'

'My dear chap,' said Cecil, refilling my glass with champagne, 'you surely did not take me seriously. That was a remark made in the heat of the moment. You are our most valued columnist.'

'However that may be,' I said, 'I have already applied for another job. Lord Beaverbrook told me at his birthday party recently that if ever I decided to change from the *Mirror*, I should let him know. So I have left a cable in the wire-room telling him that I am free to take up his offer if he is still interested.'

'Headstrong lad,' said Cecil, shocked. 'Tell the steward to go down right away and cancel the message, or, if it has already gone, send another wire saying it was all a mistake.'

'That's all very well,' I said, 'but the fact is that the *Express* would undoubtedly pay me more than I am getting from the *Mirror*.'

'All right,' said Cecil, 'we will pay you another ten pounds a week.'

'Twenty,' I said.

'Very well,' nodded Cecil with a sigh. 'Twenty.'

That was in the spring of 1953, when a copy of the *Daily Mirror* cost 1½d – a half of 1p – so a pay-rise of £1,000 a year was a sum of money. As a matter of fact, although I had not expected the day to end on such a happy note, I had already told the radio officer not to send my message until he received further instructions from me; I knew how bitterly Cecil disliked Lord Beaverbrook.

9

It's no go the merrygoround, it's no go the rickshaw,
All we want is a limousine and a ticket for the peepshow.
Their knickers are made of crêpe-de-chine, their shoes are made of python,
Their halls are lined with tiger rugs and their walls with heads of bison.

Louis MacNeice, *Bagpipe Music*

By the time I arrived back home in the spring of 1953 the whole of
Britain was in the throes of preparation for the coronation of Her
Majesty Queen Elizabeth II. For the first time since the end of the war
there was an air of optimism in the land, and people were talking about
the New Elizabethan Age. Winston Churchill was back at No. 10
Downing Street having won the 1951 election with a little bit of help –
quite accidental – from the *Daily Mirror*; at that election the populace had
already tired of the Labour government that had been dismantling its
empire abroad and creating a state-controlled bureaucracy at home, but
the election was still a close-run thing, and it was the *Mirror* that
involuntarily tipped the balance in favour of the Tories.

The paper ran a 'Whose Finger on the Trigger?' campaign, aimed to
smear Winston Churchill as a warmonger, but the campaign misfired
because the public recognized the accusation as a monstrous calumny; so
Churchill, by that time seventy-six years old, was returned to office, the
Tories won the day, the *Mirror* had to pay damages to Churchill and the
Labour party was pushed into opposition from which it did not recover
for the next thirteen years; so as it had been the *Mirror* that had been
instrumental in putting Labour into power six years previously, poetic
justice was done all round.

But in spite of its unpopular election *gaffe* the newspaper itself went
on from strength to strength, its circulation soaring. By 1953 my own
column had been expanded to occupy the whole of a page, six days a
week, and as well as this I was also writing a London Nightlife column
every day because the nocturnal acitivities of the capital were receiving
the kiss of life from the coronation excitement. Hoardings all over the
country and big advertisements on the sides of buses exhorted the public

to BUY THE DAILY MIRROR AND GO GAY WITH NOEL – a slogan that carried none of the implications that it would have in later years because the word 'gay' had not been hi-jacked and its only meaning was 'bright and lively'.

For young people living now, in the final decade of the twentieth century, the London of that period would seem as unfamiliar as the London of Dickens's time; architecturally it looked different because everywhere it was still pockmarked with bombsites and most of the high-street shops and restaurants were dowdy. The poor were still observably poor and the rich conspicuously rich in a manner that is far less evident at first glance in modern times. Then people dressed so differently – most men wore hats, few men in the street were to be seen without a tie or jacket, the cult of leisure clothes had not arrived except on holiday and the idea of any office-worker going to work in jeans would have been unthinkable, even if jeans had been invented then.

The nightlife of London, centred in Mayfair and Soho – there was hardly any nightlife in outer districts or in the suburbs, people went 'up West' – was in a curious way more naïve than it is today, and it was enjoyed by far fewer people, mostly older people because they were the only ones who had the money; youngsters of the un-moneyed classes went to the cinema or the pub for a night out, because that was what they could afford, and the subsequent proliferation of discos and realtively small-cost entertainment for young people had not even started to happen; the only time you saw a large number of young people in the streets at night was when they came to watch the film stars arriving in limousines for big West End premières; some of these were deliberately turned into minor riots by the machinations of publicity men who knew that trouble meant bigger newspaper coverage surrounding the film with which it was associated. But on the whole London at night was a remarkably safe place; night after night I would walk round the town, through main streets and side streets, often in full evening dress, sometimes until dawn, and the thought of danger would never cross my mind – I doubt if there were many old ladies who would have thought it dangerous either.

The nightlife of any town at any time is usually run mostly by villains, but by any standard the men who ran the nightlife of Mayfair in those days, when Hutch was doing cabaret at Quag's and a nightingale was singing in Berkeley Square, were a club of queer trades, including as they did an ex-pawnbroker, an ex-bookmaker, an ex-barrow-boy, an ex-fishporter and a boxers' manager. Individually they all catered luxuriously for the mink-and-diamond trade; collectively they were as varied as the contents of a chorus girl's handbag; but they all had one characteristic in common – they were gamblers.

In the run-up to the coronation summer they were investing every penny they could lay their hands on in preparing premises of ostentatious luxury as traps for the rich spenders of dollar bills, pound notes, and all the other currencies that were beginning to swirl round London like leaves in an autumn wind. They leased some of the fine houses of Mayfair, richly carpeting their drawing rooms as bars and restaurants decked with Georgian mahogany and silver; tree trunks burned in their vast fireplaces, crystal chandeliers hung from their high ceilings, heavy silk curtains were drawn at dusk by liveried footmen; a butler received members in the soft-lit hall, supervising the signing in of guests; money in terms of cash was seldom seen until the end of the evening, when it changed hands by the barrow-load.

Once when I arrived at one of these places, I was handing my overcoat to a flunkey when I discovered that I did not have a match to light my cigar, so I said to him, 'Get me a box of matches, would you please?'

''Ere,' said the flunkey, offering me a box from his pocket, 'use one of these and save yourself seven-and-six.'

It was hardly an economy because the flunkey would expect a pound note for his courtesy, and would get it.

The Meadows brothers, Harry and Bertie, set up three of these clubs, two of which were to remain among London's best-known nightspots for many years. There were three Meadows brothers, in fact, but Eddie remained in the East End looking after the family confectionary business, while Harry and Bertie moved up West for bigger pickings. When Eddie's name cropped up, Bertie used to say, 'Eddie is the one our mother still talks to.' Apart from making a great deal of money, Harry and Bertie also made themselves an unenviable reputation among the CID officers at West End Central Police Station, largely because there were always so many unaccompanied girls on their premises. 'They help to furnish a room so nicely,' Bertie would say. 'I know that anatomy is something we all have, but you've got to admit that it looks better on girls.'

Both Harry and Bertie sported guardee-type moustaches. One evening a master of foxhounds called in at Bertie's place, the splenditerous 21 Room in Chesterfield Place, off Curzon Street, to arrange about holding a hunt ball there. 'By the way,' he said, looking at the two brothers, 'were you chaps by any chance officers in the Brigade of Guards?'

Bertie smiled sadly and nudged Harry. 'We wish we was,' he said.

Bertie was known to one and all as PPB – Permanently Pickled Bertie. Over the years I cannot recall seeing him without a glass in his hand, but on the other hand I never saw him the least bit the worse for liquor. His 21 Room was widely regarded as one of the three most luxurious and lavishly decorated clubs of its kind in London; even the doorman, an Irishman called Paddy, wore an elaborate livery that had been specially designed by Norman Hartnell, the Queen's dressmaker. Its clientele was in general very rich, but somewhat on the raffish side of society.

One of Bertie's most frequent conversational topics, especially when chatting with a columnist, concerned the spectacular lavishness with which he had converted the upper storeys of the house into luxury apartments for members who wished to stay overnight. 'I used the best architect in London,' he would say. 'Brilliant job he did of it. Cost a bloody fortune. No expense spared. A lot better than Buckingham Palace, I should think, though I hear on good authority that young Philip is waking their ideas up about the old-fashioned rooms they've got there.'

There was no reason for somebody like me to go upstairs in the ordinary way, but one evening a story cropped up that would entail my catching an early morning plane out of Heathrow, so I booked in at Bertie's 21 Room for the night, just to see what it was like.

When I arrived that evening, Paddy the doorman took charge of my bag and one of the footmen took the car away – there was never the bother of parking your own car in London in those days because every club and every big hotel had a man always ready to park it for you and bring it back when you needed it again. Inside the foyer of the club the walls were lined with crimson silk and the Georgian chandeliers shed an opulent light. While I was booking in at the desk, the Duke of Marlborough came in – the present duke's father – with an extremely beautiful girl, and they waited behind me to talk to the receptionist; the duke was an exceptionally tall man with the unmistakable Spencer-Churchill features, and he wore a long coat of sable fur and carried an ivory-topped cane.

'Room 136, Mr Whitcomb,' said the receptionist, handing me the key. 'Will you be dining first before you go up?'

'No,' I said. 'I'll go up first and come down to dinner later.'

I turned the key in the door of Room 136, went in and stood there in amazement. It was one of the dingiest rooms I had ever seen. The walls were distempered in two shades of workhouse green. There was a

Woolworth's shade on the single light-bulb that hung from the ceiling. The bed looked crumpled and uninviting. The tap in the stained green washbasin was leaking.

It was the other side of the coin, the dark side of the moon of London's clubland luxury; here was the normally hidden reason why so many expensively dressed but unaccompanied girls walked amid the finery downstairs.

While Bertie ran the 21, Harry Meadows presided over the La Rue Club in Queen Street, Mayfair, and Churchill's Club in Old Bond Street. The La Rue was particularly *chic* because it was at that time a favourite haunt of the Princess Margaret Set, who would often drink pink champagne there after the theatre. The barman was a short, tubby man called Joe Francis, who was, in normal circumstances, the most courteous, correct, quick and expert barman you could find in London. Joe had only one fault: occasionally, very occasionally, he would become tired of the life of an employee and would start mixing drinks for himself as well as for the customers. This would not become apparent until at some point in the evening the cork in his bottled-up emotions would pop, and he would throw a tankard at a customer. If the customer happened to be a duke or an earl, as was often the case, because Joe was selective in his targets on such occasions, a shocked altercation would arise. Joe would then leap up on to his bar and shout, 'Go on – fuck off – all of you, fuckin' aristocratic layabouts.' Joe would then be swiftly captured by the rest of the staff and led away.

This happened only two or three times to my knowledge; even the suave and fast-talking Harry Meadows had some difficulty in persuading the customers to take it as a joke and eventually Joe was fired. Whereupon he went and set himself up in his own club, the Arlington, just beside the Ritz, where all his old clientele from the La Rue used to visit him, wondering if he would put on his old show, but the tranquillizing effect of being the guv'nor instead of a mere servant prevented him from ever breaking out again. Joe was the perfect host forever after.

I was in the La Rue Club one night during Royal Ascot week when Prince Aly Khan came in with his wife, Rita Hayworth. They were, as I was, still in their Ascot clothes, and Aly came over to me at the bar. 'Do me a small favour, Noel,' he said. 'Look after Rita for me, just for an hour or so while I go and see a man about a horse.'

Aly had been hounded by the press during his affair with Rita, before they were married, but even though I was down in the South of France when the main *brouhaha* was going on, I had studiously avoided taking part in it, because that sort of story was not my cup of tea. So Aly knew he was safe in leaving Rita with me. Safe from publicity, anyway.

Rita was still at that time one of the most beautiful women in the world. But she was terribly unhappy, because Aly was always going off with other girls, and I noticed when we went in to dinner that she was already drinking quite heavily.

Aly had not returned by midnight, so I left messages for him and took Rita off to the Ritz, where I booked her into a suite and then went home. She rang me the following day to say that Aly had still not shown up. He often used to leave her stranded like that, which was a particularly hateful experience for a girl who was acclaimed everywhere as a great Hollywood star. It broke her in the end, because the last time I saw Rita, a number of years later, she was a sight to wring one's heart.

For all that his other clubs were making enormous profits, it was Churchill's in Bond Street that was Harry Meadows' biggest money-spinner. Harry had a gleaming new Bentley with a chauffeur to ferry clients from the La Rue or the 21 Room to Churchill's and this was where they finally got so drunk that they paid colossal bills without ever looking at them, or even being able to see them in focus if they did look. Yet hardly ever did anyone complain. When the customers woke up next day, usually about lunchtime and often in some unfamiliar room untidy with make-up and scent and silk stockings on the floor, they usually felt far too ill and far too guilty to make a fuss; all they wanted to do was to make a telephone call to tell their disbelieving wives that they had been in a nasty accident.

Harry was always in Churchill's from midnight until after 4 a.m., 364 days a year; on Christmas Day he gave a party for underprivileged children from his native East End. He greeted every rich or well-known customer individually as they arrived, welcoming them as his dearest friends whom he had not seen for many years.

'My dear Sir Noel,' he would call out, any time I went in. 'This is a great privilege. What a delightful surprise to see you. Come on in, my dear sir, come on in.'

If I had friends with me he would call to the headwaiter, 'Show Colonel Whitcomb and his guests to our best table.' He always promoted me, sometimes to Brigadier. It impressed other customers in earshot. If I went in alone he would ask me to sit with him at his own table, close to the stage; he would realize that I had come in to watch the cabaret and review it in my nightlife column. After the cabaret, which was always an expensive production, Harry would send for a couple of the girls out of the show to come and sit with us. That was how I first met Audrey Hepburn, who was working there as a dancer, and Eartha Kitt, an unknown to whom Harry had given a chance as a singer.

The most frequent guest at Harry's table was Arthur Helliwell, formerly a good reporter and war correspondent, who was well known throughout the land at that time for his Follow Me Around column in *The People*. On most Sundays his column contained 'startling revelations' about what went on in London's 'Naughty Square Mile' or sometimes 'Glittering Square Mile' or, when he turned his attention to Soho, 'London's Sleazy Square Mile'. *The People* built him up as a national figure who knew about everything that happened in London at night and, as hardly any of the readers ever attended these places, he wrote torrents of absolute rubbish about them, which were avidly read from Newcastle to Penzance; the appallingly lavish wickedness of the lives of celebrities in the big city was a topic of never-ending fascination for the working classes.

Arthur was seldom sober after lunchtime, although he went on drinking usually until 4 a.m., so he did not often remember what he had seen; this was not of great importance because he invariably made it all up; there would have been little of real interest to write about otherwise. This suited the club owners well, because although he was ostensibly attacking them in his column for their pandering to the disgracefully outrageous habits of the rich, what he was doing in fact was publicizing them in a fashion that was of great value to their trade, describing them as kings and princes of London after dark.

I got on very well with Arthur if we met by chance during the mornings or at lunchtime, but by late evenings he always hated the very sight of me, and he would invariably finish up by trying to pick a quarrel. For this reason, if I chanced to come in, Harry Meadows would tactfully shift Helliwell to the table presided over by Bruce Brace, the manager of Churchill's.

Bruce was a tall and burly cockney who had come out of the RAF flat broke and had taken a job as a hire-car driver in the West End. After making £35 in tips during his first week, working nights, he discovered that the trick was to quadruple his income by delivering his passengers to selected clubs and taking a pay-off from the club proprietors. By this means he made enough money to set up a club of his own, but in the meantime he learned the business by working for the Meadows brothers. One of his tasks, apart from intimidating any customer who became difficult after seeing the bill, was to distribute largesse clandestinely to any official who needed to be pacified or squared. Plain-clothes detectives frequently visited the clubs, officially to watch out for infringement of the licensing laws or use of the premises in connection with prostitution, and some of these policemen soon became so well off that a rule was introduced in the force limiting the tour of duty of any officer in the West End vice squad to one year, after which they were moved elsewhere.

Bruce had a ribald cockney wit, and made no bones about his bribery activities. When Bertie Meadows converted the garden of his 21 Room into an open-air restaurant for coronation summer, Bruce remarked, 'No kidding, if the clerk of the weather had a London office Bertie would have me round there in no time with a cheque book, secretly buying six weeks of fine weather – name your own price.'

Churchill's club consisted of an extremely long room on the ground floor of what had been a noble house in bygone days, and all along the walls were dim lights shaded by tall red witches' hats. Bruce made up all sorts of stories about the history of the house, mostly for the gratification of American tourists who would return home with tales of the aristocratic and ancient places they had visited in London.

One night an American came over to Bruce's table and asked, solemnly, 'Is that right that Queen Victoria had her coronation photograph taken in this very room?'

'Quite right,' nodded Bruce. 'She used to come here often. That was before Harry took the place over, of course. She wouldn't come here now if she was alive – she couldn't afford it.'

After one occasion when the club had been struck off the register and fined for misdemeanours, the name Churchill's could no longer be used, so it reopened on the following night under the name New Churchill's, a big red neon sign with the new name having been hastily erected outside. Unfortunately the new sign did not work properly, and the only letters of the name that actually lit up were CHURCH. When Bruce arrived at the club and saw this he rushed inside shouting, 'Get an electrician, quick! Doesn't matter what it costs – get that sign fixed immediately. Do you know what it says? It says CHURCH! Get the bloody place a bad name!'

When I visited the club I always paid the bill because the *Daily Mirror* had a strict rule about its staff not accepting hospitality in those days, but I was probably the only journalist with an expense account sufficiently large to accommodate such bills; most of the newspapermen who patronized the place took whatever they could get without money ever changing hands.

After I ceased to write my coronation Nightlife column, which was a merciful relief, I seldom went back to Churchill's, although I occasionally saw Harry at the 21 Room. The odd thing was, I think, that he genuinely liked me, which made him one of a very small and select coterie. Most people came in time to scorn him as a sort of amateur brothel-keeper, but it always struck me that the girls in his clubs had a great affection for him, and he often used to take them on outings to the seaside or the country for picnics, in a merry group; in any case, I have never found it possible to berate such people with loud and self-righteous disapproval; I do not much care for what they do, but I dislike hypocrisy even more, and there are not many men who would qualify to cast the first stone.

The last time I saw Harry Meadows was at Royal Ascot, thirty years after that coronation summer. He asked a mutual friend, George Mitchison, managing director of the House of Hartnell, to go and find me and bring me up to his box for a drink.

'Ah, good – Colonel Whitcomb himself,' beamed Harry as I walked into the box. 'Waiter – bring a glass of champagne for the Brigadier.'

'Twit,' I said, laughing. 'You know damn well I was never even a lance bombardier.'

Harry was as dapper as ever in his morning suit with the red carnation, but he looked terribly ill. He took me aside. 'Noel, boy,' he said, 'there is something I want to say to you. I've not been well, you know. Touch of the old cancer. Well – we've all got to go some way. But what I've been thinking is that someday you are going to write a book about your life. I'd like to think that somewhere in that book will be a mention of Harry Meadows as a man who was not so bad as some people used to say. I've had a great deal of publicity of one sort and another in my life, but I'd like to think that you might give me a proper place in London history.'

'Right, Harry,' I said, trying to keep on laughing. 'That's a deal. Star billing.'

A few days later I heard that Harry had died. I doubt whether I would have written this chapter but for the promise I made that day at Ascot.

One of our favourite places to dine in that long, cold summer of 1953 was Cunningham's seafood restaurant in Curzon Street, and of all the fish in that elegant room the oddest fish was Captain Owen Cunningham, the owner. There was a touch of Falstaff about the man, because he was always telling lurid stories about how he had fought off a band of rogues, but he dressed more like a Regency buck and he had a strong flavour of Alfred Jingle. He was always in trouble of some sort. Dukes punched him on the nose. Bandits, theatrically masked, invaded his rooms and he fought them off with a cutlass. Brigands robbed him on a quiet night in Wapping. His wife, in a fury, took a razor and slashed every one of his many suits and overcoats to threads. It all sounds highly unlikely, but in fact it was all true. Melodramatic trouble followed him around.

His restaurant was expensive and excellent. Americans in London for the coronation used to bid heavily for his reproduction Hepplewhite chairs and his nearly-Sheraton cabinets. 'The furniture is not really old and the Yanks know it, because I tell them,' Cunningham used to say, 'but they still insist on buying the things. They cart them home and put plaques on them – 'Antique, from Cunningham's.'

When the lease on his Curzon Street premises was running out, the restaurant was scheduled to be knocked down for a road-widening scheme. There was little reason why the building should not have been torn down because it was only late Victorian, even though Cunningham had tricked it out to look Georgian. But when the plan was published there was an outcry; American newspapers described the plan in shocked terms as an example of British vandalism – CRAZY PLAN TO KNOCK DOWN CUNNINGHAM'S said one headline, and another said ANCIENT LONDON LANDMARK TO GO. So the council, rather than risk a stand-up fight with Captain Owen Cunningham, scheduled the premises as an ancient monument.

The swashbuckling Cunningham, who had been a captain in the Catering Corps and had opened the restaurant on his gratuity from the army after the war, had started life scrubbing kitchen floors, and in spite of the vast sums of money spent in his place by his rich and coroneted clientele he was constantly faced with the spectre of having to return to his original job because of the personal calamities which befell him with such regularity.

One morning when he was, like Captain Grimes, in the soup again, he rang me and asked me to go with him to look at some premises in St James's. His Curzon Street lease was on its last legs, he was in deep financial difficulty, but the thought of closing Cunningham's altogether and abandoning his loyal customers never entered his mind; he was planning to move into a bigger and better dream.

The house he took me to see was certainly most elegantly situated, being a fragment of old St James's between Lock's, the venerable hatters, and Berry's, the aristocratic wine merchants; but what I saw when I looked at it was a motor showroom with flats above. However, Cunningham saw it with different eyes. The estate agent, who came with us, had told him that it had once been the site of a coffee inn, like

White's, and had later been run in the eighteenth century as a gambling house of great infamy by a full-blooded old swashbuckler called Captain Pickering, who fought the last duel in London in its courtyard.

The imagery was irresistible to Owen Cunningham. He did not see the dull showroom façade. He was back in old St James's, a buck. He saw the bow-fronted window of the coffee inn and heard the clatter of the carriage wheels on the cobbles.

'I'll take it,' he said to the agent, 'bow-fronted window and all.'

'But, sir,' said the agent, 'the bow-fronted window has not been there for over two hundred years.'

'Well put it back,' roared Cunningham.

And they did.

With a little help from his friends he scraped together £6,000 for a shortish lease and then he spent £40,000 on restoration. Cunningham supervised every moment of it. The painters working on the exterior had instructions from him to work only on hot sunny days. They were slapping on thick black paint, and as they put the paint on they had to spit on it. 'On a hot day that causes it to blister right away,' explained Cunningham. 'Makes it very old immediately,'

Every piece of china in the restaurant when he opened was gold-edged Minton, and the cutlery was silver. To serve a hundred and thirty customers he had seventy-five staff. Fortunes are seldom made out of dreams of such opulence, but Cunningham had his day before he finally went down, still fighting.

Not many of those dreamers of gilded dreams ended their careers with a penny to bless themselves, even though in their heyday they were taking in money nightly by the lorry-load. The most spectacular success and ultimately the saddest failure of them all was Rico Dajou, an extremely able and experienced restaurateur who set up a club called the Casanova in a fine large Georgian house just off Grosvenor Square. Rico was a perfectionist. Everything about him had to be of the best. Even his customers were not the normal café-society crowd, because unless people were what Rico regarded as a high enough social class he simply would not let them in unless they were his special friends, no matter how much money they had.

The walls of the Casanova dining room were hung with Italian Renaissance paintings, one of which was a genuine Tintoretto; few of the members believed this and used to pull Rico's leg about his Tintoretto fake, but some of the ultra-rich fine-art experts from Bond Street, such as the Wildensteins, occasionally dined there, and one or two of them bid him big money for it. Rico would wave aside their offers impatiently, 'What else I put on my wall if I sell my Tintoretto?' he would ask. 'Nossing but Tintoretto is good enough for the Casanova.'

He was a shortish, rather pop-eyed man who normally walked around with a worried expression on his face, which would change quickly to a radiant smile when he saw a friend. He used to say that his origin was 'Souse-American', and he spoke always with the rapidity of a machine gun with hiccups, using words from several different languages so that he was not always easy to understand. If even the slightest thing went wrong he would explode into a shrapnel-bomb of words. Then he would become sad. 'Tarrible,' he would say. 'I tell you, honest to God, boy, cross my heart like a Catlic, I wish I didn't ever coming into this business. It sends you med – stark, ravink med! Warry, warry, warry, all is warry – hey, excuse me a minute, the duke's coming in . . .'

Dukes, princes, maharajahs and nobles of all nations were the staple clientele of Rico's club, and it made him very proud. He loved a lord. When stately homes came under the hammer, Rico would be there bidding for the silver, especially the Georgian silver candelabra which graced all his tables; he bought all the Lonsdale candlesticks, including those given to the Lonsdale family by George III, because, he said, 'zey give ze perfect light to make a woman lovely'.

Outside at the back, in his large garden, he introduced star-like fairy lights to hang above the dining tables, and had a special table for two built into the branches of the big tree. The Casanova was essentially a luncheon and dining club, but for the coronation Rico splashed out by turning the floor above into a nightclub called the Don Juan. During the years when he had been working as a restaurateur in Paris he had visited Versailles, and had been so dazzled by the beauty of one of the rooms there that he made sketches of everything in it: these sketches he used in the pre-coronation weeks in London to recreate that room as the Don Juan. He proudly showed me round it when it was in the final stages of completion, before the opening in time for the Queen's big day.

'Lissen, boy,' he said excitedly, chewing like a hungry rabbit at the end of a fat cigar, 'did you ever see anything like this? Pah! Never! Nobody since Louis Sixteen ever see anything like this! Is beautiful. Tiens! Lookada chandaliers! Costed a thousand quid each. And I got Josephine Baker coming over for the cabaret. The best, I got, only the best.'

To decorate the ceiling alone took 15,000 packets of gold leaf. Though all the carpenters and electricians were still busily beavering away, spreading sawdust and bits of wire all round, the rich carpet was already being laid because Rico could not wait to see how splendid it looked. The foreman said to Rico. 'It's crazy to have that carpet down and unprotected before the carpenters have finished, sir.'

'*Hein*?' shouted Rico. 'Wass dis? Crazy? Hah! So I'm crazy, hey? With ten dukes and duchesses coming to my opening, two princes, three maharajahs, a whatsa-likely-to-be a king – I'm crazy. Pah! Lay the carpet, quick.' As the red carpet unrolled, Rico beamed like the rising sun. Then he turned to me, looking suddenly deflated. 'Lissen, boy, I'm dead like a mouse, see? No sleep. Only warry. Hey – did you see my golden goblets?' He darted to a box and brought out an armful of gilded goblets. 'These costed a fortune,' he said. 'Two fortunes! And the gold champagne buckets – hah! Best in the world, eh? Thissa one from the Duke of Hamilton's place – lookada crest, huh?'

Suddenly he leapt in the air and shouted in anguish as he saw a workman hanging a painting out of true. 'Not right!' he roared. 'Thissa frame costing me one hundred and forty-four quid alone and God knows what the painting cost me – you gonna hang it wrong? Rather I don't open. Pictures sideways – pah!'

His opening night at the Don Juan was a triumph, one of the most spectacular London occasions in the immediate prelude to the coronation. At 2 a.m. he came over to my table, stuck a big cigar in my mouth, called a waiter to bring Napoleon brandy, and slumped into a chair. 'Horses,' he said, gloomily. 'That bloody maharajah wanted to bring his horses in here. I stopped him. I won't have no horses in here – no horses!'

'Horses?' I echoed. 'How could he bring horses in?'

'He takes 'em everywhere,' growled Rico. 'But I told him not in my place. No horses!'

Suddenly I realized what he was talking about. He meant whores. Alone among the nightlife nabobs, Rico had a strict code of propriety. He was a family man. He had a pretty English wife called Rosalie and a baby son on whom he doted, and they all lived very simply in the apartments – formerly the servants' quarters – at the top of the house. Nobody was ever allowed in there, not even maharajahs, because it was a million miles from Renaissance paintings and Georgian silver candelabra – it was home.

Rico was ruined some seven years later when Rab Butler's Betting and Gaming Act became law, enabling gambling casinos to be operated legally. He introduced gaming tables into the Don Juan, because so many of the other nightclubs were doing it, but it was not his scene; the crooked gamblers moved in, as they were doing all over the country at the time, and took him for a ride. He had to close down and sell up. The last time I saw him he was working as an employee at Crockford's in Carlton House Terrace, all passion spent, a broken man.

The Albany Club, run by Bill Little, in Savile Row, was the place where the big gamblers gathered in coronation year. This was the haunt of the boxing crowd, the big bookmakers and the show-business impresarios, and it was taking £22,000 a year in membership fees alone, because membership was carefully screened to prevent non-members getting in and seeing how the other half lived.

Typically of the times, Bill Little more or less won the club in a snooker game. During the war, when he was running a car-hire firm, he walked into the Empire Snooker Hall in Soho one night and gave a trouncing to the resident snooker expert, who normally beat everyone. A little man who was sitting in the corner took a liking to Bill; his name was Sam Henry, a man who ran a lot of clubs at the time and was always on the lookout for suitable managers, so he bought the Albany Club for £20,000 and put Bill in to manage it.

When Sam Henry died, very soon afterwards, he left the whole place to Bill, lock, stock and fortune. Bill later sold it to Jack Hylton, the impresario and former bandleader, who ran it mostly as a private haven for his friends, and after Jack died the house was sold to the Beatles who used it as the headquarters of their Apple Company, filling it with unshaven youngsters who wore jeans and smoked reefers: that was when I stopped going there.

Coronations and royal weddings bring out the best and the worst in the gentlemen of the British popular press; technically, from a production and display point of view, they sometimes reach peaks of journalistic excellence, but from a story-selection and writing viewpoint they invariably plumb the very depths of banality. The coronation of Her Majesty Queen Elizabeth II in Westminister Abbey on Tuesday, 2 June 1953, was the first such occasion in history on which newspapers had been in competition with television, and the fact that the *Daily Mirror* sold seven million copies of its Coronation Issue on the day after the ceremony in the Abbey is a clear indication that the news battle between the two media had not at that time been won; such a vast production of copies of a single issue of a British daily newspaper would be both unthinkable and technically impossible today.

The *Daily Mirror*, which had already hit a daily circulation peak of five million under the editorship of Silvester Bolam, was intrinsically under a completely changed management. After Hugh Cudlipp had been fired from his job as editor of the *Sunday Pictorial* in 1949 by Bartholomew, he had been taken on by Lord Beaverbrook as managing editor of the *Sunday Express*, but this had been an uncomfortable time for him because, as the wily Beaverbrook anticipated, it had merely resulted in the sudden rejuvenation of the ageing John Gordon, long-time editor of the *Sunday Express*. Gordon, vividly aware of the threat to his job posed by the introduction of a young wolf into his pack, took good care to make sure that Cudlipp had a miserable time, and gave him little chance to show his skill.

Although Hugh Cudlipp had been Cecil King's ally and protégé, King typically never even telephoned him during Cudlipp's two-year exile at the *Sunday Express*. But after Bart had been cleared out of the way, King immediately brought Cudlipp back to his old job as editor of the *Sunday Pictorial* and soon afterwards promoted him to editorial director of both the *Pictorial* and the *Daily Mirror*. This move heralded nearly two decades during which, for the first and only phase during its whole existence from Northcliffe to Maxwell, the *Daily Mirror* was a real newspaper.

It was Cudlipp who decided that my full-page column during the coronation period should be titled CORONATION SCOOP, and as the word scoop indicates an exclusive story I viewed this title with some misgiving; but in fact it turned out to be a requirement not too difficult to achieve because there was so much going on all over Britain in preparation for the great occasion. People of interest were arriving in swarms from abroad, there was a mass of constitutional matters and protocol arrangements to be decided, and the whole country was obsessed with reading about every detail of the plans.

Walter Bagehot gave it as his opinion that the English are a deferential people, and although this had become gradually less true during the intervening years there can be little doubt that the high point of English deference during the second half of the twentieth century was reached during that coronation summer: it was the year during which Stalin died, Everest was conquered, the Korean War ended, and Crick and Watson discovered DNA, but although such stories were given reasonable prominence it was the royal family who dominated the pages of the popular press; every little item concerning the Queen and her courtiers, every rehearsal for the big day, every single thing that was going on at Westminister, at Buckingham Palace and at Windsor was given the sort of space that pushed all other topics to the back of the paper.

Not surprisingly, much of what was written was the familiar royal slush, gushing rubbish of stomach-turning effusiveness and idiotic triviality in the style that later became known as 'entries for the Godfrey

Winn Memorial Prize'. Luckily for me, my sense of the ridiculous enabled me to steer reasonably clear of this emetic approach, but it was a case of swimming against the tide. To fill a page every day was hard work, especially as I was working at nights as well, so it was decided that I should be given an assistant.

The features editor of the *Daily Mirror* was a man called James Eilbeck, one of the new, younger executives then being groomed for stardom by Hugh Cudlipp. He was a tall man with flaming red hair who hailed originally from the Isle of Man and he quickly became the bane of my life. The main problem was that he had never been anywhere, and his essentially provincial background left him vulnerable to a naïve sense of excitement about being part of great events in the big city; this was unusual enough among the average seen-it-all-before denizens of Fleet Street, but additionally he had a longing to become part of what he saw as the glittering high-life of London, an ambition which was in tune with the way the readers felt but lacking in a sense of proportion for a man whose job required a more critical eye. It is not uncommon for journalists to start with such disabilities and overcome them through experience, but Jimmy had two other problems that he did not recognize in time: he was psychologically unstable to a point that ended distressingly near madness, and he was an incipient alcoholic, an occupational hazard in newspapers.

His almost prurient fascination with what he honestly believed to be the alluring delights of London's nightlife caused him to come out with me regularly at the end of the day, when his work was done and I was starting my rounds for the Nightlife with Noel column. He wanted to see it all going on with his own hungry eyes and to drink champagne among famous people, living the luxurious life of a lord and seeing himself as one of the celebrated hell-raisers – the euphemism used for drunks at that period – known throughout Mayfair as flamboyant playboys and princely hosts.

This was both an embarrassment and a nuisance to me, because he did not fool anybody in that cynical world, and the caricature of an upper-class accent that he assumed, which became louder as the night progressed, added to the high-pitched laugh which he imported from the Isle of Man, would surely have resulted in his beoming *persona non grata* at some of the more selective haunts of café society if he had not been accompanied by a columnist whom they did not wish, for commercial reasons, to offend.

Most bothersome of all, from my point of view, was that on these jaunts round the clubs he would pick up, in conversation, snippets of gossip about well-known people and bring them excitedly to me, like a dog laying a dead rat at the feet of its master, in the hope that I would use them in my column. Most of these items were either fabrications or, even if true, libellous, and in any case they were not the sort of material that I used.

On such occasions I was constrained to stay with Jimmy until the bitter end because he had the dangerous habit of returning to the office in the early hours and making changes on the feature pages. He would go straight down to the composing room, where the final London edition was in the last stages of preparation, read the proofs, and occasionally delete material, substituting material of the same length written by himself. As features editor he had the authority to do this, but his method of doing it meant that the new material was not screened by the night lawyer, and if it was dangerous material – as it usually was – the newspaper became in peril of the legal action that its normal systems took great pains to avoid.

He did this twice to my column, much to my anger and anguish, and I threatened to take the matter to the editor if he ever did it again; in fact, he did once do it again, on his very last day in the job, and precipitated the only libel action against the *Daily Mirror* that ever arose from a column that appeared under my name. But that was months later and is part of another story.

It was Eilbeck who provided me with an assistant, and in that short-lived appointment he also showed an outstanding lack of psychological understanding: he brought into my office an amiable young Yorkshireman who had recently joined the paper as a feature writer and was showing great promise. The young man's name was Keith Waterhouse.

This was a singularly gauche piece of miscasting, because Waterhouse was a writer in his own right, not a leg-man, and what I needed was a leg-man. A leg-man on a diary-type column finds stories which he writes and hands in to the man who is editing the column, who then collates all the stories that have been collected for him and presents them as a coherent miscellany of the required length. Mine was not that kind of column; it was a piece written by one man in his own individual way.

What Waterhouse did, with studied courtesy, was bring me columns that he had written in his way; they were not pieces that an editor could easily rewrite, because their value lay inherently in the style of the man who wrote them. I made the foolish mistake at the outset of trying to rewrite one of his pieces in the manner of my column, which caused both misery and offence to Waterhouse, as it would have done to me. Luckily

173

both Keith and I had enough sense to allow the idea of a collaboration column to die without any attention being drawn to the matter, and Keith quietly returned to his normal job of writing his own features. Once, later, he took over my column-space when I was on holiday, and although Keith Waterhouse is one of the relatively few natural-born newspaper columnists of this century, it did not work; Keith became celebrated as a playwright and satirist, but it was not until he took over the column-space vacated by Cassandra, after William Connor's death, that his true worth as a newspaper columnist became fully recognized and marked by awards for excellence.

Eilbeck's galloping *folie-de-grandeur* led him to start going on his champagne trail during the daytime as well as the night, and as he had it firmly fixed in is head that wherever I went was likely to be the centre of London's roistering, he took to following me around like Mary'a little lamb. I did not wish to fall out with him, but this was too much. My normal routine was to arrive in the office soon after 10 a.m., do some telephoning and clear up the mail, then write the column and leave it for my secretary to type, after which I went off for a drink and a bite of lunch, usually to the Savoy. When Jimmy Eilbeck started turning up regularly at the Savoy, calling loudly for champagne, I switched to the Ritz. I did not tell Jimmy, of course, but on the very first day I put this change of plan into operation he came striding into the Ritz Rivoli bar, shouting for champagne and claiming me as a long-lost brother. Thinking to give him the slip, I arranged to meet friends next day at the Connaught for lunch, but had not been there for more than five minutes, sipping a gin and tonic, before in came the long streak with flaming red hair, demanding vintage Bollinger.

There were two lunching-and-dining clubs in Mayfair to which I had not introduced the dreaded Eilbeck on our nocturnal revelries, so I took refuge in these. One was Les Ambassadeurs in Hamilton Place, which had been opened in 1952 by an immensely tall and elegant Pole called John Mills, with whom I was friendly; 'Les A' catered then, as now, for a mega-rich international crowd of super-tycoons such as Paul Getty and Charlie Clore, plus the more discerning among the wealthier ranks of film producers, directors and stars. The other was the International Fine Arts Club, better known as Siegi's, in Charles Street off Berkeley Square, also designed for the Rolls-Royce trade, though membership tended towards the sporting type of racehorse owner and the more respectable artists and writers who moved around in café society. Siegi Sessler, the sleek, short, round but elegant Pole who owned the club, was the best dressed man I ever met, and he had more suits in his

Definitely *not* Elvis Presley: greeting Bill Haley and his wife, Cuppy, in New York, 1957

With Frank Sinatra, as co-guests of honour at a Variety Club luncheon, in the days when teenagers swooned when they heard Sinatra's voice. Ol' Blue Eyes was the pop idol who started the swooning phenomenon – until he came along the kids had merely applauded their favourites

The Prince of Wails: singer Johnny Ray (*centre*) with Suzanne Warner and the author at the Dorchester Hotel

With Cilla Black soon after Brian Epstein (who discovered the Beatles) had noticed Cilla when she was working as a hat-check girl at the Cavern in Liverpool, where the Beatles worked, and had groomed her for stardom

Close harmony: with the Beverley Sisters

Discord: with Marlene Dietrich, re-establishing harmonious relations
(© Syndication International Ltd)

The author took this snapshot of Errol Flynn and Patrice Wymore, his third wife, aboard Flynn's yacht *Zaca* in Palma, Majorca, 1959

We're a couple of swells: dining with Judy Garland in New York

Moviola – the machine that can make time go backwards: with Jean Simmons in Hollywood, 1951

On the bluesmoke circuit: with Pearl Bailey at the Copacabana in New York

Mike Todd, son of a rabbi, Czar of Hollywood, with his wife, Elizabeth Taylor

With Eddie Fisher, Mike Todd's filmstar protégé, whom Elizabeth Taylor
married – a brief encounter before she met Richard Burton – during her period of
anguish after Mike Todd was killed in an air crash

'A triumph, dear boy!' Noël Coward with Joe Glaser (*centre*)
immediately after Coward's first-night success in Las Vegas. 'God
sent you to me,' said Coward to Glaser. Joe replied, 'I thought it was
Ernie Anderson and Noel Whitcomb.'

A whale of a time: during the shooting of *Moby Dick*, with John Huston (*centre*), Gregory Peck (*bearded*) and José Ferrer

Lady Docker, 'Naughty Nora', 1950s Pied Piper of the consumer society, wearing white mink and diamonds and driving her star-spangled golden Daimler, upholstered with zebra skin (© Syndication International Ltd)

wardrobes than any other man I have ever known, but this latter fact arose not only from personal vanity but also from an amusing chain of events.

Siegi was a compulsive gambler on horses. When his club closed soon after three o'clock in the afternoon, he would retire to his flat upstairs with a copy of the *Sporting Life* and the gleanings of his morning's conversations with racehorse owners, and he would sit in his armchair with a telephone at his elbow and play the horses. He bet in large sums and invariably ended up sending a hefty cheque to his bookmaker at the end of every week.

At about the time when he was ruefully realizing that most of his profits from the club were being channelled direct to his bookie, he was sitting at lunch with me and trying to think of ways in which he could occupy the afternoons interestingly, away from a telephone, until racing was over. I made a few suggestions – Why not get married? Why not take up charity work? – but he was still drenched in the gloom of his sad story when I had to go. 'I can't stop,' I said, 'because I have an appointment with my tailor to get a fitting for a suit.'

'I'll come with you,' said Siegi.

My old tailor in Savile Row had recently died, and I had started going to a firm called Donaldson and Williams, who originally had premises in St James's but later moved to Burlington Arcade. While Williams was doing my fitting that afternoon, Donaldson was showing Siegi some suit materials, and Siegi decided to order a couple of suits. He was so pleased with them when they were finished that he started going along to the tailor's almost every afternoon, sometimes for a fitting but usually also to order a new suit.

Within a year or so Siegi had more than a hundred new suits in his bulging wardrobes, many of which he had never even worn, but when people taunted him about his narcissistic extravagance he would shake his head vigorously. 'It's an economy measure,' he would say. 'I gave up backing horses in the afternoon and started going to the tailor's instead, and apart from getting value for money at the tailor's the amount I save in bookmaker's bills is enormous.'

The introduction of this dream customer to my tailor must have done me no harm, either, because that year I was ceremonially presented with a silver Beau Brummel statuette after having been selected by the tailoring trade as Britain's Best Dressed Journalist.

But I was far from being Britain's most contented journalist. I was out of

175

step with the *Daily Mirror*, uneasy at the way I was being dragged into sensational news stories, frequently at odds with the features department over the fact that changes were sometimes made in the wording of my column without reference; I longed to leave the paper but felt that I was so closely identified with it that I had burnt my boats. I was like an actor in a long-running television series who becomes so personally recognized as the character he is playing that nobody can imagine him in another rôle. I felt like a donkey on a treadmill.

Eilbeck, in spite of his continued lurching along the champagne trail, was becoming increasingly influential on the paper, and although he still allocated to me large quantities of space to fill daily, and my stock with him was high, there was too much dissimilarity in the way our minds worked for me to feel comfortable about the direction my working life was taking.

I was in Munich, writing a column about the Oktoberfest, when I heard on the telephone the good news from London: Eilbeck was being promoted to assistant editor; this would get him out of my hair, because Jimmy, with his magnified sense of self-importance, would surely move into a position of more overall responsibility as assistant editor, and would cease to be so engrossed in my affairs; he would have bigger fish to fry.

Heaving a sigh of relief I flew on to Hamburg and wrote a couple of columns from there, deciding not to return to London until Jimmy was safely out of the features department. But it was coming up towards the weekend, and Jimmy was not due to take up his new appointment until the Monday, so I moved on to a strategic position in Paris, deciding to send my Sunday-for-Monday column from there and then fly back to London when the coast was finally clear. This was a fateful decision.

In Paris, in circumstances that I shall describe in the next chapter, I met Isabel Patino, younger daughter of Don Antenor Patino, a Bolivian who was at that time one of the richest men in the world. Isabel, who was angry with her father, told me the strange story of her family history. Her grandfather, Simon Patino, had been a humble Cholo Indian from Cochabamba who had one day stumbled across an abandoned tin mine in Bolivia. Having got it working almost single-handedly and become richer than the Bolivian government, he was appointed Bolivian minister to France. When he died he left a fortune worth £75,000,000 to his son, Antenor, who married a Bourbon princess, a niece of King Alfonso of Spain, from whom he later separated; this was Isabel's mother, the Duchess of Durcal.

Antenor became so obsessed with the grandeur of his aristocratic position in European society that he assiduously protected both his daughters from association with people who were not high born. Isabel's story about the unhappiness that this had caused her elder sister, Cristina, when her father had prevented her from marrying an American in Madrid and brought her back to Paris to marry a prince who was the eldest son of one of France's oldest and most aristocratic families, had a vein of tragedy reminiscent of Emily Brontë's *Wuthering Heights* and I asked her permission to write it as a column: for reasons of her own, she willingly gave it to me.

I telephoned the column to the *Daily Mirror* on the Sunday morning, speaking briefly to Jimmy Eilbeck before I put it over, in order to tell him what the column was about. It was Jimmy's last day as features editor, and he was euphoric. 'I am going out of this job in a blaze of glory,' he said to me. 'Tomorrow's features will be the most sensational ever.'

I should have been alerted by that remark, but at the time it rang no warning bells in my ear.

What happened then in London was that Jimmy Eilbeck gave a champagne and caviare party at lunchtime, with his successor as features editor, Mike Randall, as guest of honour. According to Mike, the caviare ran out but the champagne kept flowing. It developed, as was customary with Eilbeck's parties, into a drunken thrash.

Returning to the office, the first thing Eilbeck saw on his desk was a copy of my column. Taking out the red ballpoint pen that he used for making marks on copy, he 'improved' my story.

It was in some ways lucky for me that Eilbeck had used his red pen, because when, months later, Don Antenor Patino's libel suit against the *Daily Mirror* came to court, my name was removed completely from the action as soon as it was discovered that most of the offending phrases had not appeared in the original typescript, but had been added to the copy in red ballpoint handwriting.

Whether Don Antenor would have pursued his action if my column had gone into the paper as originally written is open to question: I think he probably would, because I had portrayed him unequivocally as an egregious snob. But I doubt whether he would have won his case, as he did on the day, being awarded £20,000 damages against the *Daily Mirror*.

Hugh Cudlipp, knowing the circumstances, treated me kindly and told me not to worry, because he knew I was distraught at the outcome. But Jimmy Eilbeck kept out of the affair altogether. He ignored me. His career was still advancing and he was appointed editor of the new

Woman's Sunday Mirror, a short-lived publication that was later retitled as *Woman's Mirror,* and was edited by Jodi Hyland, who become Hugh Cudlipp's third wife.

Eilbeck's mental illness was fast making him intolerable as an executive, and eventually Cudlipp had to fire him. Although he had not spoken to me since the libel case, Jimmy immediately telephoned me as though I were his best friend, and asked me to intercede with Bertie Meadows so that he could use a room at the 21 Room as a home and as an office, as he had left his long-suffering wife. Never having been able to bear a grudge for long, I did so. I also lent him money for food, because he was penniless, although I should have known – probably did know – that he would spend the money on champagne.

From his dingy room at the 21, with manic energy, he set about starting a daily newspaper called the *Sun* – a title not then in use – and an evening paper called the *Mayfair Moon*. It was all dreams, of course. There was no possibility of Eilbeck being sufficiently responsible to start or edit a newspaper. Yet his persuasive tongue in madness convinced several important financiers to take him seriously. One morning, wearing a dirty shirt and an old pair of trousers, which were the only clothes he had left, he walked barefoot, having lost his shoes, from Mayfair to the City, to keep an appointment with the general manager of the Westminster Bank. He was seeking a loan of half a million pounds.

During all these days he telephoned me constantly, asking me to come and see his dummies for his new papers, commissioning columns and articles from me, which, of course, I never wrote. One morning he telephoned me and said only five words: 'Jimmy here. I'm sorry, Noel.' Then he put down the telephone.

Later that day his body was recovered from beneath an electric train on the London Underground.

He was thirty years old.

10

In lives of leisure
The craze for pleasure
Steadily grows.
Cocktails and laughter,
But what comes after?
Nobody knows.

Noël Coward, *Poor Little Rich Girl*

One story with which I became entangled at that period has been retold in widely differing versions time and again in magazines all over the Western world, partly because it is a love story in the classic tradition of Romeo and Juliet with counterparts of the Montagues and Capulets, and partly because the young man concerned in the story has since become rich and famous as the international business tycoon Sir James Goldsmith.

Some of these magazine accounts that I have read claiming to be the inside story of the Goldsmith-Patino elopement are confections of fact and fiction, embellished from the imagination of the writer; but as far as I know James Goldsmith has never taken any action to correct them: this may be because the sequence of events as it unfolded in reality was far more bizarre than any of the ornamented versions. The story still stands today as the textbook elopement of the twentieth century, and part of its interest lies in the fact that it reflects so vividly the customs, the behaviour-standards and the public attitudes of its time, all of which have changed radically during the nearly four decades since it took place.

I have never before written an account of the affair since it ended, although I have received many offers to do so because I happen, by chance, to be the only journalist in the world who is in a position to write about certain aspects of it from personal experience; but in any account of my life as a newspaperman this story has to be a waymark, so I will recount it now through the eyes of a privileged reporter.

179

Even today, it is a story that would make an enthralling play, because it is such a compendium of theatrical elements and devices.

Act I takes place in Mayfair and in Paris, in the milieu of the gilded youth of the post-war period, the golden girls and the fashionable playboys of wealthy upper-middle-class families, dancing till dawn and chasing hell-for-leather after thrills in a setting redolent of Noël Coward; but the frivolity moves smoothly into drama when two of the young people fall in love, and the girl's father, who is one of the world's richest men, tries to use his wealth and influence to frustrate the romance: he swiftly and secretly sends her far away, guarded by a duenna. The young man, in a frenzy, chases after her, and after an exciting comedy of errors he finds her and sweeps her off to Scotland in an elopement that might, if the story had been fiction, have been based on Scott's verse-romance of Young Lochinvar in *Marmion*. This brings the curtain down on the first act, leaving the audience sitting on the edges of their seats.

In Act II the scene switches to Scotland, where the tension heightens because the chase is under way. While the angry parents of the young heiress set up headquarters in Edinburgh, surrounded by lawyers instructed to prevent a marriage at all costs, the young lovers themselves are hounded across the moors and through the glens by a predatory pack of pressmen from all over Europe, in a hair-raising pursuit that – if the story had been fiction – would surely have been said to have been plagiarized from the sinister pursuit of Richard Hannay through Scotland in John Buchan's *Thirty Nine Steps*. Act II ends in triumph for the young lovers after a pulse-quickening finale in which they outwit their pursuers and get away, hidden in an old pig-van, to be married quietly at last in a sleepy little Lowlands town, far from the madding crowd.

The play could satisfactorily end there; but in real life there was a third act, which began idyllically back in Paris but ended in stark melodrama some months later when the girl died in childbirth.

I first met Jimmy Goldsmith in the autumn of 1953, in Paris. He was twenty years old, six-feet-four-inches tall, elegantly dressed, of patrician appearance, with the style and accent of a scion of an old English noble family: all of which was misleading because his family was of German origin; his grandfather, Adolphus Goldschmidt, had been born in Germany of a family that, like their cousins the Rothschilds, had been money-dealers in the Frankfurt ghetto at the time when William Shakespeare was writing *The Merchant of Venice*.

Adolphus had come to England as a young man, liked the country, married an English girl, bought an estate in Suffolk, invested his considerable fortune in Germany and Russia (which was to prove a misfortune for his heirs), and settled down to live the life of an English country gentleman; the birth certificates of all his four children bore the name of Goldsmith, not Goldschmidt.

The youngest of the four, Frank Goldsmith, read law at Oxford, took a house in London, became a member of the London County Council and a well-known and popular man-about-town, and later became member of parliament for the Suffolk constituency in which his parents lived. He took a commission in the Suffolk Yeomanry and was, to all intents and purposes, an English squire.

But in the prelude to the 1914–18 war, when anti-German feeling in Britain boiled up to such a pitch of hatred that even and especially Prince Louis of Battenburg changed his name to Mountbatten, all men of German extraction here began to be treated with contumely, and Frank Goldsmith was ostracized. He spent the Great War fighting with his regiment, achieving the rank of major, but when he returned to England at the end of the war he no longer felt at home: he felt alienated, disillusioned; the bitterness had gone deep. So he moved to France, married a Frenchwoman and invested in a French hotel company.

The marriage was short-lived because his wife died, but the hotel business flourished, and he took charge of the overall direction of the company, running a number of the finest hotels in France, including the Carlton in Cannes, the Hôtel de Paris in Monte Carlo and the Scribe in Paris.

His second wife was a young French girl in her late teens, less than half his age, and she had two children by him, Edward and James. Both the boys had dual nationality, French and English, and were brought up to be bilingual and bicultural: they were English boys in England and French boys in France.

Major Goldsmith, known as 'Monsieur le Major' in France, was not rich in terms of capital but he and his family lived very richly indeed, because of the luxury hotels that he controlled; they had the same sort of lifestyle as wealthy international celebrities, using suites in the top hotels in Monte Carlo and Cannes, always with plenty of servants around, and all on the firm. If you control luxury hotels you can live as luxuriously as the richest millionaires; his apartment at the Scribe Hotel in Paris was his main base in France, and when he later became a director of the Savoy Hotel Group in London, he always had a suite at the Savoy or Claridges at his disposal for occasions when the family visited London: he was one of the top hoteliers in Europe.

So Teddy and Jimmy grew up in the wealthy and pampered but artificial world of big businessmen, playboys, beautiful women and gamblers, and Jimmy was bitten by the gambling bug at an early age. He had every material thing that he could possibly want around him and at his beck and call, except plenty of cash in his pocket, and the only way he could see of getting his hands on big lumps of cash was by winning it. So from the time when he was a boy, Jimmy became a fearless punter, mostly on horses; but he was never a mug punter; he always carefully calculated the odds, studied the form, and gathered inside information from his friends; when all these three ingredients came together into a highly favourable chance, Jimmy had a ferocious bet; often he won, because not only did he possess a naturally cool and shrewd mind in appraising swiftly the balances of chance, but he also had that other asset without which no gambler can succeed – in matters concerning money he was born under a lucky star.

At school, first at Millfield and then at Eton, he showed no great promise, and was regarded as being far too preoccupied with the pursuit of a sybaritic life among his coterie of friends ever to do well academically. In fact, he left Eton when he was sixteen, celebrating his departure with a tremendous win on a three-horse bet. To his young friends whom he entertained to an extravagant farewell party he was a fine fellow, but to everyone else except his parents he was a spoilt brat.

Teddy was up at Oxford, also surrounded by a fast crowd of young roisterers and gamblers that included John Aspinall, so Jimmy went to stay in Oxford and continued his rake's progress there; once again, he was popular among his immediate circle of profligate young roués, but to disapproving observers he was nothing but a philandering libertine with the mind of a bookie and the morals of a tomcat.

His parents, kindly people with liberal views about young men sowing wild oats, were nevertheless anxious about the tales they heard concerning the dissolute life he was leading, so they recalled Jimmy to Paris and his father found him a job as a trainee waiter in a restaurant in Montmartre, as a start to a career in the hotel trade. Montmartre turned out to be not the ideal place to send young Jimmy. So Monsieur le Major decided to get him right away from the temptations of Paris and London, and sent him to Madrid to work in the kitchens of a big hotel. Madrid also turned out to have too many distractions for a young kitchen-apprentice of hedonistic bent, so the major, having paid his son's substantial debts, gave up the plan of finding hotel jobs for him and had a brilliant idea: he sent the recalcitrant lad back to England to do his national service.

This worked. Jimmy joined the Royal Artillery, was posted to Wales, and although he had never been an athletic or games-inclined type, and had always been an individualist rather than part of a team, he found a useful rôle in the army because his natural arrogance made him good at telling other men what to do and making damn sure they did it. Nobody had ever managed to discipline him before, but the army has ways of knocking the corners off a young man with a *prima donna* temperament, and Jimmy, for the first time in his life, began to think seriously about the future.

On his army papers, and on his passport, Jimmy had described his occupation as 'hotelier', but when he returned to Paris after finishing his national service he had already decided to become a businessman: he had discovered his real talent. The delighted major gave his younger son a room and an office in the Scribe Hotel, and Jimmy began to work seriously at building up a small pharmaceutical company of which the main product was a specific designed to alleviate rheumatic pain, called Lloyd's Adrenalin Cream. He showed flair, and the little company began to do well. Among the people he employed on a casual basis to advance the company's sales by means of public-relations techniques was a young man called Michael Mordaunt-Smith.

Mike Mordaunt-Smith was a friend of mine. Mike was Irish, related to the Guinness family, a former captain in the Black Watch, chronically hard up, indomitably cheerful, determined to make a career for himself and to have a good time in the process. We first met at Rico Dajou's Casanova Club in the spring of 1953, when I was beginning my pre-coronation Nightlife column, and he came over to talk to me because he had a story about the French aircraft industry that he wanted to sell to a newspaper; he was doing freelance publicity for a big French firm called Bréguet at the time, and his ambition was to get a job on a Fleet Street newspaper. He had an excellent nose for sniffing out interesting stories, and he worked diligently at finding out the details, but at that time he had not had the experience needed to present them in a journalistic manner acceptable to newspapers, so he sold his stories for other people to write.

Mike had, like me, a wide acquaintanceship in London society, so we frequently met at the parties, dinners and dances that were taking place all over Mayfair every night during that coronation summer, and he usually gave me first option on the stories he came across, although I used few of them because most were more suitable for the gossip columns. One of his kinsfolk was Caroline Blackwood, who was at that time working for Cyril Connolly on *Horizon* and was married to Lucian

Freud, so our paths also crossed frequently at the Soho haunts of the Bohemians of London's *quartier Latin* – Freud, Francis Bacon, John Minton, Nina Hamnett, John Deakin and other artists and writers – who gathered at Wheeler's in Old Compton Street or the French House at lunchtime and afterwards at Muriel Belcher's Colony Room Club. We both had a kaleidoscopic array of acquaintances, the full spectrum.

One interesting item that Mike brought to me that summer concerned big plans that were being secretly discussed by the directors of the Savoy Hotel; I asked him where he had found the information, and he told me that he had heard it from his friend Jimmy Goldsmith, whose father was a director of the Savoy: it was primarily a story suitable for the financial pages, because, if true, it meant that there would be a sharp rise in Savoy B shares when the news was announced.

The *Daily Mirror* did not have a City column in those days, and printed no company news, so my interest in the story was personal, not professional. I have always taken a keen interest in the stock market, and at that time when there was no capital gains tax I used to deal almost on a day-to-day basis, often buying and selling within the same account. My stockbroker was a clever young Old Harrovian called Peter Raymond, a junior partner in his father's firm of Raymond and Bekhor; Joe Raymond *père* was a rich man then, a member of the wealthy Sassoon family of bankers. Peter and I used to meet often and exchange information that we had heard, usually over a glass of champagne in the American bar at the Savoy, and it was – suitably enough – at the Savoy that we discussed this piece of information from Mike Mordaunt-Smith. We decided to buy strongly into Savoy B shares, and Peter dealt immediately on behalf of both of us.

In the vastly changed circumstances ruling in the City today, dealing of that sort could easily provoke a Stock Exchange inquiry; it would not quite come under the heading of insider dealing, because we were not insiders, but it would surely be classified as a leak meriting investigation, and might result in dealings being halted in the shares. However, in 1953 such deals took place so frequently that they were almost the rule rather than the exception, and many well-informed people played the market on the strength of inside tips from their company-director friends, thereby consistently boosting their income, as I did.

Within days of our buying the Savoy B shares they shot up in value, so we sold, making a handsome profit.

Mike Mordaunt-Smith, having himself made a minor killing, told Peter and me that we should go in again, because he had heard that there was more price-sensitive news still to come; so we bought again, took a smaller profit when the shares went up during the account, and once more ended up smiling. I heard later that some people who thought they were in the know had hung on in anticipation of a further rise, but suddenly the bottom dropped out of the market for Savoy B shares, and they plummeted. When I next saw Mike I told him that I hoped his friend, Jimmy Goldsmith, had not taken too much of a loss.

'Jimmy?' he said, surprised. 'Jimmy wouldn't get caught like that. Just before the shares fell he not only sold out but he also sold short, so Jimmy did very well indeed. Not that he told anyone about the news that caused the tumble,' added Mike, thoughtfully.

It was during that coronation summer of 1953 that Jimmy Goldsmith met Isabel Patino. They met in London on Isabel's eighteenth birthday. Isabel's father, Antenor, known as the King of Tin, had once held a Bolivian diplomatic post in London, before he moved to Paris for tax reasons, so he knew both capitals well, and the family celebrated Isabel's eighteenth birthday with a big dinner at Claridge's in London. After the dinner, the young people moved on to dance at Rico Dajou's Casanova Club, and that was where Jimmy first encountered Isabel; having been introduced, they danced together for the rest of the night until the revels ended.

Back in Paris, which was homebase for the Goldsmiths and the Patinos, the two young people began seeing each other as frequently as possible. They had fallen in love. But the course of true love did not run smooth, because Isabel's father kept her under strict surveillance; Isabel was heiress to several millions in her own right, under her grand-mother's will, and her father was constantly on the *qui vive* to spot fortune-hunters, of which there were many among the so-called 'debs' delights' who hunted rich prey at the season's parties and dances in London and Paris. She was a sweetly pretty girl with dark hair and dark eyes, vivacious and fun-loving, and rebellious against the restrictions placed upon her by her father; it was the heyday of society elopements, and, in the eyes of eligible but impoverished young men all over Europe, Isabel represented the catch of the season.

So when Mr Antenor Patino heard that his younger daughter was secretly meeting a young jackanapes whose father was in the hotel trade, he became very angry indeed. He had planned that his younger daughter would make either a royal or an aristocratic match, as his elder daughter had done under his guidance; and there was another factor of even more alarming unsuitability in his view: Jimmy Goldsmith was a Jew. Mr Patino forbade his daughter ever to see this young man again, and engaged a chaperone, Princess Maria Windisch-Graetz, to ensure that his orders were carried out.

Isabel was fairly typical of the rich girls of her time: not a great deal of brains but not a great deal of need for them. Some of her friends called her Gypsy, and much was made of this nickname in the newspapers during the elopement drama, giving her the entirely spurious image of being a flashing-eyed Carmen of wild and fiery passion; in fact she was a rather quiet girl, determined and courageous in her fashion, but no Carmen, and although there was an ingredient of the Carmen story in the *opéra comique* of the elopement and the ultimate tragedy that was to come in the following year when Isabel died while giving birth to Jimmy's baby, it was no part of Isabel's nature. The 'Gypsy' story arose because it was sold to the newspapers during the time when they were hungry for any titillating snippets they could lay hands on, and the people who sold the story were two young men about Mayfair who were hard up and eager to be seen as young bucks in the vortex of rich social life, although neither of them knew Jimmy Goldsmith well and Isabel Patino hardly at all: their names were Julian Plowden and Dominic Elwes. Dominic's name was to crop up again, much later, in Jimmy's life, still with little substantial link but once more with a tragic ending; some stories, trivial in origin, have a way of sending rever-berations down the years like echoes dying slowly in the hills.

Isabel's dominant characteristic was her stubbornness in refusing to obey her father's orders that she should give Jimmy up and forget him, and in the face of considerable difficulties she continued meeting Jimmy by means of subterfuge. This greatly angered her father, who knew precisely what was going on because he had two servants who were required to send him a daily written report detailing Isabel's movements; so, realizing that he was not succeeding in his commands to his daughter, Mr Patino sent imperiously for Jimmy.

Jimmy told me later about this meeting and according to his account Mr Patino demanded from him an undertaking that he would cease seeing Isabel, because he had other plans for her. Jimmy refused bluntly, and said that he loved Isabel and intended to marry her. This infuriated Don Antenor, who told Jimmy that unless he gave an undertaking to get out of Isabel's life, she would be sent away to some place where Jimmy could not find her, and added scathingly, 'It is not the habit of members of my family to marry Jews.' Jimmy replied hotly, 'And it is not the habit of my family to marry Red Indians, either.'

This reference to Red Indians was to become a key issue in the libel action that Mr Patino later took against the *Daily Mirror*, because I repeated it in the article I later wrote, and although it was technically accurate it was considered by the furious Mr Patino to be a monstrous slur.

So this was how the situation stood, although I did not know it at the time, when I decided to stop over in Paris for a couple of days on my way back to London from Hamburg in October 1953. My intention was simply to see some friends and write a column from Paris. So I checked in at the Ritz, dined there and went to bed early.

Next morning I was awakened by the telephone before seven o'clock, and was surprised to hear the voice of Olga Deterding on the line; 7 a.m. was an hour unknown to most of Olga's friends, or, if known, was regarded as extremely late at night, so I realized that there must be some momentous reason for Olga to be telephoning at such an unsocial hour. After the death of her multi-millionaire father, she was usually described in the gossip columns of the period as the richest girl in the world. She was a restless soul, always rushing from place to place in search of elusive happiness, permanently seeking to exorcise the mocking devil of guilt that she felt because of her enormous wealth and her trivial life.

'Sorry to wake you up, darling,' she said, 'but I was wondering whether you would do me a tiny favour.'

'Depends what it is,' I said, suspiciously. I had read in the paper that she was in France sponsoring an Oxford University golf team, and I had no intention of letting myself in for some golfing escapade.

'It's my car,' said Olga. 'The golf boys were going on to Madame Billy's last night, and I wanted them to take me with them, but they refused, the rotten ungrateful lot.'

'Not surprised,' I said. Madame Billy's was the top-class brothel in Paris. 'Anyway, what has that got to do with the car?'

'Well, I sort of left it in a hurry,' she said in her helpless-little-girl voice. 'It's in the Champs Elysées, up by the Etoile.'

'You mean you left it in the middle of the road?' I asked.

'Well . . . you know, darling – I've never been very good at parking.'

I had a vision of this beautiful sports car surrounded by outraged Paris flics as the traffic roared round it in the busy Champs Elysées, with French drivers hooting like maniacs in the traffic jam it would be causing, and I understood immediately why Olga did not wish to appear on the scene herself.

'Did you leave the key in it?' I asked.

'No–o–o. I have it here.'

'They'll put you in the Bastille for life,' I said.

187

'Yes, I know, darling. That is what is worrying me. But I have to fly to Monte Carlo this morning because the boys have a golf match down there. I suppose you wouldn't be an angel and drive it down to the Hôtel de Paris for me?'

'You suppose right,' I said. 'I'm a working lad. But I'll tell you what I will do. Leave the keys at your place in an envelope addressed to me and put in a note authorizing me to take the car away. I will go and find it and buy it back from the *flics*.'

After breakfast I set off on my mercy mission. Sure enough, the car was still there. It had been bumped into the side of the road by the police, and there was one fierce-looking cop standing guard over it, awaiting the return of the miscreant. A substantial sum of money changed hands, and I drove the car to a garage belonging to a friend of mine, in a side street just off the Place de la Concorde.

As I was walking back past the Hôtel Crillon I decided to go in and say hallo to my old friend Sam White of the *Evening Standard*, who used a corner of the Crillon bar as an office and was such a good customer that they had even given him his own telephone on the bar. Sam was not there when I went in, but several other people I knew were having a pre-lunch livener, and I had just joined them in *une coupe de champagne* when who should walk in but Michael Mordaunt-Smith.

'Well I'll be damned,' he said, 'this is providential. I was just about to ring you in London and ask you to come over. The fact is that Jimmy Goldsmith finds himself in a very tricky spot, and he needs all the help he can get. I told him last night that I would ring you and ask you to bring the mighty brain to bear on finding a solution.'

Mike had a touching faith in my ability to come up with ingenious ideas. I, being in my early thirties, was more than ten years older than his young friends, and Mike regarded me as an experienced man-of-the-world who could quickly come up with Jeeves-like solutions that would outwit parental opposition and smooth the path for the young lovers so that wedding bells would finally ring out.

He led me to a quiet corner of the bar and, in conspiratorial tones, outlined the story of the problems and obstacles that were being placed in the way of the true love of Jimmy and Isabel. This was the first time I had heard about the Goldsmith-Patino romance, and although I listened attentively I had difficulty in not smiling at times because there was a strong scent of Blandings about the way Mike told it. When he got to the part where Isabel's father had sent her to the rambling old Château d'Haroué, deep in the French countryside, and Jimmy, having discovered where she was, had followed hotfoot on the next train, I fully expected to hear that characters such as Hugo Carmody, Catsmeat Potter-Pirbright and Roderick Spode were already installed in the castle, posing as other people.

I did not see how I could be much help in what was, after all, a family matter, but Mike was a good chap and I did not wish to disappoint him by dodging away from the problems of his friends, so I agreed to go along with him right away and talk to Jimmy. We took a taxi to the Scribe Hotel.

In the absence of his father and mother, Jimmy was holding a council of war among his friends in Monsieur le Major's suite, known to everyone in the hotel as *Le Siège* – the seat of justice. There was an air of tension in the room, and Jimmy was striding round, full of nervous energy, angrily relating the schemes and strategems to which Mr Patino was resorting in order to discredit him.

'Do you know, my dear fellow, that Senor Patino has actually spread a rumour that I am a *pédéraste*. Me! He is a wicked man, but I will not have him making a *maquereau* out of me!' Jimmy frequently used French words in his English conversation in those days, especially when he was excited. I had a strong feeling that he was, in a curious way, enjoying the drama that he had precipitated, and revelling in the sensation of being an equal adversary of one of the world's richest men. There was no doubt at all in my mind from the first time I met him that Jimmy was mesmerized by money, and took pleasure from being at daggers drawn with a mega-millionaire.

The other people in the room were all likeable youngsters, slightly overawed by the perilous battle in which Jimmy had become engaged: there was Digby Neave, younger brother of Airey Neave, who had been at Eton with Jimmy and had subsequently mediated to get him out of a number of scrapes – Digby had set up in Paris in the motor insurance business, and had a flat on the Ile de St Louis; Peter West, son of Air Commodore Freddie West, the last RAF holder of the VC from the 1914–18 war, was there with his fiancée, Davina Portman; and, of course, Isabel herself, clearly thrilled to be in such a desperately forbidden place as Jimmy's father's suite. Isabel's alibi that morning was that she had taken her dog for a shampoo to the dog shop in the Avenue Georges V. 'Poor little chap, he is the most shampooed dog in France,' she smiled.

I sat talking with Isabel for a while, and as she related details of the life of her family under the austere and – to her eyes – tyrannical rule of her father, I began to realize why I had been invited there. This was a perfect story for the *Daily Mirror*. I was not exactly being set up, but on the other hand I felt sure that Jimmy Goldsmith had encouraged Mike to bring his journalist friend, in full realization of the fact that a newspaper story revealing the eccentric snobbishness of Senor Don Antenor Patino would do no harm to the Goldsmith cause; Jimmy was only twenty years old but he was already a Machiavellian strategist.

All the same, while I was aware of the ulterior motive, the story itself was a tale that Willie Somerset Maugham would have relished, for it contained all the ingredients of a typical Maugham short story. Isabel, eighteen years old and brimming with vitality, had been brought up in the repressively protective environment usually associated with Spanish aristocratic families of the seventeenth or eighteenth century; her father, the grandee, had treated his two daughters as valuable possessions who would, in time, advance still further his social position among the highest-born families of Europe. They were to have everything that life could offer, except freedom. So, in natural consequence, freedom was the only thing they wanted.

'It is all so silly and so fraudulent,' said Isabel, 'because we are not really an old Spanish family at all. My grandfather was a Cholo Indian from Cochabamba in Bolivia, a poor and humble man who became very rich because, by chance, he stumbled upon an abandoned tin mine and, through his own hard work, turned it into a great fortune.'

That was the key fact that Isabel's father did not wish to see published in a newspaper, and it was also the key fact that Jimmy Goldsmith did wish to see published, because it undermined Mr Patino's objection to an alliance with the middle-class Goldsmith family, and exposed it as social snobbishness without a valid reason.

In his own quest for social aggrandisement, Antenor Patino had married the Duchess of Durcal, a niece of King Alfonso of Spain and therefore a member of the royal Bourbon family, and both their daughters were given the Bourbon name on their birth documents – Cristina and Maria Isabella Patino y Bourbon. The marriage had not been a happy one, and, to the sadness of the two young daughters, their mother and father had separated in the midst of acrimonious legal battles, leaving them in the care of their father, whose strictness they feared. Not surprisingly, both girls rebelled, or tried to. Cristina fell in love with an American, and asked her father's permission to marry him; but he refused, so she eloped with the American to Madrid. Her father arranged for her to be brought back to Paris, and that was the end of that.

Soon afterwards, a young man called Prince Marc de Beauveau-Craon went to see Mr Patino and asked for Isabel's hand in marriage.

190

Although of noble birth, being the surviving heir of one of the oldest families in France, Marc was in a much reduced financial state; he was working in Paris for the Mercury Travel Agency, a subsidiary of one of the companies controlled by Jimmy Goldsmith's father, for a salary equivalent to about £10 a week. His ancestral home, the Château d'Haroué near Nancy, was a crumbling country mansion of which only three rooms were still in use.

In Senor Don Antenor Patino's eyes, Prince Marc was an eligible man, but Marc was in his thirties and Isabel was only seventeen; so Don Antenor refused permission for Marc to marry his younger daughter, but at the same time he invited Marc to his house in Paris and introduced him to his elder daughter, Cristina. A marriage was arranged. The wedding was one of the most lavish and glittering events of the Paris social calendar in 1952. Antenor provided his new son-in-law with an enormous allowance, suitable to his aristocratic position in society, and set about restoring the family seat, Château d'Haroué, at gigantic expense. The young couple went to live there.

When Cristina – or Christine as she was known to her friends – became pregnant, Don Antenor's financial munificence to his son-in-law increased, and arrangements were made for the birth in the tradition of European royal and noble families, among which was the provision for the father to attend the birth; at the American Hospital in Neuilly a room was booked for Prince Marc for the period of the confinement. (This arrangement was later changed in order to falsify my published account of the preparations.)

Isabel had been sent by her father to the Château d'Haroué, to get her out of Paris, and had been forbidden ever to see Jimmy Goldsmith again; but she had smuggled out a letter to Jimmy, telling him where she was, and Jimmy had gone rushing down to the château, where he was curtly refused entry by Prince Marc, who was carrying out the strict instructions of Mr Patino. Jimmy had no option but to return to Paris, chafing angrily. And soon after that, because Christine was in the late stages of her pregnancy, Isabel was also whisked back to her father's house in Paris, and kept under constant surveillance, although from time to time she managed to give her two chaperones – a noblewoman and a princess – the slip, and run off to assignations with Jimmy. Her great fear was, so she said, that her father would have her put into a convent, possibly abroad, for a period of years, in the hope that her love for Jimmy was a mere infatuation which would shrivel and die with the passage of time.

I felt sorry for her, as I would have done for any girl who had been treated so imperiously, but I had no intention of writing anything about her or about Jimmy Goldsmith; what interested me from a column point of view was the grotesquely out-of-date snobbishness of the relatively *nouveau-riche* Mr Patino, and the lengths to which he would go in order to ensure that his daughters married aristocrats and lived in a style suitable to a family with royal connections. The circumstances that Mr Patino had decreed surrounding the birth of Cristina's child, which, if a boy, would be the heir to his millions, were a clear example of his obsession with royal protocol, because it was startlingly unusual in 1953 for an ordinary father to attend the birth of his child, so I decided to write a column on that theme. Not for one moment was I unaware that by doing so I would be walking across a minefield, because Mr Patino, in the fashion of some rich men whose unsureness about their own background pushes them towards a form of paranoia, was a lightning hand with a writ, and he was in the habit of resorting to the courts of law in the way that other men obtain their excitement in casinos.

Before I left the Goldsmith apartment in the Scribe that morning I told Jimmy what I had in mind to do, and arranged that we should dine together that evening, inviting also Digby Neave and Michael Mordaunt-Smith

'*Parfait!*' exclaimed Jimmy, delightedly. '*Parfait!*'

I spent the afternoon checking details of the story, and during dinner I went over the details again, item by item, making as sure as possible that there was no misunderstanding or inaccuracy. After that I wrote the column, and went to bed confident that although it would surely not please Mr Patino, there was no likelihood of his being able successfully to take any action about it.

I reckoned without the 'improvements' that were to be added by Jimmy Eilbeck before the article went into print: when I read the resultant column in the paper, and saw the headlines and presentation, I realized immediately that the minefield had not after all been negotiated without casualties, and I went straightaway to see the chief of the *Daily Mirror*'s legal department, a wily old lawyer called Mark Goodman.

Mark listened carefully, and then delivered his opinion. 'No doubt we shall receive a writ,' he said, 'because of the inaccuracies that you have pointed out. But Mr Patino is unlikely to bring the matter to court if his daughter, Miss Isabel Patino, is willing to give evidence for us that the substance of the story is accurate.'

'She will,' I said. 'I telephoned her this morning, and she assured me of that. I took the precaution of recording the conversation.'

'In that case,' said Mark, 'the *Daily Mirror* will defend any action that may be brought. Our case will stand on the evidence of your witness.'

Although Mr Patino's solicitors issued a writ forthwith, the matter was not viewed with much anxiety inside the *Daily Mirror*, particularly because of events that transpired during the following couple of months, which I am about to describe. In fact it was not until after Isabel died during the following year while having Jimmy's baby – a girl, also christened Isabel, who lived – that Mr Patino brought his action against the *Mirror* into court, and although my name had been removed from the plaintiff's case I can still recall the chilling words of Mark Goodman on the morning the trial began. 'We shall almost certainly lose,' he said, 'simply because our chief witness is now six feet under the ground. If she were still alive, it would never have been brought to court.'

In the days and weeks that followed the arrival of Mr Patino's writ, during October 1953, I went on working in the usual way, writing columns and travelling hither and thither, and all thoughts of the brief interlude in Paris faded from my mind. Jimmy Goldsmith had said at dinner in Paris on the last night that I had seen him that if Mr Patino continued his implacable opposition to the marriage, he, Jimmy, would elope to Israel with Isabel; if I thought about the matter at all during those following weeks, it would have been to suppose that I would wake up one morning and read in the papers that young James Goldsmith had eloped to the land of his fathers with the heiress daughter of a Bolivian mining tycoon. Privately I wished them luck, but professionally I had no interest whatever in the matter. It would be an item for the gossip columns. Or so I thought.

It was just over two months later, on 9 December, that the telephone rang in my study at home and I heard the voice of Mike Mordaunt-Smith on the line. 'I'm ringing from Jimmy Goldsmith's flat in Paris,' he said, 'and I thought I had better let you know that things are hotting up here, and we may need some help. Papa Patino sent Isabel off abroad somewhere this morning – we don't know where – and his lawyers have been to see Jimmy demanding a signed undertaking that he will not try to find her. Of course Jimmy refused. He was hopping mad. He is here at the moment, and I can tell you that few caged tigers have ever paced up and down as much as Jimmy is doing right now. Poor Jimmy is frantic with rage and anxiety. Patino has sent old Princess Windisch-Graetz with Isabel to ensure that she does not try to telephone Jimmy and tell him where she is. Jimmy is determined to find her and marry her as soon as possible, whatever the obstacles. The fact is, old boy, strictly between ourselves, Isabel is pregnant.'

This was a fact that I never at any time revealed to anyone; but it obviously put a different complexion on the matter entirely: I knew enough about French law to realize that if Jimmy now found Isabel and took her away from her appointed guardian, Mr Patino could slap a writ on him for *détournement de jeunesse* or *détournement de mineur* – Isabel was still a minor under French law – and this could be very serious, because it was a crime that could carry a prison sentence. Overnight the story would cease to be a gossip column paragraph and become an international *cause célèbre*.

'Give Jimmy my regards and tell him that if there is anything I can do to help, he can count on me,' I said. 'Tell him to take care, too, because he is up against a powerful and ruthless enemy.'

'Thanks, old boy,' said Mike. 'I'll keep you in touch.'

I debated with myself whether I should tell the *Daily Mirror* anything about the story that seemed likely to break soon, but decided against it: although I have been a newspaperman all my life, I have never trusted newspapers.

Two days later Mike rang me from Paris again. 'Isabel is in Casablanca,' he said. 'Jimmy had a scribbled note in the post from her this morning, asking him to go there quickly. He telephoned Croydon Aerodrome right away and chartered a de Havilland Dart for £1,000. It is being flown over to land at Le Bourget this evening, and will fly Jimmy straight down to Morocco. Digby Neave and John Train are going with him. I am staying here in Paris to look after this end. Isabel is a clever girl. She told Jimmy in her note that she had managed to slip out and get a British visa stamped on her passport.'

'Wish them good luck and keep me in touch,' I said. This was clearly brewing up into a story with explosive potential.

At eight o'clock next morning Mike rang again. 'You wouldn't believe what has happened,' he said. 'Jimmy managed to get a message taken to Isabel's hotel in Casablanca yesterday, telling her to put on as many warm clothes as possible and be at the airport at dawn, where he would pick her up in his chartered aircraft. But the message was intercepted by one of Mr Patino's spies, and as soon as old man Patino heard about it he commanded that she should be brought back to Paris immediately. So Princess Windisch-Graetz bundled her on to a Comet bound for Paris right away.

'Now listen to what happened next. Jimmy's chartered plane had to wait for clearance to take off from Le Bourget last night because a Comet was coming in to land. As soon as the Comet landed, Jimmy's plane took off. But Isabel was on that Comet! She was actually walking across the tarmac to the arrival gate while Jimmy's plane was revving up for take-off.'

'Where is she now?' I asked.

'In her father's house. She has just telephoned me. They think she is sleeping after the journey and all the excitement. I checked that she still had her passport in her handbag, so I am going over there now in a taxi, because Isabel is going to try to slip out. If she makes it, I will take her straight to the airport and try to smuggle her out of France before the balloon goes up in the Patino household and they discover she is missing.'

'Where will you take her?' I asked.

'To London, of course. There is nowhere else she can go. She has a Bolivian passport with a visa for Britain on it, but strictly speaking she cannot leave French territory without an exit permit, so we are going to need a lot of luck. As soon as Mr Patino finds that she has run away he will have every port of exit closed to her, so it will be tricky timing.'

'You can't leave her in a hotel in London,' I said. 'She would be discovered within hours. You had better bring her here to my house. Ring me from the airport in Paris and I will meet you with the car at Heathrow. My wife will look after her until we can get hold of Jimmy and tell him where she is.'

Luck was on their side. Isabel managed to slip out of the house unobserved, Mike was waiting up the road in a taxi, they drove straight to the airport where Mike bought a couple of tickets to London in false names on a flight that was just about to leave and within hours they were sitting in front of the fire in our drawing room. Isabel was shivering and it was not only because of the weather: the poor girl was terrified.

Mike and I went off to my study and set about making several telephone calls to Casablanca, where I had made a number of good acquaintances on previous visits, asking them to try to locate Jimmy Goldsmith and tell him to ring me at home in London. The plan worked. We were sitting at dinner that night when Jimmy came through.

'Noel,' he shouted. 'Isabel's in Paris.'

'No she's not,' I said. 'She's here.'

'Where?'

'At our house in London.'

Jimmy gave a wild whoop of joy. 'Marvellous!' he cried. 'Oh, what a relief. I cannot tell you what wonderful news that is – I've been worried out of my mind since I discovered that she was no longer in the hotel here. We have only just found out that she had been taken back to Paris. Please keep her there until I can join you in London. I will set off back right away – we had a terrible journey here, had to re-fuel at Bordeaux and at Madrid, so it will take me a little time, but I will be as quick as I can. Is she all right?'

'Hang on a moment,' I said, 'and you can have a word with her.'

Isabel had left her father's house in Paris with nothing except the clothes that she was wearing, a twin-set and pearls and a half-length coat of ocelot fur; so next morning my wife took her out to the shops to buy a few things that she needed. Soon after they returned, one of the shops telephoned to say that the young lady who had been in with Mrs Whitcomb to buy some stockings, had dropped a necklace, and they had put it in the safe for her in case it was valuable. I went to collect it. It was Isabel's pearl necklace, worth some £50,000.

Jimmy arrived towards early evening, unshaven, clearly very tired, but full of excitement and delight at seeing Isabel again. He had decided not to stay overnight, but to take Isabel away immediately and head for Scotland; his lawyers had discovered that in Scotland it was legal for people over sixteen to marry after fifteen days' residence and a further seven days of published banns. So, after reaching Scotland, provided they could stay in hiding for the next twenty-two days, they could legally be married and then there would be nothing that anyone could do about it.

I telephoned a reliable hire-car driver, who could be relied on to keep his mouth shut; he quickly arrived in a Rolls Royce and they set off, heading north.

It was clear to me that when the story broke, as it inevitably would during the ensuing month, it would be a very hot potato indeed; even today, as I write, the elopement to Scotland of a beautiful eighteen-year-old Bolivian heiress to millions with a twenty-year-old Etonian who had the reputation of being a playboy, would receive considerable notice in the newspapers; in 1953, when the attitude of the general public towards every aspect of such an escapade was so extraordinarily different, the story was a ticking bomb. As I saw it, I had an obligation towards my new young friends to protect them as far as possible from the added difficulties that would arise for them if the press got hold of their story too soon; but on the other hand I had a duty towards the *Daily Mirror* to ensure that the *Mirror* would be streets ahead of all the other papers when the story eventually broke.

Undoubtedly Mr Patino would be searching for his daughter, but I guessed that he would do this as quietly as possible, taking every precaution to prevent the newspapers from hearing of his search. If that guess were accurate, and if he did not discover Isabel's whereabouts during the next fifteen days, it would be only on the sixteenth day, when banns for the marriage had to be published in Scotland, that he would find out where Isabel was. I had no doubt at all that he would find out about the banns within hours of their being published. So once again I decided to wait and see what happened, telling nobody, but taking precautions to make sure that I would know if Mr Patino arrived in Britain. I ringed in red the date 29 December in my diary, which was the date on which the banns would have to be published in Scotland, and then set about having a happy Christmas with my family at home.

On 29 December I telephoned an old friend of mine in Edinburgh, not a journalist, and asked him to check for me what notices of marriage had been published in Edinburgh that day. He rang me back with a list that included the names of James Michael Goldsmith, bachelor, hotelier, of 14 Drylaw Crescent, Blackhall, and Isabel Patino, spinster, of 14 Church Hill, Edinburgh. That announcement could not possibly go unnoticed for long. So I wrote a confidential memorandum of seven pages to the editor of the *Daily Mirror*, outlining the details of the affair, pointing out that it would not be in the newspaper's interest to break the story until I gave the go-ahead, and promising that if they sat tight and awaited developments I would ensure that the *Mirror* had the inside track when the race started. I took this memorandum into the office personally, and it caused the sort of stir that I had anticipated. Only a handful of senior editorial executives were allowed to read it, and one or two of them were in favour of breaking the story right away, but the rest realized that the whole thing could blow up in their faces unless they took care, and they had no option but to trust me, and do it my way; so, with difficulty, they controlled their impatience.

In fact it was not until Sunday, 3 January, that I received the news that I had been expecting. The hall porter of one of London's biggest hotels, the former valet of a friend of mine, telephoned me. 'Mr Noel,' he said, 'you asked me to let you know if Senor Patino from Paris came into the hotel. Well, he checked in this morning. But he is not staying here – he is off to Scotland. I have just booked him on the night train to Edinburgh, tonight.'

So the chase was on. The secret was out. All the newspapers would soon be running the story that Mr Patino was bound for Scotland in search of his daughter. But the *Daily Mirror* would have the whole story, the full story with the background detail, first. I sat down and wrote it, leaving out all mention of my own connection with it, and telephoned it to the *Mirror*, together with a brief memo to the editor telling him that I was on my way to Scotland and would be in touch from there with follow-up material. Then I, too, caught the night sleeper to Edinburgh.

When I arrived there next morning I bought all the daily newspapers and discovered that the *Mirror* was the only one that carried no mention of the story at all. All the other nationals had small items announcing the bare fact that a rich Bolivian called Antenor Patino was on his way to Scotland in search of his runaway daughter. This did not surprise me. All Fleet Street newspapers in those days had spies in the camp of every other national paper, and this meant that a copy of the first edition of every newspaper was secretly rushed to the offices of all the other papers as soon as it was off the presses; any newspaper that had a big scoop would be milked by all the others, who would shamelessly rewrite the story for inclusion in their own later editions, thereby aborting the scoop of the originating paper. The *Mirror*, with its enormous print-run of five million copies in London alone (it did not then print in Manchester), started printing earlier than most of the other nationals and was therefore particularly vulnerable to this barefaced robbery technique; when the *Mirror* had a really big story all to itself, it would hold it until the later editions, when it was too late for its rivals to steal the story.

This is what the *Mirror* had done the previous night. Its later editions carried the story all over the front page and the back page: HEIRESS ELOPES – ALL-NIGHT DASH BY MILLIONAIRE FATHER screamed the headline. The *Mirror* had wiped everyone's eye, much to the fury of all the other papers.

I went straight to the Caledonian Hotel and took a room there, having first established that this was where Mr Patino would be staying. Then I went for a walk and took a room at another hotel as well, booking it in the name of Mr Bernard, my middle Christian name; then I visited an old friend in the city and arranged for him to hire a self-drive car in his name and hand it over to me. These George-Smiley-type precautions sound absurdly over-dramatic, but it must be remembered that my face at the time was one of the most readily recognizable faces in the country, because a photograph or a drawing of it appeared on my column at least three times a week in a paper that was read by fourteen million people; newspaper columnists of my kind were treated as film stars, and were frequently stopped in the street for autographs. So what I needed in Edinburgh was as much anonymity as I could get, because I knew that as soon as the other newspapers saw the *Mirror* story they would put two and two together and quickly guess that I had been responsible for it, even though the *Mirror* had sensibly honoured my request to leave my name off it; they would then tell their reporters to

198

follow me as well as Mr Patino, in the hope that I would lead them to the elusive young couple. Which I had no intention of doing.

Jimmy Goldsmith had left me the names of two lawyers in Scotland whom he had engaged to advise him, Iain Smith and James Mounsey. I telephoned James Mounsey and told him where I could be contacted if any help was needed. 'I think we are going to need all the help we can get,' he said, 'judging by the way things are going at the moment. Jimmy was staying with me here, at my house, until 29 December, and Isabel was staying with my friend Charles Sinclair and his wife nearby. But after they completed their residential qualification, and the notice had been posted in Coates Terrace that any valid objection to their marriage must be lodged within seven days, I advised them to seek shelter in some part of Scotland where they would be less easily located. Truthfully, I do not know where they are at the moment, and do not wish to know for the time being. Jimmy will contact me when it is necessary. As far as I can see there is nothing in Scottish law to stop them getting married after 10 a.m. on Wednesday, and there are two hundred registrars in Scotland who could perform the ceremony, provided they have the licence with them. It may possibly be that getting the licence to them without attracting too much attention may be the difficulty, but Jimmy suggested to me before he left that you might be able to help with that.'

'Certainly,' I agreed. 'You can count on me. But knowing what I do about Mr Patino, I doubt if that is likely to be the only difficulty. I will keep in touch with you.'

That day in Edinburgh there began the most astonishing media circus that I have ever witnessed in the whole of my career, and I have seen a fair few. Reporters and photographers began to pour in from all over Europe, all battling for any scrap of news they could find about the runaway couple. Soon there were hundreds of them, all searching Scotland from their base at the Caledonian Hotel, checking in every hotel, poking into every boarding house, fighting each other, bugging each other's telephone calls, spending mountains of money and becoming more and more frantic as they found less and less information. What happened during that week in Edinburgh is hard to believe today – too comic to be true; but while it was in progress, a *Daily Mirror* reporter called Norman Martlew was making detailed notes of what went on, and when it was all over he gave me a copy. I have it before me now. It is a period piece, written in the breathless, short sentence, Hemingway-pastiche style that was affected by many of us who worked on tabloids at the time, and using a method of punctuation almost as reliant upon dots and dashes as Morse Code.

The reporter in Martlew's narrative is portrayed as the anti-hero, in the manner of the private eye as depicted by Raymond Chandler, a loyal, hard-working, underpaid employee, indestructably honest, who uncomplainingly allows himself to be subjected to hardships that would break the spirit of an Arctic explorer, but who battles on through pain and adversity in selfless dedication to the paper. To some degree we all had this sympathy-seeking approach at the time, and it arose from the welfare-state mentality which was already entrenched in Britain in 1953 and which continued for the next three decades during which the unionized workers saw themselves as being cavalierly forced to bite the bullet.

Martlew's account of what happened in Scotland during the Goldsmith elopement, apart from being complementary to mine because we saw it from different vantage points, shines an interesting sidelight on the gangsterish way in which newspapers behaved then and the cut-throat behaviour they encouraged in their editorial staff when working on a big story: this cynical approach of newspaper managements to questions of morality in news-gathering and journalistic codes of conduct has not changed fundamentally during this century, although the rising clamour of outraged public opinion has forced most newspapers to pay lip-service to the achievement of higher standards; indeed, the oldest and most dubious news-eliciting technique of all, which requires the use by the reporter of the iron fist in the velvet glove, is still frequently apparent even to the unpractised eye in television news interviews. News-gathering is never likely to become an occupation for shy violets with tender hearts. By its nature it is red in tooth and claw. To put it mildly, it is no trade for a gentleman.

Martlew titled his report THE PATINO STORY, and I will quote extracts from it to set the scene. He began like this:

This is the story of a story . . . it is incomplete; yet from a reporter's point of view it still holds fascination.

It is a story told by the men and women of the *Mirror* . . . the story of a love affair between a boy named Jimmy and a girl named Isabel, and, on the other hand, of the girl's father, Senor Patino, a rich man. A story of a colleague who reached new glory because of the love affair – Noel Whitcomb.

But, hell, it's the story of some ordinary boys and girls called *Daily Mirror* Reporters.

The TEAM from the *Mirror* was there!

Then Martlew goes on to describe the electrified and fizzing atmosphere that began to crackle inside the *Daily Mirror* after I delivered my seven-page memorandum, although neither he nor any of the other reporters knew at the time that the memorandum was the reason for the excitement. They all thought somebody was going to be fired. He tells his story well, every sentence bitten off and spat out like a Texas cowboy with a five-cent cigar. He captures the cops 'n' robbers atmosphere in a style of writing that has its raincoat collar turned up and the brim of its grey fedora pulled well down over the eyes – the Lemmy Caution school of journalism. 'Now and again Noel Whitcomb came in. Even his carnation was wilting. But he didn't slot into things. Something big was happening. Something real big.'

Senior executives of the paper moved into huddles, whispering, but nobody else could discover what the tense excitement was about. Until the Sunday when I sent to the editor the story that Don Antenor Patino was at last on the move, and that I was tailing him on the night train to Edinburgh. Then the balloon went up.

Reporters and photographers were being dispatched with great urgency, not only to Scotland but also to Paris and any other place where background or clues to the runaway couple might be found. Martlew himself was sent on a particularly wild goose chase to a place called Brightlingsea in Essex, where Iain Smith, one of Jimmy Goldsmith's two lawyers, had been staying. Missed him. Just left. Catching the night train to Scotland. Martlew hurtled through the stormy night and scrambled aboard the train as it was moving off.

When he arrived in Edinburgh he checked in at the Caledonian Hotel and picked up a message that most of the rest of the *Mirror*'s editorial staff were rushing on their way to join him there. Tired and baffled, he sat down to breakfast. His narrative continues thus:

At 9.30 Whitcomb arrived in the dining room to join Martlew's breakfast. Noel is sore. 'I don't think it is of much help all you reporters and photographers coming up here,' said Noel. A great welcome for an ordinary reporter. After taking all that punishment. Noel swallowed a sausage. 'I don't know where the couple are now,' he said. 'Nobody knows. But as soon as I find out I shall disappear for two days. I shall see no one around here. I shall not speak to the office.'

Then up came a fellow with a wad of black hair and he said, 'Good morning, Your Highness.' He bowed to Noel. He was Mike

Mordaunt-Smith, Jimmy Goldsmith's mate, Noel's mate . . . the marriage-maker.

At 10 a.m. Noel and Mike went out of the hotel for a conference with Mr Iain Smith. He'd arrived. That was the last they saw of Noel until late Thursday night. He kept his promise. In fact they didn't see him for four days. What Noel thought when he heard that still more *Mirror* boys and girls were arriving is terrible to think.

Martlew's wryly ironic reference to me at this point was highly understandable because they were all having a terrible time except me, and in the fiercely competitive world of Fleet Street it was hardly surprising that nobody would have wept too bitterly if I had broken a leg; furthermore none of them knew what was happening and they suspected – rightly – that I did know what was going on, and the feeling of frustration that this caused them did nothing to increase my popularity.

By midday on that Monday the Caledonian Hotel began to be invaded by what Martlew called 'the most memorable army of pressmen ever to gather under one roof'. They swarmed in not only from Britain but also from all over Europe and the United States. They started by bribing the hotel staff with fistfuls of notes. But they got nowhere – no news. They bugged each other's telephones. They drank and they fought until the hotel management threatened to clear out the lot of them.

They knew that Jimmy and Isabel were somewhere in Scotland, but they had no idea where. They knew that Mr Patino was occupying most of the first floor of the hotel, with his army of lawyers, but they could not get near the first floor because it was sealed off and guarded at every entry point. The only other thing they knew was that the London editions of the *Daily Mirror* had carried what Martlew called 'a screaming splash on the Patino affair', leaving every other paper floundering.

Although the growing regiment of *Mirror* reporters and photographers in Edinburgh knew that this story had come from me, nobody else knew it because there had been no byline on the story. So all the troops of Midian who did prowl and prowl around from all the other papers turned their attention to the *Daily Mirror* mob and followed them wherever they went. They had no other leads to follow.

Martlew describes it like this:

Martlew went to the register office in a big Humber. So did twenty other reporters. Mortars was casing a hotel exit. So were twenty

202

other reporters. Craig cased another exit. Twenty reporters from other papers watched Craig. Mary Malone went to powder her nose and half the women reporters in Fleet Street followed her into the Ladies . . .

Into the night the vigil stuck. Rupert and Dave, blue with cold, casing the hotel. With them Denny and Jock and Freddie. Blue with cold. No food, no drink. They could not leave the place because they knew Papa Patino was playing smart. They were the ordinary boys on the job. The team. They were opposed not only by the hotel staff, Patino, and the couple, but by hundreds of pressmen who were ganging up on them . . . anything to break down the cold, shivering Mirrorites. Where the hell was Noel?

No one knows where the couple are. A thousand and one pressmen had done the rounds . . . solicitors, register offices, hotels, boarding houses, friends of the couple, police, airlines, hire-car operators, coach firms, railway booking offices, restaurants, pubs, clubs, private eyes, law courts, consulates, marriage-guidance councils, private photographers, banqueteers, Moss Bros. Nothing. Not a line.

That magnificent chaos continued for two days during which more and more aircraft landed with more and more pressmen arriving from London and the Continent and another battalion from the USA. They all fell in and followed the *Mirror* squad, like Mary's little lamb – whithersoever thou goest . . .

Then at last a news story exploded. Martlew calls it a bombshell. Mr Patino gained an injunction preventing the wedding from taking place next day. Such a judgement had never before been recorded in Scottish legal history. The judge sat to hear Mr Patino's petition at 11 a.m. on the Tuesday in the registrar general's office. He granted an injunction. The hearing was in open court but not one single reporter was present, although any of the hundreds who were scouring Edinburgh could have walked in if they had been smart enough.

Norman Martlew's account of the frenetic goings-on among the turbulent tide of newspapermen in Scotland continues in a rising key of hysteria for page after page. Journalists from other newspapers tried to bribe the *Mirror* staff for information, offering them enormous sums for crumbs of information, which infuriated the *Mirror* reporters to an almost unbearable degree because – although they were not admitting it – they did not have any information to sell; a *Daily Mirror* aircraft arrived at the local airport and was met by the throng of international press representatives that would normally gather for the arrival of a head of state – but only one *Mirror* photographer stepped out of the aircraft. So many contrivances and forms of bribery among telephone-exchange employees were tried for the purpose of intercepting or listening to *Daily Mirror* telephone calls that the senior executives in the *Mirror*'s London office devised intricate codes for use by staff in Edinburgh, which resulted in heightened confusion and chaos; and it was not only in Edinburgh that these Keystone Cops antics were going on, because cohorts of pressmen fanned out throughout the whole of Scotland in their search: all to no avail.

Towards the end of Norman Martlew's narrative he is under the impression that I had missed the big story that was the climax of the affair, and it would be understandable if that thought did not cause him too much anguish, because from his point of view and the viewpoint of all his colleagues I had been the cause of all the trials and tribulations that had afflicted the *Mirror* team during the preceding five days. The first story I had sent the *Mirror* concerning the Goldsmith elopement, which had been published on the Monday, had been bylined, 'From *Daily Mirror* Reporters, Edinburgh, Sunday' and although there was not a single *Daily Mirror* reporter in Edinburgh on that particular Sunday – not even myself, because I telephoned the story from London and did not arrive in Edinburgh until the Monday morning on the overnight train – it was this byline that led the rest of the press to persecute my colleagues under the impression that they knew what was happening. In fact, of course, they never at any time knew any more than their rivals; apart from the details of Mr Patino's legal struggle to prevent his daughter's marriage, which unavoidably became public knowledge, nobody knew what was going on except Jimmy and Isabel, Jimmy's lawyers, Mike Mordaunt-Smith and me.

At the climactic peak upon which Norman Martlew ends his tortured tale I was sitting quietly in my room in a house on the outskirts of Edinburgh (shades of Pappenhacker!) typing out the story that was to be the third and by far the biggest world-scoop printed by the *Daily Mirror* during that week.

Factually, here is an account of what went on, unknown to the hordes of pressmen in Edinburgh, during the five days when the story was in the headlines.

When Mr Patino arrived in Edinburgh on Monday, 4 January, he was already aware that his chances of preventing his daughter from marrying Jimmy Goldsmith in Scotland on the Wednesday were slim. He had heard about the banns soon after they had been posted on 29 December, and had spent the next four days consulting lawyers from

Paris, London and Edinburgh concerning ways in which the marriage might be prevented; the advice he received was that there was no precedent in Scottish law for stopping the marriage by legal process, although it was possible that it might be delayed.

This meant that his only serious chance of achieving his object was to persuade his estranged wife, with whom he had been at loggerheads in European courts for several years past and who was seeking from him a divorce that he was unwilling to give her, to go to Scotland with him and play on Isabel's very real love for her mother; he knew that his own appeals would continue to fall on deaf ears. This was a strategy he hated, because he bitterly disliked his wife, but he had no other option. So his lawyers, some thirty of whom were working on the affair by that time, contacted the Duchess of Durcal, and she, because of her love for her daughter and her belief that it would be a mistake for Isabel to marry a Jewish boy in trade, agreed to go to Edinburgh with her husband and put on a front to the world as though they were a united family.

One vital ingredient of this plan was that it should be carried out with as much secrecy as possible; any leak to the press before the Patino lawyers had found Isabel and arranged a meeting with her mother could seriously complicate matters. On the Monday when the Patinos arrived in Edinburgh, private detectives engaged by their lawyers had already been scouring Scotland for four days in search of the runaway couple.

The appearance of my story in the London editions of the *Daily Mirror* on that Monday was therefore a hindrance because it destroyed the secrecy element of the plan; it meant that the search for Isabel would now be joined by hundreds of chaotically stampeding pressmen from all over Europe, and that the Patino campaign would henceforth be conducted in the glare of unwelcome publicity; but it did not change the strategy.

Realizing this, I decided to go to ground for a couple of days, and leave the coverage of Mr Patino's legal injunction – which was never more than a delaying tactic – to my colleagues in Edinburgh; it was only fair, because this was the only news throughout the whole affair that they or their rivals managed to lay their hands on.

Mike Mordaunt-Smith was already in Edinburgh on the Monday morning when I arrived there on the same overnight train from London that Mr Patino had caught. After our breakfast as described by Norman Martlew, who had also arrived in Edinburgh that morning on the same train – although rather less comfortably according to his account of the journey – Mike and I went to see Iain Smith, Jimmy's Goldsmith's lawyer, who had also arrived from the south that morning on the same popular train.

Iain Smith, in full agreement with my contention that it was important for me to lie low and remain out of sight, cancelled the small-hotel room that I had booked earlier that morning under the pseudonym of Mr Bernard and arranged for Mike Mordaunt-Smith and myself to have rooms in a safe house four miles away from the centre of the city.

This was Prestonfield House, a fine old country mansion tucked away discreetly in its own extensive grounds; it had been owned by the Dick-Cunyngham family from the early 1600s, but at the time we went there it was being run as a guest-house by a former Life Guards officer called Roddie Oliver. It was the ideal place for us as a hideout, and indeed it had been used for a similarly clandestine purpose in the past: hanging on the wall of the dining room was a framed receipt for 100 guineas from Bonnie Prince Charlie, in payment for the time he had spent in hiding there after his defeat at Culloden.

My task for the rest of that day – in sharp contrast to the tasks of Norman Martlew and my other colleagues – was to sit in front of a big log fire in the Tapestry Room reading a book, while Mike Mordaunt-Smith stayed in contact with Jimmy Goldsmith's lawyers, monitoring events.

Iain Smith had told us that, after the banns had been posted in Edinburgh on 29 December, he had placed his Standard Vanguard car at the disposal of Jimmy and Isabel, and had advised them to disappear until Tuesday, 5 January, which was the day before their wedding could take place under Scottish law. He had advised Jimmy not even to contact him by telephone until the Tuesday, unless he was hunted down by the Patino agents before then. Mike Mordaunt-Smith and I had arrived at Prestonfield House on the Monday, so we expected no activity on the Goldsmith front until the morrow.

Following Iain Smith's advice, and having nowhere particular to go during the last lap of their waiting, Jimmy and Isabel had set out on a holiday tour of the Highlands. They stayed at big hotels, signing their own names in the hotel registers and making no attempt at concealment. They continued to do this from 29 December onwards, throughout the days when squads of Mr Patino's private detectives and hordes of rampaging pressmen were scouring Scotland for them.

Technically speaking, they should not have been difficult to trace. One experienced private detective sitting at a telephone and ringing round the big hotels of Scotland should have found them within hours.

But none of them did. As far as the press was concerned, as has always been customary on this type of stampede, more drinking than thinking was done; most of the pressmen were staying at the Caledonian Hotel in Edinburgh, and as they were all residents the drinking went on legally round the clock; I would be surprised if there has ever been a week in the long history of the Caledonian Hotel during which it has sold more liquor. In their frustration at finding no news of any consequence apart from the legal proceedings, most of the reporters spent much of their time talking among themselves, watching their rivals, and seeking to bribe anyone in sight who might possibly know anything. For the hotel staff, showered with largesse, it was Christmas.

Jimmy Goldsmith abided by the instructions of his lawyers and did not telephone Iain Smith until the Tuesday. Smith, by this time aware of the injunction that Mr Patino had obtained much to the surprise of Scottish lawyers, decided that it was time for Jimmy and Isabel to seek a safer haven, so he told Jimmy to go to a place called Blair Adam, home of a friend called Captain Adam, DSO, RN, from which Mike Mordaunt-Smith and I would collect him the following day.

I had not been in contact with the *Daily Mirror* in London nor with any of its staff in Edinburgh since the Tuesday morning, but when I received Iain Smith's message that Mike and I were to pick up the young couple on the following day, I decided that it would be only fair to the *Mirror* to let them have the first and only exclusive picture of Jimmy and Isabel in Scotland; but I had no camera with me, of course, and, being no sort of photographer, the only camera that I knew how to use was the camera I had at home, a 35mm Leica. So I strolled out of the grounds to a telephone box and rang the *Mirror* in London, asking them to arrange for Freddie Reed, the photographer, an utterly reliable old friend of mine, to meet me at a given spot in Edinburgh that night and hand over a Leica to me. They eagerly agreed.

Naturally I had chosen, for the meeting with Freddie, a spot in Edinburgh that I thought would be unfrequented. I parked my hired car in a dark place, and walked round the corner to the agreed meeting place. Freddie was there. He handed me the camera, spent a few minutes making sure that I knew how to use it, and then departed. I walked back towards the car, but as I rounded the corner I ran smack into four reporters, who immediately recognized me. They were, not surprisingly, clearly very angry with me. They saw me as one of the major causes of all the harassing troubles that had been causing them to run round in circles. One of them was a *Mirror* reporter. His eyes were blazing with fury. 'We'll teach you a lesson, you bastard,' he shouted, and, lurching forward, he took a swing at me. He was a stocky man with a beer belly, by no means athletic, and when he came for me I had plenty of time to duck under his fist and give him a sharp jab in the solar plexus, just hard enough to double him up. But in doing so I dropped the camera. Grabbing it from the pavement while the three other reporters held up my howling colleague, I ran to the car, jumped in and drove off.

This incident had two effects: the camera would not work and my hired car was now recognizable. There was no time or opportunity to change the car, so I had to take a chance on that; and there was no time to get another camera, so I had to take another chance: I stopped at a call box and rang Freddie Reed at the Caledonian. He had just got back. I asked him to go out to a callbox and ring me on the number of the callbox in which I was standing. He did that, and I asked him to go on the following day to Blair Adam, making sure that he was not tailed, and wait for me there at a given time with his camera ready. That was how the *Mirror* obtained their first world-scoop picture, which was later rushed by Arthur Sidey to the waiting plane at the airport, Arthur in a plain van that was followed by a cavalcade of cars containing pressmen.

Next morning, the Wednesday, Mike and I set out soon after 5 a.m. in my hired car, having decided on the early start so that we could travel in darkness for most of the way to Blair Adam; the roads were icy as we drove out through Dunfermline and Cowdenbeath, but we made good time. Blair Adam was a romantic old house concealed in the mountains, and as we drove up a muddy cart track towards the house we saw, parked strategically beside the track, the Standard Vanguard that everyone in Edinburgh was seeking. Jimmy and Isabel were in it. Jimmy signalled to me to keep going and both cars headed up the track for the house. Freddie Reed was waiting there and took pictures of all of us as we stepped out of the cars and gathered in the drive.

'We have been traced here,' said Jimmy, calmly. 'I doubt if we have much time. Let's get going.'

We could see the road for a long distance below us, so I left Freddie to keep an eye on the road and shout if he saw any cars approaching, and went into the house with Captain Adam to arrange a small precaution: I telephoned to a hotel in Loch Awe, far away in the west of Scotland, and booked two rooms there in the names of Goldsmith and Patino. On the scribbling pad beside the telephone I wrote the telephone number of the hotel, surrounding it with squiggled doodles. Then I explained to the enthusiastic Captain Adam and his wife that this was intended to leave a false trail, and asked him to allow any pressmen who arrived to use that telephone.

Then, leaving one of the servants to park the Vanguard in a locked barn, we all set off very fast indeed in my hired car, Mike in the front with me, and Jimmy and Isabel in the back.

Along the narrow roads that wound over the purple hills and through the glens of the wild moorland country, we made a forty-mile detour to avoid going through Edinburgh, and arrived safely at Prestonfield House unnoticed by anyone on the journey except for a rural postman who had stood in the road in front of the car on a hilltop, flagging us down and forcing me to pull up; but all he wanted was to know whether we had seen a grey horse that had strayed.

As soon as we were in the house I telephoned Captain Adam at Blair Adam to find out if anything had happened, and he was chuckling with amusement. 'Within fifteen minutes of your departure,' he said, 'an enormous fleet of press cars began gathering in the drive. They were all asking, of course, whether the young couple were here, and I told them that they had been, but had left some time ago. Then they wanted to telephone to their offices, and the first one who went to the telephone saw the number that you had left on the pad. He rang that first, just in case, and when he put the telephone down he let out a whoop of triumph. All the others realized that he must have a clue, so when he rushed out to his car they all followed, and they swarmed down into the glen like a pack of foxhounds on the scent.'

Later I telephoned the hotel in Loch Awe to cancel the two rooms I had booked, and the receptionist was surrounded by such turmoil that she could hardly hear me. 'I don't know quite what's happening here,' she said in a precise Edinburgh accent, 'but we have an invasion going on at the moment. Every newspaper that I have ever heard of, and some that I have never heard of, has representatives here, and they have descended on us like a plague of locusts. Already, I am sorry to say, we have had to send for further supplies of whisky.'

So all was going according to plan. We all spent the evening quietly. After dinner we sat in the Tapestry Room. Isabel, still wearing the clothes in which she had left my house in London three weeks before, was reading a book called *Desirée* by Annemarie Selinke, the story of a rich businessman's daughter who became the mistress of Napoleon; Jimmy was reading Bertie Russell's *History of Western Philosophy*; Mike and I played chess. Towards midnight we had a telephone call from Jimmy's lawyers to the effect that Mr Patino had offered to withdraw his objection to the wedding if Isabel would agree to meet her mother before any ceremony took place.

Isabel agreed eagerly. 'It has hurt me terribly to know how anxious and distressed Mummy must have been,' she said, 'so I would love to meet her tomorrow. But I think she should know beforehand that nothing she can say will change my mind.'

A meeting in secrecy was arranged between Isabel and her mother to take place on the following day, and we all went off to bed feeling more hopeful than we had felt for a long time. The family problems were melting like ice in the sun; but the problems of the pursuing press still remained: Jimmy wanted a quiet wedding.

Next morning, Thursday, all the newspapers were in the dining room at breakfast time; all except the *Mirror* were still carrying the story of Mr Patino's search for the young couple. The *Mirror*, under the byline '*Daily Mirror* Reporter, Somewhere in Scotland, Wednesday', carried a front-page interview with Jimmy and Isabel, together with one of the pictures that Freddie Reed had taken at Blair Adam. EXCLUSIVE shouted the *Mirror* above the headline that read NOTHING WILL ALTER MY LOVE FOR JIMMY. And it added for good measure THE MAN FROM THE *MIRROR* WAS THERE.

Jimmy asked me, laughing, 'Aren't they ever going to reveal who The Man from the *Mirror* is?'

'Tomorrow,' I said. 'Tomorrow I shall be unmasked as the most unpopular man in Fleet Street.'

While we had all been asleep, the lawyers and the Patinos had been busy through the night. At 4.30 a.m. the night porter at the Caledonian Hotel had been told, 'Send up eight rounds of sandwiches and two pots of white coffee to Room 108.' Mr Patino and his wife ate their sandwiches and drank their coffee while they were packing their suitcases, then they were smuggled out of the hotel by the linen lift to a waiting car, and drove off into the darkness: the hotel lounge was still full of reporters, but nobody knew, nobody noticed.

Five hours later, at 9.30 a.m., in the Appeal Court in Edinburgh, Mr Graham Guest QC told the presiding judge that Mr and Mrs Patino wished to withdraw their petition objecting to their daughter's marriage. It was a formality and took only five minutes.

During the next half-hour, John Sinclair, one of the partners in the firm of lawyers representing Jimmy, with the press in full cry behind him, walked to the office of Mr W.S. Cockburn, the registrar, and collected from him the wedding licence. He returned to his office with it, and the press laid siege outside. Nobody could go into that office and come out again with the licence without being seen and followed by the press. They now knew that the wedding would take place that day, but they did not know where.

Back at Prestonfield House, we were busy solving this problem. Roddy Oliver had a rusty old green van that was normally used for taking pigs to market. We put a couple of deckchairs in it, and the bride and groom laughingly took their places in the deckchairs.

'See you in Kelso at five o'clock,' I said to Jimmy, as I shut the doors of the van and it drove off with Mike at the wheel.

Isabel's meeting with her mother was scheduled to take place, in secret of course, in Kelso during the afternoon. There was no likelihood that anyone apart from ourselves and the lawyers would get to hear of this. There was only one problem left, and that was how to arrange for the licence to be taken out of the solicitor's office in Edinburgh, and then rushed by road to Jimmy and Isabel in Kelso, without any of the watching eyes outside the office realizing that the licence had been removed from there.

I thought of the story by G.K. Chesterton in which people were watching the door to a building and swore that they had seen nobody go in or out; but the postman had been in; nobody noticed the postman. So I telephoned Jimmy's lawyers and we set up a little charade. They got in touch with their office charlady. She went in with her mop and bucket, in the usual way. But when she came out again an hour or so later, still with the mop and bucket, she also had Jimmy and Isabel's marriage licence tucked into the pocket of her overall.

Nobody took any notice of her. She walked down the street and round the corner. She passed a parked car in which a man was reading a newspaper, with his driving-side window open. As she passed, she dropped the envelope containing the licence into the car. Without even picking it up from the car floor, I drove off. Alone.

It was some forty-odd miles to Kelso, and I kept an eye on the rear mirror all the way; but the coast was clear. Hundreds of pressmen and women were still camped out on the pavement outside the solicitor's office in Edinburgh. We had all got away.

Isabel had the meeting with her mother in a solicitor's office in Kelso. When I arrived in the little granite town on the border, the first thing I did was pick up Freddie Reed, whom I had telephoned earlier telling him where to meet me. Then Freddie and I walked to the office of Mr James Mabel, the registrar, and Jimmy arrived with Isabel at the same time, spot on five o'clock, as arranged. We all went into the little brown room that was the registrar's office. I handed the wedding licence to Jimmy and he gave it to Mr Mabel, who sat down and began to write out the wedding certificate.

It was not what could be called a dressy wedding. Isabel was wearing the same twin-set and pearls that she had been wearing ever since she ran out of her father's house in Paris; Jimmy was wearing his last clean shirt, which he had saved for the occasion; the registrar was in grey flannels and a sports jacket; Freddie Reed, busy taking pictures of the ceremony and the simple scene in the little room, was the tidiest of us all. We were all very pleased that it was over.

Jimmy had decided that he and Isabel would go to the George Hotel in Edinburgh and behave normally, with no further attempt at concealment, as though nothing in particular had happened, so Mike drove them there in my hired car. I drove the pig-van back to Prestonfield. So that was the end of that.

Next morning, the *Daily Mirror* came out triumphantly with the story all over the front page, all over the back page and all over the middle two pages; my forecast to Jimmy of the previous morning had turned out to be accurate, because the front-page headline in gigantic type was ISABEL WEDS HER JIMMY AND NOEL WHITCOMB IS THERE. A quarter of the splash was taken up by Freddie Reed's world-exclusive picture of the young couple and the registrar in the little room in Kelso, signing the register. It was not merely a scoop for the *Mirror* but a complete whitewash of all the other papers. As had been said in past years of Eclipse, the incomparable racehorse, it was the *Mirror* first and the rest nowhere.

I caught the first available train home because it seemed a long time since I had seen my own wife and baby daughter. I felt satisfied about the way things had gone, happy about Jimmy and Isabel and pleased about the big show I had received in the paper. But I was far from exultant. Some niggling worm of self-criticism inside kept reminding me that this was not the sort of achievement that I had hoped for when I set out on my career to be a writer; not even the sort of story with which I had hoped to make a name when I had settled for being a journalist: it was good in its way, but the wrong way.

The *Daily Mirror* was understandably cock-a-hoop. The first three letters I opened when I went in were congratulations from Cecil King, congratulations from Hugh Cudlipp and a scribbled note from Jimmy Goldsmith, saying. 'I do not know how to thank you for your extreme kindness and understanding. Again I stress that I would not have known what to have done without you.'

For the first time, and I think probably the only time, in the *Mirror*'s history, Hugh Cudlipp wrote a bulletin for the noticeboard. Headed THE ELOPEMENT STORY, it read:

We do not normally write bulletins in Geraldine House, but I must do so today.

What a splendid week for the *Mirror* – the *Express* described the Patino-Goldsmith romance as 'The Elopement of the Century'; the *Mirror* has therefore scored the scoop of the century in this class of story.

Today's issue has never been bettered in our past. Here is journalism at its best – completely thrilling, completely satisfying, a tonic for a bitterly cold morning.

Cudlipp's bulletin went on to enumerate all the ways in which 'every other paper was pipped at the post'.

For a journalist, it was a good reference. And I was grateful to him for his generous words. But, foolishly perhaps, arrogantly some might say, I kept uneasily recalling the words from Eliot's *Love Song of J. Alfred Prufrock*:

> This is not it at all,
> That is not what I meant, at all.

11

A serious writer is not to be confounded with
a solemn writer. A serious writer may be a
hawk or a buzzard or even a popinjay, but a
solemn writer is always a bloody owl.

Ernest Hemingway, *Death in the Afternoon*

At the start of one of his novels P.G. Wodehouse soliloquizes amusingly
about how much he should tell his readers about the previous goings-on
of the characters in his book; should he, for instance, explain all about
Sir Galahad Threepwood and Lady Constance, Sir Roderick Spode and
the efficient Baxter, all of whom had appeared frequently in his
previous novels, or should he assume that the reader will merely yawn
because he knows it all.

This is a problem that besets not only great novelists but also your
run-of-the-mill Joe who is knocking out a portrait of himself as a
survivor from the Fleet Street jungle that has since fallen to developers,
because the cast of characters about whom he is writing, although
household names in their time, have become nothing but faces in a dusty
picture, their importance blurred or even obliterated by the passage of
time.

My own solution to this dilemma is to write about the people who
kept occurring in my life as if they were fictional characters in a
multi-part serial, like members of the Pickwick Club, and rely upon the
absurdity of the incidents in which they were involved to gloss over the
fact that they were real flesh-and-blood human beings who took part in
the factual occurrences I describe.

Another difficulty that confronts an old tusker who is staying on as
one of the last survivors of a dying breed and seeking by reminiscence to
recreate the atmosphere of the jungle through which he plunged is that
the period of which he writes is too recent in historical terms to have
become readily recognizable to his younger readers: the period of which
Dickens and Surtees wrote, with its horse-drawn cabs and its tall
stovepipe hats and long frock coats is recognizable even to children

today, through films and television; the period of which Agatha Christie and John Betjeman wrote, with its elegant motor cars and country houses, green lawns and 'flappers' drinking cocktails until dawn in what Scott Fitgerald called the Aspirin Age, is familiar for the same reason – it has an identifiable brand-image.

But the post-war years of the mid-1940s to the early 1960s, from the senescence of Winston Churchill to the birth of the Beatles and the dawn of the Permissive Society, do not yet have a distinctive character in the minds of people who have become adult in the closing decades of the century; it is the too-recent past, a fuzzy gap of time that has not yet assumed a personality of its own and is identifiable as a specific period of interest only by students of political and social evolution.

Yet although the visual picture of the period that we gather from clips of newsreel seen in television documentaries is not vividly different from our present world, the thought-processes of people who were living in Britain at the time were as different as a push-bike is from a Porsche. Our dominant fear of the future lay in 'the Bomb', and the seeming near-certainty of Armageddon in our time was at the root of how we behaved; now that the bomb is a political back-number, leaving only an uneasy wonderment about how we can sweep these infernal monsters under the terrestrial carpet so that they will not go off by accident in years to come and blow our grandchildren to smithereens, we have a qualitatively different worry; in the post-*glasnost* years of *perestroika* our thought-processes are conditioned not only by bewilderment about the unpredictable outcome of cataclysmic events in Eastern Europe and the ominous conundrum of South Africa but also by more subtle fears about the frail grip that life itself has on the planet that we and our forbears have been destroying in the name of technical progress, and even an unease about the nature of time itself. The scientific or pseudo-scientific programmes on television that are offered almost nightly have an unsettling effect upon the public mind and make the world a far more confusing place than it appeared to be half a century ago.

All this may seem to have little to do with the story of a man who has spent most of his life working for popular newspapers, but in fact it has because people of different generations bring a different eye, conditioned by changed thought-processes, to the newspapers they read; which means that although the types of story that the tabloids print have never greatly changed, their readers look at the newspapers with a more sophisticated or a more jaundiced eye, no longer believing or trusting anything they read but chewing the daily pabulum as a form of comic relief from the menacing tide that they nebulously fear is already lapping erosively at the very shores around them.

When I was a child some schoolmaster told me that it would be possible to get the entire population of the world on the Isle of Wight: as we had just returned from a family holiday on the island during Cowes week, this statistic impressed itself upon my mind and I imagined millions of men dressed in white trousers, striped blazers and straw boaters standing shoulder to shoulder with their wives in Liberty-print dresses while millions of their children crawled around like ants on an ant-hill building sandcastles on Ventnor beach.

Although this child's-eye view of a safe and middle-class world would bring hoots of laughter from televiewing toddlers today, accustomed as they are to seeing pictures of starving millions in a world desperately struggling with a population explosion, it is an indication of how one ordinary child pictured the world in those days, and the child is father to the man. Throughout all age-groups working people were less cynical and more naïve because Mum was still at home doing the housework, sexual behaviour had not been revolutionized by the discovery of the contraceptive pill, football was still a sport that was played for fun, pop-music did not have a political dimension and Dad was still reading the *Daily Mirror* as if it were the *Revelations of St John the Divine*.

So the superficial similarity of the period in terms of a type of civilization to the technically advanced life we lead half a century later is misleading, because the thoughts of every generation are so strongly influenced by seemingly trivial aspects of its daily life.

To give a few random examples of the trivia that affected the popular mentality in 1951, when I had been writing the column for five years: everyone in Britain still had to carry an identity card; people still queued for food such as tea, sugar, butter, bacon and confectionary; there were no supermarkets; the weekly ration of meat was to the value of a few pence per person; top-selling brands of cigarettes such as Players, Gold Flake and Woodbines were still 'under the counter' – filter tips were seldom seen and people smoked heavily without fear; drinking formidable quantities of beer was considered a sign of manliness because alcoholism was a word little known outside medical circles and drunkenness was not a matter of public concern but still a joke to laugh at.

These may seem insignificant matters but my point is that they exercised considerable influence on the thought-processes of the man on the Clapham omnibus: even the pound in his pocket had a tangentially different significance because the public attitude to money and what it must be used to buy arose from a set of values that would seem eccentric to young people today. Comparative price-statistics are never more than an indication of the normal run of inflation, but spiralling prices have consistently been a major topic of conversation in the post-war years and the amazing cheapness of yesteryear provides a nostalgic theme that never fails in its attraction. Go into any cockney pub at night and you can hear snatches of conversations such as, 'O' course, in my dad's time you could get a bottle of Scotch for twelve-and-six and a packet of Woods for tuppence,' or, 'When me and Lil first started goin' on holiday to the Costa Brava you could get one of them bloody great glasses of the local cognac fit to blow yer 'ead off for threepence – ole Lil could get pissed for a tanner in them days'; less frequently recalled is the fact that for those reading my *Mirror* column in 1951 the national average wage was just over £6 a week and even by 1960 it was still under £12, and although at that time we were still congratulating ourselves on having won the war the majority of the population was still socially and economically in chains.

Such circumstances, which in themselves are no more than minor details in the process of change and evolution, nevertheless condition the thought-processes that a population brings to the reading of its newspapers; some stories that once hit the headlines with a nationwide impact would seem commonplace to young people who are accustomed to accepting divorce and one-parent families as a norm, and cause them to wonder what all the fuss was about.

However, although the attitude that readers bring to their popular newspapers has changed, the attitude of the people who produce those tabloids has altered far less: the ingredients that they need for baking their daily cake are still contained in pots marked Greed, Hatred, Envy, Sex, Passion, Prurience, Intolerance, Xenophobia, Sudden Riches and Sudden Death; the success of any popular tabloid has always depended upon a capacity to irritate and infuriate as well as to entertain, and from time to time it must touch an exposed nerve on a tooth in the population, thereby causing a shout of outraged pain so loud that the paper's circulation benefits from the publicity surrounding the *brouhaha*; this is the main reason why privacy laws that are framed to curb the excesses of the popular press are never likely to succeed, because although tabloid proprietors and editors solemnly pretend to welcome such laws they never have any intention of allowing them to get in the way of increased circulation. Even if Parliament brought back the rope as a penalty for editors who overstepped the line, the only result would be that tabloid editors would receive extra pay as danger-money, and there would be no shortage of tabloid journalists prepared to take the risk. They rely upon atavism and merely genuflect to superficial change.

Anyone who writes for the popular press must be aware of this, unless he is a moron, and it is the endless attempt to rationalize it that causes the sublimated unease in the minds of journalists like me: we take the money and go home to a gentler world, a tidy and well-ordered world that is psychologically a million miles away from what Aldous Huxley called the moral equivalent of a slum. It is the money that sings a lullaby to the conscience; I always needed money in above-average quantity, and the *Mirror* had plenty to lavish upon journalists who served their purpose well. As I always had the freedom to avoid personal involvement with stories on the seamier side of the trade, I convinced myself that it was a fair bargain – or nearly convinced myself, but never quite.

Another reason why I stayed was moral indolence. The work I was doing was so absurdly easy and yet was so well received that there seemed no point in going to the trouble of finding out whether I might succeed in work that would present a greater challenge. Privately I was aware that this was mere casuistry, an *apologia pro vita mea* on a noticeably less exalted plane than Newman's, and that it was a line of meretricious reasoning that always sings a siren song to the intellectually lazy; but I was as cunning as old Rumpole when arguing the case for my own defence. What I kept telling myself was that there were fifty thousand other writers all beavering away, and all but a handful of them over-estimating the quality of their work. In any hundred tons of words there is never more than one ounce of fine gold – so why should I bother to join the hungry ranks of scribblers who take themselves too seriously?

At any rate, all Jesuitical cant apart, the fact remains that I never did take any chances by allowing myself to jettison a well-paid job and seek to discover whether I might be happier in the pursuit of success on a more disciplined literary plane which might have entailed comparative poverty; the maverick genie that whispered its messages in the back of my consciousness insisted that to be broke was an accident that could happen to any man, and did not necessarily alter the accustomed lifestyle, but to be poor was altogether different and completely unthinkable. And in any case I enjoyed the work during my early column days. What I did not enjoy so much was constantly being in the public spotlight, in the way that pop stars are today, to the extent that it was nearly impossible to go anywhere without being recognized and hailed as a piece of public property.

My wife found the publicity that surrounded us even more

burdensome than I did, being a far more private person than I; furthermore, over the years she came increasingly to dislike the popular tabloids and most of the people associated with them, and occasionally she urged me to take a job elsewhere. My reaction to this was to dismiss it as snobbishness of the kind that arises from a Tory Party conference as pungently as the smell of fried kippers, but secretly I realized that it arose from her belief that I was capable of earning a living in a way that would make my life happier, and that it was my own peace of mind and self-respect that she was unselfishly seeking to restore. Unlike myself, but in common with many wives whose husbands' jobs thrust the family into the limelight, she rated money fairly low in the catalogue of life's priorities, and frequently pointed out that we could manage easily on far less; but although in later years I was making as much money from dealing in the City as I was from journalism, I was reluctant to admit this to my wife, and told her – sometimes angrily – that she would find a disagreeable difference if I chucked the job: which we both knew to be untrue.

A psychologist might have little difficulty in unearthing the real reason why I hung on in Fleet Street right up to the final curtain, and left the theatre dark without applause, and perhaps this reason had something to do with a basic insecurity, a deep-rooted fear of change; but being more concerned with facts than theories, there is one thing I know for certain and this is that from the time I joined the *Daily Mirror* at ten guineas a week in the mid-1940s, to the time in the late 1970s when the paper was paying out well over £150,000 a year to cushion my life from needless discomfort and thereby ensure my continuing loyalty, I always felt that part of the money was compensation for living in a goldfish bowl.

Luckily the public memory is short, and even film stars quickly achieve anonymity when their screen appearances become less frequent. Shortly before he died James Mason told me that he had been strolling in Dublin one day when a polite but curious Irishman came up and said, 'Beg your pardon, sir, but wouldn't you be James Mason in his later years?'

Columnists fade even more quickly than actors; there is something in the chemistry of a daily newspaper column which ensures that it blooms for a day and then forever dies, like the cistus or rock rose; columns written for periodicals, even weeklies, can survive for generations, and lustrous names such as Addison, Steele, Hazlitt, Swift, Lamb and even Chesterton have used the form with enduring success, but it is intrinsic in the daily medium that today's newspaper is tomorrow's wrapper for fish and chips; it is the nature of the beast.

Much of the writing that appeared on news pages during the post-war decade would bear comparison with the best journalism of any era, because cramped space in smaller newspapers ordained that it must be crisper and more simply phrased; some of the feature articles and columns would now sound as stilted as the voice on a *Pathé Gazette* newsreel and as stylized as the acting of the *Comédie Française*, but that is not among the reasons why no samples of my early prose appear in these pages – I am no Orpheus fearing to look back: my reason is purely practical because I find that when others among the thundering herd of memoir-writing journalists in whose dust-cloud I gallop across the well-trampled Fleet Street veldt reproduce their past work in books, those are the passages I feel it safe to skip.

There was an enormous amount of excellent, skilled and honest work done in Fleet Street, and naturally I have a professional respect for that, but I have never been able to feel starry-eyed about the place itself or maudlin about its demise; publicly kissing the street goodbye with all the theatrical business of Pope John Paul II descending from an aircraft is not for me.

The most I can hope to do is attempt to paint in words an impressionist picture of the Fleet Street circus in the days when I toured with it, describing the ringmasters and the high-wire acts, seeking to tell the story behind the story by depicting myself as one of the clowns who tumbled around in the sawdust ring but who were also able to observe what went on backstage, rather in the way that Laura Knight had a paid job in a circus which enabled her to leave a legacy of canvases that show the faces and scenes under the Big Top in her time. The danger of taking this approach in a non-fiction book is that it can make facts sound like fiction, as if it were set in a place as real and yet unreal as Mrs Gaskell's Cranford, and peopled by characters who are merely based on fact like the men and women who worked in the arcane Circus of George Smiley; however that is a hazard I find difficult to avoid because my working world always seemed more theatrical than real to me, a world in which the Barnums and the Baileys cracked the whip and in which there was a hint of Pagliacci behind the greasepaint of nearly all their clowns.

This is not an idle analogy in my case because during the Cudlipp years on the *Daily Mirror* I was increasingly cast in the rôle of the dancing bear, and when I delivered essay-type columns – lines pennyeach – they were unwelcome, so I became prone to bouts of frustrated depression of the kind that Winston Churchill called The Black Dog. It was the end of the era when dilettanti who could turn their hands to any type of writing were needed on newspapers, and the blossoming of the period when expanded editorial staffs brought in officially encouraged restrictive practices so that every journalist was typecast as a specialist of some kind.

It suited the *Mirror* to project me as the *soigné* man about town who knew everyone and went everywhere, a journalistic Fred Astaire dancing exuberantly down Piccadilly in white tie and tails and turning up in a grey topper at every royal wedding and gala celebration in the world: I was the readers' link with the glamorous life they dreamed of living, acting out their dreams by proxy. It was a popular act as far as circulation was concerned, so it was not surprising that the *Mirror* kept me firmly anchored to this image, because if a management has a comedian with an act that can fill the house every night it seldom takes the chance of allowing him to play King Lear at matinées.

I accepted the logic of it but never ceased to find the limitation irksome, even though in my case it was more in the nature of silken handcuffs than a straitjacket, and when an opportunity arose some years later to leave the *Daily Mirror* and write more varied material of a better kind for a new newspaper in the group I grasped it eagerly, believing that I had escaped for ever but subsequently finding that I was only a ticket-of-leave man with a five-year exeat. I returned cheerfully enough and without my tail between my legs because by that time the *Mirror* was happily agreeing to pay for the purchase and training of my racehorses in return for my writing about them in the paper, and to pick up the bill for holidays in extreme luxury that my wife and I took in favoured haunts of the rich around the world, provided I went as president of a racing club that I had set up for the paper. Whereupon I stopped being a pernickety fellow and wallowed in my good fortune until Robert Maxwell bought the newspaper and – rising like the demon king through a trap-door in a cloud of green smoke – announced in the pantomime snarl that is forever Alfred Marks that this had got to stop.

Not before time. When Maxwell told me that I was costing him one million pounds a year out of his own pocket, his arithmetic was wrong but his general appraisal of the situation was plainly right: we were all living in a world ruled by Pantaloon; somebody had to sweep through Fleet Street like a hurricane devastating a Caribbean island so that new order could be built out of old chaos, and the task fell to Maxwell and his far cleverer contemporary Rupert Murdoch. The industrial mayhem entailed in the process was facilitated for both of them by the earlier undermining of union power by Eddie Shah, a national newspaper proprietor of less lasting consequence, but Maxwell and Murdoch were the two men who took the final trick and won the rubber.

As the vanguard of the new army of newspaper proprietors, both men were fearless gamblers, but whereas Maxwell had no immediately observable talent for running newspapers Murdoch was a hands-on proprietor who had the word PRINT running through his bones in the way that the word BRIGHTON runs through sticks of Brighton rock. Hard as carborundum, obsessive, single-minded, intolerant of weakness, a dangerous man to have as a friend, Murdoch bore much more similitude to the men who ran the business in my time, because, like Murdoch, they were not merely businessmen but were also expert in the craft of newspaper production. In terms of provenance and morals those old press barons had a lot in common with the journalists they employed, and they shared their journalists' identity as outsiders, though some of them shared it with bombastic reluctance.

Lord Rothermere of the *Daily Mail*, for example, was an immensely rich man; a nephew of Lord Northcliffe, he was an old Etonian with a fine house in London and an estate in the country where he entertained on an extravagant scale, yet he was sniffed at by the Establishment and had to find his friends among the wealthier show-offs of café society. Randolph Churchill, Winston's son, described him publicly as 'the Pornographer Royal', and even his photographers saw him as being indelibly common, which must have been hard to bear because there were few lower forms of life in British society at that time than photographers.

Sir William Carr of the *News of the World* was known as Pissy Billy because he was so seldom sober, a disability he shared with most of his journalists without sharing their ability to conceal it.

Lord Southwood of the *Daily Herald* was dubbed the tender tycoon but he nearly bankrupted his own papers and those of some of his rivals by starting circulation wars and giving away life-insurance policies and encyclopaedias to attract readers.

Lord Beaverbrook of the *Daily Express* was described by King George V as 'this common little Canadian adventurer', and was mocked by Evelyn Waugh (briefly one of his employees) in the character of Lord Copper; a former insurance agent and bond-salesman, he made his first million out of a deal in Canadian cement, but he was a newspaperman by nature and he built the *Express* into Britain's top-selling national daily of the pre-war years. He was on intimate terms with many important politicians, including Lloyd George and Winston Churchill, because he used his newspapers to their advantage; it was Lloyd George who gave him his peerage for helping to engineer a political *coup* that brought down Asquith's government, and Churchill gave him ministerial office in the wartime national government for services rendered. Oddly enough none of his own major political campaigns succeeded, and in that respect he ended his life as a failure among the mounting ruins of the newspaper empire he had created.

Physically Beaverbrook was an ugly man, and psychologically he was spiteful; his vendetta against the Mountbattens made him enemies at Windsor, and it surprised nobody when Prince Philip called the *Daily Express* 'a bloody awful newspaper'. Although a few of the people who worked for him, notably Michael Foot the Labour poltician and A.J.P. Taylor the historian, saw him as an admirable and even loveable character, most of the journalists he employed detested him. I came to know him fairly well, as did most journalists in my kind of job, and first met him soon after I started writing a column for the *Mirror*, when he invited me to his flat in Arlington House near the Ritz for a drink, presumably to have a look at me; during that interview I decided that I would need to be very poor indeed before I took a job from him. There was never a great deal of difference between working for one popular newspaper and another, but during the Cecil King and Hugh Cudlipp years the *Mirror* was marginally more honest than the *Express*.

The oddest facet of Beaverbrook's character was that, although himself a brilliant newspaperman, he was jealous of the best journalists he employed. He gave Arthur Christiansen his big chance as editor of the *Daily Express*, and boasted about paying Chris £15,000 a year when the average pay for a reporter was about £1,000 a year, but when Christiansen became deservedly famous in his own right Beaverbrook mercilessly humiliated him, deposed him as an editor and finally destroyed him as a man. Having shown Chris who was the boss, Beaverbrook appointed Edward Pickering as editor in Chris's place. Pickering, too, was an outstandingly talented journalist and also a top-class managerial executive, which was a rare combination of qualities in Fleet Street, but although these were the very qualities that Beaverbrook had recognized before he made the appointment, he soon became jealous when Pickering started to receive public praise, so the vicious old man sought to undermine Pickering's authority as well; although, as Sir Edward Pickering, Pick went on to become chairman of the *Mirror* and later deputy chairman of *The Times*, this action of Beaverbrook's was greatly to the disadvantage of the *Daily Express* because the paper was subsequently saddled with a succession of inferior editors from which it never recovered; but it was a power-stroke that gave Beaverbrook great personal satisfaction. Beaverbrook was even jealous of his own son, the wartime flying ace whom we all knew as 'young Max', but although young Max was always a model of filial piety his father treated him with a contempt that disgusted all who saw it.

Noble blood and high moral tone are always as rare among press tycoons as orchids in the desert, but during my early period on newspapers it would have been hard to point to any other industry in which the lunatics were so obviously running the asylum. Cecil King of the *Mirror* was the odd man out among them, and even he would have made irresistible source-material for a Maugham short story. In fact, that nearly happened to him: once when I was in the South of France and staying briefly at the Villa Mauresque as a guest of Willie Somerset Maugham, Cecil was visiting friends along the coast, and Maugham suggested that it might be amusing to invite Cecil over for luncheon; but when Maugham's secretary telephoned, Cecil had already set off back to London, and I felt slightly relieved about that because a couple of hours in Cecil's company might easily have resulted in a Maugham short story with a central character along the lines of Powder-Puff Percy in *The Door of Opportunity* or the missionary Mr Davidson in *Rain*.

Cecil King towered above his contemporaries physically and intellectually but financially he was their poor relation; it was this that made him a horse of a different colour because although, as chairman, he exercised the same authority over his publishing empire as his peers did over theirs, he neither owned it nor was even a major stockholder in the companies that controlled it. He shared their megalomania, their narcissism and their predilection for intrigue – it was King's Claudius-like sense of political destiny that ultimately brought him low – but throughout his working life he was always a salaried employee of the companies he governed. When he was ousted from the chairmanship in 1968 his annual salary was £45,000, a trivial income among his peers, and when he died in 1987 he left £3,000,000, a sum that most newspaper proprietors at the time would have regarded as the price of a fashionably-bred yearling or a canvas painted by a second-rank Impressionist.

At the time when Cecil King was toppled from the chairmanship of what was then the biggest publishing corporation in the world, his career having been assassinated in traditional *Mirror* fashion by an internal raiding party spearheaded by his friend and protégé Hugh Cudlipp, King remarked that he had been dismissed 'like a clerk who had been caught with his fingers in the till'. It was wry humour, typical of the man, yet it was in its way a telling reaction, because under King's management almost all the employees of his newspapers did have their fingers in the till, some of them up to the elbows. Tacit dishonesty of one kind or another was rife throughout the *Mirror* organization, from top to bottom. Members of the printing and mechanical unions had become flagrantly corrupt, thieving from the company nightly by means of bogus payslips and other devious forms of crookedness, and even by barefaced burglary – portable equipment such as vacuum cleaners vanished weekly in large quantities and so many typewriters were stolen that eventually all typewriters were chained to the desks; criminals, upon leaving prison, made a beeline for Fleet Street, seeking jobs there because the pickings were so rich. Little was done by management to stop this, because feeble attempts to curb such excesses were met by threats from bandit union leaders to bring production to a halt, and in the newspaper industry where the loss of a night's product means the total loss of a vast sum of money that cannot be replaced, blackmail was a weapon that always worked.

There was another, more insidious reason why these blatant malpractices were not tackled more courageously, and this was the fact that so many employees in other departments were engaging in fiddles of their own that to point the finger of accusation at others might endanger the accuser, or at least be described as the pot calling the kettle black. For example, there were members of the management and executives who invested their salaries monthly and lived on their perks and their expenses; and the majority of the journalists were more interested in the level of their expenses than in their pay, because expenses were tax free.

On foreign assignments it was customary for journalists to draw a liberal supply of money before setting out, and then, if they found it unnecessary to spend too much of it, return only a token few pounds when they came back: 'thieve a little, leave a little' was the widespread advice to newcomers who were not familiar with the system. When I first went round the world with Cecil King in 1953 all expenditure abroad by businessmen or journalists was limited under exchange-control regulations; each of us drew the maximum permitted allowance, which was approximately the 1990 equivalent of £750 a day. Cecil was less profligate with the money in his pocket than I was, and often left me to pay the bills for both of us; furthermore, on visits to places such as Australia or Canada where the *Mirror* had subsidiary companies, it was not unusual for those companies to pick up the bills for their visiting firemen from London, which left the fortunate visitor with a comfortable surplus. ·

225

Once, on our way back from New York, Cecil showed me a charming little piece of Chinese porcelain, probably Ming, that he had acquired on our travels.

'By God,' I said, admiringly, 'I bet that's valuable.'

Cecil looked down his nose disapprovingly. 'The Chinese is the highest taste,' he said, loftily, seeking to turn my mind to the aesthetics of the matter rather than dwell upon the question of whence came the money to buy it.

It was during my brief but happy time as a vintage correspondent that I ran across the perfect analogy for journalists' expenses. In the course of making cognac, the spirit is placed in wooden barrels and left to mature; during the maturing stage, some of the spirit evaporates into the atmosphere. This is known as 'the angels' share'. In the small region of Cognac, the angels' share amounts to twenty million bottles a year, and this was a quantitative comparison with the share of newspaper profits that evaporated annually in the form of journalists' and executives' expenses. In the late 1970s there was a year in which the amount of expenses paid out to employees of the *Mirror* and its sister newspapers came to a sum in millions of pounds that was greater than the entire profits made by *Mirror* Group Newspapers during that year.

Week by week, flights of hyperbolic imagination were devoted to the writing of expense sheets, the major items referring to entertainment; nobody seriously believed that the names of people who were claimed to have been entertained had in fact been the recipients of this munificence. Hugh Cudlipp once explained the system to a new writer he had engaged: 'As far as entertainment expenses are concerned,' he said, 'put down anyone you like except the Archbishop of Canterbury – he's mine.'

From time to time an edict was sent round requiring that all claims for entertaining expenses must be accompanied by bills that had been paid: all this accomplished was the growth of a small industry in the purchase and sale of restaurant bills; enterprising journalists would acquire from waiters the paid bills that had been left on tables by ordinary customers, and then sell them for a small fee to their colleagues. On Monday mornings, when most editorial employees made out their expense sheets for the previous week, the cry could be heard on all sides – 'Anyone got any spare bills?'

There came a time when the Inland Revenue, staggered by the amount claimed to have been spent on food and drink by newspaper staffs, threatened to assess entertaining expenses as part of salary; this caused such a flurry of outrage that the then managing editor of the

Mirror designed a new expense form on which the claimant had to sign a declaration that every amount claimed had been spent necessarily and exclusively in the performance of duties for the company. Everybody signed, the managing editor was congratulated, and the tax inspector was sent packing with egg on his face. There was a general feeling that it served him right for interfering in a private matter; until the 1980s national newspapers in general and the *Mirror* in particular had special arrangements with the Inland Revenue, and even people who never worked outside the office made out weekly expense sheets claiming the 'reimbursement' of sums that had never been spent but which were paid tax-free.

Like the newspaper proprietors whose riches did not protect them from being scorned in certain sectors of society, everyone who worked on a mass-circulation newspaper was aware of the exiguous and seldom-mentioned but nevertheless inescapable stigma entailed. The *Daily Mail* was always known as 'the Daily Liar', the *Express* was always suspect because of the way in which Lord Beaverbrook brazenly blackened the characters of people he disliked and the *Daily Mirror* was generally regarded by the respectable Tory middle classes as a Communist rag. Such reputations die hard, largely because few people in the middle class read the newspapers they vilify.

Hugh Cudlipp turned the *Daily Mirror* into a newspaper of political responsibility and editorial quality, maintaining its essential ebullient vulgarity, which he called brashness, while at the same time requiring a higher standard of conduct and work from his journalists. Although this improvement was recognized among people who took a close interest in newspapers, it was naturally not noticed by people who knew the past reputation of the paper but never read it; if the *Daily Mirror* had been taken over by the staff of the *Church Times* and run as a Bible-teaching publication there would still have been people who raised their hands in horror at the mere mention of the title.

For various reasons I seldom encountered this reaction, so on the two occasions when I did come face-to-face with it I was more surprised than might have been expected. The first occurred one evening in the foyer at Covent Garden when I was chatting during the interval with Garrett Moore, who later, as the Earl of Drogheda, became chairman of the Royal Opera House and also of the *Financial Times*. Ralph Vaughan-Williams, the composer, whom I had never met before, came shambling over and Garrett said to him. 'Oh, hallo, Ralph, I expect you know Noel Whitcomb of the *Daily Mirror*.' Vaughan-Williams jumped inches into the air, looked at me in naked terror, and ran. He did not simply hurry

227

away – he fled. My face must have been a picture of astonishment because Garrett roared with laughter. 'Presumably he's not one of your fans,' he said.

My other brief encounter of this startling kind came at a book-launching party at the house of John Murray, the publisher. I had been talking for some time to Dorothy Sayers about her translation of Dante's *Divina Commedia* and we were getting on rather well, when she casually asked me, 'What sort of things do you write?'

'I write a column for the *Daily Mirror*,' I replied.

The effect was electric. She shied away as if someone had lighted a firework under her tail, and began pushing her way through the crowded room, spilling people's drinks and shouting, 'I say, I say, we have a spy from the yellow press in our midst!'

Most of the other guests found it a highly diverting interlude, and several moved over to chat to me as a gesture of amends for Dorothy Sayers' embarrassing behaviour; but although I found it a disagreeable experience at the time, in retrospect I understood the reason for it: I was probably one of the few people in the room who knew that Miss Sayers had had an illegitimate child by a motor mechanic and had subsequently married a journalist on the *News of the World*. These were matters of no interest to me, but people who have secrets of which they are ashamed are often thrown into horrified confusion when they find themselves accidentally talking to a newspaperman. Fear of exposure is the trigger, and they are wise to fear, because if I had a secret to hide I would avoid talking to journalists; they are trained to sniff fear in the wind like hounds scenting a fox.

Another celebrity who had an almost paranoid detestation of the press was Noël Coward. Fleet Street and the theatre generally got on well together for reasons of self-interest; from the journalists' point of view, stories about showbusiness were the easiest to find and were good for circulation because of the readers' voracious appetite for news and gossip about the stars; from the performers' viewpoint, publicity was vital for continuing success: so newspapermen were greeted with gin and *bonhomie* from Shaftesbury Avenue to Broadway, even by theatrical people who privately regarded them as God's punishment upon mankind for the sin of Adam. Columnists were particularly welcome.

But Noël Coward was among the few who seldom made any attempt to conceal his antipathy; he was convinced throughout his life that the press – the British press in particular – was consistently unfair to him. With hindsight, this was probably true. At times Coward suspected that British newspapers were unreasonably scathing about his work because

228

he was homosexual, and there was a measure of truth in that, too, because Fleet Street with its macho image delighted in mocking what were then called nancyboys, even though it had to be done in a guarded fashion because homosexuality was still a criminal offence.

Of all the newspapers, the *Daily Express* and the *Daily Mirror* were the two he hated most, and although his loathing of the *Express* arose from understandable reasons because the *Express* always treated him abominably, his prejudice against the *Daily Mirror* was rooted in a different cause. The *Mirror*, self-proclaimed champion of the working class, had been the newspaper with which he had grown up as a boy. It was his mother's favourite paper. Son of a South London piano-tuner, Coward had been raised in the suburbs by a mother who was determined to push her son into the theatre as a means of getting him out of the dreary surroundings of the family. Mrs Coward was the archetypal theatrical mum. When Noël was ten years old, in 1909, his mother wrote to the *Daily Mirror* about an article concerning child actors and this letter led to an audition which resulted in Coward's first stage appearance, in a play called *The Goldfish* at Crystal Palace. Coward never made any attempt to conceal this, but there is no doubt that he would have been happier if it had been a higher-class newspaper that was instrumental in launching his career. It is hard to forgive favours when they come from people with whom you do not wish to be associated.

Coward's spectacular career in the theatre during the 1920s and 1930s brought him not only fame but also the social acceptance in high places that he so greatly prized, and even though he realized that the dinner invitations he received from members of the royal family were sent with the implicit proviso that he would subsequently sing for his supper, he nevertheless treasured his acquaintanceship with the royals. His wartime film, *In Which We Serve*, based on Lord Mountbatten's courageous exploits in HMS *Kelly*, was an affectionate gift in return for Mountbatten's friendly patronage.

However, after the war Coward's career in the theatre appeared to be a spent rocket; his sophisticated work fell out of fashion and, as he admitted in his diaries, he was virtually a back number. In 1946 he attempted a comeback with a high-budget musical called *Pacific 1860* at Drury Lane, but it was dreadful; as one of the reviewers in the theatre on that first night, even though I had no reason to be ill-inclined towards Coward, I could think of nothing to say in its favour. It closed very quickly, having had what Coward himself described as 'more of a convulsive stagger than a run'.

229

The large amount of money that Coward had made in his days of fame was rapidly diminishing and the future looked bleak. In 1948 he had to sell his Rolls Royce and he was constantly strapped for cash. Coward was nearly fifty, and the party was over. His name slipped out of the papers. Oblivion beckoned.

One Saturday afternoon in June 1951, Coward was helping as usual with the garden party in aid of the Actors' Orphanage, of which he was a patron. Normally he signed autographs for cash at this annual fund-raising affair, but his name had become of so little consequence to the new generation of showbusiness fans that he decided not to take the chance of getting few takers for his signature. Instead, he put up a notice outside a tent, *Noël Coward, At Home. Admission: three shillings*, and with Norman Hackforth at the piano sang a selection of his once-popular songs.

It was a riot. A rainy afternoon brought an unusually large crowd into the tent and they were so delighted by what they heard that they would not let him go. He sang for hours. He did a dozen twenty-minute spots. It was one of the most remarkable occasions of its kind that I have ever experienced, ranking alongside Danny Kaye's first night at the London Palladium, when the curtain was due down soon after 10 p.m. but the audience simply refused to let Danny leave the stage and kept him singing until the early hours of the next morning. Coward's triumph in the charity tent was of that order. It was splendid, and he was superb.

Part of the impact was its unexpectedness, because Noël Coward was not known for this type of work. He had never done cabaret because it was far beneath him. During the war he had gone on several tours to entertain the troops, singing his songs with Norman Hackforth at the piano, but he had received a mixed reception because his material was too polished for most of the camp-concert audiences. But on that rainy afternoon in the tent it was clear to all who heard him – for the present-day equivalent of fifteen pence a head – that he was a cabaret artist of scintillating talent.

Sitting on the wooden garden-chair beside me in the tent that afternoon was a man called Louis Maggiora. We were friends – I had recently been a guest at his wedding – and I saw him often because he was the manager of the Café de Paris in Leicester Square, where I often dined. Louis was a nephew of the Quaglino brothers, who were restaurateurs in London, and after the war he had been given the task of restoring the Café de Paris to its former popularity as a high-class nightspot. The Café, as it was known, had received a direct hit from a Luftwaffe bomb on a Saturday night in the spring of 1941, and in a terrible scene of carnage and destruction eighty-four people had been killed, including the owner and also the bandleader, a popular figure called Snake-Hips Johnson. This tragedy had left a pall over the place and when it was rebuilt and reopened by new owners something special in the way of a new policy was needed to lure back the free-spending socialite clientele it had formerly enjoyed. Maggiora had achieved this by instituting a cabaret that consisted of one performer only, one great star to attract five hundred diners nightly.

It was a bold policy, not only because big stars are expensive but also because there were few top names capable of delighting a blasé after-dinner audience for an hour or more single-handed. But it paid off. Swiftly the Café re-established its reputation as the smartest cabaret nightspot in London, and, with a new cabaret star appearing every month, it was full every night. Harry Roy's band played for dancing, most of the cabaret stars were imported from Europe or America, tables had to be booked weeks ahead, royals and celebrities dined there and it was acknowledged as the most elegant late-night venue in town.

As Louis Maggiora and I walked together out of the tent at the charity garden party after watching Coward's performance on that rainy Saturday afternoon, Louis said, 'Are you thinking what I'm thinking?'

'No doubt about it,' I nodded. 'He's perfect for your place.'

'How much do you think he would want for a month?' asked Louis.

'The real question is whether he would agree to do it,' I said. 'He might regard it as too much of a comedown to appear in a restaurant as a cabaret act. It's a far cry from being known as 'The Master' in the international theatre world. Depends how much he needs the money. My bet is that he would want five grand at least.'

My bet was wrong. Louis wrote to Coward next day offering him £4,000 for a month and Coward jumped at it. His opening night at the Café was brilliant. It was summed up best by Kenneth Tynan who, reviewing it in the *Spectator*, wrote: 'To see Coward whole, public and private personalities conjoined, you must see him in cabaret, romping fastidiously, padding down those celebrated stairs on black suede-clad feet and baring his teeth as if unveiling some grotesque monument before giving us *I'll See You Again* and all the other bat's-wing melodies of his youth.'

Coward in cabaret at the Café was such a big hit that he stayed six weeks. He was back with a bang. But only in London. His international reputation was not restored. Outside the West End he was still the forgotten man, one of the big names of yesterday. His career in the theatre had a momentary flare-up with a revival of his *Relative Values* at the Savoy, starring Gladys Cooper, and although Coward was braced for the customary shower of rotten eggs and tomatoes from the London press, it did not happen. Coward wrote in his diary: 'Well, well, what a surprise! Rave notices. Quite a lot of them irritating and ill-written but all, with the exception of the dear little *Daily Mirror*, enthusiastic and wonderful box-office.'

The dear little *Daily Mirror* had done it again. He loathed the *Mirror*.

There was another problem, too, and it was a problem that caused me some embarrassment. My column in the *Mirror* was a big popular success, and the *Mirror* were plugging it for all they were worth in an advertising campaign. My grinning face leered down from hoardings and from the sides of buses, accompanied by the legend: NOEL – ONLY IN THE *DAILY MIRROR*! The Christian name Noël (I myself never used the accent in print) was not so frequently encountered in those days as it is now, and that is the only circumstance of which I can think to explain the fact that Noël Coward started receiving a large amount of fanmail concerning matters that had appeared in my column while I received the odd letter asking for a signed photograph – 'You know, the one in the spotted dressing gown with the long cigarette holder.'

This was the last straw as far as Coward was concerned. His secretary, Lorn Loraine, would send the bundles of letters to my secretary, Phyl Vinicombe, and the appalling mistake was kept from his attention as far as possible, but he knew about it and he hated it. I must say that I sympathized with him, because I would not have liked it if I had been him, either. The general public at large have always been notorious for making identity errors of that sort, and Coward knew it, but it was no solace; I honestly think he would have preferred it if thoughtless idiots had addressed letters to him at the *Police Gazette* or even the *News of the World*. The *Daily Mirror* seemed to dog his footsteps, and, as it happened, the *Daily Mirror* was to commit one final, unpardonable sin. It was instrumental in leading him to the greatest success of his whole life, although that fact and the way in which it happened were never mentioned in the newspaper, or anywhere else either, for that matter, until now.

One night in 1954 I was entertaining some friends to dinner at the Café de Paris. Among them was a man called Ernest Anderson. Ernie Anderson was a press agent; he was the best press agent I have ever met, and I must have met hundreds. Ernie worked only for a few carefully selected clients whom he regarded as men of quality, men such as John Huston, Humphrey Bogart, Mike Todd. He did a Rolls Royce job for them because Ernie's clients were not the sort of people who wanted

232

publicity at any price; they wanted a decent measure of dignity in what was written about them, and dignity was Ernie's speciality. He was an American from California and had been a highly rated expert on jazz music in his early days, but after his marriage broke up he came to London with his twin daughters, Allie and Marnie, and settled down quietly in Chelsea, operating as a freelance. In the newspapers and in showbusiness, he dealt exclusively with his friends.

Ernie had not seen Noël Coward in cabaret before that night, although Coward had done three separate months there since his first appearance at the end of 1951; we were all impressed, as usual, by Coward's dazzling performance, but I noticed that Ernie was looking particularly thoughtful after the applause had died away. He leaned over to me and said quietly, 'Hey, Noel, this feller's pretty good. I have an idea and I'll ring you about it in the morning.'

The idea about which he rang me the following day was that Coward would be a sensation in Las Vegas. I had been to Las Vegas a few times, and I was not so sure, because Vegas was a tough marketplace. But Ernie was insistent. He was utterly convinced. And as Ernie was a shrewd judge of such matters, I agreed that he should come round to my house right away and we would ring Joe Glaser in New York.

Joe was a friend of Ernie's and an acquaintance of mine. He was a theatrical agent in a fairly big way, one of the top agents in New York. I had met him first in Chicago, several years before. He had run a nightclub there on the Strip in his early days, but I was introduced to him at the races, where I had gone with Jimmy Schnozzle Durante, who was – oddly enough – working in cabaret at the Café de Paris in Chicago at the time. Joe was a very tough egg indeed, a Damon Runyon character in the flesh.

At any rate, I put through a call to Joe in New York, and when he came on the line I explained to him that Ernie and I had come to the conclusion that Noël Coward had all the makings of a sensational hit in Las Vegas. At first he thought we were kidding. When he discovered that I was serious he thought we must both have gone mad.

'Be your age, Noel, boy,' he said. 'Are you seriously suggesting that I should bring this elderly English singer to Vegas? I should lose my brains! Look, I have the greatest stars in the world going down on their knees to me for the chance of a spot in Vegas. I have turned down some of the highest-paid acts in showbusiness history because I did not consider them suitable for the hall. Vegas is special. I even wondered about Sinatra. Yet you are asking me to engage this English light-opera performer who nobody in the United States has ever heard of apart from a few ageing fairies on Broadway. Listen, boy, I am always pleased to hear you, but I have to tell you that I would sooner retire and give my business away than do a stroke that would have everyone in show-business from New York to California laughing at me. Give my regards to Ernie and tell him he has gone mad. How is the weather with you?'

'Joe,' I said, 'don't be too hasty. I am going to send you a recording of Coward singing some of his songs. Will you listen to it?'

'For you, baby,' said Joe, 'I would listen to Mozart.'

So Ernie and I got hold of a copy of a new LP that Coward had recently made and mailed it to Joe. We heard nothing for over a fortnight until one lunchtime the telephone rang in my study at home and it was Joe on the line from New York.

'I been thinking, son,' he said. 'Ernie is a very smart operator and you are no mug. Right?'

'Right,' I said.

'So maybe I oughta have a look at this feller Coward and see if I could fit him up with a few gigs. Hey?'

'Good thinking, Joe,' I said.

'OK. So here's what we do. You and Ernie send your boy over here to New York and I will audition him. Howzat, huh?'

'No dice, Joe,' I said. 'Noël Coward may rate as a has-been in the United States, but he is still a big name here, and since he started in cabaret he is the hottest ticket in town. There is not a chance in hell that he would take a trip to New York to be auditioned. The idea would strike him as ridiculous. He would turn it down flat.'

'Zat a fact?' said Joe, puzzled but impressed. 'OK, tell you what I'll do. I'll come to London and see him. Get Ernie to fix a meet.'

So Ernie and I went along to the Café again that night, and after the cabaret I sent a card in to Noël Coward, with a note on the back asking him for a short talk right away. He received us in his dressing room, wearing the famous polka-dot silk dressing gown.

'Do sit down, dear boy,' he said, waving me to a chair. 'How very good of you to look in.'

He switched on the old Chinese smile but his eyes were glittering a bit so I came straight to the point and told him that an American agent called Joe Glaser, who was a friend of ours, was interested in talking to him about the possibility of his doing cabaret in Las Vegas.

This surprised him considerably because he had supposed that I wanted to see him for the purpose of writing a piece in the column.

'I cannot say that the suggestion sends me wild with enthusiasm, dear boy,' he said. 'Las Vegas has always sounded to me rather an exasperating place. All those one-armed bandits and those awful people, you know.'

'The fees are very high indeed,' I said.

His mind was working quickly on this very point, and although he disliked the idea of such a suggestion coming from me, because it was none of my business, he was reluctant to cast it aside merely for that reason.

'Very well, dear boy,' he said at last. 'If you would be so terribly kind as to get in touch with Lornie and arrange an appointment for this friend of yours to come and see me, I will give the matter a little thought.'

Ernie fixed the appointment for the following week, and when Joe arrived at Heathrow we both went to meet him in a hired Rolls Royce. We took the Rolls to bolster Joe's confidence, because although Joe was king of the castle in New York he always felt uneasy in London; Joe looked on England as a little cottage-industry country full of stuffed-shirt lords and ladies who looked down their noses when they heard his Bowery accent, and he privately thought that people spoke to him in Mayfair English just to make him feel uncomfortable.

So we took him to lunch at Jack Isow's in Soho, where he could get good chopped liver and all the food was strictly kosher, and we ran into Jack Solomons, the boxing promoter, and, at a different table, Jack's sworn rival, Harry Levene, and by the time we had finished our meal Joe was revising his views about London being a town of snobs in top hats.

'That automobile you got – that Rolls Royce,' said Joe, thoughtfully, 'that's British, ain't it?'

'Sure is, Joe,' I said. 'Best car in the world.'

'Huh!' snorted Joe, giving me a sideways look. 'Can you buy 'em off the peg here or do they have to tailor them to you?'

'Off the peg,' I said. 'You want to look at some?'

Joe nodded, so off I went and telephoned the Rolls Royce showrooms in Conduit Street and made an appointment for us to see a Mr Cra'ster, the export manager of Rolls, at three o'clock.

When I returned to the table I wrote the name Cra'ster on a card and gave it to Joe, so that he would know whom he was talking to. Joe read it incredulously. 'Cra'ster?' he said. 'With a apostrophe in the *middle*? How come a guy gets a apostrophe in the *middle* of his name? I hearda plenty English guys who gotta hyphen, but this is the first guy I ever heard who's got a fuckin' apostrophe. What is he – a duke?'

At the showrooms we were greeted courteously by Mr Cra'ster, and Joe's eye was immediately taken by a showroom model of the Rolls

Royce H.J. Mulliner Drophead Foursome Coupé. He walked round it with evident approval.

'Swell,' he said. 'Very elegant. I like it. Does it come in red?'

'Any colour you wish, sir,' said Mr Cra'ster.

'Good,' said Joe. 'Ship one over to me in New York. Soon as possible. Here's my card.'

'Very good, sir,' said Mr Cra'ster.

We were just about to leave the showroom when Joe had a thought and turned back. 'Make it two,' he called. 'It's my mother's birthday in a coupla weeks and this would be something different for a little gift.'

'Very good, sir,' said Mr Cra'ster. 'Both in red?'

'Both in red,' nodded Joe, and off we went to leave him at the Savoy Hotel for a rest.

That night Ernie and I took Joe to the Café to see Coward doing his cabaret, but we had not told Coward he was going to be there because Joe wanted to remain incognito until the meeting. He wanted to make his mind up about the act before he spoke to the performer.

It was a glittering audience as usual, and, also as usual, Coward was superb. Joe did not applaud, of course, but on the way back to the Savoy he said, 'It's crazy, and it don't make sense, but he's got it.'

'What's he got?' asked Ernie.

'Boxoffice,' said Joe, shaking his head. 'Big boxoffice.'

Next day we all went in the Rolls to Coward's house in Gerald Row, Belgravia, and when we had left our coats we were shown into a room full of people. Joe muttered to me, 'What the hell's going on? You said this was to be a private meeting but it looks like what I've come three thousand miles for is a goddam cocktail party.'

Coward came towards him with arms outstretched and the famous smile, 'My *dear* Joe,' he said, 'how *terribly* good of you to come. Let me introduce you. This is my British accountant. This is my London lawyer. This is my accountant for foreign affairs. This is my American attorney. And this is the splendid advocate who looks after all my overseas contracts. Will you drink champagne?'

'Coke,' said Joe. 'I don't drink.'

Joe was grinning broadly because he immediately saw through the theatrical charade that Coward had set up to impress him. 'Let's siddown and talk,' he beamed.

The talk ended, half an hour later, with Joe agreeing to pay Coward thirty-five thousand dollars a week for two shows a night at the Desert Inn in Las Vegas. It was more money than Coward had ever earned in his life. It was also, although nobody knew it at the time, the biggest turning point in the whole of Coward's career.

Joe flew home with Coward's signature in his pocket. On the drive with Ernie and me to Heathrow, he said laconically, 'That guy doesn't know who his friends are.'

Soon after Joe's visit, Coward confided to his subsequently published diary: 'I regret, dear journal, this unworthy, sordid preoccupation with money, but I have worked hard all my life, I am £15,000 overdrawn in London, I am fifty-five years old and I fully intend to end my curious days in as much comfort, peace and luxury as I can get.'

That was the excuse Coward made to himself for dealing with Joe Glaser, whom he patronized abominably and privately regarded as not being good enough for him. It was Glaser who chanced his own reputation in America on a contract that resulted in Coward becoming rich again, far richer than he had ever been, and far, far richer than he ever expected to be. Yet, so far as I know, Coward never admitted how it all happened. He mentioned briefly in his diary that Glaser had called on him in London, but that was the first mention of the Las Vegas affair, and it came in more or less as an aside, among other things he was doing. He wrote: 'A character called Joe Glaser flew in from New York to sign me up for Las Vegas. A typical shrewd, decent, sharp agent type. The discussion was satisfactory financially, everything being contingent on whether or not I like Las Vegas, so he is escorting me there for a couple of days so that I can case the joint and decide which room I prefer to play in, if any.'

In a later diary item Coward wrote about Joe: 'He is . . . naturally over the moon with delight at having got me under his wing. My name is big prestige stuff for a brisk little Jewish go-getter who hitherto has mostly booked coloured acts and promoted prize-fights.'

I was always glad that Joe never read that diary entry, because, if he had read it, Coward would never have appeared in Vegas. Joe was not proud but he had his dignity, and the truth was that Coward's name did not add up to a row of beans in Las Vegas at that time. Coward was a dead duck all over America, and it is unlikely that any other agent would have touched him with a bargepole as far as a booking for a multi-million dollar entertainment industry was concerned. As it was, Joe had the greatest difficulty in selling the idea to the Desert Inn, and it was not until after Coward's opening night there that the promoters woke up to what they had got.

That first night is now showbusiness history. Coward made the biggest hit of all time in Las Vegas. The critic of the *New York Times* wrote: 'No entertainer within living history has ever been received so

237

well in the United States.' The audience went wild. It was such an extraordinary triumph that the tape of his act is still available in almost every big record shop throughout Britain and America. It is one of the great classics of its kind.

After the show at the Desert Inn on that first night Coward took twelve curtain calls, and the rapturous applause was still roaring on as he returned to his dressing room and slipped into a white silk dressing gown decorated with black stars. He was very excited. Joe Glaser came strolling in, and the grateful Coward rushed towards him, embracing him and kissing him on both cheeks. 'Joe, my dearest Joe, now I know God sent you to me.'

'Izzat a fact?' said Joe, smiling slowly, 'Well, well, well – and there was me thinkin' it was Ernie Anderson and Noel Whitcomb.'

That night restored Noël Coward's reputation to the very highest in the world at one single stroke. He never again lost that superstardom until the day he died. And he was rich again. In his diary for that week, Coward noted:

I have had screaming rave notices and the news has flashed round the world. I am told continually, verbally and in print, that I am the greatest attraction that Las Vegas has ever had and that I am the greatest performer in the world, etc., etc. It is all very, very exciting and generous, and when I look back at the grudging dreariness of the English newspaper gentlemen announcing, when I first opened at the Café de Paris, that I massacred my own songs, I really feel that I don't want to appear at home much more. I have just had a batch of notices from London of Larry and Vivien's *Macbeth* at Stratford, and their ignorance and meanness and cruel, common abusiveness have made me sick. I *know* they can't be right, but even if Larry and Viv were not perfect (which I doubt), the tone of the notices is beneath contempt. Much the same as I usually get from the mean, envious little sods.

Hallo campers! With Sir Billy Butlin (*centre*) at a party to celebrate his knighthood in 1964

What we need is a couple of good winners: William Hill and Teasy Weasy Raymond at a Punters Club party

His amazing Grace: with the Duke of Norfolk, prized patron of the Punters Club, in the winner's enclosure at Ascot

His ill-fated Majesty: the Shah of Persia, dining at a nightspot

'O frabjous day! Callooh! Callay!' With Mirror Boy in the winner's enclosure
after his victory in the Andy Capp Handicap at Redcar, 1980

Living the life of Reilly: Punters Club members in the grandstand at Longchamp

Happy horse, sad story: with Trooper Smith

The horse that won thirteen races – but not with this jockey up! Even Up being ridden around a muddy field in Ireland in 1970, before he went into training

Rake's progress: Annigoni's caricature of the author in a Rowlandson setting

All dressed up and somewhere to go: with Sally at the Debs' Ball

Funny hats run in the family: schoolgirl Kate in the garden at Hampstead

Messing about in boats: Sally sailing on the river at Henley

Graduation day: proud Ma and Pa with daughter Kate, BVSC, MRCVS

'Gladys's house' – the house on the river at Henley

12

God be thanked, the meanest of his creatures
Boasts two soul-sides, one to face the world with,
One to show a woman when he loves her!

Robert Browning, *One Word More*

Life at home was different, very different, a far cry from Fleet Street. Life at home was serene and comfortable, and although this was the kind of life that one side of my nature yearned for, the fact that we achieved it was entirely due to my wife.

We were living in Hampstead, where we had bought a house for cash soon after I started dealing on the Stock Exchange. It was a pretty house, small but ideal for us, being the library wing of a Georgian mansion, formerly known as Frognal Grove, which had been converted into four houses including the stable block by a local builder after the war. It had been built in 1741 by an architect called Henry Flitcroft, who redesigned Carlton House for the Prince of Wales, designed Woburn Abbey for the Duke of Bedford, redesigned Wentworth House for Lord Rockingham, designed and built St Giles-in-the-Fields as the parish church of Holborn, and then built Frognal Grove for himself, later selling it to the Duke of Norfolk.

This grandeur of occupancy was upheld to some degree by our next-door neighbour, Robin Balniel, who was at that time member of parliament for his uncle Salisbury's Hatfield constituency, but who, on the death of his father, became Scotland's premier earl, the 29th Earl of Crawford and Balcarres. (When Lord Home – Sir Alec Douglas Home – relinquished his peerage to become prime minister, and there was much criticism about the job going to an old aristocrat, Robin remarked, 'I can't see what all the fuss is about – after all, he's only the *fourteenth* earl.')

The house was set upon an eminence, one of the highest points in London, and from the top floor you could see into ten counties on a clear day; one of our flashier neighbours had an altimeter fitted in his Aston-

Martin. But it was a beautiful and tranquil place, and had always been a magnet for artists and writers; John Constable's cottage was a few hundred yards away, a stone's throw from Romney's house; Keats, Shelley and Leigh Hunt, who had lived nearby, used to stroll on summer evenings along the drive that led to the house, which was flanked by lime trees that had been planted by Flitcroft and was carpeted all round with daffodils in spring.

Our daughter Katie was a toddler then, and it was a perfect place for children, like being in the country. In 1820 an artist called William Collins, RA, had painted a picture of children swinging on the wooden gate at the end of the drive and called it *Happy as a King*. When, later, I saw it hanging in the National Gallery of Victoria in Melbourne, it brought a lump to my throat because it captures timelessly our own idyllic days, when the house was always full of children. Although we had only one, most of our close neighbours, being roughly the same age as ourselves, had young families, and my wife was extremely popular with all the children, providing them with sausages and taking them for picnics and walks. One day in Sainsbury's, when she had only Katie with her, the man behind the counter asked, 'Where's all the rest of your family today, then?'

Beyond the fence at the bottom of our garden lay the rest of the garden that had belonged to the house when it was Frognal Grove, some six acres of it, set with trees and shrubs, pools and follies, all a mass of flowers in summer. Robin Balniel's daughter, Bettina, was the same age as Kate, and Anthony Caro, the sculptor, who lived in the stable block, had two sons, Timmy and Paul, who were also about the same age, so they all played together in this enchanted garden, completely safe, throughout their early years, because it was not developed for houses until several years later.

Katie went to a little school that was more or less at the bottom of this big garden, and although she preferred to walk there by herself, I would sometimes accompany her, hand in hand, as she scampered busily along in her grey uniform and hat, carrying her satchel. The school was a fairly big Victorian redbrick house set in a large garden with a long lawn, and I remember that lawn well because it was the scene of one of my few sporting triumphs, although my wife would not agree with that description.

In the summer term of Kate's first year at school we received an invitation to sports day, and although I had previously arranged to fly to Munich on the day in question, I cancelled all engagements. This was important – a family milestone. On the big day itself my wife was busy during the morning, so it was not until we set out that she noticed the finery that I had selected to wear for this occasion. It was a sunny summer's day, and we were going to a gala affair, so I had decided to wear a white suit which I had purchased in Deauville the previous August after a prudent investment in the Prix Jacques le Marois; perhaps it may have been more suitable for Deauville than for a school sports day, because there was undoubtedly a touch of Gatsby about it, but as there would be races at the place where we were going I felt it was appropriate. But my wife was horrified. 'You look as though you are going along to do the cabaret,' she said. 'For God's sake go and change into something more suitable for school.' But there was no time, we were already getting late.

It was a splendid setting in the gardens when we arrived – union jacks and bunting fluttering in the breeze, the big lawn marked with white lines ready for the races, a small band playing in a fashion reminiscent of the Llanabba Silver Band of happy memory on Dr Fagan's great sports day, a white marquee for refreshments and the whole scene peopled with proud mothers wearing Ascot gear and fathers wearing blue pinstripe suits, some carrying neatly rolled umbrellas. It was clear that my decision to add a flavour of Deauville to the occasion had not been well thought out. My wife whispered, 'Try to keep out of sight as much as possible.'

This was not easy because we knew many of the other parents and had to mingle in the usual sociable way, but the most difficult moment occurred when the headmistress announced that there was to be a parents' race. As soon as we heard this, I started walking with an exaggerated limp, but this cut no ice with the headmistress. She lined us all up with no argument.

'Right,' she said, picking up the loud-hailer but not needing it, 'I want all the mummies and daddies over here, please. All the mummies will be given a balloon which they will blow up until it is near to bursting, and they will then hand it to daddy, who will climb into one of the sacks over there and – without letting the balloon go down – will then jump to the winning line.'

The sacks, lying in a pile, appeared to have been used previously for potatoes. Not the ideal thing to put on over my white suit. But there was no way out. We were all lined up and under starter's orders. The headmistress fired a toy cap-pistol and we were off. The mummies started puffing like mad into the balloons. I will admit that our balloon was no more than three-quarters blown when I removed it from my wife and with one hand deftly made a knot in the neck, a talent I had

241

perfected when young while blowing up balloons for cricket dances. Then I made a dive for the sacks.

I had noticed that one sack was wider than the others, so I grabbed it and climbed in. It was the dirtiest sack of the lot, but this was no time to be choosy about that. One daddy was already three jumps down the course, so – using a technique that had once brought me success in the lower fourth – I stuck one foot in each corner of the sack and shuffled forward at a lively clip, passing the early front-runner at the halfway mark. I could hear Kate shouting, 'Go on, Daddy!' and I put everything I had into a late run. I won pulling up and crossed the line to applause that sounded to me like Cheltenham on Gold Cup Day, although I realized later that much of the noise was coming from kids jeering at fathers who were coming in with the washing.

Stepping out of the sack, I stood modestly aside while my wife arrived to join me for the prizegiving ceremony. The trophy was a small bon-bon dish inscribed 'A Present from Bognor', but as far as I was concerned it was the victory that counted. I have a competitive nature.

My wife was trying to smile as she discreetly drew my attention to my formerly white trouser legs, which were now muddy brown right up to the waist from the mud that had been in the sack. I took it in my stride, of course, laughing with the rest when my beaten rival was heard to remark that this would teach me to bring my own white sack next year; but I must admit that there was a fraught moment when he came up to me in the tea-tent later and said, 'According to the headmistress's rules we were supposed to jump, you know. You didn't jump – not one single jump. You shuffled. You should have been disqualified. If you try any tricks like that next year I shall have my eye on you.'

This particular daddy was a local magistrate, Sir Alfred Something-or-other, and I could see from the look in his eye that if ever I got hauled up in front of him on a parking offence I would surely get five years' hard labour without the option.

As things turned out, we did both turn up for the school sports again the following summer. I was properly dressed this time, in the regulation blue pinstripe, and it was again a beautiful day, but I could see that the old acrimony still rankled because Sir Alfred came up soon after we arrived and said, 'I see you are here again. No hanky-panky today, hey? What?'

My wife had delivered a similar ultimatum before we set out.

I had a look round for the sacks, but there did not seem to be any, so I asked one of the other children, a boy of about twelve, if the headmistress was planning to have a parents' race again this year.

'Oh, yes,' he said. 'From what I hear the old battleaxe has set up a different sort of Chinese torture for today. We don't know exactly what it is yet, but my friend Julian, Sir Alfred's son, is making a book on it, and he has his dad as evens favourite because the old boy has been in training for this event. He doesn't like coming in second. I've got sixpence on him to win.'

'What price is he offering about me?' I asked.

'You've gone out to three to one since he saw you in a blue suit,' said the boy.

'Well,' I said, 'I disapprove of children betting, and I am sorry to hear you are wasting your pocket money in this way. But if you must do this unwise thing I advise you to have a couple of coppers on me as a saver.'

After the children's races were over, the headmistress strode to the centre of the track and made the big announcement. 'Now we come to the race for mummies and daddies,' she roared. 'This year we shall give each mummy a sheet of newspaper.'

This cheered me up no end. Knowing a bit about newspapers, I thought it might give us a head start. But it was not to be.

'After I have fired the starting gun,' went on the headmistress, 'every mummy will fold her newspaper into a pirate hat. I am sure you all know how to do it. When the hat is made each mummy will pin it with three pins which she is to receive, and then she will put it on daddy's head. Daddy will then run to the winning post, but if his hat comes off – he's out.'

We were all circling round at the far end of the lawn like runners in the Grand National before the starter calls them in to line up. There was a fair tail-wind running and the chances of anyone getting to the wire with his hat still on looked slender. The sheets of newspaper and the pins were already being distributed. My wife has always been good at making things, so I knew we would be in with a squeak on the first part of the contest. And so it proved. She had a pirate hat made and neatly folded in double-quick time, and she was just about to put in the third pin when I spotted my old rival of last year already cantering to the start with his paper hat on. I crammed on our hat and set off in hot pursuit. There had been no time to fix the third pin, so my headgear was flapping in the breeze – fortunately on the side over to the far rails (the judges were on the stands side).

Sir Alfred took a bit of catching, but soon there were just the two of us out on our own, both of us having slipped the field. There was a fair bit of cheering going on, too, and I was just coasting up nicely beside him when suddenly I felt the side of my hat – the part where the third pin was

243

supposed to be – coming apart. With lightning resourcefulness I grabbed a handkerchief out of my pocket and dabbed my brow, just in time to catch the hat neatly on the far side and stop it from coming off.

Sir Alfred was looking across at me as we ran, and he shouted, 'I saw what you did!'

But I was going strong, full of running. We came mighty close together at the ten-yard pole, but I managed to stay just in front of him up to the line because he was a lot bigger than me and he kept the tail-wind off my hat. But it was a damned close-run thing, not far off a photo-finish. I was already pulling up with a diffident smile and savouring the applause when I heard Sir Alfred bellow from behind, 'Headmistress – objection! Where's the stewards?'

'Stewards, Sir Alfred?' said the headmistress, bustling up, 'What stewards? And what objection?'

'Taking my ground in the last ten yards, holding his hat on and trying to weigh in without his full quota of pins.'

The headmistress was on home ground now. She saw what the problem was. Turning to me she said, 'May I see your hat, please?'

I handed it over.

'There is certainly one pin missing,' she said.

'Must have just come out,' I said, scrabbling on the grass with my foot. 'Shall we try to find it?'

Some of the tail-end-Charlie daddies were still straggling over the finishing line, and a couple of unseemly cat-calls had been heard, so the headmistress swiftly made up her mind that she was going to brook no arguments on sports day, and came up with a solution that would have done credit to Solomon.

'Prizegiving!' she trumpet-called. 'All gather round, please. This year I shall call upon Sir Alfred to present the prizes . . .'

We lived happily in Hampstead throughout Kate's schooldays and, as well as going down to take her out for permitted weekends when she was at her preparatory school in Bexhill and later at Benenden, I do not think we missed a single school occasion to which parents were invited. This lustrous attendance record was made possible by the fact that my wife always regarded my work as a mild inconvenience which had to be tolerated because I was unaccountably interested in it, but which must never be allowed to interfere with any matter of real importance such as our private life. This suited me fine, and I agreed entirely with her attitude. Luckily for me I was nearly always in a position to choose what I did and to go where I wished, so it usually presented no problem for me

244

to adjust my diary so that more vital matters such as school occasions took precedence over work.

I can recall only one occasion when I nearly came unstuck on this. It happened when Kate was at her prep-school in Bexhill, which we had chosen for her largely because the headmistress, Miss Margaret Huxley, was such a clever woman and had a natural talent for interesting the children in literature, poetry and the arts, which seemed to be Kate's inclination at the time. Miss Huxley, a sister of Aldous and half-sister of Julian, bore some resemblance in appearance to the actress Margaret Rutherford, and was known to some of the children as 'old Bloomers' because of her Edwardian taste in underwear, but she shared the capacity of her brilliant family for explaining difficult things in a way that made them sound not only easy but fascinating.

One summer term when we were due to attend speech day on the Saturday, I was in the Middle East during the week. I had left what I thought was plenty of time to get back for the big affair but, as so often happens in the Middle East, a good deal of shooting broke out, and it became clear that I would be cutting things fine to get back by the Saturday. King Hussein of Jordan was, as so often, one of the key figures concerned, and as I knew him very slightly – I had once been instrumental in his achievement of an ambition to play the drums in a London nightclub, and the bandleader concerned was later appointed stud manager for all the royal horses in the Hashemite kingdom of Jordon – I flew from Beirut to Amman to see him.

However, there was also unrest in Amman, and by the time I had completed the work in hand all scheduled airline flights out of Amman had been suspended. It was Friday. To be in time for the start of speech day in Bexhill I had to be there by two-thirty on the following day. My mind was made up. I would get there somehow, by hook or by crook. As things turned out it happened to be by crook, although I did not know it at the time.

Kim Philby, who was then working for the *Observer*, also wanted to get out of Amman and he told me that there was a rickety old Elizabethan aircraft gathering dust in a hangar on the airfield at Amman; he said he had friends who could charter it if only he could rustle up the sensational sum in cash that the owners required. The *Observer* was not in that financial league, but the *Daily Mirror* was.

'I'll pay,' I said. 'My paper requires me back very urgently.' And off I went to send a cable to my wife: SEE YOU OUTSIDE BEXHILL RAILWAY STATION TWO OCLOCK SATURDAY.

The old Elizabethan had been laid up for months with engine trouble, waiting for a spare part. But our pilot – whose native tongue, incidentally, was Russian, though this did not strike me as odd at the time – managed to get it cranked up and out on the runway, not without difficulty because it was all rusty and in a terrible state. Amidst a cacophony of creaking and groaning the old Elizabethan at last rattled down the runway that evening, finally achieving lift-off with only inches to spare above the roofs of buildings beyond the far end of the runway. After a hairy flight during which Philby, who was as petrified as I was, drank a whole bottle of Scotch, we landed bumpily on one engine at Nicosia.

Kim was too tired and emotional to fly on, but I hung around the airport drinking coffee and after a couple of hours or so I managed to get a stand-by seat on a flight to Rome. Things were looking up. In the small hours of that Saturday morning I rang my wife from Ciampino airport and told her not to worry. 'I'm on my way,' I said, 'and all you have to do is get to Bexhill and wait outside the station. I'll be there at two o'clock.'

Although there was no available flight from Rome that would get me to London in time, I was able to get a seat on a flight to Paris. Everything was coming up roses. However, when we arrived at Orly I found that there was a strike in progress which affected all flights to London; all were temporarily grounded. Foiled again. But KLM told me that they had a flight leaving Amsterdam that would get me to London in time, and they not only reserved a seat on it for me but they also helped me to charter a light air-taxi to get me to the airport in Amsterdam in time for the connection. Pausing only to telephone London and arrange for a car to meet me at Heathrow, I was off again. Still in the game with a chance. I boarded the KLM aircraft at Amsterdam with ninety seconds to spare, and we touched down at Heathrow dead on half-past eleven.

I was lucky to get through customs quickly, and the driver was waiting for me. As we raced towards the car, I said to him, 'Set your compass for Sussex and put your foot down. I have to be outside Bexhill railway station by two o'clock.' He was magnificent. He told me that at one time he used to race against Prince Bira at Brooklands and I believed him. Bexhill station clock stood at five minutes to two when we pulled in. My wife was waiting.

'You look awful,' she said. 'You haven't shaved. Have you had breakfast?'

'Yes, thanks,' I said. 'Two aspirins and a glass of Moët on the plane.'

'I brought you a clean shirt,' she went on, 'and a decent suit – not a white one – and I've taken a room in the station hotel across the road so that you can change there. Better hurry. You have fifteen minutes.'

In fifteen minutes I was changed, shaved and ready for the fray.

'How do I look?' I asked my wife.

'Clean, bright and slightly oiled,' she said, smiling. 'Come on – we'll just make it.'

A church clock in the distance was chiming the half-hour for half-past two as we walked towards the front door of the school and I rang the bell. To my surprise it was the headmistress herself who opened the door.

'Good morning, Miss Huxley,' I said.

'Good afternoon, Mr Whitcomb,' she replied. 'How nice to see you. Have you come to take Katie out for the afternoon?'

'No,' I said. 'We've come for speech day.'

'Speech day?' said Miss Huxley. 'Speech day? Speech day is *next* Saturday.'

In those Hampstead days when Kate was small we usually went to Greece for our holidays, or otherwise Italy or France. One summer when she was eight years old we were wandering round the zoo at Vincennes when Kate saw some men and women in white coats gathered around a hippopotamus.

'The hippo must be unwell,' said my wife. 'Those men and women in white coats are obviously veterinary people.'

Kate stood watching them with keen attention. My wife and I kept walking on for a few yards and calling to her, but she would not move.

'Come on, Katie, you'll miss your lunch,' I said. This thought would normally have brought her running, but she still stood watching, fascinated. Eventually, after about half an hour, a hoist arrived. The hippo was loaded on to a lorry and departed with the people in white coats.

Then Kate walked slowly back to us and said, thoughtfully, 'That's what I'm going to do when I grow up. Doctor animals.'

We assumed it was a childish fancy. Nobody in our family was concerned with medicine. Kate herself showed promise at school only in arts subjects. She loved books above all, and some of her childhood writing showed a glimpse of poetic imagination. My wife was always afraid that she might be attracted to newspapers. In fact, when she was at her public school we went down for one hobbies' day and found that she had produced and edited a school magazine. My wife was not too pleased but the Queen, who was also present as a parent because Princess

Anne was at the school, took a copy home with her. The *Daily Express* picked this up as a news item and printed a few paragraphs about it, praising the magazine for its journalistic excellence and commenting in a friendly aside that the editor was clearly carrying on her family tradition.

My wife was not too happy about that, either, and even I was a trifle anxious. But we need not have worried. Kate never deflected from the decision that she took at the age of eight at Vincennes Zoo, and today, as I write, she has her own veterinary practice only a few hundred yards from where my wife and I now live in Kensington.

Throughout my life I have always avoided writing about our friends, if only for the practical reason that to do so would have been the best way to end up with no friends; and because this meant that there were many, many interesting and sometimes amusing stories that I deliberately kept out of the newspaper, my resolution on this matter was occasionally hard-tested.

Among our friends in Hampstead, for example, were a family called the Robinsons; quiet, kindly, witty conversationalists, very well off but unobtrusive people of the sort who hated publicity in any form, Philip and Marjorie Robinson were among our favourite neighbours. Philip was an antiquarian bookseller of considerable distinction. He and his brother Lionel, in their scholarly fashion, advised upon and looked after the libraries in several of the oldest stately homes of England. Shortly before we met them they had paid what was an enormous sum at the time, something in the region of one million pounds, for what was left of the books and manuscripts of a man called Sir Thomas Phillips.

Sir Thomas, an extraordinary man who had died in the latter part of the nineteenth century, had been a bibliomaniac. His declared ambition had been to own one copy of every book in the world. Like the ancient King of Pergamus, who had the same ambition two thousand years before, Sir Thomas Phillips nearly succeeded. He had bought books and manuscripts all over the world on a massive scale. Starting as a very rich man, he had become impoverished by his obsession for owning books. When he died he had been living almost in penury, but he owned millions of books and manuscripts; they filled houses, church halls and barns all over the Home Counties, the Midlands and Yorkshire. No other single individual in the world owned so many books.

It took decades to sort out his estate. During the forty years after Sir Thomas's death, many of the world's top book experts sorted through the mountains of his literary possessions, and a succession of week-long sales were held by major auction houses in England, Europe and America. Millions of pounds were realized.

By the time the Robinson brothers entered this remarkable story, there was one barn full of books and manuscripts left. It was the final residue of a colossal treasure-house that had been meticulously scrutinized by professional bibliopoles for nearly half a century. To pay a million pounds for it was a tremendous gamble.

The Robinsons did not use their expert staff to wade through their purchase. They took off their coats and did it themselves. It was hard work but, loving books as things of beauty, they savoured every minute of it. Soon they reaped the harvest. They came upon some startling treasures. They found original manuscripts of Robert Herrick's poems; Sir Walter Raleigh's diaries, written in his cell in the Tower of London while he was imprisoned awaiting execution; the love letters of Lord Essex to Queen Elizabeth I – their sharp eyes uncovered wondrous treasure that had been missed through all the earlier years of searching. Within a relatively short time the Robinsons had paid back to Barclays Bank some half a million pounds that they had borrowed to finance their purchase, and they still had a small mountain of books and manuscripts left through which to sort. It was a romantic story but, even today, it is scarcely known outside the dignified small world of the antiquarian book trade.

One evening the doorbell rang in our house at Hampstead. My wife was out and I was alone in the house. I opened the door, and there on the step was Philip Robinson.

'My dear Philip,' I said, with genuine pleasure at seeing him. 'What a nice surprise. Come on in.'

'I have foolishly left my keys at home,' he said, 'and Marjorie is out so I can't get in until she comes back. But I knew that you would give me sanctuary.'

I took his coat and hat and hung them up but was slightly surprised to notice that he carried a brown-paper parcel with him into the drawing room and placed it beside his chair. 'I have had a busy day, dear boy,' he said, as I poured two glasses of champagne. Then he told me what had happened.

'I was sorting through some books and manuscripts this morning as usual,' he said, 'when I came across a manuscript that made me jump. I could scarcely believe my eyes. I thought I knew what it was, but I could not be sure. It seemed so incredible. So I telephoned the curator of the Pepysian Library in Cambridge and asked him a favour. I asked if I might be allowed to come in and look at the *Caxton Manuscript*.'

The *Caxton Manuscript*, as it was known, was volume I of the first two volumes that Caxton printed. It was one of the most valuable books in the world. Volume II had been lost for centuries, presumed destroyed. But even volume I alone, without its companion volume, was prized as a bright jewel in the crown in England's historic art heritage.

Philip had wrapped up his manuscript into a brown-paper parcel and hastened by train to Cambridge. In the Pepysian Library, volume I of the *Caxton Manuscript* was awaiting him on a lectern. He unwrapped his manuscript from the brown paper, and laid it alongside. No doubt about it. This was it. This was volume II.

The curator walked over to ask Philip whether he had everything he wanted. He glanced at the lectern. He saw the two volumes, side by side. Then he let out a whoop of amazement and rushed for the telephone.

'There was only one thing for it,' said Philip, sipping his champagne. 'Within ten minutes the whole of Cambridge would have been descending on us. I did not wish to become the centre of a big scene, so I hastily wrapped my manuscript up again in the brown paper, slipped out of a side door and came straight home.'

He cast a glance at the floor beside him and added, 'Now you will understand why I was presumptuous enough to bring a parcel into the drawing room.'

Philip was well aware that his discovery was a news story of international significance. He also knew that I worked for the *Daily Mirror*. But I doubt if it ever crossed his mind, bless his old heart, that my values might be so far out of focus as to allow his story to become a sensational news scoop in the *Daily Mirror* and cause the hounds of Fleet Street to lay siege to his house for interviews and pictures. And he was right. The announcement of the discovery appeared some weeks later in the proper place, on the front page of *The Times*, and as far as I can recall the name of Philip Robinson did not appear in the account.

During those early years in Hampstead I travelled abroad a good deal, working often in foreign countries, but my wife at that time was usually too busy with home affairs to come with me. So I always returned home bearing gifts, such as little dresses for Kate and trinkets for my wife. Sometimes I came back wearing some small item that I had bought for myself because it was typical of the place I had been visiting – a Hawaiian beach shirt, perhaps, or a green Tyrolean hat with a shaving brush in the side – but these exotic articles of apparel were seldom greeted with more than two cheers at home. Sometimes no cheers at all. There was a definite coolness in the house about a Russian astrakhan hat to which I was very attached; my wife refused to go out with me while I was wearing it, saying it made me look like a stallholder in Petticoat Lane during the Christmas rush.

One morning when I was in New York I was walking down Broadway when I ran into Joe Glaser, whom I had not seen since the apotheosis of Noël Coward in Vegas several months before. Joe greeted me warmly.

'Whaddayaknow, boy,' he said. 'Great to see you. Gee – that's a swell suit you are wearing! Doubtless a little number you had run up for you in your Say-vile Road in London, hey?'

'Matter of fact, yes,' I said. 'It did come from Savile Row.'

'Those boys sure do turn out some snazzy duds,' said Joe, appreciatively. 'Ernie tells me I should come over and get myself a couple of their ensembles, but I am very satisfied with my fellow, Levinsky, who can run the Say-vile Road bozos to a close finish when he is on form. Levinsky built for me this suit that I am wearing. Whaddaya think? Not bad, huh? Bespoke, of course. Hand-sewn buttonholes.'

'Very stylish, Joe,' I said. 'Particularly the shoulders and the drape. You couldn't get a better suit than that anywhere, not even Savile Row.'

'Hah!' said Joe, pleased. 'And lemme tell you – it's all-American. Even the material. Here – feel the quality. It don't have no wool or cotton or old-fashioned stuff like that – it's all pure nylon.

'Tell you what,' he went on. 'I've just had a great idea. Why don't I walk you down to Levinsky's shop so he can measure you up for half a dozen suits like this. With my compliments, of course.'

'Oh, no, Joe,' I said. 'It's very kind of you but I wouldn't dream of it.'

'Listen, boy,' said Joe. 'Don't take it the wrong way. I musta made half a million bucks outa that Noël Coward deal that was given to me on a plate by you and Ernie. I am not suggesting that you get yourself a commission but just do me a small favour, hey? To tell you the honest God's truth it would not cost me, because I would tell Levinsky what Ernie told me, which is that you got some sort of a Oscar for being England's best-dressed newshound, and Levinsky would do it for the honour. He'd hang a notice in his window – by special appointment to Noel Whitcomb who has been decorated for being one of the sharpest dressers in Say-vile Road, England, in Europe.'

I could see that Joe would take it as a gratuitous affront to the American tailoring trade if I went on refusing, so I said with a laugh, 'Well, thank you, Joe. It is a very kind thought. But there is one point on which I must insist. Only one suit. I have a good reason for that. It's not that I don't like the cut of American suits – I do. But I shall be travelling round the United States for a fortnight after the end of this week, and I just could not manage six more suits in my baggage.'

At the end of the week I picked up the suit from Levinsky.

'It's a masterpiece,' said Levinsky, as I stood in front of the looking-glass, wearing the finished confection. 'We got a real winner there. The pants alone will win you another medal, mark my words.'

In fact I was very pleased with it. It was different. If Bertie Wooster had turned up at home wearing a suit like that, Jeeves might have almost imperceptibly raised an eyebrow. If pressed to offer an opinion, Jeeves might have said, 'Well, sir, the shade of blue is perhaps more suitable for the Florida area where the light is so much brighter than is normal in our northern climate. Also, if I may say so, sir, the jacket is a trifle longer than we usually wear them, and the lapels and drape are more similar to those we see at the cinema being worn by the gentlemen in Chicago who were concerned with the bootleg liquor trade.' But to hell with such stuffy criticism, I said to myself. I liked it.

In my pocket I had an invitation to a big banquet that was to take place in Texas; it was being given by a mega-rich oil tycoon called Amon Carter, who also owned newspapers in Dallas and Fort Worth. Mr Carter was a flamboyant figure even for Texas, and this banquet was described as being in honour of The World's Great Newspaper Columnists. It was an ego-trip for Amon Carter, because his news-papers were not important and he was really a big fish in a little pool, but he had appointed a panel of editors to select well-known columnists from countries around the world, and one of the editors on the selection panel was Basil Walters, for whose paper I had once written a boxing column in Chicago, so I assumed that this was the reason why I had received an invitation. Normally I would not have bothered to go, because it was only a mutual back-slapping fiesta, but I was on my way to Mexico City so I decided to take it in on the way.

It was the usual lavish affair, and most of the best-known syndicated columnists in America had been flown in for it, which meant that Amon Carter would get the nationwide publicity he desired. I knew most of them, so it was a pleasant evening, and at the end of it we were all presented with a magnificent Texan ten-gallon cowboy hat and a pair of pearl-handled six-shooters.

So I flew off to Mexico next morning wearing my new bright-blue Palm Beach suit that had been a present from Joe Glaser, and my new Texan ten-gallon cowboy hat. I was still wearing this colourful outfit when I arrived back at Heathrow, and when I emerged from customs I was carrying the pearl-handled six-shooters because I had needed to do a fair bit of explaining about them when I declared them to the customs officer. My wife was waiting for me at the airport and her face was a picture as I strode happily to greet her.

'What the hell do you think you're wearing?' she asked. 'Here – give that hat to the driver and let's make a beeline for the car before anyone sees you.'

'What do you mean – before anyone sees me?' I said. 'This is my favourite suit.'

'I don't doubt it,' she said. 'If you are planning to take a job as a stand-up comic in cabaret at Al Burnett's Stork Club it will be the ideal thing. But if you think that I am going to be seen walking round Hampstead with a man who looks like Max Miller with firearms, you have another think coming.'

I never did have the opportunity of wearing that excellent suit again. While I was away in Naples some weeks later, it was accidentally sent to a church jumble sale. Unaccountably the Stetson hat went missing, too. Sometimes I used to wonder whether Winston Churchill, who throughout his life had a highly individual taste in hats, ever had the same sort of trouble with his wife. One never knows.

13

Is this a dagger which I see before me,
The handle toward my hand? Come, let me clutch thee . . .

from the Scottish play, by William Shakespeare

The White Hart in New Fetter Lane was for many years the *Daily Mirror* pub, but it was never known by its proper name: everyone called it 'The Stab', short for the stab-in-the-back. This was no idle witticism because The Stab was notorious as the place where reputations were knifed. Plotting and intrigue to bring about the downfall of colleagues was always a cottage industry inside the *Mirror*, the family newspaper that presented such a breezy, jolly, open face to its readers, conducted its own internal affairs in an atmosphere reminiscent of Brecht's *Threepenny Opera*. Any book that detailed the inside stories behind changes in the *Mirror*'s top staff would read like an account of operations planned by Machiavelli on behalf of his old employers, the Borgias. Few careers died a natural death.

Although I took care to avoid becoming too deeply involved in office politics, I always had a ringside seat from which to watch the contestants dancing round each other and awaiting the moment to deliver the killer blow. Furthermore, hot news about the progress of these machinations always reached me on a private grapevine because I had a mole in the field: my secretary, Phyllis Vinicombe, had a talent for obtaining secret information that would have led her to a glittering career if she had been employed by MI5; as it was, she stayed working for me for nearly thirty years, and few bosses can ever have had a more loyal and efficient secretary and friend.

After Cecil King had successfully organized the hatchet job on Harry Guy Bartholomew, and then brought back his centurion Hugh Cudlipp who quietly disposed of the body of Bish Bolam, everything changed. Most of the old generals were left dying on the battlefield and a new high command was established at staff headquarters behind the battle lines.

As an outside man, in more senses than one, I observed these changes with a thoughtful eye. Cecil King was a friend of mine, but I was not so sure about Hugh Cudlipp. I had known him for several years by then but had never been one of his cronies. Cudlipp seemed amiable enough, but by nature he was abrasive and sardonic, talented but ruthless. Success mellowed him a little but if anyone took him on for a fight he always went straight for the jugular. Once during the speeches that followed a dinner that had been set up to celebrate Lord Beaverbrook's birthday, Hugh Cudlipp and Randolph Churchill began one of their periodic slanging matches, shouting angrily at each other across the tables. Both men were masters of verbal abuse, both were drunk, and they hated each other. The frail old Beaverbrook, who had employed them both, stood up to intervene and publicly rebuked Cudlipp.

'You're too rough, Hugh,' he said. 'That's your big trouble – you've always been too rough.'

Coming from Beaverbrook, who had the nature of a street-fighter, this was regarded by most people at the dinner as a remarkable tribute. It had taken Cudlipp the best part of a quarter of a century to fight his way up from the job of a junior reporter on the *Penarth News* at five shillings a week to the position of editorial director of Mirror Group Newspapers at £28,000 a year, and he had not achieved it by affecting tennis-club manners. He was a bruiser, and he did not care who knew it. One of his friends, Rex North, used to call him Dillinger, after a notorious Chicago gangster who had been in the habit of gunning down anyone who opposed him, but although Cudlipp would never stand for overt disrespect he privately accepted this nickname as a compliment. It was widely held by people who observed him closely that behind his deliberate cultivation of an aggressive image was a deep-rooted fear of being thought a cissy; perhaps for some reason dimly remembered from his Cardiff boyhood, he associated the name Claud with a timid, namby-pamby, Little-Lord-Fauntleroy type of man, and in heated moments he would sometimes say, 'My name's not Claud, you know!'

He strode round the *Mirror* offices, always walking fast, the upper part of his body bent forward from the hips in predatory fashion, a large cigar clenched in his teeth, aware that all eyes were upon him. He was an actor playing the part of the charismatic newspaper boss. Apart from the cigar, which gave an unintended impression of Groucho Marx, his act had the appearance of being based on the performance of Orson Welles as the newspaper tycoon in the film *Citizen Kane*. Many years later, when I saw Anthony Hopkins playing the part of the newspaper boss in *Pravda* at the National Theatre, I watched in wrapt fascination because that hunched walk, that hooded reptilian stare with the head pushed forward, that wide smile which turned to a snarl, all were authentic hallmarks of the Cudlipp persona.

When Cudlipp returned to the *Mirror* from his brief exile he brought with him a number of his friends, including several who had worked with him when he edited the forces' newspaper *Union Jack* in the Western Desert during the war, a cabal known as 'the men with sand in their shoes'. Some of these became columnists, but although most of them were *soi-disant* specialists, whereas I was a general dogsbody who wrote about anything that came my way, I had trouble with these new colleagues from time to time. The reason was that every one of them stood over his specialized patch with the vigilance of a Dobermann pinscher guarding a safe deposit, and if anyone else on the paper chanced to write on a subject that they considered to be their preserve they would go running to the editor or to Cudlipp shouting, 'It's not fair!'

My reaction was always to reply with the same observation that I made to the children when they complained in similarly tearful tones: 'Life is not fair'; but this did little to enhance my popularity, especially as my right to choose the subjects about which I wrote was usually upheld – not, I may say, because any of the editorial executives concerned was likely to send me a Valentine but simply for practical reasons of circulation.

People who deal in the written word tend to develop an exaggerated sense of their own importance; even great writers such as Kipling talked at times like demigods; Wilde and Wells became ludicrously egotistical, and the Bloomsbury Group so pompous that sometimes their world now sounds almost as comic as that of Mr Pooter; Evelyn Waugh and Dorothy Sayers in their time suffered from raging *folie-de-grandeur* and the coterie of contemporary writers that includes Harold Pinter and Salman Rushdie all suffer from the same malaise even though their much-publicized work is of a lower literary standard: the condition is endemic. But of all the writers of all kinds and qualities across the spectrum, there is no doubt that newspaper columnists take the biscuit. At the top end of the trade you hear exponents of this very minor art referring to 'm'column' in the way that Etonians used to refer to 'm'tutor', and lower down the scale the words 'my column' are used with an air of deep importance that Michaelangelo would have hesitated to assume when talking of 'my ceiling'. Women columnists are, in my experience, the most embarrassing in this respect, but in any race for boasters open to all categories they would have the hot breath of boxing columnists on their necks all the way to the line. Why this should be so is not readily susceptible to explanation, but the facts as I have observed them show that writers and critics who concern themselves with the noble and manly art tend to be fragile blossoms at heart, sometimes ending up as born-again Buddhists or animal-rights campaigners or romantic novelists, and all are as touchy as electric power cables.

The first example I encountered of this eccentric anthropological species was a man called Tom Phillips, who was chief boxing writer for the *Daily Mirror* during my early days on the paper. Tom was a Geordie from the Newcastle area, and a great friend of the editor, Bish Bolam, who came from Durham. It was Tom's custom to send in long, blow-by-blow accounts of boxing matches late at night, when all the inside staff were working at full stretch to get the copy down to the composing room in time for the final edition. In such circumstances it was not surprising that the occasional word or even sentence of Tom's prose was deleted to make the copy fit the space available, but this offended Tom's literary sensitivity so deeply that he stormed into the editor's office and demanded to be made assistant editor in charge of sport, a position that would enable him to fire anyone who had the temerity to lay a finger on his copy.

The editor, being an old friend, agreed. This caused chaos. Tom would return to the office after the box-fights very late at night, inflamed with Scotch whisky and artistic enthusiasm, and create merry hell if so much as a comma in his copy had been misplaced. Worse still, he would sometimes rewrite at greater length, causing his boxing column to extend to a whole page or more; there were occasions when this required the sudden removal of the race-cards for two or three meetings, and that all the racing tips be dropped. The whole sports department was horrified, but there was nothing they could do about it because Tom was the boss.

By an odd chance, I inadvertently played a minor part in the drama of Tom's downfall. I was in Chicago for a week at a time when a world championship heavyweight fight was due to take place there; as one of the contestants had previously fought in England, and I had seen the fight, the managing editor of the Chicago *Daily News*, a man called Basil Walters, asked me to write a boxing column for his paper during the days of the run-up to the fight, and to report the fight from the British angle when it took place – to which I agreed with pleasure.

On the day before the fight the usual weigh-in took place, and in this case it was located in Goldblatt's department store. All the camp-followers of the two contestants poured into Goldblatt's, and the manager, observing that some were decorated fashionably with cauliflower ears and others with razor-scars on their cheeks or guns tattooed on their forearms, decided to hold the ceremony in garden supplies rather than in the jewellery department.

It was an informal occasion. The two boxers came on stage accompanied by a blonde in a pink bustle and an actor wearing Gay Nineties costume. Ezzard Charles weighed in at 182lb and Joe Maxim at 181½lb and immediately the blonde canary began singing, 'I dowanna live without you baby – and can YOU afford to live without Goldblatt's?'

The whole production was sufficiently different from the average British weigh-in to provide me with material for a light-hearted column in the *Daily News* next day; extracts were picked up by the agencies and some were printed in the diary columns of the London evening papers, giving the customary credit to the *Daily Mirror*. The thought that somebody else on the paper was writing about boxing so outraged Tom Phillips that he marched into the editor's office and demanded that I should be fired. The editor pacified him and said he would send me a warning cable. That was not good enough for Tom, so he wrote a letter to the chairman, Cecil King.

The editor's cable read: CONGRATULATIONS YOUR CHICAGO STUFF BUT PLEASE LAY OFF BOXING STORIES. By the time it caught up with me I was ensconced in a suite at the Beverly Hills Hotel in Hollywood, writing columns about film stars – which, if I had thought about it, was by that time the heavily defended territory of our new showbusiness columnist, Donald Zec.

It was some time later, when I was tramping over the moors in Scotland with Cecil King, that I heard about the outcome of Tom's letter. 'Mr Phillips came to see me,' said Cecil, 'and made it clear at the start that he was the best sports columnist in the world. I seldom read sports columns, but I agreed that this might be the case. He went on to demand that his salary should be doubled. I told him that this might present some difficulties because it would make him far more highly paid than the editor, but that there were precedents for such things happening in newspapers.

'He then demanded to have a car and driver at his disposal twenty-four hours a day, seven days a week. This, I told him, would be an expensive item because it would require the employment of three drivers on shifts, but such an arrangement was not unknown.

'Finally he said that he would agree to remain on the paper only if he received a written undertaking that every word he wrote would be printed in the *Daily Mirror*. I pointed out that this could not only present legal difficulties but also great technical problems. He appeared to be inclined to argue so I fired him on the spot.'

A brace of grouse fluttered up in the distance and Cecil dispatched both birds with a swift left and a right.

'How do you get on with Cudlipp?' he asked as he reloaded.

'Oh, first class,' I said. 'David and Jonathan. Damon and Pythias.'

'Caesar and Brutus,' added Cecil, drily.

The abrupt demise of Tom Phillips left a gap in the paper which Cudlipp filled by bringing in his old friend Peter Wilson, who became the best boxing columnist of his day, but who also had that strain of paranoia about his column that is endemic in the vocation. Peter, an old Harrovian whose father had worked on the *Mirror*, was a bulky man with a soup-strainer moustache and a fruity saloon-bar chuckle, and he strode around wearing a Sherlock Holmes cloak with a fancy waistcoat beneath it, brandishing a heavy sword-stick.

His approach in print was always appropriately pugnacious. There were other columnists who fearlessly exposed the chicanery of the boxing world, but Peter did it with such belligerence that Cudlipp dubbed him 'The Man They Can't Gag': a description that Peter had no difficulty in justifying either in conversation or in print. When reporting big fights he went in for a florid type of prose that dripped with the blood of Titans: reading his reports of heavyweight contests you could hear the crunch of breaking bones as the courageous warrior hit his opponent with a mighty right that would have demolished Battersea Bridge, and you could hear the liquid hiss as the champ spattered his victim's nose over his face like a squashed pomegranate, squirting his gore in a crimson fountain over the sporting gentlemen in the ringside seats. Peter's stuff was very popular. It was like reading about a road accident.

He was a prodigious drinker, famed for his prowess in this respect even in that period when the competition was at its zenith. If annual Fleet Street awards had been made in this category, the *Daily Mirror* would have won the *victor ludorum* year after year. If at that time you had taken all the liquor consumed inside the *Mirror* building in any week, and poured it into Loch Ness, the level of the lake would have risen by several inches and the Loch Ness monster would have surfaced singing *When Irish Eyes are Smilin'*.

Under the Cudlipp regime, every director, every senior executive and every top columnist had a well-stocked private bar in his office, and these bars were used almost solely for entertaining colleagues on the paper; sometimes the editor or one of the directors would have guests in from outside, but in general the liquor was consumed by the staff. These bars were status symbols, and the hosts would offer hospitality to their less privileged friends on the paper, the cost being charged to the company under the heading of entertainment.

These conferences or meetings ('Mr Smith is in a meeting – can I give him a message?') usually started in mid-morning and went on sporadically all over the building throughout the day and often far into the night. One of the most talented page-designers I ever met, a man called Harold Keeble, always kept his office refrigerator stocked with bottles of Pouilly-Fuissé, of which he was particularly fond, but he also kept an oxygen cylinder beside his desk for use at any time when an important job cropped up. Visitors from more disciplined industries were sometimes heard to wonder how a newspaper could be produced under such conditions. They were sternly reminded that although drink was always available, drunkenness was frowned upon. The word alcoholism was never used except to describe the sad affliction sometimes to be found among dossers who drank methylated spirits and slept underneath the arches. International statistics at the time showed that Ireland had the lowest incidence of alcoholism in Europe, and the same system of counting was used in the *Daily Mirror*.

The day's drinking inside the *Mirror* was interrupted by the lunch hour, when everyone would go out for a drink. The lunch hour usually began about 1 p.m., and for quite a large proportion of the staff it habitually ended at about 4 p.m., when lunchers would return from the Wig and Pen Club or similar hostelry with afternoon licensing facilities and invite colleagues into their offices for a drink while they discussed the work in hand.

I personally spent as little time as possible in the office, mostly because it was an essential part of my job to be out and about, but partly on the advice of our local undertaker, who did a brisk trade in newspapermen. In any case, although I was fully accepted as an old pro who could turn his hand to anything and never missed a deadline, I was always regarded inside the office with the faintest air of suspicion; slightly foreign.

The one type of celebration to which I was frequently invited, however, more as an acknowledgement of seniority than through any deep longing for my companionship, was the big office lunch. In Bartholomew's time such luncheons took place infrequently, mostly on festive occasions when somebody of consequence was to be ritually fired, and were savoured as such, like public hangings at Tyburn. But during the Cudlipp years the ceremony of the office lunch was elevated to a fine art, and they proliferated until they became almost as common as feast days on the Calendar of Saints; seldom did a week go by without one or two office lunches in the diary, and the point about them was that they were paid for by the office.

These luncheons were held in private banqueting rooms at big hotels or restaurants – the Ritz, the Savoy, the Café Royal – and when they were arranged to mark some special occasion, such as a new appointment, a promotion in the upper echelons, an anniversary, a circulation landmark, a forthcoming campaign or a retirement, they were extravagant and spectacular productions: the walls would be decorated with six-foot-high blow-ups of appropriate photographs, and four-page menus with pictures and specially written stories in the form of the newspaper would be printed.

They all ran to a traditional ritual. Staff would arrive at 12.30 for 1 p.m. and stand around chatting and drinking dry martinis or gins and tonic until about 1.15 when Hugh Cudlipp would come striding in with the editor. Hugh, waving his cigar, would then say, 'Let's have a glass of Charlie.' Waiters would then hasten to open several dozen bottles of Bollinger which had earlier been put on ice in readiness for the command. When these had been consumed we would all sit down to lunch, usually about half-past two.

The food was usually ordinary but the wines were always excellent. We would start with generous helpings of a white Burgundy, a Corton-Charlemagne or a Montrachet, and then move smoothly with the meat course to a first-growth red Bordeaux, usually a vintage Château Latour. Latour was Cudlipp's favourite claret, and when we reached the brandy-or-port stage he would usually wave the brandy aside and say to the waiter, 'Let's have another glass of the old Lat.' In preparation for this, several more magnums of Latour would already have been decanted and placed on the tables alongside the bottles of cognac and carafes of vintage port. In Cudlipp's vocabulary the expression 'a glass of' was used figuratively and when he called for 'a glass of' it usually meant 'a case of'.

The speeches began on the customary note of mutual admiration, but Cudlipp soon tired of this, and introduced an element of mayhem. People who had made some harmless remark were savaged by his brutal invective; I have seen guests of honour, old colleagues who were retiring, torn to shreds and left for dead after the speech that Cudlipp made in their honour. It was a ritual. Everyone present enjoyed this savage cabaret except the poor fellow who had been verbally crucified. Sometimes Cudlipp went too far and fired the individual concerned, but he always took him on again next morning. After all, these were fraternal occasions.

Although I can recall two or three of these lunches that ended at 7.30 p.m. more often they concluded around 5 p.m. when members of the staff would straggle from the room, some bearing in their side pockets the unfinished bottles of brandy, whisky and gin that had been left on the tables, rather than leave them to be pinched by greedy and dishonest waiters. Evening pub opening time in the Fleet Street area was five o'clock, so lunchers who still had unfinished business to discuss would pop in for a refreshing pint or a gin and tonic on their way back to the office.

After Silvester Bolam finally staggered from the building, manfully struggling to wrench the dagger from between his shoulderblades, Cudlipp appointed Jack Nener as the new editor. Jack, being a Welshman with hollow legs, was much more suitable to the task in hand, which was to revolutionize the *Daily Mirror* into The Paper with Heart – the good, old-fashioned sentimental friend of the people, the paper that loved charladies, patted doggies, cooed at babies, drank beer with miners, stuck two fingers in the air at bosses, gossiped familiarly about members of the royal family and stood for no nonsense from uppish foreigners. (This last quality was exemplified in a full front-page message in enormous type to Mr Khrushchev after he had stormed out of a summit meeting: DON'T BE SO BLOODY RUDE, MR K! WHO DO YOU THINK YOU ARE – STALIN?)

Jack Nener would not have been everyone's choice as an editor, but he was ideal for Cudlipp's purpose for three reasons: first, he was technically well qualified for the job, having worked his way up through the subs' table to the back bench; secondly he was so Welsh that whenever a dinner was given in his honour the assembled company had to sing *Land of My Fathers* and *Sospen Fach*; thirdly, and most important, he knew his place – he was no danger to Hugh Cudlipp and was happy to do the donkeywork of editorship while Cudlipp took all the major editorial decisions. Cudlipp always employed people who were good at their jobs, but if anyone on the staff ever showed signs of being good at Cudlipp's job, that man soon found himself seeking employment elsewhere. Jack Nener listened to his master's voice and did as he was told.

To a certain extent through frustration, but more because it was in his nature, Nener ruled his underlings with a ferocity that would have drawn a nod of approval from Attila the Hun. He tyrannized over his inside staff, putting the fear of God into his deputies, growling with menace at his assistants, tongue-lashing his departmental editors and bullying his back bench of editorial executives who had been his erstwhile equals. His columnists, however, were hardly ever on the receiving end of the Caligula tactics, and I was one of the people to whom he was unfailingly polite.

Jack Nener looked the part of an editor. Tall, white-haired, well dressed, he presented a distinguished appearance, and to people who were meeting him for the first time he was quite impressive; until he spoke: then the spell was broken; his language was hair-raising. It was not merely on occasions of stress that he sprayed the world around him with a blistering fire of four-letter words; that was not unusual at times of pressure in Fleet Street. Jack did it all the time. He even used four-letter words in the speech he made to the guests at the reception following his wedding to Audrey Whiting. Like the fish-porters at Billingsgate or the guardsmen in barrack-rooms at Pirbright, Jack seldom completed a sentence without a four-letter word in it.

He lived in Wimbledon, and the local domestic agency eventually had to tell him that they could no longer find daily women who were prepared to work in his house, because they were all so shocked by his language. So Jack was put to the necessity of importing a foreign girl to do the housework. She spoke practically no English when she arrived, but one reason why she came to this country was, of course, to learn the language.

One Sunday morning when she had been working in the house for a few weeks, the telephone rang and she answered it. Reg Payne, then features editor of the *Daily Mirror*, was on the line. 'I want to speak to Mr Nener, please,' he said.

'Is not possible,' said the girl.

'Not possible?' repeated Reg. 'Why? Isn't he there?'

'Oh, yes, is here,' said the girl.

'Well – you go and tell him it is Reg Payne on the line. Tell him it's urgent.'

'No,' said the girl. 'Is not disturb.'

'Not disturb?' echoed Reg. 'Why is not disturb?'

'Because he is mending ze fuckin' Hoover,' said the girl.

The domestic lives of *Daily Mirror* journalists were often beset by complexity, because the exigencies of office life and the requirements of life at home were seldom compatible. House-ownership was far less widespread in those days, of course, and almost unknown among the working class; few journalists owned the property in which they lived, and, even of those who could have afforded to do so, most preferred to spend their money in other ways and lived in rented flats or small semi-detached rented houses in the suburbs.

Hugh Cudlipp, different in this as in so many other ways, lived in a fine Georgian house in Cheyne Walk, a house that belonged to his second wife, Eileen Ascroft, who had previously been married to a film director. But Hugh was a sociable and gregarious man who liked to have his colleagues and henchmen around him, and to make them feel more at home he had arranged for part of the ground floor to be converted into a replica of a *fin-de-siècle* saloon bar, complete with brass rail and all the period accoutrements. His wife used to serve behind the bar wearing the low-cut white blouse and black split-skirt of a typical Edwardian barmaid, and in the corner was an old-style honkytonk upright piano around which on many convivial evenings happy guests would sing *Wales, Wales, Glorious, Glorious Wales* until one evening Wolf Mankowitz was sick into the works, after which the tone was never quite the same. (When Cudlipp finally retired, the *Daily Mirror* staff contributed towards buying him a barrel-organ as a leaving present.)

Cudlipp, a generous man with his own money as well as with the firm's, was unusual in inviting colleagues from the paper to the house, and few of the rest of us did it. In our own case, my wife always maintained that it would only cause trouble by upsetting them, and this turned out to be an accurate assessment on the only occasion when the editor came to visit. I was laid up at the time, recovering from some minor illness, and Jack Nener arrived at the house unexpectedly with a bottle of brandy as a get-well present, accompanied by Reg Payne.

My wife did social work in Hampstead, looking after the old and infirm, and two other local women who were concerned with this work, one the wife of a Mayfair art-dealer and the other a rich American widow, were having tea with us in the drawing room on the afternoon when Jack Nener arrived.

The drawing room was on the first floor and we could all hear Jack's loud and deep voice as he talked to Reg Payne on his way up the stairs. 'Jesus Christ almighty, Reg,' said Jack, 'this is posh. How the bloody hell do you suppose Noel got a bloody lovely place like this? . . . Oh, excuse me, ladies,' he added, as he was shown into the room, still looking round in surprise. 'Didn't know you had company, Noel.'

'Let me introduce my editor,' I said. 'This is Jack Nener.'

'Do you live in Hampstead, Mr Nener?' one of the women asked.

'Christ, no,' said Jack. 'I live in an ordinary fuckin' house in Wimbledon.'

There was a ten-second silence, and then the other woman said, 'Ah, Wimbledon. How convenient.'

'Convenient?' echoed Jack, giving her a suspicious look.

'For the tennis,' she said.

Jack had about as much interest in tennis as he had in Egyptian archaeology or Renaissance art.

But the subject about which he proudly claimed to know nothing at all whatsoever was pop music: Jack abominated pop. One morning he came into my office and closed the door behind him in a conspiratorial manner, looking round the room in cloak-and-dagger fashion as if searching for hidden microphones. 'Noel,' he said in a whispered growl, 'I've just been up with Hugh Cudlipp and we have a special job we want you to do. Very secret.'

'Righto, Jack,' I said. 'Delighted. At your service.'

'Nobody must hear about this,' he went on. 'Nobody. This is for your ears only.'

'You know me, Jack,' I said. 'Silent as the grave. Say on.'

'We want you to fly to America tonight on a terribly secret mission.' (Incidentally, when reporting Jack's conversation from now on I will use the system employed by transcribers of the Watergate tapes – expletives deleted.)

'Sure, Jack,' I nodded. 'What's the story?'

'We want you to bring back the pop-star feller,' he said.

'Which pop-star feller?' My own knowledge of the pop world was scanty enough, and I was beginning to think that somebody more expert than me should be employed on this assignment.

'You know the feller I mean,' said Jack. 'The one that all the kids are stark raving crazy about.' He went into a grotesque sort of mime, strumming an invisible guitar and jumping up and down on the carpet as if writhing in pain.

'Elvis Presley?' I asked.

'*That's* the boyo,' said Jack. 'I knew you'd know. We want you to bring him to this country to do a concert tour.'

'Does he know about it?' I asked.

'Don't bother me with details,' said Jack.

'But look here, Jack, I was reading a piece about Elvis Presley the other day and according to the writer he has a Svengali-type manager called Colonel Tom Parker, an old Barnum-type showman who has made a hundred million dollars out of Presley in America and who has gone on record saying that Presley would come to Britain over his dead body.'

'How you arrange it is your affair,' said Jack. 'If we didn't think there might be a few difficulties we wouldn't be asking you to do it, would we?'

I digested this pretty compliment and tried another tack.

'Who is setting up this concert tour?' I asked. 'This Presley chap is the hottest ticket in the entire world, and if he came on tour round this country it would take more organizing than the second coming of the Messiah.'

'All that part of it is taken care of,' said Jack. 'Hugh has been talking to Suzanne this morning. Lew and Leslie have arranged the theatres and the dates. It's all set up ready. The *Daily Mirror* will sponsor the tour, exclusive. Our story. Nobody else gets a look-in. That's why it's all so secret. But apparently this chap' – Jack went into his guitar-strumming and jumping-up-and-down mime again –

'Presley,' I said.

' – that's right,' said Jack, 'apparently he has not signed on the dotted line yet, and is being a bit difficult, which is why we want you to go over there in dead secrecy and just arrange the final details and then bring him back with you.'

'Oh, yes,' I nodded. 'Now I see it all. I can see the headlines – PRESLEY KIDNAP. BRITISH JOURNALIST HELD.'

'Don't be squeamish,' said Jack. 'You're booked on the six o'clock flight to New York. Don't come back without him.'

All the way home in the car and all the time I was packing my bag I kept puzzling about this odd assignment; there was something strange about it, something that did not quite fit. Jack had said that Lew and Leslie had arranged the whole deal and set up the tour, and that meant it was entirely possible, because Lew and Leslie Grade were the biggest variety agents in Britain; the Grade Agency handled every big act that came over from the United States, and Suzanne Warner set up all the publicity for them. I had known all three of them very well for years and I decided that, in spite of Jack's warning about dead secrecy, I would telephone one of them and find out the background: after all, if they had set it up they must be in the secret.

I was halfway through dialling Lew's private number when a small voice in the back of my brain counselled caution, and I put down the phone; all three of them, Lew, Leslie and Suzanne, were also friends of Hugh Cudlipp, and whichever of them I rang would be on the line to Hugh within minutes of the end of any conversation I had with them.

Lew and Leslie Grade and their brother, Bernie Delfont, had come to England with their mother as refugees from Jewish persecution in

Eastern Europe early this century; there was a story current in showbusiness that when the three boys landed at the London docks they had been very, very poor indeed – for ten minutes. Lew and Bernie had become hoofers on the variety stage – Lew had won a Charleston dancing championship – but soon they moved into the managerial side of the profession and became richer by the day.

In the early 1950s, when commercial television was in its infancy in Britain, Lew and Leslie were in virtual control of the powerful Associated Television company, of which Cecil King bought ten per cent on behalf of the *Daily Mirror*. The inside story of the financial in-fighting and political intrigue that surrounded this commercial *coup* has been amusingly told by Clifford Davis in his book *How I Made Lew Grade a Millionaire*, but the upshot was that in later years everyone concerned with it – including Suzanne Warner – became immensely rich. I myself bought some shares in ATV for a few shillings each in the early days and later sold them when they had reached about £14 a share; that was the period when Lord Thomson described the ownership of a commercial television franchise as a machine for printing money.

The point about all this is that on the day when I was packing to fly off to America to bring back Elvis Presley there was already a strong link between Hugh Cudlipp and the Grades, not to mention Suzanne Warner, and this meant that I needed to proceed with delicacy in the matter of my latest assignment: to put a foot wrong could cause a lot of trouble; so off I went to the airport without telephoning anyone.

In the VIP lounge at Heathrow I ran into Jack Hylton, whom I had known since the days when he was a bandleader, and who was by this time one of London's biggest theatrical impresarios.

'Where are you off to, Noel?' he asked.

'Oh, just slipping over to New York for a few days,' I said. 'Catch a few of the new Broadway shows, meet a few friends, nothing special.'

'Where are you staying?' he asked.

'Haven't booked,' I said. 'Probably dig in at the St Regis.'

Jack took a bunch of keys from his pocket and tossed them to me.

'Stay at my apartment in New York,' he said. 'It's very convenient, up by the park. You'll like it. Nobody else there at the moment except my butler, Fred, who is a very useful man.'

Normally I would have turned down an offer of this sort, because it is never a good idea for a columnist to be under an obligation to anyone in showbusiness; but Jack Hylton was a very old friend and was not the sort of man who would try to exact payment in kind for a good turn; furthermore the use of his flat would save me the necessity of putting my name on a hotel register, thereby shrouding my visit in even greater secrecy. So I thanked him and accepted. Jack wrote a note on one of his cards to tell his butler, Fred, that I was a guest, and off we went on our separate ways.

It was a beautiful apartment, ideally situated for my purpose and richly furnished, and Fred turned out to be the perfect stage butler, reminiscent of Beach, Lord Emsworth's worthy man.

I spent the next morning finding out that Elvis Presley was in California, that he had a schedule of firm arrangements for appearances in the United States that extended for at least the next six months, and that his minder, Colonel Tom Parker, was in Hawaii on holiday: not a promising prospect. The plot thickened.

As I strolled along Fifth Avenue, deep in thought, I heard my name called from behind, and looking round I saw Midori, Mike Todd's Japanese girl secretary. 'Great to see you, Mr Noel,' she said. 'What a nice surprise. Does Mr Todd know you are in town?'

'No, I said. 'I only got in last night and I haven't got around to ringing anyone yet.'

'Mr Todd sure will be pleased to hear this news,' said Midori. 'Where are you staying?'

There was no point in sounding shifty about my whereabouts, and to shilly-shally would have seemed either furtive or unfriendly, so I gave Midori my address and telephone number. Mike Todd was a big-time film producer, but I had known him way back in the days when he was down to his last million; in fact, among all the hundreds of aquaintances I had in movies, Mike was one of a handful – the others being David Niven, Errol Flynn, Humphrey Bogart and John Huston – whom I regarded as friends.

Mike, John Huston and I shared a keen interest in horses, but whereas Huston preferred hunters, Todd was mad about thoroughbreds. He was so interested in racing at one time that he bought the Del Mar Racetrack from Bing Crosby. The day he opened it he distributed free to all racegoers a leather-bound copy of Damon Runyon's book *Horseplayers Die Broke*. After a short time of daily playing the horses on his own racecourse, Mike not only lost all his money but he also lost the track. I have known many men who lost heavily on the horses, but Mike was the only one I knew who had actually lost a racetrack.

After lunch I sauntered back to the apartment, and Fred shimmered out of his quarters to greet me with a message. 'Mr Michael Todd telephoned, sir,' he said, and although Fred's face remained as impassive as that of an Egyptian mummy I could hear from the tone of his voice that he was impressed. 'He asked if you are doing anything this evening, sir,' went on Fred, 'because if you are not Mr Todd would like to come in for a drink after dinner with Miss Elizabeth Taylor.'

'Sure,' I said. 'Sure – ring back and tell him I'll be delighted.'

Fred gave a modest cough and added, 'He said he would have some friends with him, if that would be all right.'

'Tell him it's Liberty Hall here,' I said. 'His friends are my friends. Tell him he can bring whoever he likes. Especially Elvis Presley,' I added.

'I do not think that you would care for Mr Presley, sir,' said Fred, disapprovingly. 'None of my gentlemen has ever entertained Mr Presley.'

I spent the afternoon going round museums and galleries, trying to think of a convincing story to tell Jack Nener about why I had failed his trust in the matter of E. Presley Esq.. This would be my first failure in such a matter, and I knew it would not go down well. I dreaded to think of Jack's language when I broke the news to him. Deciding to postpone the evil hour until next day, I finally wandered back to the apartment at about the cocktail hour. Letting myself in with Jack Hylton's latchkey, I was confronted by a remarkable sight in the hall. It looked as though somebody had bought the entire stock of Moyses Stevens' flower shop and delivered it. There was also a mountain of cases of vintage champagne.

Fred bustled up busily, wearing a green baize apron, and I asked him what was going on. 'Are you hiring this place out for wedding receptions and barmitzvahs during the master's absence, Fred?' I asked.

'Oh, no, sir,' he said, shocked. 'Mr Todd sent these. I assume he thought that we might possibly be short of flowers and champagne in Mr Hylton's absence. Not that we are, of course, but it was a kind thought. He said they would be here about ten o'clock, sir,' added Fred. 'I have laid out your dress clothes in readiness.'

At ten o'clock I was ready and waiting in a new tuxedo and the guests started arriving. Noël Coward was the first to arrive, with Alfred Lunt and Lynn Fontaine, and he was clearly startled to be greeted by me, because he had been expecting to see Mike Todd and Elizabeth Taylor; but he was no more surprised to see me than I was to see him.

'Come in, dear boy, come in,' I said. 'Mike and Liz will doubtless be here in a couple of minutes. Meanwhile let us begin the revelry.'

In fact, Mike and Liz did not arrive for another half-hour, during which time the apartment filled up with what appeared to be a star cast for Academy Awards Night. Almost everyone who was anyone on

Broadway or in Hollywood was there. An invitation from Mike Todd, even at a few hours' notice, was not one that any star in his or her right mind would turn down. Fred was in his element. He was deploying the small staff of waiters he had engaged for the night with the panache of Lord Cardigan sending in the Light Brigade, and the crush and the noise in progress must have been not too different from Balaclava.

'Very gratifying, sir,' said Fred, as he refreshed my glass. 'I wish Mr Hylton were here. Almost everyone else is. Mr Sam Goldwyn is over there, talking to Miss Shirley Maclaine and Mr David Niven. Excuse me, sir, I must attend to the door. That is Mr Todd arriving with Mr Zanuck and Miss Marlene Dietrich.'

To list the illustrious names who were present would be tedious; suffice it to say that everyone was there. It was, for sure, the best party I have ever given – if that is the right way to phrase it – and it was four o'clock in the morning when I bid goodbye to the last departing guest and retired to my couch.

The bedside telephone awakened me shortly after 10 a.m. and, picking up the receiver, I immediately recognized the voice on the other end of the line: Ralph Champion.

Ralph Champion was bureau chief of the *Daily Mirror*'s New York office. I could hear from the tone of his greeting that he was not pleased, and I was not surprised: for a columnist like me to come to New York without letting him know that I was in town was rather like the Cardinal Archbishop of Westminster visiting Rome without telling the Vatican; it was an unforgiveable solecism.

'Ralph,' I said, 'my dear Ralph, I know what you are thinking.'

'I doubt it,' he said, coldly.

'You must realize, Ralph,' I said, 'that I am under strict instructions from Jack Nener. He impressed upon me before I left London that my visit to New York must be kept absolutely secret. I was to tell nobody. I was to keep the whole thing under wraps.'

'Well,' said Ralph, 'you have not entirely succeeded, but we may be able to limit the damage. There are probably eighty million people in the United States this morning who know you are in New York. If we play our cards right we may be able to keep it a secret from the rest of the population.'

'What are you talking about?' I asked.

'Your party last night,' said Ralph. 'And by the way – thanks for the invitation. It must have got lost in the post. According to Walter Winchell, who used his whole column on it, it was a very spectacular do. Cholly Knickerbocker says in his column that *le tout New York* was there and that it was the biggest high-society bash of the season. You certainly do have a modest way of keeping quiet about your presence.'

'Steady on, Ralph,' I said. 'It wasn't my idea, it was Mike Todd's. Mike decided to give a little welcome party for me, as an old mate, and he asked if he could hold it here. He said he was just bringing a few pals – I didn't know he was going to bring *le tout New York*.'

'Well, however it happened the fact is that he has blown your cover in a spectacular way,' went on Ralph. 'Walter Winchell's column is syndicated to newspapers all over the United States, and Cholly Knickerbocker's column appears from coast to coast. Most of the London papers who have bureaux here feed bits from Winchell to their own diaries, so it will not be long before Jack Nener hears of your lavish hospitality to the drinking classes in America. It is just lucky that you will not be needing to send him the bill for last night's saturnalia, because he might feel disinclined to sign it.'

I groaned.

'What *are* you doing over here, anyway?' went on Ralph. 'Working for the Deuxieme Bureau?'

'Listen, Ralph,' I said, deciding that it was now impossible not to let him in on the secret, 'I will level with you. You must promise to keep this under your hat. Jack Nener asked me to come over here and take Elvis Presley back to London.'

'What a nice idea,' said Ralph. 'It would certainly result in the outbreak of World War III, and that would get you into the record books because nobody is expecting the next war to be between Britain and America. It would make a lot of work for all of us. You would be shot at dawn, of course.'

'Very droll,' I said, coldly. 'But let me tell you that the whole thing has been set up through the Grade Agency, and Hugh Cudlipp has arranged that we have the inside track, exclusive. Hugh has fixed it with Suzanne Warner.'

'Suzanne!' roared Ralph. 'Now I see it all. Suzanne was over here last week and she told me in strict confidence that the *Mirror* would be sending Pat Doncaster over to take back Bill Haley.'

'Bill who?' I asked.

'Bill Haley is the second hottest property in the world, after Elvis Presley,' explained Ralph. 'He is top of the pops with a number called *Rock Around the Clock* and all the kids are wild about him. But apparently he is playing hard to get because he has heard that the fans in Britain are red in tooth and claw, and he figures they will tear him limb from limb. He wants danger money.'

271

'But Ralph,' I said, weakly. 'Jack definitely told me Elvis Presley.'

'Did you ever know Jack Nener get anything about pop music right? The last time Jack knew the name of a popular singer it was Enrico Caruso.'

'I'll murder that bastard Nener,' I growled.

'If you ever do perform that service to humanity,' said Ralph, 'you will find no shortage of colleagues willing to come forward and swear that they were playing poker with you on the night of the crime.'

After the Baskerville shadow of Hound Dog Presley had been lifted from my life, the task of putting Bill Haley under starter's orders seemed as simple as selling Tower Bridge to a Texan oil tycoon.

Haley was a timid man with a kiss-curl, and when I ran him to earth he was evasive. 'You'll have to talk to my manager,' he said. 'He likes to be called Lord Jim.'

'Ah,' I said, 'he's fond of Conrad, is he?'

'Oh, no,' said Bill, 'he's not that sort of man. He's married.'

It was somewhat like dealing with Martians, but I soon had Bill Haley and his band, the Comets, loaded aboard the liner Queen Elizabeth and off we sailed for England, home and beauty. Mission accomplished.

In those days there were several of us who were regulars in the Queen boats on the transatlantic run, and it was more like a club; most passengers in the first class knew each other. On this trip there were several actors and actresses I knew, plus a couple of City financiers and a brace of film directors, so we all settled down for four days of restful amusement. Twice during the voyage I won the sweepstake for guessing the mileage of the day's run, and the two sums added up to the present-day equivalent of the price of a Jaguar car, so I was having a splendid time.

I made a slight error of judgement in giving a party in my stateroom for Bill Haley, because although it was a happy social occasion nobody among the several dozen guests apart from Jack Buchanan and Victor Mature had ever heard of Bill Haley; which deepened his foreboding about England. But I had been sending columns daily to the paper, speaking well of our client, and the *Daily Mirror* had been displaying them in a fashion suitable for a coronation or a royal wedding, so Bill cheered up when we arrived at Southampton and he saw the welcome that awaited him.

Looking down from the deck it appeared that a cup-final crowd from Wembley had been joined by the crush from Epsom Downs on Derby day: tens of thousands of teenagers had turned up to greet their idol, all screaming their heads off; it was an astonishing scene and the noise was stupefying. The *Daily Mirror* was treating its triumph in capturing Bill Haley in a manner more suitable for the celebration of Wellington's victory at Waterloo, and the paper had arranged a special train to take the conquering hero back to London.

With a sigh of relief I handed Bill Haley and his band over to my colleague, Pat Doncaster, the *Mirror*'s pop-music expert, and slid quietly off to a waiting car that took me straight home.

Life returned to normal. I told Jack Nener that the next time he wanted Elvis Presley kidnapped he had better get in touch with Cosa Nostra, and Jack replied with a remark about pop stars in general that would have shocked a stud manager.

Day after day for the next few weeks the front page and two or three inside pages of the *Daily Mirror* were blazoned with stories about Bill Haley's sensational tour around the country; Bill was mobbed in Manchester, beleaguered in Birmingham, besieged in Bradford, chased by howling hordes in Cardiff, rough-housed in Liverpool; everywhere he went he was embroiled in the pandemonium of a seething, scrambling, screaming mass of teenagers. Riot followed riot. The *Daily Mirror* was naturally delighted about this eye-catching success. After all, Bill was their boy. If the original manuscripts of all William Shakespeare's plays had been discovered in an attic during that period, the news would have been given a small space in the *Daily Mirror* somewhere towards the back of the paper: Bill Haley was king, and no other news got a look-in.

Knowing how scared Bill was of the British fans, I read the accounts of his tumultuous progress with a smile on my face. There was only one item on his agenda with which I had agreed to be associated, and this was a special *Daily Mirror* ball in honour of Bill Haley at the Hammersmith Palais. It was to occur towards the end of his tour, so if the fans tore him to pieces in Hammersmith, which seemed to be on the cards, no serious damage would be done. I was quite looking forward to it.

On the evening before this ball was scheduled to take place, I had a telephone call from Leslie Grade. 'Noel,' said Leslie, 'have you got time to come over for a drink?'

'Sure, Leslie,' I said. 'I have a dinner date later so I'll come right over now.'

I assumed that he wanted to see me about some help he was giving me in fund-raising for charities that looked after underprivileged children in London; Leslie was a good-natured man and, like so many Jews in showbusiness, he was always generous in helping a good cause. So I was mildly surprised to see Suzanne Warner in his office when I arrived.

Suzanne was an extremely good-looking girl. She had come to London from her native California with Jane Russell, to publicize Jane on behalf of Howard Hughes in a film he had made called *The Outlaw*; having coined the catchphrase 'mean, moody and magnificent' for Jane, Suzanne did such a fine job that she herself became well known in the process, and she had married a journalist friend of mine called Freddie Mullally. Together with Freddie, a handsome young man with a taste for the high life, she had set up a publicity agency in Hay Hill, off Berkeley Square, and they had quickly become the top agency for handling American stars who came to London under the aegis of Lew and Leslie Grade.

When I walked into Leslie's office, Suzanne was talking about constipation, which has never figured high in my estimation as a topic of conversation. 'I can't go,' she was saying. 'I keep taking things but they don't work. It's the worry that does it, don't you think so, Noel?'

'Oh, yes,' I nodded. 'Martin Luther had the same problem.'

'What did I tell you, Leslie?' said Suzanne. 'It happens to everyone in the business.'

Leslie was looking unhappy and I was in a hurry so I prompted him. 'Was it about the children's charities that you wanted to see me?'

'Oh, no, Noel,' he said. 'The fact is that Lou and I have been talking about you. We are planning to set up a new programme for television on which big stars will be interviewed, and we thought you would be ideal for the interviewer. Isn't that right, Suzanne?'

'Dead right, Leslie,' nodded Suzanne.

I looked at them both in surprise. It did not strike me that I was an obvious choice, except that I had a good name as a popular columnist. There was something slightly odd about the offer. So all I said was: 'How kind, Leslie.'

'It would be a smash, I know it would,' he went on. 'We would start you off with thirteen half-hour programmes, all live, and we would provide you with such great names to interview that the Noel Whitcomb show would soon become the Ed Sullivan show of Great Britain. I know you are already famous and I know you are well off, but this would make you very famous and seriously rich. Suzanne would handle all the publicity. Isn't that right, Suzanne?'

'Dead right, Leslie,' she nodded.

It was an offer that many of my colleagues would have snapped up like hungry crocodiles, but I already had enough experience of tinsel fame to be dubious about the advantages of such an idea; most of the chat-show hosts I knew were even more bogus than I was, and the

274

thought of becoming a sort of Archie Rice on television did not have an immediate allure.

Leslie saw my hesitation and went on. 'We could make the contract for twenty-six half-hour shows,' he said. 'You would make a fortune – and it would be great for the paper. The *Mirror* would love it.'

By this time I realized that there definitely was something odd about the proposition, so I said, 'Come on, Leslie, what's all this about?'

He looked more unhappy than ever. Finally he said, 'Look here, Noel, the fact is that our boy Bill Haley has refused to appear at your big do at Hammersmith Palais tomorrow night, and we need your co-operation in getting us all out of this difficulty. Unless you help, we are all in *schtuck*, including you and the *Daily Mirror*. We cannot go to Hugh Cudlipp about this because it would put him in an impossible position. But if you were to write a nice piece in tomorrow's paper saying that poor Bill Haley has lost his voice due to the wonderful work he has done for the British fans, and is going home immediately to see his doctor, everyone would believe you and we would all be in the clear.'

It was serious, but I could not help laughing. 'Not if you offered me fifty-two shows at a million pounds a show, Leslie,' I said, shaking my head.

'Listen, boy,' he went on, miserably. 'I know how you feel about this and, believe me, I feel the same way about it myself, but the truth is there is nothing I can do. Bill Haley has flatly refused to appear, and from yesterday the little bastard has even refused to talk to me. He says his life will be in danger. The fans have torn about twenty suits off his back and they have even started taking scissors to chop bits of his hair off. He is absolutely convinced in his own mind that even if you were to bring in the entire police force tomorrow night as protection, the fans would kill him. Between you and me he has already chartered a plane to take him home tomorrow morning. His mind is made up. There is nothing more that any of us can do. Except you. You could save us all by writing a column in tomorrow's paper that would put the whole teenage population into deep mourning for poor Bill Haley. Be reasonable, son.'

'May I use your telephone, Leslie?' I asked. 'I want to cancel my dinner engagement. I am going round to the Savoy to talk to Bill.'

Bill Haley and I talked until two o'clock next morning. There was no acrimony. Patiently and courteously I explained to Haley in painstaking detail precisely how I would set about destroying his career across three continents if he failed to turn up for the Hammersmith gig.

That following evening Bill fulfilled his engagement at the Hammersmith Palais. About half a million teenagers stormed the doors

275

but the occasion was a considerable success and we managed to get Bill out alive. I never heard anything further about the television series.

14

You cannot hope
to bribe or twist
thank God! the
British journalist.
But, seeing what
the man will do
unbribed, there's
no occasion to.

Humbert Wolfe

By the mid-1950s, when I had been writing the column for a decade, it had become unusual for me to find myself at any gathering of so-called celebrities without being at least on nodding terms with all of them: I knew who they were and they knew who I was, even if that knowledge did nothing to improve their evening. My life had taken on a pattern along the lines that Anthony Powell devised for Nicholas Jenkins in his *Dance to the Music of Time*, inasmuch as a cast of characters kept occurring in the course of my life and interacting with each other and with myself in a seemingly random fashion that nevertheless had a traceable theme which arose from our acquaintanceship.

Among the jumble of names in this *dramatis personae* were Mike Todd, Noël Coward, Pietro Annigoni, Norman Hartnell, Trevor Howard, Orson Welles, Peter Sellers, Dominic Elwes, Robin Douglas-Home, Gerald Hamilton, John Huston, Billy Rees-Davies, the Maharajah of Cooch Behar, Ken Tynan, Muriel Belcher, David Milford Haven, Nancy Mitford, John Betjeman and Nina Hamnett.

Gerald Hamilton was an engaging rogue who revelled in the reputation of having been an important international intelligence agent – he claimed to have been arrested on Paddington station, disguised as a nun – and he was the source-material for the character Mr Norris in Christopher Isherwood's novel *Mr Norris Changes Trains*.

Muriel Belcher was a grotesque woman whose portrait was painted by Francis Bacon in her Colony Room Club in Dean Street where she presided over the dying days of London's Bohemians, but I first knew her when she ran a club called the Music Box in Leicester Street, off Leicester Square.

Nina Hamnett, a *habituée* of the Colony Room, was an artist of some quality, and I met her first during my Wardour Street working days when we used to meet with Dylan Thomas and Julian Maclaren Ross and others among the last relics of the Fitzrovians in a pub called the Wheatsheaf. In her later years she became poor, near derelict and desperate for money, and she once painted a portrait of me in Victor Berlemont's Soho pub – the French – for which she demanded, 'Pay me in gin, deah.'

Pietro Annigoni also made a sketch of me in Soho, surrounding it with caricatures in the style of eighteenth-century Rowlandson – he was fascinated by the Soho characters, seeing them as images from John Gay's *Beggar's Opera* still living on in London. At that time he was painting a portrait of the Queen, working at Buckingham Palace, Windsor and Balmoral. It all seemed such a strange world to him that he wrote daily letters to his little daughter, Ricciarda, in Florence, describing what happened to him. These letters, illustrated with enchanting drawings, were written in the form of stories about the adventures in London and at court of *Messerpulcio* (Mister Chicken). Pietro showed me some of these letters before he sent them off – they were exquisite – and he agreed to my writing a column about them. When he read the column he was so delighted that he wrote: 'My dear Noel . . . I feel as to thank you very much . . . really it was the finest article!' As a gesture of gratitude he gave me a drawing of *Messerpulcio* (himself) dressed in a kilt at Balmoral, which he drew specially as a present for my own three-year-old daughter, Katie.

Several of the people listed above became my friends because of the theatre and film connections, but with a few of them I became associated in schemes to make money that would have captivated the heart of Stanley Featherstonehaugh Ukridge. For instance, with Billy Rees-Davies, then a member of parliament as well as a QC, I was a director of an international business services company that offered multilingual communications facilities for businessmen visiting London – an idea that was ahead of its time. With Bhaya Cooch Behar I planned an Anglo-American agency for conducting intrepid tycoons on tiger hunts in India. With David Milford Haven I set up an international tiddleywinks championship – an idea that turned out to be not so daft as it sounds.

The point about all these characters in the context of the Nick Jenkins analogy is that they kept criss-crossing my life: among them were my Stringham and my Templer, my Moreland and my Quiggin, my Sunny Farebrother and my General Conyers, my Molly Jeavons and my Gypsy

Jones, with Hugh Cudlipp as my Widmerpool. Cudlipp cropped up in almost every chapter.

To ingratiate the *Daily Mirror* with its readers Hugh Cudlipp would frequently devise what he called 'a bit of fun', which usually entailed bringing several dozen representatives of some unsung sector of the populace such as charladies, paper-boys or miners' wives to London for a spectacular dinner and ball at one of the big hotels. The usual scenario at these occasions was that the newspaper's senior executives and a few celebrity guests would get drunk amiably – although Cudlipp himself sometimes became truculent towards the end – and the bemused charladies or miners' wives would be given what was described as 'a jolly good time'. These functions were wildly expensive, partly because of the extravagant requirements of the staff who attended them, and my part in the proceedings – a task which initially fell to me because I was the only adequately senior member of the staff who could look as though he were enjoying it when meeting readers in the flesh – was to appear in evening dress and act more or less as host.

This presented no problem for me because I did in fact get on quite well with the readers. The problem arose because it also became my task to write the accounts of these occasions for publication in the paper. If only I had made the first one sound pedestrian I would have saved myself a great deal of trouble, because somebody else would then have been assigned to the job; but unfortunately I treated the whole thing as a variation of Cinderella, which was not an original approach but was highly acceptable, and I wrote such glowing panegyrics about the scintillating success of these often rather boring affairs that both Cudlipp and the editor insisted upon my handling these in-house stories every time they happened. The fact that I frequently wrote the account of the night's proceedings on the day before it took place made no difference, because my account of what happened was always much more exciting than what did actually happen. Nobody minded this because it made life easier for everyone. I would go into the office and the chief sub-editor would say to me, 'Oh, Noel – you've got an Oh-What-A-Night! to do tomorrow, haven't you? Can I have the copy now?'

It was no part of my grand design to become the poet laureate of the office binge, but this hidden talent that I had unwittingly revealed for making dreams sound like reality led to my being requested to cover all kinds of big occasions at which the imagination of the writer and his dazzling command of adjectives were more in demand than the facts. It was a testing time for me because once again my so-called career had taken an unexpected lurch down another blind alley, but I soldiered on.

There was a spate of royal weddings and colourful state occasions all over western Europe during this period, and wherever the ageing remnants of the *Almanac de Gotha* gathered in their medalled finery, there also went I, the Boswell of the deposed and chronicler of the fancy-dress cavortings of the *ancien régime*. This enabled me to browse as a privileged observer in many great houses and palaces full of objects of art, and to spend time in cathedrals and museums where there was much of exquisite beauty to be seen, so I consoled myself with the thought that even if this job was doing nothing for my prose style it was at least improving my education in aesthetics; and also it kept me out of London, far from the madding crowd that jostled around Hugh Cudlipp: happy the subjects distant from their prince.

Florence and Venice were the places I visited most frequently, and although not all the columns I sent were received with rapture by the editor – I recall one particularly blasphemous telephone call from Jack Nener after I had sent him a lyrical piece on the subject of Donatello and Brunelleschi – the primary purpose of my visit was usually a news story that saved the day and elicited the more customary telegram of congratulation. One such was the wedding in Venice of Princess Ira Fuerstenberg and Prince Alfonso Hohenlohe.

The interesting thing about this small country wedding from the viewpoint of the *Daily Mirror* and similarly high-minded newspapers throughout the western world was that the bride was fifteen years old, a girl of exceptional beauty, and the groom was a thirty-two-year-old motor salesman of impeccably noble lineage but definitely no Adonis, nobody's idea of young Lochinvar. Editors of popular papers all over Britain, France, Italy and the United States shipped off hordes of ravening reporters and photographers to investigate this matter.

Ira's father, Prince Tassilo *zu und von* Fuerstenberg, had been an officer in the German army during the war, but.had never been a supporter of Hitler or the Nazi rabble, and after the war he had retired into the quiet life of a country gentleman. When the mass invasion of his small estate near Venice by the world's press began, he took the whole thing with elegant aplomb. They trampled over his flower beds and he smiled; they damaged his lawns and he did not complain; they camped out in vast numbers in the drive that led to his front door and he sent out servants with trays of wine for them: but when he read the outrageous fabrications they were writing, his patience snapped. He ordered them away from his demesne.

There was little news of interest to report during the week before the wedding, and, as is usual in such circumstances, the reporters were making up their stories. I was staying at the Hotel Gritti Palace in Venice, having an agreeable time, and had decided to go nowhere near the house and to do nothing about the story until the day of the wedding, which promised to be a colourful affair of the type in which I had become a reluctant specialist.

However, to my astonishment I received a telephone call from Prince Tassilo. The press were driving him mad and he wanted to find somebody from among their number who might be able to persuade them to behave less like savages. This was a pious hope, and I told him that any interference from me would probably only make things worse by infuriating my colleagues who, thinking that I must have inside information, would doubtless make his life an even greater misery. But I did think of a plan, which I offered to him.

The reason why Tassilo had telephoned me was that we had met some time before at a masked ball that had been given by a man called Charles de Beistegui at the Palazzo Labia in Venice. This had been an occasion of such conspicuous extravagance that even the old Aga Khan, who was in his mid-seventies at the time, was quoted as saying that it was the most lavish party he had ever attended in all his life. Notable party-goers had flown in from all over the world to be seen there and the only reason I was present was that some weeks previously I had been talking to some friends in Harry's Bar in Venice when Charles de Beistegui came in and discovered that two of the people with me had been at school with him, so he invited us all.

Even though the scene on the Grand Canal as the guests arrived was most beautiful, with all the gondolas richly decorated and the gondoliers in the livery of the once-great families, I did not greatly enjoy the evening because these ultra-opulent parties always attract the world's least likeable people; elderly women of great wealth with their gigolos, coroneted confidence-tricksters, septuagenarian multi-millionaires with nineteen-year-old model-girls and a colourful sprinkling of popinjays have never seemed to me the ideal guest-list for a happy night out. I chatted with a few of the British contingent including Willie Somerset Maugham, Noël Coward, Oliver Messel and Cecil Beaton but I had already decided that I had had enough when an amusing diversion occurred: a senior diplomat from the British embassy in Rome was leaning over a table to help himself liberally from a bowl of caviare when one of the candelabra set fire to the headdress of scarlet ostrich feathers he was wearing and the sight of a diplomat with his hat on fire caused a great commotion.

Prince Tassilo was standing next to me at the time, and as we had been introduced he knew I wrote a column, so he said, laughing, 'That will surely make an item for your English newspaper tomorrow.'

'Possibly,' I replied, 'but it will not come from me. I don't write society gossip. Some of the stuff I write is trivial enough in all conscience, but I am not yet reduced to rushing for a telephone just because some silly ass accidentally sets fire to his ridiculous hat.' We both laughed about this, and perhaps Tassilo remembered it; at any rate, it subsequently seemed to me the only reason why he thought of me when he was beleaguered by the press.

The plan I suggested to him for reducing the excesses of the European and American newshounds and photographers around his Palladian villa was the old and tested system of offering to give a set number of press conferences and photo-opportunities at specific times in exchange for assurances that he and his family would be left in peace at all other times; if anyone broke the agreement, all further co-operation would cease. This does not always work, but if it is backed up by threats it usually has some effect, and in this case the result was to restore order until the day of the wedding when the world's press went stark raving mad as usual.

Princess Ira was a spirited girl with a mind of her own, and the reason why her family had agreed to her marriage at what would normally have been considered an immature age was that she was a spectacularly early developer; she had been at a girls' boarding school in England but at the age of fifteen she had only too evidently become a physically mature young woman who attracted wolf-whistles from every boy who set eyes on her, and the family doctor advised her parents that if she were not married soon they would almost certainly have a serious problem with which to deal; she was fond of Prince Alfonso, and he was in love with her, so the marriage was agreed.

Set against the incomparable beauty of Venice, with ribboned gondolas moving towards the church along the streets paved with water, it was the prettiest wedding I have ever seen, even though the vast army of photographers hired every available craft except gunboats in which to follow the bridal gondola; even at their worst and most intrusive, there was nothing the press could do to spoil the elegance of that day, and it was a triumph for the good manners and shrewd management of Prince Tassilo.

In common with most other papers, the *Daily Mirror* gave a big display to the story and I received the usual telegram of congratulation from

Jack Nener for sending him a string of adjectives that would have earned me a pat on the back from Dr Roget.

Some months later I spent a happy week as guest of Ira and Alfonso in the quiet and unspoilt Spanish fishing village of Marbella where Alfonso had the only house of any size; his mother, Princess Max, who lived in Mexico, had asked Alfonso to arrange for the development of the hillside looking down on the sea, which was land of little value that she owned, and over dinner one evening I agreed to buy one of the villas that he was planning to build on this land, for the sum of £3,000. But when I returned home my wife opposed this plan, on the grounds that we did not want to go to the same place every year, so I passed on the opportunity to a stockbroker friend of mine; this was not one of my cleverer financial deals because I understand the villa was sold in later years for a sum in the region of half a million pounds.

But I did not see Prince Tassilo again until about a week before the wedding in Monte Carlo of Prince Rainier and Grace Kelly, in the spring of 1956. In contrast with Princess Ira's wedding in Venice, this was a gruesome affair. Representatives of the world's press were there in battle strength as usual, giving what was known as blanket coverage to this sweet story of the reigning prince and the Hollywood film star, but internecine war soon broke out among them, and the in-fighting between the reporters and columnists who swarmed in the little gambling principality of Monaco became strident and vicious.

The root of the problem was that Prince Rainier was hard up; his little tax-haven on the fringe of France was down on its pasterns; the post-war world had passed it by, and the outlook for Monaco was bleak. So when Rainier had visited the Cannes Film Festival, just along the coast, and had met Grace Kelly, the beautiful, famous and rich film star, a solution to all his problems stared him in the face: marry Grace, and the whole western world would come flocking to Monaco; the biggest blaze of organized publicity since the allies won the war would bring a tidal wave of dollars flooding in to Monte Carlo, and all his problems would be little ones.

So the marriage was arranged. Everyone knew it was a *mariage de convenance*, but it was a superb story. The bride's father had once been an Irish labourer and had made his fortune in America; the groom was a reigning prince in a tin-pot little European principality that lived off gambling, but he was a scion of the Grimaldi family who had come from Genoa centuries before, and he had a fairytale palace on top of a rock. Admittedly Rainier, who was thirty-two at the time, was not the average housewife's idea of love's young dream: his trousers were baggy and even when dressed in ceremonial uniform he looked as though he had just slipped out of the stagedoor for a smoke during a performance of a Ruritanian musical; but there was nothing shabby about his business acumen, and once the marriage had been arranged he set about using the occasion to restore the family fortunes. Nothing was to be free; nothing, not even news.

Grace Kelly had worked for Metro-Goldwyn-Mayer in Hollywood, so MGM bought the film rights to the wedding for a start; the *Time-Life* Organization moved in and bought another piece of the action, taking exclusive rights on all news pictures that were likely to be worth having; the Peter Pan Brassière Company in the United States bought the radio rights; anyone who wanted to buy anything that was left had to pay heavily for it or fight for it. A number of American columnists lavished hospitality on down-at-heel barons and counts who had drifted into Monte Carlo with the rest of the world's senior con-men, jewel-thieves and pickpockets, but as most of them had never even met Prince Rainier and did nothing but eat and drink in unaccustomed luxury, this ploy failed dismally. The rest of the press ran hither and thither in ever decreasing circles, drinking vast quantities of Scotch or dry martini but getting nowhere; so they fought. There were several ugly scuffles between the photographers and the Monegasque police, but the reporters and columnists fought among themselves with bitter jealousy. Monte Carlo, a sad place at the best of times, became a cut-throat marketplace for news items.

Among British newspapers, the *Daily Express* deployed the biggest battalion, partly because its proprietor, Lord Beaverbrook, had a villa along the coast at Cap d'Ail; it must have delighted Lord Beaverbrook to observe that his employees were all at each other's throats – he enjoyed strife. When the *Evening Standard*, also a Beaverbrook paper, sent its woman columnist Anne Sharpley to join its Paris bureau chief, Sam White, Sam walked out of Monte Carlo in a huff: it was more like a war than a wedding.

Most of the more acceptable stories that appeared during the pre-wedding period were complete fabrications. When Grace Kelly arrived on the SS *Constitution* from America, all the reporters except one described her in their stories as radiant and smiling; the odd man out wrote that she arrived in floods of tears, and his story was given the biggest show of all the news stories that appeared next day. He received a telegram of congratulation from his editor, and most of the other reporters received severe reprimands for missing the story. The story was not true, and everyone knew it was not true, but it was the best story of the day because that was the story the public wanted to read: a happy bride is good for circulation but a bride in tears is even better; and the world's housewives were already waiting to read volumes into this seeming sign of sadness as a veiled hint that one of the most beautiful girls in the world had chosen position above love. It was a clever story.

However, it clearly did not please Prince Rainier's entourage. His personal chaplain, Father Tucker, an Irish-American priest with a taste for high society, hit back. During his sermon at mass, Father Tucker wept movingly as he made an oblique but unmistakable reference to the fact that Prince Rainier had given up his former girlfriend, Gisèle Pascal, in order to do his duty and restore the fortunes of his people by marrying Grace Kelly. 'Jesus will be there at the wedding on Thursday,' went on Father Tucker, adding another distinguished name to the guest-list.

Outstanding among the non-acceptors for the big race were all members of the British royal family, who clearly did not wish to get mixed up with quite such a blatant publicity stunt; it was said jokingly at the time that Lady Docker, Britain's pre-eminent symbol of opulent vulgarity of that decade, would be in the cathedral to represent the Queen, and when Norah Docker heard this rumour she did not deny it; after a few dry martinis she held a press conference in the bar of the Hôtel de Paris, which was unusually well attended because liquor was expensive and all the drinks were on Norah, and a couple of Americans filed a story about the English queen's representative, having nothing else to send.

The bar at the Hôtel de Paris, normally a dignified place, began to look more and more like a Silver Ring bar at Epsom racecourse on Derby day; liquor was spilt all over the tables, cigarette ends smouldered on the carpet, torn newspapers and scraps of screwed-up copy littered the floor: the press had taken it over as headquarters. The head barman, half shocked and half elated, became the man with whom they all wished to ingratiate themselves, and they left enormous tips on the bar in the hope that he might pass on any snippets of gossip that came his way. Randolph Churchill, always loud-mouthed and seldom sober, held court there, surrounded by American columnists who assumed that, because of his distinguished connections, he must know something.

Grace Kelly's relations, who were staying at the hotel, were shunned by the rich European residents because they were so often dressed as if for a barbecue on Waikiki beach, but for the press they became like a magnet in a tray of iron filings. The hotel became known as the Grace-and-favour residence – if you knew Grace they would do you a

285

favour – but as I did not know Grace or anyone of consequence in the Grimaldi circus I was as much in the dark as nearly all the rest of my colleagues. The *Daily Express* contingent had managed to buy tickets for entry to the cathedral for the wedding, but I did not even have a ticket. I began wishing I had not bothered to bring a top hat.

Furthermore the columns that I was sending to the *Daily Mirror* were not of the genuflecting sort that would help me to gain any preferment in Monaco; I found it impossible to take the story seriously. When an announcement was made that a civil wedding ceremony would take place at the palace on the Wednesday, followed by a church ceremony on the Thursday, I sent this news, adding a conjecture that a third ceremony might take place on the Friday – on ice.

The French destroyer *Kersaint* sailed into the harbour and fired off a twenty-one-gun salute, which was returned by a twenty-one-gun salute from the ramparts of the palace; the noise of the booming guns was startling, because few people knew what it was all about, so on my way to lunch I slipped into the bar and confided to the head barman that war had broken out at last between France and Monaco over the long-standing dispute about Monaco's tax-free status. A posse of American columnists were rushing towards the bar as I left.

Although it was funny I was not enjoying it. The people were awful and the ostentatious display of wealth so offensive that it seemed surprising that the whole working population of Monaco did not march off *en bloc* to join the Communist Party; and apart from being socially provocative it was degenerating into a shambles. Reflecting on this aspect of the affair in one of my daily columns, I forecast that unless Prince Rainier could quickly find some organizer who would bring order out of chaos he was likely to get a bad press for his wedding, and I referred in passing to the recent wedding of Princess Ira in Venice, suggesting that what was needed was a man like Prince Tassilo to handle the arrangements with debonair aplomb.

Whether by coincidence or because some official at the palace heard about this suggestion – they read all the European and American reports avidly – Prince Tassilo arrived in Monte Carlo two days later, having been requested to take over the arrangements for the wedding and advise on protocol. Apart from saving the day for His Serene Highness Prince Rainier, because arrangements for the wedding immediately improved and were set upon a far more disciplined basis, it was also a stroke of luck for me: to my astonishment I received an invitation to the wedding plus a ticket for a seat in the cathedral and an ornate card inviting me to the reception at the palace after the ceremony. At first I thought they must have been sent to me by mistake, but when I next saw Tassilo he winked, so I thanked him.

'One good turn deserves another,' he smiled. 'In any case, Rainier and I are distant kinsmen, so I would not like to see him get a bad press for his wedding.'

In the days immediately preceding the wedding I received two other unexpected invitations. The first was a dinner invitation from a girl whom I knew slightly, who was staying at La Reserve in Beaulieu, just along the coast. Her name was Barbara, and I was delighted to hear her on the telephone inviting me to dinner because she was an exceptionally charming girl. The only place we had met before was at the Savoy Hotel in London, where I occasionally used to see her in the press office. The press office – in the famous Room 205 at the Savoy – was run by an American girl from the Kentucky bluegrass country, name of Jeanne Gilbert, and it was one of the most popular corners of the hotel because it was more of a social salon than an office, and it was usually swarming with pretty girls; among these girls was Barbara Taylor, who was an executive on a women's magazine, and in my estimation she was the best-looking of the lot, although I may have been prejudiced because she was a Yorkshire girl and I have always been partial to Yorkshire girls.

So I was looking forward to this dinner, and on the morning of the day when it was to take place I was writing a column in the sitting room of my suite at the Hôtel de Paris when the telephone rang and I was utterly astonished to hear the voice at the other end of the line because I recognized it immediately: Lord Beaverbrook.

'Noel,' he said, 'I want you to come to dinner tonight. Eight o'clock.'

It was not exactly an invitation because Beaverbrook did not give invitations to British journalists, he issued commands, and I had to think quickly because complying with this would mean giving up my projected dinner at La Reserve. The old man was obviously not going to offer me a job, because he did not like me; he was a man who demanded to be admired, and he always sensed immediately if anyone in his presence did not think much of him. I knew that he considered me to be nowhere near deferential enough, so I realized that he must have some reason for requiring my presence, and my curiosity about what that reason might be overcame my disinclination to chuck the dinner date *chez* Barbara. I accepted.

Barbara was out when I telephoned La Reserve to give her my apologies, so I left a message regretting that work would prevent me from turning up for dinner.

As I drove the couple of miles along the coast to Cap d'Ail that evening, I was still trying to puzzle out why Beaverbrook had invited me. The old man never did anything without a reason. He was in his mid-seventies at the time, and was not so active in running his newspapers as he had been, but he was still a giant in my world. It seemed unlikely that there was anything I could do that could not be done equally well by one of the many employees of his organization who were swarming along the Côte d'Azur. It was all very odd.

Beaverbrook's villa, La Capponcina, was a rich man's house although it always struck me that it would look more at home in Walton-on-Thames than on the French Riviera; it was furnished expensively with the heavy taste of a man who is not greatly interested in the objects that surround him so long as they are manifestly costly. I had been there three or four times in the past so I knew my way around. Mead the butler let me in and Miss Rosenberg, the old man's secretary, showed me into the room where the Beaver was talking to other guests; he greeted me amiably but without warmth, and I realized more strongly than ever that I had been invited for a purpose, whatever that purpose might be.

Most of the people in the room I knew by sight, except for two Frenchmen whom I had never seen before. I stood chatting for a few minutes with Beaverbrook's current mistress, but the old man quickly came over and took her away; she was a pleasant and good-looking woman who later committed suicide after Beaverbrook had ditched her. The little nut-brown man was widely rumoured to have great sexual attraction for women, but the few women I knew who had been around his house and had been subsequently rejected all spoke of him as a dirty old man. He was a malign influence on those over whom he exerted power, and even in his geriatric years one of the few pleasures left to him was to hurt and damage people who were powerless to fight back.

After we had sat down to dinner I soon discovered why I was there. I was placed close to the two Frenchmen, who were discussing in loud voices the iniquities of Prince Rainier, alleging all sorts of financial and political impropriety, and talking of a plot that was being hatched to get rid of him. This sort of gossip had been current in the principality for a long time, since financial irregularities had been unearthed, and it was clear to me that Beaverbrook had invited me so that I would hear details of the machinations that were going on to oust Rainier. If I had not felt angry I would have laughed: the idea that the wicked old man had assumed that I would help to do his dirty work by passing on this rubbish to the *Daily Mirror* made me want to wring his ugly neck. I did not know whether he had a particular grudge against Rainier – perhaps he had not received an adequately important wedding invitation or had suffered some similarly trivial slight to his overweening pride – or whether he was simply trying to take pleasure from damaging Rainier at a moment that would otherwise have been triumphant. Either way I had no intention of allowing this detestable old schemer to use me as a pawn, and as soon as it was reasonably polite to do so I left the villa and headed back to Monte Carlo.

On my way to the hotel I stopped at an all-night café for a cup of tea. Sitting by himself in the far corner was Aristotle Onassis. Every newsman in Monte Carlo knew Ari Onassis, because he was an approachable man who shrewdly took care to keep the press on his side; among his investments outside shipping he had bought a controlling interest in the Monte Carlo Casino, a deal that had temporarily saved Prince Rainier's financial bacon but had not improved personal relations between the two men because it had made Onassis as important in the principality as Rainier himself. Ari waved to me as I went in and I went over and joined him at his table.

We sat there talking until four o'clock in the morning. Onassis was a strange man, lonely even when he was surrounded by a crowd, and he had the physical advantage that is so noticeable in very rich men; he needed no more than two or three hours' sleep in twenty-four. This quality had enabled him to start his fortune, because he told me that when he was a young man working as a night cable-operator, he occasionally read in the cables information about company deals that was market-sensitive, and as he possessed a naturally clever financial brain he acted upon this news on his own behalf, buying and selling stock before world markets had woken up to the news that would send prices soaring or plummeting.

I told him about the conversation at the dinner table, because there had been nothing confidential about it and I owed no favours to Lord Beaverbrook, and Onassis, who knew all about it, was amused. 'You would be unwise to send that story to your newspaper,' he said, 'because Prince Rainier is no fool even though some people think him stupid, and he will be running this country long after he has disposed of these disgruntled snipers.' Which turned out to be true.

Before we parted, Onassis asked me to lunch on his yacht later that day – it was 5 a.m. when I got to bed.

Onassis's yacht, the *Christina*, was the biggest and most luxurious private boat in the harbour, the subject of some jealousy on the part of Prince Rainier whose *Deo Juvante* was smaller and less richly appointed. The handrail of the staircase in the *Christina* was made of lapis lazuli, and objects of immense value were scattered around the rooms, some of them beautiful pieces of great antiquity, because Ari was a man of taste; on the wall in front of his desk hung an El Greco deposition, and he loved it not only for its value.

The guests at lunch were the usual mixture of celebrity and wealth, film stars and ballet dancers, bankers and duchesses; but the only interesting thing about it that I recall, in retrospect, is that the lives of so many of the people who were present later ended in tragedy, disaster, murder or suicide: the whole of Monte Carlo at that time abounded with immensely rich people whose lives were to end in misery and wretchedness.

When I arrived back in the bedroom at my hotel, the telephone was ringing. It was Barbara, calling from La Reserve. She was hopping mad. She had not received my message cancelling the dinner date of the previous night, and she did not believe that I had sent one, so her fury was very understandable. I tried to explain but could not get a word in edgeways. Barbara was in full flood. I had thought that she would have other guests, but apparently the dinner had been planned as a *diner à deux*, and she had hung about waiting for ages, getting more and more furious. In the course of an eloquent disquisition upon my contemptible and scurvy character, Barbara gave it as her opinion that if ever a British Olympic team were picked for rotten, low-down heels, I would surely be selected as captain, and she added that if she ever set eyes on me again it would be purely accidental. Then she hung up.

In fact I have never since that time seen Barbara in the flesh, if I may use that expression, but, some thirty years later, I saw her on television. I arrived home one evening at our house in Kensington and my wife was watching a television programme; on the screen, being interviewed, was an extremely good-looking woman.

'I know her,' I said.

'Oh, for God's sake,' said my wife. 'I suppose she is another of your oldest friends.'

'Not exactly,' I said. 'I never knew her well but I once stood her up on a dinner date.'

'A likely story!' exclaimed my wife. 'Do you know who that is? It's Barbara Tayor Bradford, the famous woman novelist whose books sell in more millions than almost anything except the Bible.'

'Well, well, well,' I said, thoughtfully. 'Well, well, well.'

That Rainier wedding in what became known as Kelly's Kingdom was not the happiest time of my life. It acted as aversion therapy for the most inveterate name-droppers because there was such an *embarras de richesse* of names all round that one became sick of them; and most of the names were attached to such miserable faces, with expressions of jealousy, cupidity and despair – as was to be expected in a little country that relied for its livelihood upon a casino.

I have no objection to casinos, although I have seen too many people ruined in them to consider them an embellishment to civilized life; the atmosphere inside them is usually about as jolly as the last act of *Romeo and Juliet*, and even the Monte Carlo Casino, famed in legend and song as one of the world's most romantic places, has always struck me as having roughly as much glamour as Paddington station; but it was on one of my visits to this chandelier-hung mausoleum of dead bank-balances that I had my most memorable *mauvais quart d'heure* of the whole trip, by courtesy of Lady Docker.

When the definitive history of the mid-twentieth century is written, Norah Docker deserves to be noted in a vignette because she was the drum-majorette who cavorted flamboyantly at the head of the march that was to lead in later decades to the consumer society; towards the end of a post-war period of rationing and shortages in Britain, when the majority of the population was sick and tired of austerity and restraint, Norah hoisted the banner of nonsensical extravagance and led her army of admirers onward and upward into the fantasy world of Harold Macmillan's land of you-never-had-it-so-good: she was the gold-plated spearhead of the thrusting new Britain, the flagship of the tawdry fleet that sailed on into the 1990s.

The popular newspapers loved her because she was the Cinderella with a taste for Bollinger who kicked her shoes off at the ball and went on to marry three princes of industry and commerce, all of them stinking rich. Born Norah Turner in a flat above a butcher's shop in Derby, daughter of a car salesman who committed suicide, brought up in a pub run by her mother, she became every overworked housewife's dream of the poor girl who had made it into the promised land of mink and diamonds. She came to London as a club-hostess, working the ritzier nightspots, and she had stood bereft in widow's weeds beside the graves of two millionaire husbands before she married Sir Bernard Docker; third time lucky.

When their engagement was announced, one of Norah's girl friends said to her, 'But my dear – he's got one foot in the grave!' 'Yes,' nodded Norah, 'but he's got the other foot in Cartier's.'

Sir Bernard, an amiable, bumbling, ineffectual old Harrovian, was chairman of the then mighty Birmingham Small Arms Company, an armaments-to-motorbikes industrial giant; he was also a senior director of the Midland Bank, and of many other companies, all of which eventually kicked him out because of Norah's meretricious antics, but he never ceased to be loyal to her: through thick and thin, throughout her erratic, comet-like progress across the sky of notoriety, trailing a tail of outrage and disaster, he loved her dearly.

Norah was the first of the female hell-raisers, during a period when the description 'hell-raiser' was used by the newspapers as a euphemism for a drunk; she was the lush with the delicate air, and her wheedling little-girl voice concealed the arrogance of a robber-baron and a determination to get her way unsurpassed even by the Marquise de Pompadour.

She flaunted her 'golden' Daimler motor car which she had persuaded Sir Bernard – who was a director of Daimler – to have specially made for her, with gold-leaf on all the parts that were normally chromium-plated and gold stars on the bodywork. She claimed that she was gaining valuable publicity for her husband's company, but the dignified Daimler company did not see it that way, especially as their shareholders were paying for it, and ultimately they fired Sir Bernard.

In those days before television had become the new opiate of the people and newspapers still held centre-stage in the communications business, the mass-circulation Sundays ran stories and pictures of Lady Docker's antics as an ongoing serial, and the 'pop' dailies – the *Express*, the *Mirror* and the *Mail* – vied with each other in giving Norah her daily fix of publicity. She particularly courted columnists, but I managed, without difficulty, to keep her out of my column during the first half-dozen years of her notoriety; it was not until just before Christmas in 1951 that she fired a sighting shot across my bows to remind me that I had been remiss.

An enormous hamper arrived at our house in Hampstead, delivered from Fortnum and Mason in Piccadilly, containing champagne and cognac, claret and Burgundy, Christmas puddings and liqueur chocolates, game pies and cold roast pheasants, vintage port, cigars and Christmas crackers. Inside the hamper was a note: 'Merry Christmas, dear Noel, with love from Norah and Bernard.'

My wife looked at it with astonished displeasure. 'We don't even know the woman,' she said. 'What impudence! Does she think we need food parcels?'

'No,' I said. 'It is intended as a bribe.'

So we sent it to a hospital, with a note to the bursar asking him to thank Lady Docker for it and tell her from whom it had come.

Some days later I was in the editor's office talking to Jack Nener when

I mentioned that I had received this gigantic hamper of goodies from Lady Docker. My colleague Bill Connor, Cassandra, was also in the room, and he said, 'I got one, too. She sends them to all the columnists on all the papers at Christmas, you know. She's a very good-hearted old bag.' Bill shared the general view that Norah Docker enlivened the scene in a dreary world, and it was a view that the *Daily Mirror* supported, because she was a heroine in saloon bars all over the country.

Jack Nener, looking thoughtful, merely said, 'Doesn't she know that it is the editor who decides what goes into the paper? Someone ought to remind her about that.'

Bill Connor was a typically honest journalist of the period; although you could not have bribed him with an offer of fifty thousand pounds in used notes, there was very little he would not do for half a pint of bitter, especially if it were handed to him with a friendly smile; so when he heard that I had not kept my hamper he was mildly irritated by the implication that he had put himself under an obligation by keeping his, and he said to me, 'I think you are just being a sanctimonious idiot. You'll find that you will be writing about the old girl soon, anyway.'

'I have a fiver that says I won't,' I said.

Fortunately for me he did not accept my bet, because he turned out to be right.

Every big casino employs a *physiognomiste*, a man who never forgets a face; it is an important job because all sorts of people try to get into casinos who are *persona non grata*, and it is the job of the *physiognomiste* to spot them before they get into the gaming rooms and thwart their intention of entering, helping to chuck them out if they argue. Norah Docker slapped the face of the *physiognomiste* at Monte Carlo Casino shortly after my conversation with Jack Nener and Bill Connor, and as these chaps do not care for losing face in such a fashion there was a fair old set-to: as in the case of the celebrated Linares bullfight in which the result was headlined as 'Bull 1, Manolete O', Norah lost the contest. She had not enjoyed her evening, she was boozed up to the mascara, and she was raring to go fifteen rounds with any official who appeared to be memorizing her face. She demanded that the man be sacked, but Prince Jean-Louis de Faucigny-Lucinge, president of the Casino Sporting Club, was called in as referee and ruled against Lady Docker on a technical knock-out. This decision was followed by another scuffle in the ring, which ended with Norah and Sir Bernard being unceremoniously bundled out and told by Faucigny-Lucinge not to darken his doors again.

These high jinks were reported with great relish in the London evening papers, and I was reading the reports at home when my telephone rang. It was Jack Nener calling from the office. 'Noel,' he said, 'Hugh wants you to go over to the South of France right away and talk to Lady Docker. She and Sir Bernard have shifted their yacht out of Monte Carlo and taken it to Cannes.'

'All right, Jack,' I said, without enthusiasm. 'I happen to know that there are no flights to Nice at this time of the evening, so I'll catch the first plane tomorrow.'

'That's too late,' said Jack. 'Go tonight and take the *Dove*.'

The *Dove* was a four-seater aircraft that the *Mirror* kept at Croydon aerodrome in readiness for use in emergencies. As I drove to Croydon, cursing Norah Docker and all who sailed in her, a heavy mist began gathering over the fields. It was no surprise to find, when I arrived at the airport, that all planes were grounded.

I found our pilot sitting, with a pint of beer in front of him, in the little private bar they called the club. 'Relax, old son,' he said to me. 'I'm waiting for a met report before I can get permission to take off. May as well have some supper.'

He had four more pints before he decided that we were going to take off without permission. 'I have been on the phone to Jack Nener,' he said, cheerfully, 'and Jack offered to get me fired if I don't get you there tonight.'

The *Dove* was more like an oversized seagull than an aircraft, and before our pilot took off he shouted to me through the door that separated his seat from the passenger seats: 'I've got a bet on about this trip. My pal in the club bet me that this little crate can't get to the South of France on one tank of fuel. I've never tried it before but I bet him a quid that it can.'

Over the Alps the little plane butted its way through an electric storm, bobbing about like a ping-pong ball on a jet of water, and I was relieved when, some hours later, the pilot finally made his approach to a runway. The engine had been giving an occasional ominous cough for some time past. Then suddenly, just as we were about to touch the ground, the little plane soared up again almost vertically, and the pilot shouted through his door, 'Ooopsadaisy! Nearly put up a black there. Wrong airport! That's the old airport at Cannes – I was looking for Nice.'

If I were to add up the number of nights that I have spent in the Carlton Hotel at Cannes they would total well over a year of my life, but it was eventually at this comfortable caravanserai that I laid my weary head for the remaining few hours of that night. When I awakened I wrote a note to Lady Docker asking her to see me, and sent a *chasseur* to

294

take it to her yacht. Within an hour she was on the telephone.

'Dear Noel,' she cooed. 'Come to lunch on the *Shemara*.'

The *Shemara*, an 863-ton yacht with a crew of thirty, was one of the biggest private yachts in commission at that time; she was not a beautiful boat, but she was the pride of Norah Docker's life. Norah welcomed me aboard as if I were the prodigal son and called for pink champagne. She herself was drinking dry martini with the air of a desert-wanderer slaking a terrible thirst, constantly refilling her glass from a big cut-glass jug. I could see trouble ahead, because dry martini was gunpowder to Norah, but she was looking radiant and full of excitement; she was nearly fifty at the time (Sir Bernard was ten years her senior) but was one of those people whose rare metabolism prevents them ever having a hangover. (In my experience this is not always as lucky as it sounds because most such people die young, but Norah proved to be an exception to this rule because she lived to the age of seventy-six.)

'Bernard and I are thinking of buying Monte Carlo,' she said, 'to teach them all a lesson.'

This was a newsworthy introduction to any conversation. Sir Bernard nodded with the wan smile of a businessman who recognizes a silly idea when he hears one, but Norah was full of her plan for retribution.

'The first thing we would do,' she went on, 'would be to get rid of Prince Faucigny-Lucinge and dismiss Monsieur Rebuffel, that ill-mannered physiognomist.'

Although it sounded ridiculous, there had been an occasion in England when Norah had been dissatisfied with the service at a restaurant in which she was dining so had the following day bought the restaurant and fired the staff; clearly the idea did not seem ridiculous to her. But among my fellow guests at luncheon were Mr Medley, the Dockers' English lawyer who had flown in specially from London, and Monsieur Neveu, Sir Bernard's French legal advisor, and both of them were looking unhappy because they realized that even if the Dockers could have afforded to buy Monaco, there was surely a law in the principality that would prevent them from doing so; and if no such law existed Prince Rainier would damn soon get one passed.

'I think,' said M. Neveu, 'that we should issue a statement to the effect that we are seeking an amicable settlement. You must remember, Madame, that heated tempers cool in time. *Tout s'arrange dans la vie*,' he added with a shrug.

Norah snorted, but Mr Medley also tried to pour oil on troubled waters. 'I think you should consider carefully before you decide upon any serious steps,' he said. 'The point Sir Bernard must bear in mind is the existing currency-control regulations.' Mr Medley turned towards me with a thoughtful look. 'You are aware, of course,' he went on, 'that Sir Bernard and Lady Docker pay for everything ashore out of their winnings at the casino. Everything aboard ship is paid for in sterling.'

'Oh, yes, that's right,' said Norah, suddenly realizing that she was swimming in shark-infested waters. 'We didn't have a very good night last night, because we only paid for our dinner and showed a profit of about twenty pounds, so unless we do well tonight we shall have to go carefully.'

We all remained silent for a few moments after this, because we all realized that under British currency regulations then in force no British citizen was allowed to take more than £25 out of the country, except on business, and twenty five quid would not go far towards buying Monte Carlo.

The fact was that nearly all the British people on the Riviera at that time were finding a way round the currency regulations and pretending that they won their French francs in the casinos. It was an open secret. Norah Docker had lost several thousand pounds at roulette some nights previously, and this fact was being widely publicized by members of the *Shemara*'s crew, one of whom had a wife and five children to keep on his weekly wage of £6.10s.

Mr Medley respectfully reminded Norah that her heavy losses were becoming a subject of gossip, and she turned on him angrily. 'If I were to lose a thousand pounds a week for the rest of my life,' she said, 'would I be poor?'

'Possibly not,' replied Mr Medley, 'but if you did it in France that would be an academic question, because you would surely be in gaol.'

I strolled back to the Carlton after lunch and sent the *Mirror* a carefully worded story about the Dockers' dilemma, stepping delicately through the minefield of possible libel actions with which the whole affair bristled; even so, the tongue-in-cheek copy was not unamusing, and the *Mirror* knew a good joke when they saw one, so they splashed it all over the front page next day, under the banner headline WILL THE DOCKERS STRIKE? THEY ASK IN MONTE.

This had an effect that nobody, including myself, anticipated. The Treasury realized that they could no longer continue to turn a blind eye to the currency infringements that were flagrantly taking place on the Côte d'Azur, so they decided to send investigators to the Riviera to look into the spending habits of British visitors. The *Daily Mirror* headline next morning was PROBE INTO BRITONS' HOLIDAY CASH STARTS PANIC ON THE RIVIERA.

The word panic was no exaggeration. It was like the flight of the Israelites out of Egypt. All Cannes went quiet. Only the airport was busy. My hotel was suddenly deserted. Everyone went home. The *Shemara* weighed anchor and sailed into the sunset. I was not a popular fellow anywhere, but aboard the *Shemara* my name must have been murkier than mud. Everyone in England was laughing, but Norah was not amused.

Not surprisingly, no hamper from Fortnum's turned up for me the following Christmas. Whitcomb was *chez la maison des chiens*. Which was the way I preferred it. Bill Connor had been right in his forecast that I would write about the Dockers, but I did not propose to make a habit of it. I doubt if I even saw Lady Docker again during the next three years; not, in fact, until she turned up in Monte Carlo for the Rainier wedding: she had been forgiven by the casino management, who had lifted the ban on her and had decided to take her money again, but it was widely known that she was still conducting a vendetta against Prince Jean-Louis de Faucigny-Lucinge. Norah never admitted defeat.

On the pre-wedding night in question I had been invited to a birthday party by a family of French people I had met on the Onassis yacht. The party was to take place in the nightclub below the casino and it was due to start at 10 p.m.; I finished dinner about nine o'clock and as I had nothing else to do I strolled across the road to the casino. The gaming rooms were crowded. I changed some money into chips and decided to play chemmy for an hour.

All the places round the *chemin-de-fer* tables were occupied, and there was also a crowd of kibitzers standing round each table, placing an occasional bet, so I joined one of these crowds and stood watching for a while. A moment arrived when there was a sizeable pot in the bank, but none of the players sitting round the table was accepting to fade the bank for its total worth, so on impulse I called, 'Banco!' A woman's voice behind me also called, 'Banco!' but the croupier said, 'The gentleman was first.' Sliding the cards swiftly out of the shoe he scooped up two cards on to his *palette* and shovelled them in my direction.

My two cards added up to nine, which is the winning number, so I tossed them face upwards on the table and the croupier pushed a big pile of chips over to me: it was no more than an ordinary everyday win of the sort that happens dozens of times a night in the casino at Monte Carlo, but even so it represented the price of a small cottage in the country. I gathered up the chips, mostly big-denomination *plaques*, and decided to take them straight to the *caisse* to cash them in. As I turned away from the table I saw that the woman who had called 'Banco!' just too late was Lady Docker. Luckily looks are not lethal because otherwise I would have been lying dead on the floor.

When I had collected the large bundles of new French banknotes from the cash desk I walked back to the hotel to put them in my *coffre-fort*, and then I read the papers for half an hour until it was time for me to go across the road again for the birthday party. On the way across I fell in with Jean-Louis de Faucigny-Lucinge, who had also been invited to the party, so we walked together down the stairs to the nightclub.

The first thing I saw as we walked in was Norah Docker sitting at a table with Sir Bernard and a couple of English columnists. She spotted us, too, and as the *maître d'hôtel* led us towards the table of our host she jumped to her feet and started shouting. 'Gauleiter Whitcomb!' she bellowed. 'Look at him! That's the man who betrayed us!'

She was jumping up and down with fury, and as I sat down at the table I apologized to our host for the rumpus that my presence had caused.

'Take no notice,' said our host. 'The lady is pissed, *comme d'habitude.*'

Norah was later barred from the nightclub, barred from the casino, barred from Monte Carlo, barred from the South of France and even barred from her local pub in Jersey where the Dockers had a house, but she went on making headlines until the day she died. There was a trace of Madame Bovary as well as of Diamond Lil about her; perhaps some day in the future some librettist will chance upon the story of her tumultuous life and set a Broadway musical around her; it would be a fitting epitaph because, as Shaw said about Ireland, the only thing you could ever do about Norah Docker was put footlights round her.

15

We are all in the gutter, but some of us
are looking at the stars.

Oscar Wilde, *Lady Windermere's Fan*

David Niven used to say that there was one point on which Errol Flynn
was utterly reliable – he would always let you down. This has been a
noticeable characteristic in some of my friends throughout my working
life, from Arthur Allighan onwards, although that may be more of a
comment upon myself than upon them. I was always amused by
unpredictable people, if unpredictable is the word I am looking for;
purists might choose a less tolerant word.

Time and again Flynn walked away whistling from an awkward-
looking situation and left me to do some fast talking. He thought it was
funny, and sometimes it was. The very last time I saw him before he died
he put me in a spot. I had invited him to a big ball that the *Daily Mirror*
was having at the Dorchester – one of Hugh Cudlipp's 'bits of fun' – and
Flynn telephoned me from the Savoy to say that he would love to come
but that his girlfriend had nothing to wear.

'Is that a problem?' I inquired.

'Be serious, sport,' said Errol, sternly. 'This poor kid can't go to one
of your million-pound publicity stunts looking like Cinderella before
the pumpkin scene. I'm not kidding – you'd get fired if you let it happen.
Listen, sport, a bloody great rich newspaper like yours can certainly
afford to make sure that its guests don't turn up looking as though they
have walked there from Skid Row. How about you ringing up Norman
Hartnell and getting him to run up something simple for her – something
with a few tiny diamonds on the bodice, what?'

Flynn knew, because it had been mentioned prominently in the paper,
that I had already asked Norman Hartnell to design a ball gown for the
girl who was to be our guest of honour, but I had no intention of
extending this privilege to all our female guests. So I said to Flynn, 'Look
here, Errol, I'll tell you what I'll do. You send your bird along to Moss
Bros, where they have a selection of very high-class gear in the way of

ladies' evening wear, and let her hire what she likes. Put it down to me.'

Flynn's girl nearly stole the scene when she arrived at the ball because, over a pretty low-necked dress, she wore a spectacularly long white fox-fur that was not only elegant but obviously very expensive. Everyone had eyes for her and all the women were talking about her gorgeous fur, which she flashed around with theatrical *élan*, much to Flynn's amusement.

On the morning after the ball, Errol telephoned me again from the Savoy. 'Listen, sport,' he said, 'can you believe that this poor kid could be so unlucky? She's lost that goddam fur.'

'No, I cannot believe it,' I said. 'Now you listen to me. Tell her to take that fur back to Moss Bross immediately or we will sue her.'

Flynn laughed heartily. 'That would look really swell in the papers,' he said. 'The publicity would do her a power of good. But unfortunately she cannot have that publicity because the fur is on your account, sport. Remember? It was your instructions. And – don't forget – the *Daily Mirror* is insured.'

However much trouble he caused me, Flynn always made me laugh. He never took life seriously. Even on his yacht, *Zaca*, he flew a white pennant with nothing but a big black question-mark on it; it was Flynn's proclamation to the world that he wondered what life was all about. He was a wicked fellow in some ways, as he himself was the first to admit, but there was a serious side to his character; surprisingly, he read a good deal of philosophy; and when he was on the yacht, playing with his little daughter, Arnella, or the dog called Fubar (so named by Errol because the dog looked Fed Up Beyond All Recognition), and eating Pat Wymore's delicious cooking, Flynn was a different man, a charming, ordinary man, who laughed at himself and his absurdly flamboyant Hollywood image. It was all a joke, sometimes an ugly joke but always a joke.

Flynn's yacht *Zaca* – *zaca* is the Samoan word for 'peace' – was the setting for another Flynn escapade that I found anything but peaceful. It was my fault. Or perhaps it was Hugh Cudlipp's fault, because it arose from another of Hugh's 'bits of fun'.

Cudlipp had decided that we should stage a gigantic seaside promotion to publicize the paper and, at a meeting in his office of people who would be concerned, he outlined his plans. 'We are going to put on a *Daily Mirror* week in Blackpool,' he said. 'It will take place in Scotch Week, which is the biggest week of the holiday season. We will take over the whole town. We will take on every showbusiness personality in the place and have them helping with our promotions or performing on

Blackpool beach under the *Daily Mirror* banner. We will plaster every square yard of the town with *Daily Mirror* posters. We will have banquets and balls and firework displays, and to start it off with a bang we will have a big parade through the streets, a spectacular procession like the Lord Mayor's Show, headed by the *Daily Mirror*'s beauty queen of Blackpool riding in state in a horse-drawn coach with Noel in his top hat as her escort. OK?'

Everyone nodded enthusiastically except me. The idea in general sounded good, but the bit about me togged up in Ascot gear and waving to the cheering crowds from a barouche sounded less attractive and likely to cause some ribaldry among the massed ranks of lads wearing kiss-me-quick hats.

'It's a brilliant plan, Hugh,' I said, 'but don't you think we might get a more volcanic explosion of enthusiasm from the holiday crowds if we fired it off with a wildly exciting opening?'

'Such as what?' said Cudlipp, who never liked to have his ideas queried.

I was thinking on my feet. 'Such as bringing a big Hollywood star . . . such as . . . such as' – and then the idea hit me. 'Such as getting Errol Flynn to sail into Blackpool on his yacht, with a flotilla of seagoing craft of every kind to meet him and sirens blaring everywhere, and then having him airlifted off the deck in a helicopter and landed by a rope and tackle outside the town hall to declare the *Daily Mirror* Blackpool Week officially open, to the deafening cheers of a deliriously excited multitude.'

If I had had more time to think I might have made it a shade less like the scenario for an Errol Flynn movie, but the damage was done. In a flash I could see that it was now going to be left to me to arrange it.

'Smashing idea, Noel,' said Hugh. 'Go and see Flynn and fix it with him right away.'

'But Flynn is on his yacht somewhere in the Mediterranean, probably in Majorca,' I said.

'I don't care if he's in Timbuctu,' said Hugh. 'You get him today.' He called to his secretary in the adjoining room, 'Hey – Mary – get the office car round to the front door right away. Mr Whitcomb is going to the airport.'

There was a flight to Majorca just over an hour later, and I was aboard it. I had a few necessities in an overnight bag that I always kept in the office, but I was still wearing a blue business suit because I had been planning to go on to a board meeting in the City of a small company of which I was a director.

301

At Palma airport I told the taxi driver to drop me near the Yacht Club, and from there I walked along the harbour, looking out to try and spot the *Zaca*. Suddenly somebody slapped me on the back and nearly sent me flying. It was Flynn.

'Hallo, sport,' he said, 'what are you doing here – and what's the idea of the heavy disguise? When I saw a feller in a blue suit walking purposefully in the direction of my boat it gave me a nasty turn – I thought it must be a tax inspector.'

'I've come over specially to do a deal with you,' I said.

'If there's money in it, the answer is yes,' grinned Errol. Flynn was financially in the soup again at the time. 'Come aboard the bucket and have a touch of gin,' he added. 'I never do business with a feller who is cold-stone sober.'

So we went aboard his yacht and had a few touches of gin – what Errol called a touch of gin would have made a roomy home for three goldfish – while I put the proposition to him. Flynn had been in a fight the previous night and his right hand was in plaster, but he was managing to jot down some figures with his left hand and I could see that he was preparing to ask a ridiculous price for doing what we wanted, so I said that I would go and dig in at a local hotel for the night and come back in the morning for a detailed discussion.

'You'll do nothing of the kind, sport,' said Flynn. 'Jaime here, my butler, will cook us a splendid dinner and he will prepare for you a cabin. He will also put out some of my leisure togs so that you can chuck that bloody blue suit over the side, and you can relax for a day or so while Patrick works out what it would cost to sail the yacht to Blackpool.'

Patrick Corfe-Cother was the skipper of Flynn's yacht and he looked uncomfortable while we were discussing the plan over dinner. I guessed that he was simply not keen to sail out of the Mediterranean. I guessed wrong.

When I awoke next morning in my cabin the first thing I heard was the thump of the engines. We were moving. I went up on deck and looked round. No land in sight. I'd been shanghaied.

'I couldn't tell you last night,' said Flynn, as we breakfasted on champagne and aspirins, 'because you might have cut and run, but I have been planning this expedition for some time. We are going to be rich, sport, rich beyond the dreams of avarice.'

With a conspiratorial air Flynn took from his wallet an ancient scrap of parchment. It was a map, a very old map. 'I pinched this out of the museum in Ibiza,' he said, deadly serious. 'That big black X in the middle marks the spot in the ocean where a Spanish galleon laden with

Inca gold sank in a storm in the days of Hernando Cortés and Francisco Pizarro. Those thieving bastards filched it from the poor bloody Mexicans and Peruvians. You and I, sport, with the help of a couple of divers, are going to put history straight by getting it back again.'

'But we're not Mexicans or Peruvians,' I said.

'Don't quibble,' said Errol. 'My research tells me that the wreck lies in shallow water. When we have found it unofficially we will first take a load of bullion down to North Africa where we will dispose of it quietly, then we will sail back and find the wreck officially, by accident, and be acclaimed as public benefactors while the Spanish government fights it out with the Peruvians and the Mexicans as to who gets what's left. Meantime you will be able to buy the bloody *Daily Mirror* and the *Daily Express* as well if you fancy it, and I shall be able to pay off my debts with a few million bucks to spare for alimony.'

'You're more likely to end up in a Spanish gaol,' I said. 'This is piracy.'

'Too right, cobber,' nodded Flynn. 'I've always suspected you of having a puritan streak. That's why I couldn't risk letting you go ashore and then have people asking questions about where I'd gone. It could have messed up my timing. We are due to pick up the diving gear and a couple of world-class divers under cover of darkness tonight off Formentera. So before we sailed I sent Jaime off to the cable office with a cable to your office, signed by you, saying that you would be delayed for a week or so owing to difficulties about the Blackpool project and that you would be out of touch. By the time you are back in touch again you will be able to buy Blackpool and give it to Cudlipp as a present in lieu of notice.'

It is a matter of record, of course, that we never found the treasure, but we did find a wreck. On the second day of our odyssey one of the professional divers came up with some shards of amphora, probably Roman. The water was so clear that you could see the rippled sand on the sea bed, and it was obvious that if any wreck were there it would be buried beneath centuries of silted sand. But Flynn was not dismayed. I had been passing the time by helping him write a couple of chapters of his autobiography, but when the bits of amphora came up it was action-stations all round.

'It looks likely,' said Flynn, 'that we have found the wrong wreck. But there might be a few dollars-worth of saleable gear in this one – you never know – so here's what I suggest we do. I will take one diver and the double-ender and reconnoitre the waters south of here while Noel and Paul scrabble about on the seabed here and see what they can find.'

What we did find was a heavy cylinder of metal encrusted with barnacles. Flynn found something much more interesting: when he returned from his sortie in the double-ender he had with him an extremely pretty French blonde. He had seen her swimming off the coast somewhere and had invited her to dinner aboard the yacht. Dinner, he said! She was wearing a bikini and had nothing else with her, but she didn't need anything else. In fact it was only at mealtimes that she needed the bikini. Her name – and you are not going to believe this – was Fifi.

Luckily for me, Flynn's new interest in this splendid modern discovery took his mind off more ancient treasure trove, and he agreed to put me ashore on a strip of coast that was part of a salt mine on the island of Ibiza. I was immediately arrested on suspicion: the local policeman thought there was something fishy about a man carrying a blue suit trying to find a telephone in a salt mine, and one can see his point. I could cheerfully have murdered Flynn.

Back in London I managed to pull my chestnuts out of the fire by persuading the Beatles to perform on Blackpool beach as part of our *Daily Mirror* jollifications, and as there were about fifty thousand teenagers on the promenade that night the Beatles went down rather well. It was touch and go whether we brought 'em back alive.

The teenagers of that period had become particularly hard to handle, unusually rebellious, and pop music had become the medium of their anarchy; they were the parent-generation of the football hooligan, the pathfinders for the juvenile drug addict, and they began to represent a serious socio-political problem which the tabloid newspapers handled with predictable irresponsibility, pretending to be shocked by their behaviour but at the same time egging them on. At times when their pop idols were performing the youngsters sometimes went on a rampage of destruction that was uncontrollable except by means that were unacceptable to a so-called civilized society. A few pop stars such as Cliff Richard, who recognized the danger in what was going on, were careful not to excite their fans to the point of hysteria, but most pop merchants worked on the principle that the bigger the riot the bigger the publicity and the more they earned; part of their fee for public appearances was danger money.

Johnny Ray was a pop-singer who could bring the house down in more senses than one, and so when the *Daily Mirror* decided to bring him over from America to do cabaret in a ballroom full of teenagers, everyone with a nose for danger could sniff trouble in the wind. The occasion was the last of Hugh Cudlipp's 'bits of fun' in which I was a reluctant accomplice, and it was called the *Daily Mirror* Debs Ball.

The Queen was in the process of abolishing the formal presentation at court of débutantes because it no longer fitted in with the social pattern of the time; so, arising from a suggestion by Marjorie Proops, the *Mirror*'s agony auntie, Cudlipp decided that we should run a big ball in London for ordinary teenage girls and call them the *Daily Mirror* debs. All they had to do was to send in their photographs and fifty would be picked to come as débutantes to the ball, each accompanied by a boyfriend escort. One of my tasks was to assemble a panel of judges to choose fifty from the tens of thousands of photographs that poured in, and on judging day in a private room at the Savoy Hotel we set about the work. I had chosen people in the public eye as judges, and the panel consisted of Raine Legge, Barbara Cartland's daughter who later, as Lady Spencer, became Princess Diana's stepmother; Pietro Annigoni, who was painting a portrait of the Queen; Teasy-Weasy Raymond, who was at the peak of his fame as a hairdresser; and the Duke of Bedford, who was seeking to publicize Woburn Abbey as the prototype of all theme-park stately homes.

It should have been easy, but the judging went on all day and far into the evening largely because Raine Legge picked all the peaches-and-cream blonde English types of girl while Annigoni selected all the dark-eyed Giacondas, and as chairman of the panel I had great difficulty in getting them to agree; in fact, by the time we adjourned there was still no agreement about the selection of the final girl – Raine Legge was holding out for a blonde girl and Pietro Annigoni was adamant that it should be a Renaissance Florentine type. I ended the proceedings by ruling that the editor should have the final say, although I had no intention of bothering him with it. I intended to put both photographs face down and pick one blindfold.

Back in the office I was clearing up a few things on my desk when the door opened and in came Teasy-Weasy. 'Noel,' he said, 'I'm sorry about barging in like this but I just wanted to ask you if you would choose the blonde girl. I think she is an absolute smasher. If she came into one of my salons and asked for a job as a model I would take her on without another word. In my view she is the best of all the fifty.'

'Sure,' I said, laughing. 'It doesn't matter to me which one it is, so long as we get fifty. Consider it done. It saves time, anyway. What's her name?' I picked up the photograph and looked at the name on the back. 'Her name is Rosalie Ashley,' I said. 'Right. That's settled. Miss Ashley is number fifty.'

Rosalie Ashley was certainly a good choice. She looked a picture at the ball. Teasy-Weasy met her there for the first time. A few months later they were married. That was over forty years ago, and, as I write, they are still married, and every Christmas I still receive a card written in a feminine hand and signed 'with love from Rosalie and Raymond'.

The ball itself presented one problem that was less easy to solve. When Johnny Ray arrived in England to do our cabaret he was front-page news in all the popular papers; vast crowds of young people laid siege to the hotel where he was staying, screaming and swooning and crying real tears for Johnny, the Million-dollar Teardrop. When I asked him to come and have a look at the ballroom in which he would be performing, so that he could approve the lighting and the microphones, we had to smuggle him out in heavy disguise through a back door. Incidentally, Derek Nimmo was his 'roadie' – his tour manager.

Johnny walked into the ballroom and stood looking round for about a minute. Then he said, 'Noel, boy – no deal.'

'What do you mean – no deal?'

'I mean that nothing in this wide world would persuade me to sing in front of a hundred kids in these circumstances. They will kill me. I'm not kidding. I know. They will tear my pants off first and then they will tear my balls off for an encore. You must be stark raving mad. I am insured for a million bucks against injury by fans, but if I walked out on to this open floor and sang in front of a roomful of kids I would not be covered for a cent, because it would be direct provocation. I am sorry, boy, but get yourself another singer.'

'Look, Johnny,' I pleaded, 'I can assure you that you will be as safe as if you were in Fort Knox. I have a secret weapon.'

'What's that?' he asked.

'The black tie,' I said. 'It never fails.'

When I had explained my plan to him, Johnny reluctantly agreed to take a chance and try it. It was very simple. And it worked. On the day when our young guests arrived in London, all the girls were fitted into pretty white ball gowns, just like Queen Charlotte's. The girls were not so much of a problem because, as every parent with a toddler knows, if you have a party attended solely by little girls you have no difficulties, but the minute you introduce one boy into the room, fighting breaks out. So it was the boys I had my eye on. They looked an unpromising bunch of young villains. Some wore zoot-suits and one had a bicycle chain in his pocket. Some had knuckle-dusters. Few had left home without a knife of some description. So the first thing I did was to have them all relieved of these impedimenta and the next thing I did was to have them all shipped off in taxi-loads to Moss Bros, where they were kitted out with hired dinner jackets and black ties.

When all the youngsters trooped into the grand ballroom, with its crystal chandeliers and banks of flowers and tables set with white napery, it was a most elegant scene. Throughout dinner they all behaved better than would have been the case with upper-class youngsters at a hunt ball; but I was still slightly anxious about what would happen when Johnny Ray came on; the pop star known as the Prince of Wails was powerful chemistry with youngsters anywhere and sparked off atavistic passions.

The moment came. The lights flicked down. The drums rolled. In swept Johnny. There was a tumultuous round of applause. But only applause. Apart from clapping and cheering, nobody moved. Johnny went into his first number and there were screams and squeals from all over the ballroom. But they all sat tight. Johnny sang for forty-five minutes, went off to deafening applause, then came back and did four encores. When he finally went off, nobody rushed the stage. Nobody so much as asked him for an autograph. Johnny Ray was the most puzzled man in London that night. He even wondered whether he might be slipping. But it was the black tie that had done the trick. None of those lads had ever worn evening dress before, or danced under chandeliers with girls in white ball dresses, and the utter strangeness of the setting had caught them all off balance. It is not that the offspring of the poor are better mannered than their counterparts in the middle class, but simply that they are more easily intimidated by unfamiliar circumstances. They lose their self-assurance, and self-assurance is, above all, the attribute for which wise parents pay the fees at Eton.

Soon after the ball I was back in France and, walking through the foyer of the Ritz in Paris, I ran into Errol Flynn, whom I had not seen since our seafaring treasure hunt. Knowing that he had been excited about our find of the heavy tubular piece of metal, being convinced that it was a cannon off a Spanish galleon, I asked him what had happened about it.

'Well, sport, I sent it to the Spanish Maritime Museum,' he said, 'as a foundation gift for the Errol Flynn Archaeological Bequest. I told them that Mr Noel Whitcomb, the well-known expert on Doric columns, was associated with me in this discovery – so that both of us would get a medal pinned on the chest by a grateful president of the Spanish Fine Arts Commission.'

'So what came of that?'

'I got this letter,' he went on, taking the letter from his pocket and handing it to me. The letter read: 'Dear Mr Flynn, Thank you for your gift of the metal object. Regrettably it is not a cannon from a galleon but a drainpipe from a merchant vessel of recent date.'

We both burst out laughing. I said, 'It was a good try, but I doubt if either of us is ever likely to get any medals.'

'Story of my life,' nodded Flynn. '*Tout est bien qui finit mal*. Never mind. Let's have a touch of gin.'

While in Paris I had dinner with Mike Todd, who asked me to play what he called a 'cameo part' in the film he was making of Jules Verne's *Around the World in Eighty Days*. As there were 68,894 people from thirteen different countries appearing in this historic motion picture, it was not a big deal, and Mike asked me to do it simply as a friendly gesture and because almost all the vast army of actors and artists concerned with the film were friends of both of us. It was a family affair. I told Mike that I would let him know because I had to get permission, due to a clause in my contract with the *Mirror* that required me to obtain clearance from the editor before doing any film or television appearances.

This was normally a formality, and I had never known permission to be refused before, but when I mentioned the matter to Jack Nener, the editor, he looked doubtful. 'I'd better send a memo to Hugh Cudlipp about it,' he said. 'I don't think he likes Mike Todd.'

Cudlipp did not even know Mike Todd, and had never met him, but I think there was something about Todd's enormous success as a showman of which Cudlipp was, in a curious way, jealous. At all events, he sent a one-line memo back to Jack Nener, saying, 'Ask Noel to make his mind up whether he wants to be a journalist or an actor.' Nener was most apologetic about it, but there was nothing he could do, and I decided that it was too small a matter to make a fuss about. But I remembered it on the morning after the London première of *Eighty Days*.

Mike Todd had given a gargantuan party in Battersea Festival Gardens to follow the first night of his film. The film itself had been greeted on all sides as a sensational success and the party that followed had been the most spectacular and celebrity-packed junket of the decade. Stories and pictures about it were all over the morning papers. My wife and I did not get home from the party until nearly five in the morning, and I was awakened soon after nine by the telephone. It was Hugh Cudlipp.

'Noel,' he said, 'I want to lunch with Mike Todd today. Will you fix it?'

'If he's free,' I said. 'Which I doubt.'

This was the most triumphant and busiest day of all Mike Todd's life.

Everyone was after him. Movie moguls were flying in from the United States in the hope of doing deals with him; banks were sending directors to offer finance for his next picture; Mike was the most sought-after man in Britain that morning, and the whole of his professional future was being shaped by decisions he took that day. Yet when I, feeling rather a fraud, telephoned him and passed on Cudlipp's request about luncheon, all he said was 'Sure, Noel, sure – bring him along. See you at one o'clock here.'

Cudlipp decided to bring Bill Connor – Cassandra – as well, with the idea that Bill would write a column about Todd. We arrived slightly early and, while we were waiting for Todd, Hugh and Bill sank a big jug-full of dry martini between them. It was fighting-juice for both of them and my heart sank as I sipped my champagne. It seemed a pity to spoil Mike's big day but I could see that we were getting to the moment when seat-belts should be fastened.

It started amiably enough, with congratulations about the success of the film, but that soon stopped. Cudlipp and Connor began being gratuitously rude to Todd, asking him all sorts of personal questions about his private life. They behaved like juvenile delinquents. Todd took it all in a good-humoured way, answering some of the questions and side-stepping others with politeness, but naturally he was rattled. Clearly he was wondering what he had done to me that had caused me to let him in for this extraordinary inquisition, especially as it came from one of Britain's top newspaper executives aided and abetted by a major columnist who was famous as a verbal mauler. Towards the end of lunch Mike lit a cigar. This was unusual, because he had given up cigars some time previously at the request of Elizabeth Taylor who thought smoking was doing him harm.

It was, as it happened, Elizabeth who broke up the lunch. She came into the room and was about to say hallo to everyone when she saw Mike smoking. 'Oh, Christ!' she shouted – Elizabeth's language was always overripe – 'it's that fucking Whitcomb who has started Mike off smoking again!'

She never forgave me, and I never explained. All I did was keep out of her way as much as possible, which was not difficult. But Mike forgave me for the ugly lunch and during the next few years he would always telephone me when he was in London or Paris, and sometimes he would write to tell me what he was doing.

One morning, at home, I opened a letter from him. He wrote:

I have been looking through some press clips, and thinking once again it is ironic that the greatest single press break I ever received should have your name on it. Nothing could have pleased me more, for reasons that it is better for me to tell you face to face, which I would like to do when I return to London. [He continued with news about Elizabeth Taylor, his wife, with whom he was still deeply in love, and then ended:] I am making a career of being happy, and God knows I have all the ingredients for it. This is the best time of my life. I hope you, my friend, are enjoying life as much as I am.

Later, when I went out to get the papers, they all carried the same front-page headline: MIKE TODD KILLED IN AIR CRASH.

One man who had particular reason to be grateful to Mike Todd was Kevin O'Donovan McClory, whose substantial fortune was founded in an unconventional way. Kevin was earning £7 a week as a boom operator at British Lion Studios when I first met him, soon after the war. His father had been an Irish actor and Kevin had been born in Dun Laoghaire, but he had been at a Catholic school in Finchley until he was fifteen when he joined the merchant navy as a seaman, later returning to London as an Irish building labourer. More Irish than the Irish, almost professionally Irish, Kevin claimed descent from the Brontës of Haworth – Charlotte, Emily and Anne were Irish on their father's side of the family, as was their brother Branwell who became an archetypal Irish drunk.

When Kevin found the job at the studios he also found his true love: he fell heavily for the film business. Carol Reed gave him a trial job on production where he was spotted by John Huston who employed him on *Moulin Rouge, The African Queen* and *Moby Dick*. It was during the filming of *Moby Dick* off the coast of Ireland, where Kevin nearly ended his days prematurely during the shooting of one of the whale scenes in turbulent waters, that we began meeting frequently, usually with John Huston and Ernie Anderson. Ernie was Huston's press agent, and he did a similar job for Mike Todd, so when Todd came to London to sign up talent for his *Around the World in Eighty Days*, Ernie and I took Kevin McClory to see him. Todd liked him right away, and gave him a job as thirty-third assistant director on *Eighty Days*. Kevin quickly became thirty-second assistant director and ended up as the most important assistant director on the film, having flown 45,000 miles on location for the movie and helped Todd to edit it in Hollywood. Kevin was moving into the big time.

We used to meet often at Les Ambassadeurs or Ruby Lloyd's club in Shepherd Market because Kevin had started producing a film of his own and Ernie Anderson was helping him as press agent. The film, set against the background of Tower Bridge, was called *The Boy and the Bridge*, and due to Ernie Anderson's skilled work it was generally tipped to be a masterpiece – until it opened: after it opened it was generally tipped to be a turkey, which proved to be the case. It died the death.

The man who put up the money for *The Boy and the Bridge* was Ivar Bryce, an old Etonian who had been known to some of his friends at school as Burglar Bryce, and who had married one of the richest women in America, a member of the Huntington-Hartford family who owned the A & P 'five-and-ten' stores.

As a medium for investment in film business Bryce had set up a company called Xanadu Productions – he had a house in the Bahamas called Xanadu – and Kevin's film was his first big venture; he was ultimately to sustain a heavy loss on this début as an 'angel', but that disagreeable shock was still in the future when, during the euphoric days of pre-opening publicity, he discussed with Kevin and with his old friend Ian Fleming a far bigger production to follow – a James Bond film.

Even before this plan crystallized, Kevin was already planning a second film. He had taken a house in Belgrave Place, and his girlfriend, Bobo Sigrist, who was one of the richest heiresses in England and whom he later married, was living in the mews nearby. Ernie Anderson and I were frequent visitors to the house in Belgrave Place because it was the headquarters of the Woodpeckers, a society that Kevin had modelled on Frank Sinatra's Clan; Shirley Maclaine and John Huston were also Woodpeckers and Peter O'Toole was chairman of the Connemara branch. Much of our discussion there centred on Kevin's plans for his second film. Kevin had picked up some cans of underwater footage that had been shot off the Bahamas, and the working title for the film was *The Treasure of Gorda Cay*. Shooting was to be done using Mike Todd's Todd A-O process, which Kevin had learned to use when working for Mike on *Eighty Days*. The story concerned the finding of a Spanish silver ingot at Gorda Cay, part of the lost treasure of King Philip IV of Spain which had been sunk in a storm off the Bahamas when it was on its way from Colombia to Spain in the seventeenth century.

The whole thing smacked a bit too much of Errol Flynn for my liking, but Kevin managed to get some influential people interested, including John Steinbeck who wrote him a five-page letter explaining exactly how Kevin ought to go about it. I find that I still have a copy of that letter among my McClory souvenirs, which also include a subpoena issued at the instigation of his solicitor, Peter Carter-Ruck.

311

There was another movie idea that we discussed, an original story called *Earthquake* that had an Andalusian setting; but the story-line we discussed most often was a Bulldog Drummond type of drama, in preparation for which Kevin had several big blow-ups of pictures of a vintage green Bentley car that was to figure in the chase; we all came up with different suggestions for a plot, and I suggested *Thunderball* as a title, but no definite theme emerged until Ivar Bryce introduced Kevin McClory to Ian Fleming, with the idea that McClory might make a James Bond film.

Bryce and Fleming had been at school together and had been good friends ever since. Fleming was a journalist, having started at Reuters in the 1930s, but he had done particularly well during the war as personal assistant to the director of naval intelligence, which was the period when I first met him. He had become a popular man about town, and after the war he was employed by Lord Kemsley as foreign manager of Kemsley newspapers, later also writing the *Atticus* column for Kemsley's *Sunday Times*. By the time the film project came up he was already beginning his rise to fame as the creator of James Bond, and his early James Bond novels were selling well, but none had yet been turned into a feature film.

After McClory's *Boy and the Bridge* film turned out to be a failure, it became apparent to all of us – with the possible exception of McClory – that Fleming had doubts about the wisdom of putting the Irish charmer in full charge of the movie that would launch James Bond on the big screen; he liked McClory, with reservations, but as his friend Ivar Bryce had already lost a packet through backing McClory he was wary of becoming the instrument through which such a disaster might happen again. He wanted an experienced producer who would use McClory as director of the film. We all knew this, once again with the possible exception of Kevin, who was far too excited about the project to entertain any doubts about his suitability. At all events, Fleming agreed to work on a plot and story-line with McClory and an experienced screenwriter called Jack Whittingham – and a script was produced. Then Fleming went abroad and Whittingham completed the screenplay and the treatment under the working title of *James Bond, Secret Agent*.

Ian Fleming had a house in Jamaica called Goldeneye (Noël Coward, a neighbour, dubbed it Golden Eye-Nose-and-Throat, and Alastair Forbes suggested that it should have been named Rum Cove), and Ian had a clause in his contract with Kemsley that enabled him to spend two months of every year at Goldeneye, which was where he wrote his James Bond novels. During the year in question he wrote a James Bond novel called *Thunderball*, which was in effect the story of the film on which he had worked in collaboration with McClory and Whittingham.

All of us were convinced – once again with the exception of McClory – that Ian honestly believed he had a perfect right to do this, as the onlie begetter of James Bond; but McClory, who by this time was aware that control of the production of the proposed movie was slipping out of his grasp, decided to take legal action against Ian Fleming for infringement of copyright – an action which in effect alleged plagiarism – and against Bryce for breach of contract.

It was nearly two years before the case came before the court, during which time Ian Fleming's James Bond novels became more valuable properties than ever, and Ian had entered into a contract with two important film-makers, Harry Saltzman and Cubby Broccoli, assigning to them the film rights to all James Bond novels for which such rights were still available.

The court case went on for ten costly days, during which Fleming visibly aged ten years; he was angry at the imputation that he had stolen what he considered to be his own work, but the core of the issue was whether McClory and Whittingham had contributed ideas towards the story of *Thunderball*, and it became evident from statements made by witnesses including myself that this was indubitably a fact. On the tenth day, Bryce decided to settle, leaving Fleming no sensible option but to do the same.

Under the terms of the settlement demanded by Peter Carter-Ruck, McClory's solicitor, Kevin received a *pourboire* of £35,000 from Ivar Bryce as damages for breach of contract and infringement of copyright, but it was what he received from Ian Fleming that made him seriously rich: the film rights to *Thunderball*. *Thunderball*, which was made into a film by Saltzman and Broccoli with the name of Kevin McClory on the credits as producer, took millions at the box office.

After the settlement a victory celebration party was held in the upstairs bar of Paddy Kennedy's Star Tavern in Belgrave Mews, where an Irish tricolor was flaunted behind the bar and the revellers included Britain's most distinguished reformed burglar, Eddie Chapman, as well as a couple of highly regarded reformed confidence tricksters, Gerald Hamilton and Guido Orlando. A toast was drunk to James Stephens and *The Crock of Gold*.

When I next saw Ian Fleming, at a party unconnected with films or books, he waved to me cheerily from across the room; I think that if I had been him I would have turned my back. Fleming lived all his life in a fantasy world of dangerous adventure and immense riches, which was a prime advantage for the creator of James Bond; yet the riches of which he dreamed came to him in surprisingly meagre quantity while the megabucks resulting from his work were creamed off by men of less talent and imagination but greater shrewdness. When Fleming died, the James Bond industry was making millions upon millions, but Ian himself left only about £300,000.

I remained on friendly terms with McClory, although he spent increasingly less time in England, and when we had a house on the river in Henley he brought his daughter Bianca to see us, and later his new wife, Elizabeth, daughter of Vincent O'Brien the multi-millionaire Irish racehorse trainer. He also invited me to a party at which a band of Irish fiddlers – violinists – played jigs while he announced the preparation, in association with Richard Harris the actor, of a film about Michael Collins, the Sinn Fein leader who was killed in an ambush between Bandon and Macroom in 1922; but as the names of possible stars in this production included not only the hell-raising Richard Harris but also the hell-raising Oliver Reed and the hell-raising Trevor Howard, plus the then hell-raising Anthony Hopkins, I decided that my health was not robust enough to take any further interest in the project: sometimes one gets a premonition.

Ernie Anderson kept cropping up in my working life, usually on escapades with John Huston, but the oddest episode involving Ernie occurred in 1956, after the Russians had shocked the world by crushing with tanks in Budapest the Hungarian freedom movement. André Deutsch, the publisher, a Hungarian by birth, invited Gerald Lascelles and myself to luncheon to outline plans for a big concert at the Festival Hall in aid of the Hungarian Relief Fund. Gerald was presumably invited because he was a cousin of the Queen, and a royal interest was hoped for, and I was there as a columnist with many million readers. It had been arranged that Norman del Mar would conduct the Royal Philharmonic Orchestra, and that high prices would be charged for seats; there was little doubt that the most expensive seats would sell quickly, but the Festival Hall is a big room and there was some doubt about how readily the less well-placed of the seats would sell. That was the problem, filling the whole hall at high prices.

Towards the end of lunch I had an idea. How would it be, I suggested, if we persuaded Louis Armstrong and some other virtuosi among the greatest names of the world of jazz to join the Royal Philharmonic as a group inside the orchestra, playing specially arranged passages of the symphonic works on the programme: that would bring in the big battalions and have them queuing to pay high prices for inferior seats.

André Deutsch shook his head. 'Norman del Mar would not stand for it,' he said. 'To him it would look like a gimmick.'

But Gerald Lascelles, who was a keen jazz man and who wrote a column on the subject for the *Tatler*, liked the idea. 'I think it's worth a try,' he said, 'although I doubt whether Louis Armstrong would agree to it.'

My reason for thinking that Louis might be persuaded was that Joe Glaser was his agent, so when I returned home after luncheon I called in Ernie Anderson, rather in the way that Sherlock Holmes used to send a telegram to Dr Watson when he had a difficult case in hand. Ernie was an authority on jazz, not merely an *aficionado* but a jazz historian to be compared in that field with George Melly or Benny Green; he knew as intimate friends all the big names from Duke Ellington and Fats Waller to Django Reinhardt and Stéphane Grappelli, so when I told him about the idea he knew exactly how to go about setting it up. He was very excited about the plan. 'Great idea, Noel,' he said, seriously. 'This could be historic. But first we have to get Joe on our side, because he decides everything for Louis.' So we telephoned Joe Glaser in New York and I put the proposition.

'Are you crazy, Noel?' he asked. 'Are you seriously suggesting that my boy should fly to London to play for a bunch of classical freaks? You must be off your head. Louis is the biggest jazz name in the world. He is booked up solid for the whole of the rest of the year. What would be the fee?'

'No fee, Joe,' I said. 'It's for charity.'

Joe laughed so raucously that I thought he was going to choke. 'No fee!' he repeated, between gasps. 'No fee! For Louis Armstrong, the world's greatest, to appear with a no-name combination of *nebbish* Beethoven strummers! My life! It's not just ridiculous – it's . . . ridiculous. Looking at my watch and counting five hours forward I realize that you must have been out to lunch with Ernie. It's Ernie's idea, isn't it? Hit him for me, would you? Ernie should go and get his brains tested and you should give my love to Sally and then go and get your head down until the lunch wears off.'

'But Joe,' I said, 'Princess Margaret will be there. It will be a big prestige occasion. Louis will be mixing with royalty.'

'Princess Margaret, huh?' said Joe. 'Would she be seen to be very friendly with Louis?'

'Sure would,' I said. 'She is one of his greatest fans.'

'Huh,' said Joe. 'Huh. Lemme think about it.'

Next day he rang me back to say that Satchmo would 'do the gig and also pay all costs entailed in his visit to London.' The costs of such a visit were considerable, because wherever Louis Armstrong went he took a big entourage with him. All Louis's relations and all his wife's relations had jobs with 'ole Satchelmou', because Louis was a kindly and generous man; one of his wife's relations performed one single duty, which was to launder and iron Satchmo's white linen handkerchiefs, of which he used dozens a day to mop his brow and dab his lips while playing the trumpet; he also took Doc Pugh everywhere, simply and solely to prescribe aperients.

As André Deutsch had forecast, Norman del Mar took a great deal of convincing, and he nearly walked out as conductor; but, through the good offices of Ernie Anderson, George Gershwin worked on one of the musical arrangements with Leonard Bernstein – a symphonic arrangement of *Summertime* from Gershwin's opera *Porgy and Bess* – and on the night a group of some of the greatest jazz musicians in the world took their places in the orchestra under the baton of Norman del Mar. Nothing of the kind had ever happened before in Britain, and it was a phenomenal success. The house was packed to capacity and seldom have I heard such tumultuous applause. It was a triumph in every way. After the concert Princess Margaret spent an hour in the dressing rooms talking to Louis Armstrong and his family, so everyone was delighted, including Joe Glaser, who was well aware that this night had added a new dimension to his client's fame.

On the morning when Louis and his party were due to fly back to New York, Louis telephoned and asked me to come and see them off. As they were about to walk on to the tarmac at Heathrow, Brown Sugar, Satchmo's wife, kissed me on both cheeks and whispered, 'Honey, Louis knows that he owes this symphonic triumph to you, and he won't forget it. He done gone loves them British classical cats. And, honey, just do one more thing – give Princess Margaret a big hug for me.'

Brown Sugar died suddenly three months later, and Louis was disconsolate for the rest of his life. But from the night at the Festival Hall onwards, Louis Armstrong became another of the characters who kept flitting in and out of my personal dance to the music of time; whenever he came to Europe he would telephone and invite me to come and hear him play, and there was one occasion, some years later, when he gave a private recital for an acquaintance of mine: as usual, that was a sketch with an improbable cast, a brief comedy in the world of the poet and the lunatic.

When Yevgeny Yevtushenko, the Russian poet, first came to England, he came at the invitation of the British Council. At twenty-eight, Yevtushenko was already becoming highly regarded as a poet, his 'Babi Yar' having recently appeared in an English translation. As I had read it, and thought it splendid, I went to the press reception when he arrived intending to write a column about him.

The British Council had requested Stephen Spender and Peter Levi, at that time Father Levi, to look after Yevtushenko for the whole of his visit, accompanying him wherever he went. At the press reception, despite the fact that Yevtushenko spoke little English and I spoke practically no Russian, we managed to have a long conversation and we got on very well. When Spender and Levi came over to introduce a couple of minor English poets, Yevtushenko said with beaming Russian ebullience, 'This my good friend, Noel – he very good chap.'

Neither Spender nor Levi looked too pleased about this; it was not part of the image that they had been instructed to promote. Yevtushenko's schedule had been arranged so that he would meet mostly poets, professors of poetry, the more reliable sort of literary editor and a number of hand-picked intellectuals; the *Daily Mirror* did not rate high in their requirements. But worse was to come.

'Tonight,' went on Yevgeny happily, 'Noel and I go to football match and see Arsenal play.'

'Oh, no,' said Spender, shocked. 'Oh, no. I am sorry, my dear Yevtushenko, but that will not be possible. Tonight we are dining at All Souls.'

'OK,' nodded Yevgeny, reasonably. 'Tonight we go Oxford. But tomorrow night I go with Noel to the big fight.'

'Not tomorrow night,' said Levi, with a smile; he was clearly finding the whole charade amusing.

'OK,' said Yevtushenko. 'Not tomorrow. But when do I get chance to go and see big sports? You know, before I was poet I was sports reporter.'

Spender and Levi tactfully steered Yevtushenko away from the idea of attending football games or boxing matches, but there was one matter about which he was adamant; he had made up his mind to see Covent Garden fruit and vegetable market at work in the early morning, and he wanted me to show it to him. This concession was granted, so on the appointed day I picked up Yevgeny at his hotel at 5 a.m. Neither Spender nor Levi thought that getting up at such an hour was in the line of duty, so off we went to cast an eye over the land of Eliza Doolittle. Yevgeny was enchanted. Covent Garden market had a special atmosphere that is now lost forever – raffish, intensely expert, essentially cockney, speaking its own language that so offended the ear of Professor Higgins. We had tea at a coffee stall and then hot rum at a market pub. Yevgeny bought an enormous box of flowers and then stood before a wholesaler's stand, picking up the grapefruit and squeezing them with the air of an expert.

' 'Ere, 'ere, 'ere – put them bleedin' grapes dahn,' shouted the stall-keeper, indignantly.

I explained to him, 'This is Yevgeny Yevtushenko, the celebrated Russian poet.'

'I don't care if he's the Shah of fuckin' Persia,' said the man, 'you tell 'im to take his thievin' irons off my grapes.'

Yevgeny, puzzled, asked, 'What he say?'

'He said he would prefer that you did not handle the fruit,' I said.

Among Yevgeny's heroes were two artists of a different kind: Pushkin and Louis Armstrong. As Russia's first national poet had been dead for more than a century there was no possibility of the two writers meeting, but the case of Louis Armstrong was different; Louis was visiting London and I set up a dinner for the three of us. At first glance, it might not seem the perfect recipe for a successful conversational evening – the poet who spoke mostly Russian, the great jazz trumpeter who spoke a language that was incomprehensible to most people outside New Orleans, and the English columnist: yet it was one of the most delightful dinners I can recall, all three of us talking at once throughout the evening, except when Louis played the trumpet for us.

In the course of writing this reminiscence of Louis Armstrong I looked up the files and was surprised to find no review of his concert with the Royal Philharmonic: then I remembered why. The musicians' union in Britain was in dispute at the time, threatening to strike; one of the questions at issue was whether foreign musicians should be banned from performing in the country, on the grounds that such appearances took work from British musicians. The *Daily Mirror* would not have dared to irritate the musicians' union in case the print unions came out in sympathy. This was a good example of the way in which newspaper executives were already being cowed and intimidated by union leaders, no longer masters in their own house. It was the syndrome that ended in the death of Fleet Street as a newspaper centre and the rebirth of British newspapers in a different place, after Rupert Murdoch's last-ditch defeat of print-union anarchy.

Part of the reason for the decline and fall was that, from that time in the 1950s on into the 1980s, it became increasingly difficult for newspapers to recruit men of proven ability as executives; the progressive dominance of the union leaders made the jobs of senior newspaper executives so purgatorial that highly qualified men preferred to offer their skills to other industries rather than suffer the frustration of being constantly hamstrung in Fleet Street. So the rot set in. Newspapers themselves never recovered, not even after the excesses of the unions had been curbed. The quality of editorial staff had already gone too far downhill. Low-quality executives and, as was evident in some cases unusually low-quality proprietors, inevitably result in low-quality journalists because good journalists walk away in disgust and their places are increasingly taken by unscrupulous chancers who wave the noble banner of freedom of speech but cunningly use it as a licence to behave as hooligans in print.

The labour government of Clement Attlee in the 1940s and the later administrations under the premiership of Harold Wilson laid the ground for encouraging this outcome of what Stanley Baldwin had once called the prerogative of the whore – power without responsibility – and the disease spread to television and radio because those media shared in the dilution of journalistic quality available; the message – the political message – became so much a part of almost every news item that, however covertly the trick was played, the general public became progressively aware of it and therefore increasingly sceptical of everything they read in newspapers or heard on television or radio.

The last period during which quality of any kind, or responsibility, was observed in any British popular tabloid occurred when Cecil King and Hugh Cudlipp were running the *Daily Mirror*. Cecil King described his politics as 'left of centre' and Hugh Cudlipp was then a supporter of the Labour Party; both men had close contacts at Westminster, and they brought in political advisers who helped to turn the *Mirror* into what was probably the best-informed newspaper in the country. Cudlipp became the subject of grossly flattering articles in the weekly reviews and in what were then called the posh Sundays, although the posh Sundays themselves were already beginning to plunge further and further down-market in search of the increased circulation that inevitably leads to lower quality; in newspapers as in television and radio, more always means worse, and there is never any getting away from that immutable law, whatever fine excuses and fancy claims may be made. Cudlipp was always a bright and quick man with an innovative flair, but not astute, and it was my opinion at the time that he was greatly over-estimated – although with hindsight I can see that he was a Titan compared with the generations of pygmies who were to follow.

As Cecil King's publishing empire became more grandiose, and the *Daily Mirror* itself more influential, honours began to shower on the senior members of the staff. During the Harold Wilson years, when honours were handed out like Christmas presents with a profligacy unmatched since the time when Lloyd George sold peerages, the organization swarmed with so many titles that it became a public joke. At a luncheon to mark the retirement of Ted Castle, chaired by Hugh Cudlipp (later Sir Hugh, and later still Baron Cudlipp of Aldingbourne), and attended by former political editor Sydney Jacobson (later Lord Jacobson) and *Mirror* political editor John Beavan (later Lord Beavan), not to mention Bill Connor (Cassandra – later Sir William Connor) and Marjorie Proops OBE, we had an insight into how the system worked. Ted Castle, Barbara Castle's husband, had always been a staunch supporter of the Labour Party, and in the course of the speech that Cudlipp made in his honour he received well-deserved tribute. But Hugh remarked lugubriously that he was worried about Ted's pension. Ted was retiring from a part of the organization, Odhams, where the retirement pension entitlement was far lower than on the *Mirror*. Cudlipp said, 'Ted has never been as well rewarded as he should have been – and he should have been an editor – but it is a sad thought that he is now going to be hard up. So I have decided to go and see Harold Wilson tonight and arrange a peerage for Ted, because peers get a daily attendance allowance at the House of Lords, and this should just about top up Ted's pension to a reasonable retirement living.'

Whether or not Cudlipp did go to see Harold Wilson about it I do not know, but the fact is that shortly afterwards Ted Castle's name appeared in the Honours List as a life peer.

Cecil King was offered a peerage by Harold Wilson, despite the fact that Wilson neither liked nor trusted King, but Cecil turned down a life peerage because by that time he felt that he should be given an earldom or nothing; as Harold Macmillan had already abolished hereditary titles, Wilson cheerfully gave Cecil his second choice – nothing. The link between the *Mirror* and No. 10 Downing Street had become so strong that a Mirrorman called Alf accompanied Harold Wilson everywhere Wilson went except the cabinet room and the lavatory, and a member of the *Mirror*'s political staff, Gerald Kaufman, moved to work at Downing Street as a press liaison man for Wilson.

I had never had much to do with Kaufman, partly because I was away from the *Mirror* building during a few years when I was writing a column for the IPC *Sun*, which had been launched by Cudlipp out of the ashes of the old *Daily Herald* to be THE PAPER BORN OF THE AGE WE LIVE IN. It always seemed to me that a newspaper launched with such a clumsy slogan would have to fight for its existence, but I enjoyed my time working for the paper and during this period I occasionally ran across Gerald Kaufman. I was usually guided away from political stories, although I got on well with Hugh Gaitskell when he was leader of the Labour Party; he was a neighbour of ours in Hampstead, and sometimes I wrote a column about what he was doing; but during the Wilson years I was, for obvious reasons, *persona non grata* with many of the union leaders and also with those members of the cabinet with whom I came into contact, notably George Brown – another of the *Mirror's* political advisers – whose dislike of me was heartily reciprocated. So I was surprised when I was asked if I would cover a Harold Wilson story.

Sydney Jacobson, a friend, was editorial director of the *Sun* at the time, and he had let me get away with columns mocking the pretentious antics of some union leaders, but when I was asked to cover the wedding of Harold Wilson's son, Robin, Sydney called me in for a drink and gave me a gentle warning. 'For God's sake, Noel, try to take it seriously. It is just an ordinary country wedding, a family affair, and all it needs is just a lyrical touch in a friendly way. We want it decently written, and that was why I told Harold that I was going to ask you to do it. But it must be dignified. If you let even a nuance of amusement creep into your copy, I can assure you that there will be hell to pay for all of us.'

It was a perfectly reasonable request and I reassured him. 'No need to worry, Sydney,' I said, 'it will be all hearts and flowers. I bet you Godfrey Winn wouldn't have made a better nap selection for the job. Tears of joy will run down the cheeks of all concerned as the village wedding bells ring out. You leave it to me – you'll get a dukedom out of it.'

I drove to Devon and parked the car near the church in the small seaside town of Dawlish, where the wedding was to take place. Hurrying towards me came Gerald Kaufman. I had borrowed a Penguin book from him some time before, and as my conscience reminded me that I had not returned it I assumed that he was coming over to jog my memory. But no. He was there on a more serious mission, as Harold Wilson's minder.

'Ah, Noel,' he said, 'good to see you again. Very glad to hear that you are going to write this piece. Do you know, it may sound silly but it is a long time since I have known Harold to be so concerned about a story. It may be only a family wedding, but he wants everything about it to be absolutely right. Of course we shall probably get some snide jibes from the *Express* and the *Mail*, and they will probably make a funny of it, but there is nothing we can do about that. All the same he wants to feel sure that the decent papers will do a decent job, and I can tell you that Harold is a generous man to those who do not oppose him.'

I looked at him, slightly puzzled. 'What's all this about, Gerald?' I asked. 'It's only a wedding, isn't it, not the signing of an international peace treaty?'

He looked uncomfortable. 'Yes, that's right,' he said, 'but the fact is that you sometimes write flippantly, and I would not like that to happen here. It is not a big deal but it could turn out to be a big deal for you. Have you ever thought about becoming Sir Noel?'

It reminded me so much of Errol Flynn and his medals that I burst out laughing. Kaufman was clearly put out by this hilarity. But it seemed so outrageously absurd, standing there on the pavement and talking to a man who looked as though he were furtively selling tickets for a promenade concert outside the Albert Hall. I was also a little angry.

'You can tell the Godfather that he has nothing to worry about,' I said, and turned on my heel.

I walked into the church and ran smack into Alf, the *Mirror*'s mole in Downing Street. 'Psst,' he said, taking me by the arm. 'Do you wanna Gannex raincoat like Harold wears? Free?'

'Bugger off, Alf,' I said. 'I have just been offered a knighthood that has fallen off a lorry and I am beginning to lose my starry-eyed faith in the system of prime-ministerial power of patronage.'

'Bollocks,' said Alf, moodily. 'Be your age.'

There were times, even then, when the thought flitted across my mind that I might have been wiser at the outset of my career to try my luck as an actor instead of following my father and old Horace into newspapers. The inescapable truth was that my face never fitted at the *Mirror*. It was not their fault, but mine. They were all friendly enough, in a guarded sort of way, but there was always a gulf of suspicion. Recently on television I watched Terry Wogan interviewing Immanuel Jacobovits, the Chief Rabbi, and Wogan asked him for his opinion on the reason for anti-Semitism. 'It is the dislike of the unlike,' said Lord Jacobovits with a smile, and I smiled too because I knew exactly what he meant: that had always been my problem.

Not that I hated the popular newspapers that had provided me with a good living, or that I was too eager to bite the hand that fed me; indeed, my attitude towards them is so ambivalent that I am still irritated when I hear people attacking them for ill-considered reasons: they have a part to play, and always will have while people want to read news presented in a simple and easily understandable way. But they have become too accustomed to rationalizing dishonesty because newspapers are in love with themselves, and it is a self-love affair that now exists throughout the media: the beloved, however wrong, is always right.

Although I have raced ahead into the 1960s in describing one or two of the incidents above, it was in 1958 that my life took its most unexpected lurch down a different byway. I had been in Rome, watching the filming of *Ben Hur* at Cinecitta. After lunch with my old friend Jack Hawkins at the studios, I decided that, with his brave cooperation – because he was a star in the film – I would write a column about the unnecessary cruelty to the horses that were being maimed and killed daily during the shooting of the chariot-race scenes. It was a disgusting contrivance to produce a cheap thrill, and I wrote the column – a column about which I felt so passionately that I was sad when I discovered, much later, that the *Daily Mirror* had understandably decided to spike it – on the flight to Paris, where I had decided to spend the night.

Paris has always been a fateful city for me. It was the setting for the only column of mine among tens of thousands that provoked a libel case, the Patino affair. Now it was to become the scene of a watershed in my working life. But I had no forewarning of that when I checked into the Ritz and then took a stroll over to the Left Bank for supper at the Méditerranée. I can remember now that it was a delicious supper, although I recall little else of that night. On the taxi ride back to the hotel, a drunken milliner shot the red lights at sixty miles an hour and crashed into my taxi, hitting us amidships. The taxi driver died as a result of that accident, and I was cut out of the back of the taxi by the Paris fire brigade, although I knew nothing about that at the time. I was taken, unconscious, by ambulance to a hospital in the *quartier de la goutte d'or*, the Algerian quarter, where I was laid in bed in a darkened room while my poor wife was telephoned and told that she must hasten to Paris immediately, before it was too late.

It was a terrible time for my wife. It was not bad for me, because I knew hardly anything for days, and not much for weeks, only being aware that my wife was sitting there beside me and that therefore God was still in His heaven and all was right with the world. Sometimes I had other visitors. I was temporarily blind, but I recognized their voices. One night a shadowy figure came in and stashed a bottle of champagne in my locker. 'Keep fighting, sport,' he said. 'Don't let these bloody doctors get you down. Remember we'll both get medals in the end.' Digby Neave came in and brought get-well wishes from Jimmy Goldsmith. Norah Docker sent a room-full of flowers. It was like the past life of a drowning man wafting slowly before his unseeing eyes.

French doctors were – probably still are – superbly skilled, and the specialist looking after me was a cheerful and optimistic man who, disconcertingly, spoke English with a Mayfair accent but understood not one single word when anyone spoke to him in English. It was my wife who saved my life, but the doctor helped.

'Your husband will live,' he told my wife, 'but you must be prepared for the possibility that he may live only as a cabbage. His head is badly broken and the head is like a watch – if you drop it and the works are shaken out, seldom is it easy to put it together again.'

The *Daily Mirror* wanted to have me shifted to the American Hospital in Paris, no expense spared, but my wife put her foot down because she thought I was beginning to recover where I was, in good hands. They were kind enough, the *Mirror* people, but from their own medical inquiries they were sure of one thing: as far as Whitcomb of the *Mirror* was concerned, this was the end. I was thirty-nine years old and had been writing a successful column in the *Mirror* for twelve years, but nobody lasts for ever. They printed a big piece about my Paris accident on the middle spread, with an enormous picture of me still beaming in a grey top hat, but although the message was 'Get well, Noel', there was no doubt in anybody's mind what that article really was: a good obituary.

However, luckily for me, as was the case with Mark Twain, the reports of my death were greatly exaggerated. It was my wife's fault that I lived to tell the tale. She fought like a Yorkshire terrier and she did everything right. What neither of us imagined to be possible was that when, after a surprisingly short time, she had nursed me back to health, a new sort of life was about to begin.

16

Never give a sucker an even break.

Charles Coburn

After a few weeks of being laid up in bed in a suite at the Trianon Palace Hotel in Versailles, towards the end of which my wife took me out for a walk in a wheelchair of which the wheel came off, the doctors pronounced me fit enough to travel home. This was when I discovered one of the most awkward legacies of the taxi accident. I had no memory of the accident at all – there was a hole in my memory about the incident, which is not unusual – but when I stepped into the hired car to be driven to the airport I began to shake with uncontrollable fear. It was the same in the aircraft. The sweat poured off me in my terror.

Neurologists in London shook their heads and told me that I might have to learn to live with this. 'Kathleen Mavourneen, y'know,' said one Irish shrink. 'It may be for years and it may be for ever.' I did not tell my friends at the *Daily Mirror* about this, because I was hoping to start work again. But it was a tricky problem, until I hit upon a plan for solving it. I told nobody about my plan, not even my wife, because she might have tried – very reasonably – to talk me out of it. My plan simply was to fly in planes and drive motor cars until the terror left me.

To try this experiment I needed, of course, to go abroad. So when the time for convalescence came, I said that I would go down to Cannes for a fortnight and stay quietly at the Carlton. To which everyone agreed. On the aircraft to Nice I was shaking with such naked terror throughout the flight that the woman in the seat beside me, whom I knew slightly, was extremely anxious about me. She was Miss Pugh, Winston Churchill's secretary, and she urged me to see a doctor as soon as we landed. But when we landed, Ari Onassis was waiting for her – Onassis and Churchill were great friends – and when he saw me he insisted that I should come and stay on his yacht for a few days. Which gave me a breathing space before I attempted the second half of my plan, although it was not exactly a restful few days because Randolph Churchill was also a guest aboard the yacht and he was rampaging drunk for most of the time. Onassis would have kicked him out if he had not been Winston's son.

Then at last the moment came for sitting in the driver's seat of the hired car that had been delivered to the quay. I cannot describe the fear that overtook me. I was petrified. But I put it into gear and drove at five miles an hour along the coast road towards the border, with cars hooting at me as I gripped the steering wheel and sweat poured off me.

By the time I reached Genoa I was driving at fifteen miles an hour and my grip on the wheel was less convulsive. When I drove into Rome I was doing over forty miles an hour, and when I pulled up outside the Excelsior in the Via Veneto my old friend the doorman gave me a puzzled look because I was singing at the top of my voice. It was all over. I'd won.

After spending some time with friends I thought of flying home from Rome, but decided to take no chances, so I drove back to Monte Carlo, steady as a rock and happy as a lark. Which was a lucky decision, because when I went downstairs from my room at the Hôtel de Paris and wandered into the bar for a drink, I met an American naval officer who wanted to go across the road to the casino but was anxious because he did not know the form.

'Simple, my dear chap,' I said. 'Just get your passport and a stack of money and I'll take you over and show you the ropes. There's nothing to it. Simple as falling off a load of dollar bills.'

We shot dice at the craps table for an hour, but I have always found craps a boring and baffling way of giving money away so I told the American that I was turning in early because I was catching a flight home in the morning, and wandered off. Passing a *chemin-de-fer* table on my way out I saw a situation similar to one I remembered from the past. There was a biggish pot on the table but none of the players was offering to fade the bank for its full value. So I yelled, 'Banco!' The croupier dished me two cards that added up to nine. I walked back to the Hôtel de Paris having won enough to pay for my fortnight's convalescence plus a useful chunk left over for presents to take home.

A few days later Cecil King telephoned me at home to inquire about my health and discuss my future. 'Glad to hear you are feeling well again,' he said, 'but I doubt if it would be a good idea for you to continue hurtling round the world for the *Daily Mirror*. As you know, I have recently bought my uncle's old business in Farringdon Street, and I feel sure we can find something more suitable for you there. I will talk to Cudlipp about it.'

326

His uncle's old business was Amalgamated Press, where Alfred and Harold Harmsworth, the brothers who later became Lord Northcliffe and Lord Rothermere, had made their start in publishing. It owned an enormous variety of magazines – was, in fact, the biggest magazine-publishing house in the country – and although, by the time Cecil bought it for IPC, it was known as The Sleeping Giant, it was an immensely valuable business. Its publications ran right across the spectrum from the *Stock Exchange Gazette* and *Banker's Almanac* to *Tit-Bits* and *Chicks Own* – and it was some time before Cecil King discovered that he had accidentally bought *Vogue*, the fashion magazine, too; it was hastily sold back to Condé Nast because it was not considered a suitable bedfellow for the rest of the women's magazines – too *chic*.

It was the world of the women's magazines into which I found myself pitched. Hugh Cudlipp set me up in an office in Fleetway House – much more splendid than the sort of office to which I was accustomed – and gave a party for me to meet the editors of all the women's publications. Lady Pamela Berry, an old friend, was at the party because her husband, Michael Berry of the *Daily Telegraph*, had been one of the chief negotiators in selling his family's controlling interest in AP to IPC, and Pam was greatly amused. 'They don't know what to make of you at all, Noel,' she said. 'The fact is that they are scared of all you lot at the *Daily Mirror* – Hugh walks around the place like Dr Jekyll but they fear in secret that he is really Mr Hyde.'

This was true. They had become very set in their ways and were frightened of change. Some of the women working on the magazines were in their eighties. Circulations were either stagnant or falling. Most of the staff realized that the introduction of new ideas and new blood was inevitable. But they didn't like it. And the idea of new ideas and new blood coming via the *Daily Mirror* was *unthinkable*. 'The *Daily Mirror* – my *dear*, how *awful*!'

Hugh Cudlipp said to me, 'You'd better tread on tip-toe round here for a bit, Noel. Just smile at 'em. One of the old dears has just been explaining to me that they all expect to have a week off for Whit. She meant Whitsun. I'm glad it was me she told and not Jack Nener, because Jack's reply would surely have resulted in half a dozen quick funerals. I'm not letting Jack come over here at all.'

I told Jack about this afterwards. His terse comment in four-letter words showed how right Hugh had been.

My instructions from Cudlipp were to get to know all the editors of the women's magazines and arrange to write regular columns for several that he listed. 'Make a big play to get Biddy Johnson on your side,' he said. 'She may look like Margaret Rutherford but she's red hot – best editor in the place. She runs *Woman and Home* and *Woman's Weekly* – start with those two.'

I had already for some time past been writing freelance columns and features for the *New York Times*, Japan's *Asahi Shimbun, Paris Match*, Germany's *Quick* and several other foreign publications, but I had never written for a woman's magazine and I was by no means sure I knew how to do it. New territory for me.

On the morning when I was walking along the corridor to call on Biddy Johnson, I ran into Godfrey Winn, who was the all-time king of the columns for women's magazines. Before the war he had worked as a columnist on the *Daily Mirror*, and had been accustomed to sit cross-legged on a prayer mat in his office, dictating his column to three secretaries, but I had never tried that. All the same, apart from the showmanship, he was a first-class journalist, so I was not too proud to learn my new trade from him, even though he was known in Fleet Street as Winifred God.

'Hullo, Godders,' I said, 'just the very man to give me a bit of advice. How do you set about writing for women?'

'Well, dear boy, the most important thing is that you must always be sincere.'

'That's the end of it, then,' I said. 'I've got no chance – never been sincere in my life. Not in print, anyway.'

Godfrey nodded, sadly. 'Yes, I'm afraid that is true of a lot of our colleagues – that is probably why I've never been a journalists' journalist.'

'Come off it,' I said. 'You can be a bloody sharp reporter when you want to be. What I want to know is how you do the hearts-and-flowers stuff. I mean, I know that you talk to the daffodils and get a fair bit of news from them, but the readers would soon shout me down if I started doing that. What I mean is that I've always written just for people – men, women and dogs – and I don't know anything about women in particular.'

Godfrey smiled, archly. 'In some ways, dear boy, it is just possible that you know more about women than I do.'

'Point taken,' I nodded. 'But I can't write about that sort of stuff in a woman's mag, can I? I'd get drummed out of the building – hounded out at the point of knitting needles. D'you know what one of 'em said to me the other day? She said: "We would love to have some of your delicious little funnies in our book, Mr Whitcomb – but no sexipegs, of course."'

Godfrey grinned. 'Take no notice of what they *say* they want.

They're all sex-mad in a Freudian sort of way. But remember that if you write about sex never mention the word – call it love. And another thing I've found – women are not interested in money.'

'You obviously mix with a different sort of women,' I said, dubiously. 'Half the women I know spend most of their time talking about how much they paid for their clothes.'

'Ah – that's different. That's *shopping*. Shopping is always lovely. Finance is what they find boring. If ever you see a woman reading the financial pages of a newspaper you can bet she is not one of the women you are writing for. Family stuff is what they like best. Remember that and you will still be writing columns for women's magazines in twenty-five years' time.'

Godfrey was right almost to the month. I never missed having a column in every issue of *Woman and Home* for the next twenty-five years.

It was about the projected column in *Woman and Home* that I was on my way to see Biddy Johnson. She sat me down in a floral chintz-covered armchair, poured me tea in a pretty china cup, and offered me biscuits from a dainty plate with a doyley on it. But that did not fool me. I could see that she was the sort of woman who used barbed wire for wool when she was knitting purl and plain and probably made herself pretty little bullet-proof twin-sets.

'How good of you to agree to write a column for us, Mr Whitcomb,' she said. I just smiled, because we both knew that I was under starter's orders, and neither of us had much choice about it. 'Have you decided what *sort* of thing you are going to write?' she asked.

'I will try to write whatever sort of thing you want,' I replied. 'You crack the whip – I mean, you tell me the sort of thing you have in mind – and I will hit the typewriter until it comes out to your liking.'

Biddy beamed. We understood each other. She poured me another cup of tea and I would not have been surprised if she had taken a bottle out of her drawer and sluiced a jigger of Scotch into it.

Then she took my by surprise. She said, 'Do you know yourself?'

'We-e-ell,' I said, playing for time, 'naturally I know a few things about myself . . . or I think I do . . . perhaps I do, I think.'

Biddy laughed, 'That's it!' she cried. 'Everyone thinks they know themselves until you ask them – and then they begin to wonder. Do you see what I'm getting at? Most people are surprised to find that their ordinary everyday lives have so much in common with the lives of people whom they regard as famous. You are already famous in a way to many of our readers, but they see you as a man in a top hat who mixes with celebrities. Just you write for us about the times when you are at home and not mixing with celebrities, and you'll be doing it for twenty years.'

Biddy was five years short. But she was right.

I wrote all manner of columns for the other magazines, occasionally standing in for The Man Who Knows on *Woman's Weekly*, doing smart-alec stuff for *Woman and Beauty*, even writing advice on etiquette for teenagers in *Honey* when Audrey Slaughter was the editor, but the formula that old Biddy mapped out for me on *Woman and Home* was the one that never failed.

I had been working my socks off at this fascinating new game for a few months when, one morning, the telephone rang and I heard the familiar old gravelly growl on the other end of the line.

'Jack Nener here.'

'Yes, I know,' I said. 'What can I do for you, Jack?'

'You can come home,' he said. 'I need you here on the *Daily Mirror*. I'm fed up with the readers asking where you've gone. Send me a column this afternoon and we'll set up the old shop again in tomorrow's paper.'

'But Jack,' I said, 'how can I? I've got a full-time job here.'

'Don't give me the old fanny,' he warned. 'Full time! I know how long it takes you to write those fancy pieces. Half an hour top weight. And how often? Once a week! Once a month! What sort of a life is that for a newspaperman? All frilly knickers and cups of tea. No, don't you try to kid me – it's a sabbatical. I'll tell you what – you've got a bloody lovely office there in Fleetway so you can go on doing the magazine stuff when you want a half-hour's rest in comfort, but your old office is waiting for you here as well, so don't hang about. I want the copy by five.'

So I went back to the treadmill, doing both jobs – left hand, right hand. Back to the old familiar places; Paris for the Khrushchev summit that misfired, Rome, Madrid, Beirut, Cyprus, Athens, Vienna, Cairo, Venice, Casablanca, Marrakesh, New York, Washington, Hollywood. Sometimes I was clinging on to the coat-tails of the news – riots in Africa, Bay of Pigs, Common Market negotiations, assassination in Dallas – but more often I was wearing the old top hat and watching the tiaras go by. Nearly all *déja vu*. The rheumatism of the mind that attacks all journalists after a time – the feeling that you are a ghost haunting an old battlefield – began to make the column creak. I was recycling past experiences.

Even at home in Hampstead I kept bumping into old paragraphs, like an idle browser coming across familiar antique pieces at a Sotheby's preview. Peter O'Toole had bought a house in Heath Street. Peter

Sellers had moved into a flat in a new development at the bottom of our garden, in what had been the grounds of publisher Stanley Unwin's house. Marlene Dietrich's daughter briefly rented a house along the drive from us, and Marlene ended an old feud with me that I had sparked when I thoughtlessly mentioned her age in a column. She had burst into blue flames. 'I used to like the name of Noel,' she shouted to reporters at the airport, 'but after what Noel Whitcomb has done I consider the name suitable only for rats.'

Without stirring far from home I kept stumbling over enough showbusiness acquaintances to keep a column going in *Variety* – José Ferrer, Eddie Fisher, John Huston, Marilyn Monroe – and most of them next door; the house on the south side of ours was like an outpost of Beverly Hills. It was owned by Donald Ogden-Stewart and his wife, Ella Winter, both writers. Donald had been an Oscar-winning screenwriter in Hollywood during the Frank Capra era, but he and Ella had come under scrutiny from Senator McCarthy's notorious House Un-American Activities Committee. Refusing to answer the infamous question, 'Are you, or have you ever been . . .?' and consequently left with little chance of any further work in the United States, they had left Hollywood for London, gravitating naturally to Hampstead which was then a *quartier Latin*.

Donald and I were friendly because I was still doing theatre reviewing and had given his first West End play, *The Kidders*, a favourable notice, but his wife and mine were at daggers drawn because of a long-running war about a garden wall between us. But when both our womenfolk were otherwise engaged he used to invite me in for a chat about old times and it was on one such morning that he asked me to lunch.

'Charlie's over from Switzerland,' he said, 'and I am setting up a little party for him.'

Charlie Chaplin, born a cockney in the Walworth Road, was another of the Hollywood refugees from political persecution who used Donald's place as a 'safe house' from the rat-pack of photographers when he was in England; although I personally thought him greatly overrated except as a founding father of comedy on the silent screen, he was a twenty-two-carat celebrity.

Donald's little party was like a sixth-form reunion of alumni from Sardi's. Judy Garland was sitting on one side of me at luncheon, and on my other side was another old friend, Richard Burton, then married to Elizabeth Taylor, who was renting a house close by in Hampstead.

It was evening by the time we said goodbye and Richard suggested to me that we should walk back to his place – it was only a few hundred yards away – and have a drink with Elizabeth. But on the way he had another idea.

'Let's have a swift pint in a pub before we go back,' he said. 'Do you know any good pubs around here?'

'Not really,' I said, 'because I don't often use the locals. But our daily woman speaks very highly of a pub called the King of Bohemia in Rosslyn Hill. She calls it a Thespian pub.'

'I don't want to go to a bloody lesbian pub,' roared Richard.

'*Thespian*,' I repeated, louder. 'You know – strolling players, rogues and vagabonds, minstrels, sock and buskin practitioners, resting actors like you.'

'Yes, yes, yes,' said Richard, 'no need to go on about it. This place sounds bloody awful but we'll give it a whirl.'

Our daily help was one of a number of resting actors and actresses who hired themselves out for housework by the hour under the auspices of an agency called Your Servant, Madam, which was run by a former boy film star who had left the profession soon after his voice broke. She was the first person I saw when we pushed open the door of the saloon bar. But there were several more of her colleagues also in the bar, all dressed up to the eyebrows and jangling with heavy jewellery like harness horses. When they saw Richard walk in they all stood up as though it were a royal visit.

'Good evening, Mr Burton,' said our daily, with immense pride to see that the husband of her employer was in the company of such a superstar. As we walked to the end of the bar one old dear with a hat that had a Nellie Wallace feather sticking up from the back stepped off her stool and curtsied.

Richard ordered two large vodkas and a glass of wine – the wine was for me – and then he said in a stage whisper, 'By Christ, boy, how did you find this? It's not a pub – it's a museum of Shaftesbury Avenue. Like Penny Plain and Tuppence Coloured. Bloody marvellous, boy. It's a time capsule. I wouldn't have missed this for anything. Let's get them talking.'

He moved centre stage and said in that splendid voice, 'Ladies, would you do me the honour of taking wine with me?'

The barman said, 'Eight Guinnesses and a port and lemon,' and set them up.

From that moment on we were back with Ellen Terry. We had stories of naughty old Beerbohm (Tree), dear Sir Gerald (DuMaurier), awful old George (Robey), darling Ivor (Novello), Cocky (Sir Charles

Cochran), The Guv'nor (André Charlot), Binkie (Beaumont) and a long marquee of names in lights that spanned three generations right up to Larry and Viv (Olivier and Leigh).

Richard conducted a chorus of *Burlington Bertie* following a solo sung by an immensely old lady with bright red henna-ed hair who claimed to have once understudied 'dearest Vesta' (Tilley). Then we had *If You Were the Only Girl in the World*, with Richard in fine voice, and he did a duet of *The Boy I Love is up in the Gallery* with an old dresser who said she had known Marie Lloyd. For an encore, in which we all joined, they sang *Lily of Laguna*.

Burton was loving it. He bought round after round of drinks. In what he thought was a *sotto voce* aside – but which you could have heard in the gods – he said to me, 'Look at that wonderful old bird over there – it wouldn't surprise me if she was on the bill with Richard Burbage at the Globe.'

It was late when eventually I dragged him away. He had a bottle of vodka in each of his side pockets and he suggested that we should go back to my house, but I led him up Heath Street and back to his own front door. He couldn't find his key so he rang the bell. Elizabeth Taylor opened the door.

'You bastard!' she hissed. 'And – oh Christ! – it's that fucking Whitcomb again! You know we had a cabinet minister for dinner – remember? He didn't wait.'

I didn't wait, either. I was always against intrusion into private grief. Voices were raised before I was halfway down the garden path, and after the door slammed there came the sound of breaking crockery. Home is where the heart is.

Although it appeared that the readers were still satisfied with the column, I was not. I was desolate and sick of an old passion. The dawn was always grey. It seemed to me that I had written everything at least twice. Jack Nener retired as editor, making a farewell speech – spangled with four-letter words – in which his valedictory *cri-de-coeur* brought a murmur of sympathy from the old enemies who had reluctantly contributed towards his Georgian silver salver. 'I wasn't a bad editor,' said Jack, controversially, 'but my tragedy was that I was never any good at expenses.'

Jack's successor, only my fourth editor up to that time, was Lee Howard. Lee spoke with such a languid drawl that it came as a surprise to people when they learnt that he was Polish. He had joined the *Daily Mirror* as a junior sub-editor and caption writer at the end of the war, straight out of the RAF, a tall, handsome young flyer in an RAF blazer, slim, elegant and suave. But by the time he reached the editor's chair he weighed between twenty and thirty stone and was such a grotesque hulk that he would never allow a looking-glass near him; the sight of himself disgusted and saddened him. But he was a likeable man, immensely fair. His second wife, Sheila Black, then woman's editor of the *Financial Times*, was also exceptionally large, and she once told me that they needed to have iron bedsteads specially made to support their gigantic weight.

Lee was the most accomplished drinker I have ever encountered. He drank Scotch all day and never slurred a sibilant. Because his ungainly size made him reluctant to go out more than was necessary, he sat behind his desk in the editor's office from morning until late at night, working steadily and drinking steadily. Drink did not change him; he did his work meticulously, was usually smiling, and invariably polite. I never knew a man quite like him. At office luncheons, while the rest of us drank wine, Lee would sit at the top of the table with a bottle of Scotch in front of him, and usually he finished it by the end of lunch. He would probably drink another bottle in the office before he went home, but unless you knew him well enough to observe a few tell-tale signs, you might well have supposed that he had not taken a drink all day.

He was good at choosing his staff and giving them reasonable rein and credit for what they did – an attribute rare enough among Fleet Street editors of his time to make it worthy of mention – and I think he was the first Fleet Street editor to appoint a woman as his deputy, the hard-working and highly skilled Felicity Green (a former fashion editor whom Norman Hartnell had dubbed 'Ferocity Green').

Lee knew that I was not happy on the paper, but he did everything he reasonably could to make my life comfortable, because my column was popular and he did not want to lose it.

It was during this period that Cecil King bought Odhams Press after a complex and protracted takeover battle which I personally found very profitable, because I bought Odhams shares at the start of it and sold them for a handsome profit when the dust settled; not that I was privy to any of the negotiations, but I knew for certain that Cecil King would have committed hara-kiri by falling on his jewelled sword rather than be beaten to the draw in a publishing deal by any of his peers, especially by a Canadian upstart such as Roy Thomson; so, financially, I never had a moment's anxiety.

Odhams was gigantic, the biggest magazine-publishing house in the world, and it was the magazines that King wanted – particularly the women's magazines – because several of the top-selling Odhams magazines were in cut-throat competition with his Fleetway magazines and by rationalizing the whole business he saw that he could turn IPC into not only the biggest but also the most profitable publishing concern Britain had ever seen. Which, indeed, he did. But along with the magazines he also bought the Odhams newspapers, and these were by no means so desirable; most of them were down on their pasterns, stumbling, long past their winning days.

The *Daily Herald* was the flagship of Odhams Newspapers, a TUC-controlled Labour paper which had flourished as one of the top mass-circulation dailies under the guidance of Julius Salter Elias (later Lord Southwood) in the pre-war years; but by the time it landed in Cecil King's lap it was haemorrhaging money like a burst water main, and its losses were so torrential that some wag in the City dubbed it 'King's Cross'. Trying to save a newspaper when its readers are rushing away like lemmings is usually a way of throwing good money after bad, so there was no doubt about what had to be done: the old *Herald* had to be given a dignified funeral.

In its place, the *Sun* rose. Hugh Cudlipp was given the task of launching the IPC *Sun*, Britain's first new national daily for many years. In retrospect he was clearly the wrong man for the job, because Cudlipp was essentially a tabloid journalist – far and away the most talented tabloid journalist of his era – and the IPC *Sun* was planned as a text newspaper which would appeal to what would today be called '*Guardian* readers': this requires an organ-grinder with a different repertoire.

To be fair, Cudlipp did not operate as a one-man band but brought in skilled and suitable people as departmental editors and administrators, simply exercising overall control. A great deal of money was at stake. The *Sun* was to be produced and printed on the existing presses at Odhams' plant in Long Acre, Covent Garden, and the exciting process of preparing for the birth of a new daily newspaper began.

One morning Hugh Cudlipp telephoned me and asked me to come and see him. 'Noel,' he said, 'how would you like to be a columnist on the *Sun*?'

It was like the governor of Pentonville asking one of his chief warders whether he would like to become headwaiter at the Ritz.

'Very much,' I said. 'Thanks, Hugh.'

'It will give you the opportunity of writing for a different audience, at a deeper level and on a wider variety of subjects. That's what you want, isn't it?'

'It certainly is,' I nodded.

'Good,' said Hugh. 'I knew you'd say that. Lee Howard put up the idea that you would be the ideal man to do it, and I thought it was a very generous gesture on his part. After all, he will be losing you from the *Daily Mirror* because I want you to start at Long Acre on Friday.'

'Good old Lee,' I said. 'God bless him. What a pal!'

I ran straight down to Lee's office. His secretary warned me that he was watching *Yogi Bear*, a children's programme on television, and I knew that he had issued firm instructions that he was never to be disturbed while he was watching *Yogi Bear* except for news of a government defeat or the outbreak of war. But I was so grateful to him for his unselfish action in putting me up for the job on the *Sun* that I burst straight in and shook him by the hand.

'Thank you, Lee,' I said. 'Thank you very much indeed.'

'What have I done, doll?' he asked, smiling and turning off the television.

'About the job on the *Sun*,' I said.

'What job on the *Sun*?'

'My new job there as a columnist,' I said, beginning to suspect something. 'I leave here on Friday to start there right away.'

'First I've heard of it,' said Lee, frowning. 'Have you found it tedious working for me? Are we not paying you enough? Do you find me inadequate as an editor? Have you lost all interest in the welfare of the *Daily Mirror*?'

'Oh, God,' I said, realizing that Cudlipp had played one of his sardonic jokes on me. 'No, Lee, it's not like that at all. I was under the impression that you knew about the new plans for me. I have always found it a pleasure working for you, and you know that very well.'

'In that case I am a little surprised to find you doing cartwheels with joy at the thought of leaving me in the lurch. You go on Friday, eh? I must confess that I am mildly curious as to why you did not have the courtesy to tell me this before. Without wishing to appear effusive, it may not perhaps be easy to find a replacement for your column at a few days' notice, and I think it not unreasonable to suggest that you might have given me more time. However, Noel, all I can do is wish you the best of luck.'

There was no point in trying to explain. Never explain, never complain. I left Lee's office feeling deflated and miserable. It was the sort of joke that Cudlipp enjoyed. I could have killed him.

The old IPC *Sun* – IPC being the International Publishing Company, then the biggest publishing company in the world – which lasted for five years, could hardly have been more different from the *Sun* that is published today by Rupert Murdoch's News International: it was a good paper. Not that I am suggesting that Murdoch's *Sun* is a bad paper, although it is sometimes a wicked and disgraceful paper, but it is aimed at a different readership. The trouble with the old *Sun* was that it was aimed at a readership that did not at that time exist in sufficient numbers. It was a paper with left-wing views and a radical approach, well edited and containing good writing, but it was ahead of its time in believing that this could be a recipe for commercial success; a similar recipe could be – and was – successful in a weekly such as the *New Statesman* under the editorship of Kingsley Martin or later Paul Johnson, but it was not a practical formula for a daily paper that needed to sell in millions.

Hugh Cudlipp launched the new paper with a publicity campaign of such megahype proportions that it came as a tremendous anticlimax when the first issue off the presses was absolutely dreadful – abysmal. Few daily publications in the history of newspapers have recovered from a really bad first issue, and only the deep financial resources of Cecil King's immensely rich IPC saved the *Sun* from sinking within six months. It was a matter of *amour propre* to keep it going – King and Cudlipp could not allow themselves to be seen to have produced a turkey – but the fact was that the paper improved steadily after that disastrous first issue, and went on improving for the best part of five years. To no avail. It was a costly production to run, overmanned and extravagant in the fashion of its time, and it lost a fortune. Even so, it still had about a million readers daily when Hugh Cudlipp sold it for a derisory sum to Rupert Murdoch. Cecil King had been sacked by then, and Cudlipp was so powerful that it was said of him that not only had he deposed a king but he had also extinguished the sun. But Cudlipp had powerful enemies, too. His grip on power began to slip from the moment he did that controversial deal with Murdoch, which resulted in the new tabloid *Sun* knocking the *Daily Mirror* sideways, and within a relatively short time he went into early retirement in circumstances that have never, as far as I know, been fully revealed.

But my years on the IPC *Sun* were happy. I liked working amidst the teeming bustle of the old Covent Garden fruit and vegetable market, with squashed tomatoes underfoot and cheerful profanity in the air, and I got on well with most of my colleagues. At our offices in Covent Garden we had a floral display of columnists. There was Clement Freud, who did a sports column; Jean Rook, who later made a name on the *Daily Express* and became one of the women columnists satirized in *Private Eye* as Glenda Slag; Dennis Potter, who was as tiresomely self-important as a journalist as he was in his later career as a television playwright; James

Cameron, my old friend from reporting days; Dee Wells, then married to Freddie Ayer; Robert Robinson, the broadcasting quizmaster; Geoffrey Goodman on industrial affairs; Jon Akass; Richard Last on music and opera – later to become television critic of the *Daily Telegraph* for many years; Don Cox on racing – he tipped the winners of nine Derbys in successive years: a collection of journalistic ornaments suitable to decorate a newspaper editor's chimneypiece.

Most of them had a column that appeared once a week, but I was used less sparingly and as well as my regular three-times-a-week column I frequently wrote main-page features or did reporting jobs on the other three days. It was hard work, but enjoyable. The man who daily discussed with me my working schedule was Douglas Long, who was then in charge of news and features, a first-rate journalist who told me he was earning only a fraction of what I was getting at the time but who later became chief executive of the *Mirror* Group. Like many of the really good journalists he left the *Mirror* soon after Maxwell arrived, but he then became one of the executives responsible for the successful launch of the *Independent*, and finally launched the *Sunday Correspondent* as its chairman before he died at the age of sixty-four in 1990.

I made the most of my new job on the *Sun* because I could see from the start that it would not last. But it was a pleasure to have escaped over the wall after twenty years of not particularly hard labour at the *Daily Mirror* and once again to be free to write whatever took my fancy – the odd essay and the occasional *causerie* mixed in with the Paris riots and the Ulster troubles. I wanted variety and that was what they happily offered me. All over the world, as usual.

But I was always home in England for school occasions – never missed. It was on one such day, driving home from Benenden after seeing Kate, that we made an accidental lurch into the property market. We had stopped for tea in Blackheath, and afterwards we wandered round the shops, peering into estate agents' windows; my wife and I have always been fascinated by houses, and sometimes I think that when I have finished writing this account of my working life I might start another book about our adventures in the property trade: at least it would be funnier.

'I say,' said my wife, pointing to a photograph, 'that looks rather attractive.'

'Yes,' I said. 'But we don't want to live in Blackheath, do we? It's like living in Wolverhampton – not near anyone we know.'

'Let's go and look,' she said.

The agent was lyrical. 'Finest house of its kind we have had on our books for many years,' he said. 'It was built by a multi-millionaire builder for himself and his wife, no expense spared. If I told you how much it cost him you would not believe me.'

'Probably not,' I agreed.

'The architect's plans for every single detail of it make a pile of drawings three feet high,' he went on. 'Everything about it is the most modern in Europe – state of the art.'

'But I prefer eighteenth-century houses,' I said, defensively.

He laughed. 'A quick look round this fascinating house would swiftly change your mind,' he said. 'It is enchanting. The drawing room is about fifty feet long and has enormous windows that look out on to the prettiest little garden you ever saw, all round the house. The garden was the site of Sir Christopher Wren's studio – you know – "if anyone calls, tell 'em I'm out, designing St Pauls".'

'So,' I said, putting the boot in, 'why does this multi-millionaire chap want to sell his masterpiece?'

'His wife died.'

'Sorry,' I muttered.

'The walls,' went on the agent, 'are all lined with exquisite Japanese silk. The curtains, hundreds of yards of them because they are mostly twelve-foot drop, are all new and would alone cost you the price of a small house if you were to buy them. But the owner is leaving them. He has gone abroad. That is why he wants a quick sale. For cash. Would you be cash?'

'For houses and horses I always pay cash,' I said. 'But I have to tell you that you are wasting your eloquence. We don't want to live in Blackheath.'

'Come and look,' he said.

He had not exaggerated. For anyone who wanted to live there, it was the sale of the century. My wife was captivated by the costly modernity. Even I quite liked it.

The agent urged, 'He will consider a reasonable offer. The price is already a giveaway considering what it cost, but for a quick cash sale he might come down even further.'

I thought for a moment and then I was astonished to hear myself saying, 'I will offer him exactly half of what you are currently asking and if he wants to deal he can have the money tomorrow.'

My wife said. 'Oh!'

The agent said, 'Sir, please do not be frivolous. I said he might consider an offer but your suggestion is frankly ridiculous.'

339

'Right then,' I said, smiling with relief. 'Now we can go home. Thank you for your kind help. Sorry we wasted your time.'

Late that night the agent telephoned.

'Sir,' he said, 'congratulations. You've just bought a house. I have to admit that I still find it hard to believe, but the owner has accepted your offer. I hope you will be very happy living there.'

Well, we didn't want to go to Blackheath, but a deal is a deal and there we were. Hastily we put the Hampstead house on the market. Several people immediately came to look round, and went away to consider the matter, because we were asking what agents call 'the full market price'. We refused to consider near offers. But then we had a piece of luck because John D. Wood's Mayfair office sent us Mr Fothergill.

Mr Fothergill was tall, austere and somewhat shabbily dressed because he took no interest in his clothes – his interests were similar to those of Aristotle Onassis. While walking with him round the house first time, we learned that his yacht was sailing back from Tahiti to Monaco in a hurry because he had arranged a meeting with some oil sheikhs on it during the following week. He was in oil and shipping.

After he had gone, my wife said, 'I really cannot see that our house would suit him. Surely it would be too small?'

'Privacy,' I said. 'Chaps like that want privacy. Think how secluded we are. After all, General de Gaulle ran the French Resistance from Ben McPeake's house all throughout the war – just next door but one – and hardly anyone ever knew that he was there.'

John D. Wood told us not to count our chickens because they confided that Mr Fothergill was also interested in a much larger Georgian house with garaging for eight cars, in Mayfair.

My wife said, 'If he wants garaging for eight cars, why on earth would he be interested in our house with only one garage?'

'The drive,' I said. 'Don't you see – the drive gives him perfect concealment. He could easily park eight or ten cars in the drive and nobody but the postman would ever notice.'

However, on a later visit Mr Fothergill supplied the answers to our riddles. He did not want the house for himself. He wanted it as a quiet London pad for his personal assistant. He was building an airfield on an island in the Bahamas, and his personal assistant, who was in charge of this big project, needed a discreet base in London.

Mr Fothergill came several times, always in the afternoon, usually to discuss security.

My wife said. 'If he wants Fort Knox, why doesn't he buy Fort Knox?

He's getting on my nerves. Why don't you suggest to him that he buys the Chancery Lane Safe Deposit and leaves our house for a family to live in?'

'These tycoons are all the same,' I said. 'Paranoid about security. It is the curse of the very rich.'

He always stopped for tea.

'I think he has taken a fancy to us,' I said.

'What he has taken a fancy to is Jaffacakes,' said my wife, tartly. 'He's hooked on 'em.'

Mr Fothergill's weakness was Jaffacakes, the biscuits with chocolate on one side and orange jam in the middle. They were Kate's favourite, and they were all my wife had in the house to offer him when he first stopped for tea. He used to eat a great quantity and my wife pointed out to me with some sharpness that Jaffacakes don't grow on trees.

Then things went quiet. Mr Fothergill said he had to go to an international conference in Washington where he had arranged a private talk with the American president.

One morning my wife said, 'I'm fed up with old Fothergill. That Hollywood film director who came to see the house would have bought it like a shot if Fothergill hadn't demanded first refusal. Let's go and tackle him and tell him that he has two days in which to exchange contracts or otherwise the deal is off.'

There was some question about which of his firms handled different aspects of his affairs, and the only address we had for him was Fothergill House in south-east London, somewhere near Eltham.

So we drove to Eltham and we found Fothergill House.

It was a little council house on the fringe of a dilapidated estate. Old paint flaked off the window sashes. The tiny front garden was overgrown with weeds. Propped on a dustbin outside the front door was a scrawled note: NO MILK TODAY.

My wife looked at me and I looked at her and then we both doubled up with laughter.

'Mr Fothergill,' said my wife, 'is not at home because he is out buying Piccadilly Circus.'

It transpired that Mr Fothergill was an old-age pensioner who spent most of his time travelling round London on his bus pass. His hobby was looking at houses. He would go to the public library, read the papers and scan the property-for-sale columns, then telephone the agents and make appointments to view. He had a lovely time.

John D. Wood were not best pleased when we told them the result of our inquiries. They had been dealing with Mr Fothergill for ages, expecting to sell him property worth millions.

We sold the house shortly afterwards to a Knightsbridge dealer in fine art and we moved into the house in Blackheath. It was delightful. Everything one could wish. Blackheath is a charming place and the heath itself is one of the prettiest open spaces in greater London. The only trouble from our point of view was that it seemed to us like living in the middle of the Gobi Desert. Few of our friends came to visit because although some would not have given a second thought to hopping on a plane to Paris or New York, they considered the safari to Blackheath was an expedition that required prior consultation with Lillywhite's and the assistance of native bearers.

'It's only just down the Old Kent Road,' I would tell them.

'How do you get to that?' they would ask. 'Do you have a map?'

'Snobs,' sniffed my wife. 'We're better off without them. All the same, it is a bit lonely. Perhaps we should look for a house on the river.'

We both loved the river. There is something about looking out on tranquil water that, like musick, has charms to soothe a savage breast. So from Wapping to the Isis we trailed along the river Thames, looking at every house that came up for sale and feeling like Mr Fothergill. Some were too big, some were too small, none was perfect. Until the afternoon when we went to Newbury races to watch the running of a horse called Even Up, which I had recently bought in Ireland. He won.

Shunning the motorway we drove back happily through Berkshire villages and stopped for tea in Henley-on-Thames. We looked in all the house agents' windows, of course, but there seemed to be nothing. So we pointed the car towards London and drove slowly homeward across Henley Bridge.

Just over the bridge on the Berkshire side was a small turning that we had never noticed before.

'It looks as though it follows the river,' said my wife. 'Let's drive down it.'

About half a mile along the lane we saw it. The absolutely and utterly perfect house. Divine. It was long and low and all white, like a colonial-style house in Maryland, standing in two acres of lovely garden with lawns that ran down to the river. I stopped the car and we sat looking at it, not even saying anything. We both knew. This was it.

My wife said, 'You had better go and knock at the door and ask if it is for sale.'

'Don't be frivolous,' I said. 'They would think I was a burglar. What would you think if somebody came to the door of our house and asked if we would sell it? It's not on. They'd send for the police.'

'Try to think constructively,' said my wife. 'We've got to have it.'

I drove on slowly down the lane until we came to a pair of farm cottages. A woman was coming out of one. I called to her. 'I say,' I said, 'do you know anything about the white house back there?'

'That was Dame Glady's house,' she replied. 'Dame Gladys who died. Miss Sally has it now but she doesn't live there. There's still some servants living there, though. Foreigners, I think. I did hear it was up for sale.'

So I backed the car down the narrow lane at fifty miles an hour and we parked in the big gravel drive. There was not a moment to spare. Suppose we missed it through not being quick enough?

A Portuguese maid opened the door. We told her why we had come.

'If you would like to come in,' she said, 'I will ring Miss Sally and ask her if you can look over the house.'

We waited in the drawing room. Gorgeous. There was a verandah that ran round three sides of the house, looking out over lawns and flower beds to a line of ancient chestnut trees along the river bank. So beautiful that neither of us spoke. We just looked, holding our breath.

The maid came back and said it would be all right, so she showed us round. I remember to this day the thrill of it all as we walked out on to the balcony of the room that was to become our bedroom. The view across the lawns down to the river, with horses grazing in Fawley meadows on the far bank and the Chiltern hills rising in the distance, was like a Constable painting. Heavenly. A kingfisher flashed past with a glint of blue and a heron rose lazily from the river.

We were silent, thinking, as I drove homeward, fast. I had Sally Hardy's telephone number in my pocket. At last I said, 'Thou shalt be with me in Paradise.'

'Shut up and keep your eye on the road,' my wife replied. 'Remember Lot's wife.'

Sally Hardy was the daughter of the late Dame Gladys Cooper, who had owned the house, and at that time she was married to Robert Hardy, the actor. Her sister was married to Robert Morley.

'Well, Mr Whitcomb,' she said when I telephoned her, 'the house was sold to a solicitor we know, but he rang me only this morning to say that his wife is divorcing him and he will therefore not want it after all. If you want to buy it, that will save me a lot of trouble.'

'Oh, I do want to buy it, Mrs Hardy,' I said. 'I want to buy it more than I have ever wanted to buy anything in the whole of my life.'

'That's all right, then.' she said, 'If you will tell me the name of your solicitor I will get mine on to him tomorrow and they can arrange everything.'

I danced rather than walked from my study into the drawing room with a bottle of champagne in my hand and a fifty-kilowatt beam on my face.

'We've got it,' I said. 'All fixed. Mrs Hardy says yes. We've bought it.'

My wife heaved a sigh of relief.

'What a fantastic stroke of luck,' she said. 'Suppose we had not turned down that lane, just on spec? We would never have known.'

We talked over every detail of the house, forgetting nothing. Then my wife said, 'By the way – how much are we paying for it?'

'Oh, my God,' I said, 'in my excitement I forgot to ask.'

So I rang Mrs Hardy again. She was a charming woman but not without a noticeable *esprit* in business matters.

'Dear Mr Whitcomb,' she said in her slow drawl, 'since you telephoned I have by chance spoken to two other people, both of whom want to buy the house.'

I knew she had me in a half-nelson, and she knew.

'How much?' I croaked.

She told me.

'OK,' I said. 'OK.'

My lawyer, Mr Mallord Turner, a descendant of the painter, rang next day to say that there was a reason why we must not buy the house.

'Nonsense,' I said. 'I don't care what the reason is, we're going to live there.'

He took me to lunch at the Savoy to explain. 'I have seen the deeds,' he said, 'and there is no freehold. Only a possessory title.'

'What does that mean?'

'It means that during the English Civil War, some time in the 1630s, a gentleman by the name of Henry Knapp Esquire took an enfeoffment – a sort of loan or mortgage – for one hundred pounds from another gentleman of Oxfordshire, to rally some troops in support of the king. Title to the land on which the house stands, and any buildings on the land, was handed over as security for the loan. Whether the loan was ever repaid we do not know, but what we do know is that if you buy the house, and one day somebody knocks at the door and says that he is the heir and successor of Henry Knapp Esquire – you've had it. The property is his.'

'How long would it take,' I asked, 'to get a freehold from the Land Commission?'

'Up to twelve years.'

'Well, bustle on with it,' I said. 'We can't hang about for another glass of port because you have work to do. I have never yet bought a present for my wife that was good enough for her. But I'm going to do it now. You get working on the Land Commission and I'll take a chance.'

The agent we took on to sell the house in Blackheath came to look round and asked me how much we wanted for it. I told him and he whistled. 'In that case,' he said, 'we shall have to mount a big advertising campaign. We'll take a page in *Country Life* and half-pages in the other glossies and we'll arrange display ads in the posh Sundays. Just to put a toe in the water we'll take a two-inch double column in *The Times* the day after tomorrow.'

When *The Times* advertisement appeared we were nearly knocked over in the rush. The first person to arrive, at 10 a.m., offered the full asking price and we shook hands on it. Then they poured in – one man flew over specially from Belgium – all offering more. But we had shaken hands on it and that was that.

The agent hurried over and said, 'Well, well, well – it seems that we both seriously undervalued this desirable property.'

'Some you win, some you lose,' I said, philosophically. 'But a deal is a deal.'

The house on the river at Henley, on the Berkshire bank and smack in the middle of the Royal Regatta course, was a theatrical house. It had the unmistakably stagey atmosphere of the twenties and thirties and a lingering air of Gatsby. Gladys Cooper had lived there for twenty-five years and you could sense her personality still wafting through the rooms like the fading scent of Chanel No. 5. She had been a remarkable woman and she left a pervasive wraith. The moment you walked through the front door you could hear the distant strains of a pit-orchestra tuning up. I could, anyway. She never really left the house during all the years we were there. Sometimes when we were sitting in front of the big log fire in the drawing room at night we would hear the staircase creaking for several seconds. My wife would look up, listening, and then murmur with a smile, 'Gladys.'

It was a house designed for parties. Everyone in the village remembered Gladys's parties. Seeby, the old gardener, said, 'They used to dance on the lawn in evening dress while waiters went round with trays of champagne and Mr Harry Roy had a small band playing over by the trees. Mr Coward was often here and he sometimes sang. Funny, you know, I can sometimes still hear him singing that *Somewhere I'll Find You* song. Reminds me, it does.'

'Surprising how potent cheap music can be,' I said, in an imitation of Noël's clipped accent.

'Yes?' said Seeby, looking at me sideways. 'I always thought it was nice music. Better than all this modern pop caterwauling.'

In a corner of the garden was an enormous wooden hut which was always – even after we started keeping lawnmowers and garden tools in it – known as 'Gladys's wardrobe'. When we moved in it was still full of her dresses – line upon line of them – Balmain, Hartnell, Balenciaga, Coco Chanel, Hardy Amies, Molyneux, Dior, Schiaparelli, Yves St Laurent, beautiful dresses. Sally Hardy asked if she could leave them there until she found a home for them. After she took them away I was sweeping out the hut when I came upon a sheet of paper. It was a guest-list for a party, written in Dame Gladys's hand. I laughed with delight as I read it, and then folded it and put it in my pocket. Gladys had written only first names, so I am guessing about the names I have put in brackets but they are probably right: Roland (Culver), Bea (Lillie), Noël (Coward), Gertie (Lawrence), Basil (Radford), Naunton (Wayne), Jack (Buchanan), Bobby (Howes), Binnie (Hale), Nip (Lupino Lane), Binkie (Beaumont), Robert (Morley) and Joan, Sally (Hardy) and Tim (Robert Hardy).

It was a happy house and we were happy living there.

17

Hear the voice of the Bard!
Ever since I left school
I've been three kinds of genius
And forty kinds of fool,
And when I get to seventy
I'll look back and see . . .
The geniuses weren't geniuses
And the fools were forty-three.

William Golding

So the sky was blue at home but I could hear the rumble of distant thunder in Fleet Street. My job was coming to an end because the *Sun* was slowly but surely sinking.

It was the most humane newspaper closure of the twentieth century. Newspapers traditionally behave like the old Chicago gangsters – they give you a lovely funeral but first they make sure that you are good and dead. The *Sun* sent flowers for the living. They offered big redundancy payments or the offer of a job elsewhere. Dazed journalists walked into the sunset with cheques in their pockets that paid off their mortgages. Hugh Cudlipp supervised the wake. He did it the gentle way because he knew what everyone else knew – if he had not been generous in closing down the IPC *Sun* the print unions would have closed down the *Mirror*.

Towards the end Hugh rang me and asked, 'Please stay on deck until you feel the water lapping round your ankles. Then jump.'

He did not say whether he would send a lifeboat to pick me up out of the water. But I was not worried. Financially I was comfortable. Apart from an investment income I had a healthy freelance business, selling articles and columns elsewhere. I was in a position to do as I liked.

What I did not like was the thought of going back to the *Daily Mirror* as a columnist again. I still had a very good name in newspapers but, apart from my reluctance to return, I felt that the *Mirror* no longer needed me. They had plenty of other good names. While I had been away they had taken on many different columnists – Auberon Waugh and George Gale among them – and I could see no niche into which I would easily fit. No place for Noel.

That was when I wrote my resignation note. Finished at last.

Then, while I was on my way to deliver the note, I had this new idea.

And that was the moment when, utterly unexpectedly, my career in popular newspapers suddenly took off again like a rocket into the blue for the last spectacular spurt of its long voyage of adventure. Just as I was on the brink of leaving newspapers behind me after a quarter of a century, I found myself soaring away into a new career on the *Daily Mirror*. It felt like being in an aircraft that, after a long haul, was coming in to land, but just as the landing wheels were about to touch the runway it zoomed up into the air again.

It was November when I walked into the *Mirror* building to tell Hugh Cudlipp and Lee Howard that I was not coming back to work for the paper. November is a quiet month. Not much news about. So when I mentioned that what the paper ought to do to brighten things up was to start a horse-racing punters club and rally all Britain's racing fans under the *Mirror* banner, they both pricked up their ears. No need for a long explanation. They both saw the scenario in a flash. It was like sunshine breaking through on a cloudy day.

'Smashing idea,' said Cudlipp. 'Just what we need. Noel will probably start another bloody union, but I like it just the same.'

'I wasn't thinking of it for me,' I said. 'Somebody else could do it.'

'Who else?' said Cudlipp. 'Don't be ridiculous – this is right up your alley. Look,' he went on, striding over to the table and starting to draw the front page, 'we'll headline it: NOEL WHITCOMB – FIRST OF THE STARS OF THE SUN TO COME TO THE MIRROR. How's that, eh? We won't say that you are coming *back* to the *Mirror* because we've got a new generation of readers while you've been away, so we want to make it sound like a fresh start. You'll find that everything here has changed in the past five years. Except,' he added with a grin, 'you will probably notice that everything is exactly the same – but don't tell anyone else.'

Lee Howard said, 'Right, Noel. I want the copy by three o'clock. Seven hundred words for the front page and as much as you like for the whole of the spread. Buck up, duckie, you've got work to do. Don't hang about, doll – I mean Mr President.'

Following that first announcement of the launching of the *Daily Mirror* Punters Club, two hundred thousand readers wrote in to join. There was only me and my secretary, Phyl Vinicombe, to deal with them, so I hastily assembled a small staff. Jimmy Stephenson, who had been Northern sports editor of the *Sun*, came in as club manager and Don Cox – also one of my former colleagues on the *Sun* – joined us as technical adviser. We were in business. And it looked like being pretty big business, too, because the new club was being discussed in every pub and club around the land, and new members were joining at the rate of ten thousand a week.

The point was that nobody had ever before set up an organization to represent the interests of punters. Trainers, owners, jockeys and every other sectional interest in British racing had their own associations, but the ordinary punter – the man whose money largely financed the whole sport – had not hitherto had a voice to speak up for him. We did that. And it instantly became as popular as if we had set up a stall for giving away money.

To launch the Punters Club formally, with a flourish, I booked the ballroom at the Dorchester and gave an inaugural dinner. The Duke of Devonshire and several other stewards of the Jockey Club came to support the occasion, as did the presidents of most other Jockey Clubs in Europe – they travelled to London from France, Italy, Spain, Germany and Belgium to be in at the birth of this strange new phenomenon in the world of racing. A letter to me from the Queen Mother, wishing the Punters Club good luck, was read out at the dinner.

I had never seen Hugh Cudlipp look so puzzled as he looked that night. It was all so extraordinary. He had imagined the Punters Club as a nice little winter promotion to keep the paper looking jolly during a dull period. But here we were with dukes – dukes, for God's sake! – at a *Daily Mirror* dinner, and a new department of the paper that was already threatening to become a national institution.

However, everyone of importance inside racing understood what was happening. Racing had always been a rich man's sport, but here was the opening fanfare of the march of the new world – the entry of the mass-circulation warriors. No longer could the punter be ignored. At last he had a voice of his own – the loud voice of the *Daily Mirror*.

It is hard to remember now how little the average working man knew about horse-racing in 1969. He loved horses, because that is deep in the English character, and he loved a bet because that was his traditional way of leaving momentarily the drab streets and entering the fantasy world where people counted wads of notes. But he seldom went racing. It was too expensive. He went into the betting shop, had his bet, lost his cash, and that was that. To the bookmakers, he was a machine for printing money; to the racing authorities he was one of the servants – a decent enough chap but not the sort of fellow you want to see in the Members' Enclosure.

We changed that. It was a change that was due to happen, because it had already happened in most other sectors of society. But racing had always been reluctant to acknowledge the existence of new attitudes, so it fell to us to become the catalyst in racing's social change, helping it to move out of the nineteenth century without a revolution – the British way of change. The first thing we had to do was to educate the punters about how the sport and industry of racing worked – matters that they had never previously understood – without talking down: say what you like about the *Daily Mirror*, it never talked down to its readers. In later years expert racing journalists on television – Brough Scott, Peter O'Sullevan, John McCririck and the rest – gave all British punters a university course in racing. We set up the primary school, and there never was a collection of students more eager to learn than our class of '69.

First thing we did was to provide the opportunity for them to go racing in comfort – in grandstand and Tattersalls – where they could actually see the horses, which was an advantage that few of them had before because racegoers in the Silver Ring seldom got near the horses and saw little of the races. Also we brought the cost of racegoing within their range. Nearly all the fifty-eight racecourses in Britain offered admission at half-price to members of the Punters Club, because it was good business to do so. We took our members racing by the train-load and by the coach-load, always in hundreds and sometimes in thousands, so we were a godsend to the racetracks, especially as we were introducing such a vast number of new fans to the sport.

Because of the old reputation of the *Daily Mirror* as a rabble-rouser there were plenty of people who eyed this strange new happening with suspicion, but the men of consequence in racing administration who had already sensed the wind of change were among our supporters. The Marquess of Zetland, General Gerry Feilden, General Sir Jacquie d'Avigdor Goldsmid, Lord Abergavenny, Colonel Sir Piers Bengough and other members of the Jockey Club all gave a helping hand to the Punters Club. Even Lord Wigg, then chairman of the Horserace Betting Levy Board, asked me to lunch at the Savoy and made a bid – unsuccessfully – to take the club under his own wing. But our biggest benefactor was the old Duke of Norfolk. Some people – including George Wigg – saw him as a reactionary old aristocrat who stood like Horatius barring the way to progress; but that was not how the punters saw him – he was our patron saint.

One summer in those early days I was on Ascot racecourse, talking to Nicky Beaumont, the clerk of the course, and his assistant, Tim Thompson – Tim later went on to manage the opening of Hong Kong's new racecourse at Shatin. The Duke of Norfolk, who was then Her

Majesty's Representative at Ascot – the Queen owns the racecourse – was nearby, talking to Sir Philip Oppenheimer of De Beers, the diamond company; they were discussing details of the sponsorship by De Beers of Ascot's biggest race in the late summer, the King George VI and Queen Elizabeth Stakes.

Suddenly the duke turned to me and said, 'Noel, would you like to bring your club members here in quantity if we arrange a special exclusive enclosure for them on the Queen Elizabeth II lawn? They could have their own bars, of course, and you could put up banners showing that it was your special place.'

'Thank you, sir,' I said, hardly able to believe my ears. It was flabbergasting. Normally the duke was so opposed to advertising of any sort at Ascot that he would have organized a court martial if he had seen a Wall's ice-cream wrapper on the lawn.

'I shall have to ask Her Majesty, of course,' he went on. 'The monarch has to decide.'

Nicky Beaumont and Tim Thompson were both looking as though they had seen a ghost. The idea that the Duke of Norfolk would allow a *Daily Mirror* exclusive enclosure at Ascot was too difficult to swallow – had the old boy gone off his rocker at last?

But no. He was serious. And Sir Philip Oppenheimer, not wishing to be outdone in the matter of magnanimity, added, 'And also, Mr Whitcomb, if you would care to run a competition in your newspaper for a few of your club members to join you in your box here on the day of our big race, I would happily put up some gold-and-diamond jewellery for prizes.'

Still thinking that I must be dreaming, I was starting to thank Sir Philip when the duke interposed, 'And if you wish I will present those prizes for you, Noel, in the winner's enclosure on the day. All right?'

All right! I should shay sho! My only problem, as far as I could see, was to convince Hugh Cudlipp and the editor that this had really happened and that I had not at last taken my final trip into dreamland. But in fact, of course, both the duke and Sir Philip were shrewd men who clearly understood that a racing club with nearly half a million members – which was the tally at that time – was an organization that should be encouraged to behave responsibly rather than opposed. All the world was beginning to comprehend the more sophisticated forms of publicity; and from the *Mirror*'s point of view, this was the sort of prestige publicity that money could not buy. We all knew what we were up to, including the duke.

Biggest surprise to the doubters about this dangerous new

organization in racing was that the *Daily Mirror* Punters Club members behaved so well at the races. At the start, some racecourse managements were anxiously prepared to batten down the hatches when an influx of hordes of Punters Club members was on its way. They expected football hooligans. But what they found was a cheerful army of ordinary people, properly dressed, arriving for a day out to enjoy themselves in decent circumstances – and spending a remarkable amount of money. No trouble at all. Even some of the *Mirror* executives were astonished at the gentlemanly air about it all. It is probably true to say that I was the only person concerned who was not at all amazed, because I knew from long experience that the British working class – as represented by the mass of *Daily Mirror* readers at the time – react according to how they are treated. They were all pleased to be members of a club, and they behaved like members of a club.

Even so, there were still a few whistles of disbelief when I was offered the use of the Jockey Club balcony at Epsom for Punters Club members at the spring meeting. It was all going so splendidly that other popular newspapers were furious with envy, especially as the *Daily Mirror* circulation was once again rising merrily.

One thing that quickly became clear to me from the masses of friendly letters that poured in was that the dearest wish in the hearts of all the members was to be associated with the ownership of a real, live racehorse. In tens of thousands they wrote in to say: 'Dear Noel – How about you trying to persuade the *Daily Mirror* to buy us our own racehorse for the club?'

So I began looking round for a suitable animal at a reasonable price, which is seldom easy. One weekend I was back in Northern Ireland, where I had previously worked when I was writing about the troubles, and I was driving through the countryside of County Antrim when I noticed a decent-looking horse standing in a field and looking over a gate. I stopped the car, walked across the road, stroked his nose and picked a handful of grass which he munched with relish. He was a big horse, and although I was no great expert he looked to me like a typical Irish steeplechaser. It was love at first sight. On impulse I walked to the nearby farmhouse and knocked on the door. A shortish, lean man with a red, weatherbeaten face opened it.

'I hope you will not think me impertinent,' I said, 'but I was just looking at that horse of yours in the field, and I wondered whether by chance he was for sale.' This was by way of being a politeness rather than a serious question, because in the whole history of Ireland there has only ever been one horse not for sale, and that was Arkle, the greatest 'chaser of all time which was owned by Anne, Duchess of Westminster.

'He might be,' said the man. Over his shoulder he called, 'Rosemary, bring a saddle.' Then he said to me, 'Let us go out into the field and my daughter will put him through his paces for you.'

Out came a girl with a saddle over her arm. Swiftly and expertly she saddled the horse. Her father gave her a leg up and she walked the horse round, then trotted and cantered. To my eye, he looked perfect. Then they allowed me to canter him round the field. I was hooked, and they knew I was hooked.

'He is nicely bred, by Even Money out of a Beau Sabreur mare,' said the man, 'and I would want £3,500 for him. He is four years old and has never seen a racecourse.'

'If I may,' I said, 'I would like to ask a friend of mine who knows a great deal more about horses than I do to come and look at him, and advise whether he would be suitable for my purpose.'

'Of course,' said the man, 'with pleasure, sir. Who would that be?'

'Captain Ryan Price,' I said. I saw a smile come into the man's eyes, but that did not surprise me because the name of Ryan Price was famous to everyone concerned with horses. I supposed that the man thought I was boasting.

'You could telephone Captain Price from here, if you wish,' said the man, gently.

So I did. I rang Ryan and asked him if he would come over and look at the horse for me.

'Me come over to Belfast?' he roared. 'Not likely, me boy. Bloody dangerous place.'

Ryan had been a commando captain during the war. He had been General Montgomery's personal bodyguard, and had taken part in daring exploits that would have frightened the life out of James Bond, so I realized that he must have some other reason for not wanting to come to Ulster – probably he just did not fancy the idea of leaving his beloved Sussex downs.

'Who the hell is this farmer chap who's got the horse?' asked Ryan.

'His name is William Rooney,' I said.

'Willie Rooney of Portpatrick?' shouted Ryan. 'Do you mean Willie Rooney?'

'Yes,' I said. 'Do you know him?'

'He only happens to be one of my oldest friends,' roared Ryan. 'He is also the finest horseman in all Ireland. His daughter Rosemary is a champion, too. If Willie is offering you a horse for sale you had better buy it bloody quick. You appear to have a knack of dealing only with the best people, even if it is by accident.'

'But will you come over and look at it?' I persisted.

'Will you do me a favour?' said Ryan.

'Yes, I will.'

'Right, then – I'll see you at Willie's place at midday tomorrow.'

The horse's name was Even Up, and on Ryan's advice I bought him. 'He's a bloody fine sort of individual,' said Ryan. 'He'll be a real athlete in time.'

On the flight home to Heathrow I said to Ryan, 'You'll make all the arrangements, will you? Have him shipped over to your yard?'

'No,' said Ryan. 'I will not.'

I was puzzled. 'But you'll train him for me, won't you?'

'No,' said Ryan. 'You remember that you promised me a favour?' I nodded. 'The favour is that you will send this horse for training to my neighbour in Findon, Alan Oughton.'

I knew Alan well.

'He has not been training for long,' said Ryan, 'and what he needs is a really good horse to set him up quickly – a horse that might win a big race. Even Up is that sort of animal.'

So it was arranged. Even Up went to Alan Oughton's stable in Findon and I announced in the *Daily Mirror* all the exciting details about OUR HORSE! You could almost hear the cheers that went up all over the country. We were no longer just ordinary knockabout punters – we were OWNERS! We had gone up in the world in a big way, and the members were so thrilled that their delight – expressed in terms of letters by the hundredweight – was almost indescribable.

There were one or two small technical obstacles to overcome, because the rules of racing at that time forbade club ownership or commercial ownership of racehorses; but with the help of Weatherby's, the Jockey Club's secretaries, we circumvented these problems by registering the horse in my name – even though the *Mirror* had paid for it – and arranging that it should run in my racing colours, which are black, white and flame. All I needed to do then was to announce the Punters Club colours as black, white and flame. This paved the way for a change in the rules of racing that permitted club ownership, because the old rule was out of date in the new circumstances that were developing.

Alan Oughton soon had Even Up in splendid shape. Almost daily I was writing in the *Mirror* about our horse's progress, and excitement among the readers was becoming tuned to a high pitch by the time I announced that he was ready to go racing. My task was to keep this excitement under control, to prevent the members from betting more than they could afford to lose, and I did this by constantly counselling caution. On the morning of that Friday in February when he was due to run at Sandown Park in a novice hurdle race I was particularly careful to damp down the euphoria. Reminding the readers that he was a young and inexperienced horse, I added, 'Even the most hopeful owner could hardly expect to see his number in the frame, considering the form of the company he will be in.'

It was a beautifully sunny day at Sandown Park, and the racecourse was exceptionally crowded with thousands of Punters Club members who had come – many having travelled from the north and from the west – to see our horse run. I kept as far as possible out of sight because I could see that it might turn into a lynching party if the horse ran really badly. My heart was beating in six-eight time as I gave a leg up to Graham Thorner – then champion National Hunt jockey – in the paddock, and Even Up moved out on to the racecourse among enthusiastic cheers of encouragement from the massed ranks of the punters.

'Good ole Nole!' they shouted. I wondered to myself what they would be shouting in ten minutes' time. Probably not 'good ole Nole' but something far less complimentary.

What happened next remains vividly in my mind. Even Up, an unconsidered outsider in the betting, jumped like a buck and at the final hurdle he fought his way to the front and then won superbly in a thrilling finish. His starting price was 25-1.

The whole racecourse erupted into a thunderous cheer as he passed the post. The punters were deliriously happy, even those who – on my advice – had not backed our horse. Our horse had WON!

In the winner's enclosure all the racing correspondents, most of whom were friends of mine, clustered round, chuckling. 'Well done, Noel,' they said. 'Quite a *coup*. You managed to keep that really quiet. You must have won a packet.'

'If you want to know,' I said, 'I didn't have a penny on him.'

They all smiled. Nobody believed me.

It so happened that on the next day I had to go and collect a new car that I had ordered months before. It was a decent car – a 3½-litre eight-cylinder motor – and when, on my way back to the office in the new car, I was held up at traffic lights in the Strand, a head appeared through my open offside window. The head belonged to Dai Davies, then the Press Association's chief racing correspondent. He was grinning hugely. 'Oh, my goodness, Noel,' he said, 'that was quick!'

Sadly, Alan Oughton died soon afterwards of cancer. His widow,

Diane, carried on running the stable with the help of her son, David, who later became a top trainer in Hong Kong. Under their expert care, Even Up went from success to success. Within a year I received an offer of £25,000 for the horse. Naturally I told the *Mirror* and they were horrified at the idea. 'Don't even *think* of selling our horse, Noel,' they said. 'Every single time he runs in a televised race he is worth more than £25,000 to the paper because of all the free publicity he generates for us. Everybody loves the Punters Club horse.'

And so they did. He won thirteen races for us before we eventually retired him, as a dignified old pensioner, to live out the rest of his life in comfort in a meadow in Findon.

I bought a number of other horses for the Punters Club and they all did pretty well, but most of the credit for that is down to the late Ryan Price. Ryan, known throughout racing as 'the Captain' or 'the wizard of Findon', was one of the greatest horsemasters of the twentieth century, and I was fortunate to have him as a friend and adviser. Ryan did not like newspapermen in general, and had good reason to dislike them, but he and I trusted each other unquestioningly. Occasionally I bought a horse for myself and sent it to Ryan for training, but apart from a horse called Royal Fanfare which won several races my personal forays in the bloodstock trade were less successful than the deals I made for the Punters Club. One in particular caused me great anguish.

I was in Doncaster for the St Leger meeting in September 1971, and on the Friday afternoon I was ambling aimlessly round the sales area, looking at the young horses that were due to come up for sale, when I saw an Exbury filly that filled my eye. I asked the groom to walk her round and she was a superb mover, so I gave the groom a quid and hurried across the road to the racecourse, looking for Ryan. When I found him I asked him to come over and look at this Exbury filly for me, and he agreed.

On the way over he said, 'You realize, of course, that this filly, with her breeding, will become quite a valuable animal in time even if she never wins a race. So she is likely to fetch a good sum.'

We dug out the groom and walked her round again. Ryan said, 'She would certainly look pretty nice up on the Downs. How much did you have in mind to pay for her?'

'Ten thousand,' I said, swallowing hard.

Ryan gave me a sideways grin because he knew I had intended to say five.

'Is she for the *Daily Mirror* or for yourself?' he asked.

'For me,' I said. 'The *Mirror* would have me shot at dawn if I paid that sort of money for a filly on their behalf.'

'Right,' said Ryan. 'I'll ask Jack Doyle to bid for her at the sales tonight. Mind you, I can tell you now that if you get her for that sort of money you will have stolen her.'

That night there were fewer people than usual around the sales ring. The Friday night of the Leger meeting is the night of the big St Leger dinner. Lord Harrington, who had been bidding fearlessly on behalf of Mr David Robinson, was not at the sales. Lady Beaverbrook's agents were also absent. There were vacant seats around the sales ring. Business was quiet.

Jack Doyle, the Irish bloodstock agent who bid on Ryan's behalf, stood nonchalently in his usual spot in the chute where the horses were led in. Ryan and I stood a few paces behind in the area where prospective owners take a last look at the young horses before their numbers are called.

My heart was beating so loudly that I was expecting any minute that the auctioneer would request that the Caribbean steel band should be shifted further away. In came the Exbury filly.

The bidding was slow. I thought Jack had got her at four thousand, but just as the auctioneer's hammer was hovering somebody bid another monkey. Ryan and I were lighting new cigarettes off the old ones. She was hanging fire again at nine thousand when Peter Easterby came in with a well-to-do Northern businessman and the bidding suddenly rocketed away into the stratosphere. She went for the sort of price Ryan had forecast.

I walked back to the car and drove south.

On the Sunday morning Ryan rang. 'Come down and have lunch,' he said.

'I can't – I've got guests here for lunch.'

'Well, come down and have tea.'

'Look Ryan,' I said, 'I don't particularly want to buy a horse, you know. It was just that I took a shine to the Exbury.'

'Of course you don't want to buy a horse, m'boy,' boomed Ryan. 'But I've bought forty young horses this week and I've still got the adrenalin running – I'll see you at Roy Trigg's place at four o'clock and we'll take 'em out and have a look.'

Ryan always had his new youngsters sent to Roy Trigg's stables near Horsham until his vet had checked them. We stood watching as the grooms led them round, and Ryan pointed to one.

'That colt there is just the sort for you,' he said. 'It's a St Alphage, first

357

crop. Jack bought him for me for eighteen hundred sovereign. He'll win races – guaranteed. Take him to Wolverhampton, win a couple of little races and you could turn him over at the end of the season for a profit of five grand. You don't want to keep a horse like that for long – never get married to a horse.'

I hesitated. 'He's a very plain colt,' I said.

'Don't you talk to me about fuckin' plain colts,' roared Ryan. 'I'm telling you what's value for money. I can see you've got your eye on that Floribunda colt – what you want is the sort of horse you can take to Royal Ascot with your top hat on. The Floribunda is a lovely colt but he'll set you back more than three times the cost of the St Alphage.'

For once I did not take Ryan's advice. I bought the Floribunda colt. Beautiful, he was. I named him Trooper Smith and throughout the winter I watched him furnish up into a most elegant colt. One Sunday in the following May I was walking across the Downs with Ryan when he stopped and said thoughtfully, 'I haven't said a lot about your Trooper Smith because walls have ears, but I can tell you that you're a lucky man. He's a brilliant youngster. He has all the makings of one of the best I've ever trained. I've already had nine juvenile winners this season and Trooper Smith can make them all look like hacks. I am going to run him at Kempton this Wednesday and if you want a bet I would advise you to get your money down then because I doubt if you will ever get a decent price about him again.'

I could hardly wait for Wednesday to come. On Tuesday morning Dorothy Price rang me. 'I have bad news, Noel,' she said. 'Ryan is too upset to talk to anyone at the moment but your Trooper Smith broke a leg at work this morning and had to be put down.'

I was near to tears for weeks. It wasn't the money – you can always get money but a good horse is hard to find, and I had become very fond of the horse. The odd thing was that the young horse Ryan had wanted me to buy for eighteen hundred guineas – the cheap St Alphage colt – was named Sandford Lad and became champion sprinter as a two-year-old. As a three-year-old he changed hands for about half a million.

The best horse Ryan trained for me to run on the flat as a Punters Club horse was a colt by Pieces of Eight. I bought him cheaply at the sales one night when Ryan wasn't there, and the reason why he didn't fetch much was that the Pieces of Eight blood was suspect for temperament. I named him Mirror Boy. He turned out to be the most temperamental horse I ever met – but he was a good 'un when he felt like it.

The big point about Mirror Boy was that he caused so many of the Punters Club members to consult cardiac specialists. He would start every race indolently, sauntering out of the stalls as if for an exercise canter, and would jog along until he was so far behind the rest of the field that if you were watching the race on television he was always out of the picture. Then suddenly, two furlongs from home, he would prick up his ears and start racing. He moved at such tremendous speed that he overtook all the rest of the runners one by one, leaving them for dead, and passed the finishing line to win by a short head.

Every Punters Club member on the racecourse would go straight off for a large brandy. Not to celebrate but to calm their shattered nerves. The way that horse always finished with just a whisker of his nose in front was enough to give anyone who had backed him a heart attack. But he became another great favourite with the racing crowds – another Punters Club prodigy.

From the time Mirror Boy began his racing career, Ryan Price put a boy called Joe Blanks on him as his jockey. Joe was one of Ryan's apprentices, and Joe loved Mirror Boy with a consuming passion; woe betide any other person in the stable except the Captain who dared to lay so much as a finger on Mirror Boy – Mirror Boy was Joe's horse. The two of them – the horse and the boy – were like David and Jonathan.

Mirror Boy was not an easy ride, and in fact when I later put Lester Piggott on his back he refused to exert himself for Lester. But for Joe he would always do his stuff. Joe knew exactly the moment in a race when he must give Mirror Boy the office, which was usually when they were dawdling along about a furlong behind the rest of the field, and although in all his career Mirror Boy seldom won by more than a whisker, Joe knew instinctively the potential of his pal. He never used the whip – wouldn't have dreamed of it – and he always came in smiling because although everybody else on the racecourse had given up Mirror Boy as a goner early in the race, Joe never had a moment's anxiety. He knew. Some horses are like that – they will only do their best for one human being, whom they will never let down.

Their most spectacular triumph was in the *Daily Mirror*'s own race, the Andy Capp Handicap at Redcar, which was at that time the richest handicap race in the North. I had arranged for the *Mirror* to sponsor a number of televised races, including the *Daily Mirror* Handicap at Epsom on Derby Day, but the Andy Capp Handicap was always by far the *Mirror*'s greatest occasion in the North. Everyone connected with the racecourse gave a real Yorkshire welcome to the vast army of Punters Club members who turned up on that day. Major Leslie Petch, the North's 'Mr Racing', was the genial managing director of the course, the Marquess of Zetland was its chairman and John Sanderson was the clerk of the course and they always welcomed our party with champagne, as did Lord Zetland's son, then Lord Ronaldshay, in later years. It was a fiesta.

Early in 1980 I had asked Ryan Price to prepare our horse with this big handicap in mind, and he was a master of this tactic. But, when we arrived at Redcar, Mirror Boy was not greatly fancied because the opposition was particularly strong. However, I personally never had a moment's doubt about the outcome and in the parade ring before the race I joked with young Joe Blanks, asking him to try to win by more than a short head as this habit of his was taking a heavy toll on my blood pressure.

Joe and Mirror Boy set off at a hand canter, as usual bringing up the rear, and by about two furlongs from home there was a groan from the massed battalions of punters because Mirror Boy looked to be too far back to have any chance. But then Joe pressed the button. Mirror Boy came storming past the field like an express train and won easily by one and a half lengths at 11–2.

The gigantic crowd of punters, nearly all of whom had backed him, were still cheering themselves hoarse as Joe Blanks jumped off Mirror Boy in the winner's enclosure and said to me with a grin, 'I took your advice and decided to let him win by a distance this time, guv'nor.'

That was the last time Joe Blanks rode Mirror Boy. Tragically, young Joe was killed in a fall from another horse at Brighton races shortly afterwards. Mirror Boy went off his feed for weeks. Punters Club members by the thousand sent in money in memory of Joe, as they always did when any misfortune occurred to anyone connected with the club, and it was sent to Joe's family and to racing charities. Bob Rodney, who had taken over as manager of the club after Jimmy Stevenson's retirement, arranged for us to put some money into a race at Brighton every year in Joe's memory.

In a curiously English way that sometimes happens in sporting activities, the Punters Club was becoming a kind of classless society. Everyone who cared about horses joined in the fun. The bulk of the club's colossal membership was made up of the old *Daily Mirror* readers, the newly affluent working class; but as the club advanced in public esteem an enormous number of middle-class people joined, and even some old titles. A wildfire success of this sort naturally breeds a few enemies, and we had our share, but most of them were people who had reason to be envious. When the Royal Commission on Gambling was set up under the chairmanship of Lord Rothschild the Punters Club was invited to submit evidence and recommendations for change on behalf of all Britain's punters, and our recommendations were accepted as good ideas and implemented. The club also did beneficial work for racing in general by setting up – with the help of Mark O'Connor's International Racing Bureau – championships for apprentice jockeys on the flat and for conditional jockeys in National Hunt racing. So we became – oddly enough for the *Daily Mirror* – extremely respectable.

More and more people of consequence in racing became our allies, although when I sent Mirror Boy hurdling and he beat the Queen Mother's favourite, Sindebele, in a photo-finish at Lingfield I thought we might have lost one influential well-wisher. But no. The royals are not like that. Next time the Queen Mother saw me she called me over and said, 'What a *nice* horse Mirror Boy is, Mr Whitcomb.' I think her private secretary, Lieutenant Colonel Sir Martin Gilliat, must have had something in his eye, because as she said it he looked at me and closed one eye.

Naturally the *Daily Mirror*'s top executives and directors were delighted, partly because it all added to the newspaper's prestige and partly because it was so good for circulation. Most of them liked racing, anyway, and often came racing with us on big Punters Club days. It was a period of change inside the *Mirror* building. Lee Howard retired as editor, handed in his company Jaguar, squashed his gargantuan frame into a Mini-minor – the neatest trick since the first sailor managed to get a four-masted schooner into a bottle – and drove to Rome, where, to everyone's astonishment, he settled down happily with a girlfriend.

Tony Miles, who had been a feature writer on the paper in my early days, took over the editor's chair, and when he later moved upstairs to the chairman's office the job of editor went to Mike Molloy, who had come up a long way from doing drawings for Marjorie Proops's column. Mike was the seventh of the eight editors of the *Daily Mirror* with whom I worked, and his deputy was Derek Jameson, who later briefly edited the *Daily Express* and helped to launch the daily *Star* before going on to edit the *News of the World* and – after unsuccessfully suing the BBC for libel – ended up as a BBC disc jockey. They were far from being the most talented journalists I had worked with, but they were amiable enough as colleagues.

Of all the many new ideas with which we experimented in the Punters Club, easily the most popular was organizing parties of members to go racing in foreign countries. Nobody except the rich, usually only the very rich, went racing abroad in those early days of the club's existence. There were no organized tours of the sort that later proliferated. It was virgin territory, and we pioneered it. It began in an unambitious way.

One morning Jimmy Stevenson came into my office with a letter from Peter Hayes, then chairman of Panorama Holidays in Hove, suggesting that we should set up a racing weekend in Paris for our members. It was a daring thought.

'OK, Jim,' I said, 'we'll try it. According to this letter it will cost seventeen quid a head for the weekend, but we may get a few takers. Tell him we'll give it a whirl.'

Two hundred members applied and sent cheques, so we took them all. It went superbly. The biggest advantage was that few of the members would have dared to try to do it by themselves, but we arranged everything. Don Cox and I both spoke French, so we were able to initiate the punters into the unfamiliar aspects of French racing, which has no bookmakers but only the Pari Mutuel or tote. Peter Hayes of Panorama sent one of his young assistants, Ian Fry, to act as courier. Ian had never been racing before. In later years he set up his own Horse Racing Abroad company and turned it into a big business. But on the first Paris trip we were all greenhorns, and we were all staggered by its success. The punters had such a marvellous time that when they went home they all talked about it in their pubs and clubs, and we were deluged with letters from people who wanted to come on the next trip.

One letter from a satisfied member contained a clue that caused us to take the whole operation up market.

Dear Noel, It was the best weekend that my missus and I have ever had in the whole of our lives, but if I might make a suggestion – could we stay in posher hotels next time. Our little hotel up in Montmartre was very nice and clean – nothing wrong with it – and the whole trip was fantastic value, but my missus didn't like being up in the red-light district. I think you'll find that most of the members can afford to pay more.

We certainly found that. In the course of time Punters Club members were sending in cheques totalling two million pounds a year to come on our famous racing trips abroad. When I telephoned Peter Hayes – whom I had never met – to congratulate him on our first Paris trip and tell him that we wanted higher-class accommodation next time, he assigned his air director, David Johnson, to look after the Punters Club. That was when the whole astonishing operation took off like a rocket. David booked us into the best hotels all over the world. He knew.

We were lucky to have David Johnson handling our travel operation, not only because he is one of the most expert travel agents I have ever met but even more because he had an instinctive understanding of what our punters wanted. He came everywhere with us and worked tirelessly to ensure that everything went to perfection. The members loved him. He was their best friend. He treated them all as though they were millionaires – and a few of them were. Among our enthusiastic members we had two brothers who were cockney scrap-dealers, and each of them used to arrived at the airport in a chauffeur-driven Rolls. Many of the members had to save up for the trips, of course, and count the pennies they spent, but there was never the smallest hint of money-snobbery. We had all sorts among the members who came abroad with us – owners, trainers, lords, commoners, publicans, sinners, honeymoon couples, pensioners spending their savings on the holiday they had always dreamed of, and they all got on together marvellously as good companions because they all had two vital things in common – they all loved horses and they all liked having a little bet.

Some of them occasionally had a big bet, and I recall one man who had a big bet by accident. He was a Geordie and his ambition was to speak French, but as he was pretty difficult to understand when he spoke English I did not rate his chances of success very high. All the same, he kept trying. In 1975 when we were in Paris for the *Prix de l'Arc de Triomphe* at Longchamp he came up to me in the grandstand and asked me how to say in French, 'I want to back number five to win three times.' Normally that would have meant a bet of £3. I tried to persuade him to let me write it down on a piece of paper for him, so that he could show it to the operator at the tote window – few of the tote people at Longchamp spoke English at that time – but he insisted on learning the words. So I told him how to say the words phonetically.

'Just say, "Numero sank ganyon twar fwar",' I told him.

Shortly before the big race was about to start he came back to me with his tote ticket. 'I think them buggers have short-changed me,' he said. 'Look at this ticket – have they given me what I asked for?'

They had not. For a start, he had gone to the wrong window – the 100-franc window, where the minimum bet was in units of £10.

'I'm afraid you've backed number three five times instead of number five three times,' I said. 'And as you have done it in tenners you have had fifty quid on number three.'

He nearly had a fit. Fifty quid was a fortune to him. He rushed back to the window – but too late. The race was off. He came back to stand beside me, white and shaking. 'That number three has got no bloody chance,' he said. 'I should never have tried to speak bloody French.'

But number three was a horse called Star Appeal. And Star Appeal won the race at odds of 120-1.

I shall never forget that Geordie's face as the manager of the tote came down in person to shake him by the hand and count out his £6,000 winnings in French notes. All the punters gathered round and cheered, although not a single one of the rest had backed the winner.

From those small beginnings our little acorn of foreign travel grew into a mighty oak tree. Tens of thousands of Punters Club members came on racing trips with us in luxury to beautiful and exciting places in all five continents of the globe and we had enough adventures – some of them hair-raising but most of them hilarious – to fill a book. They were great fun, of course, and remarkably affordable considering the very high standard of quality; and one of the most remarkable aspects of the whole enterprise was the warmth and generosity of the welcome the punters received everywhere they went. They were treated like ambassadors, and they behaved accordingly.

On one of our South American tours, for example, our first stop was Venezuela for racing at Caracas, a particularly beautiful racecourse. After the races we were invited to join the stewards of the Venezuelan Turf Club in their boardroom. Everyone assumed it was for drinks. But when we trooped in we found 200 chairs ranged in front of a dais. The punters were requested to sit down and I was invited to take my place on the dais, on the right hand of the senior steward.

The senior steward then stood up and made a speech in Spanish for half an hour about the long and traditional links of friendship between Venezuela and Great Britain, reminding us that British people were still the only non-nationals permitted by law to carry firearms in his country. When he sat down, to protracted applause from the punters, who had not understood a word of it, I made a brief speech of thanks for their kindness. Then we were all invited into the next room for drinks. It was a hot day and everyone was thirsty. But our hosts made amends for the delay. They put up a dozen cases – 144 bottles – of Dom Perignon champagne. And as the price of Dom Perignon in Venezuela at that time was £85 a bottle, it was a charming gesture.

In India we were greeted with elephants and welcomed by maharajahs. They gave banquets for us in Bombay and set aside their best private boxes for us on Mahalaxmi racecourse. In Delhi they made us honorary members of the Delhi Turf Club – and also told us quietly what was going to win. In Calcutta on Calcutta Cup day the big race was won by a horse called Midnight Cowboy, which belonged to the widow of an old friend of mine, the Maharajah of Cooch Behar, and she told me beforehand to tell the punters that it had a very good chance. The Bank of India had opened a branch on the racecourse especially for our group, and it did splendid business. All the women in our party were dressed as if for Royal Ascot. The president of the Royal Calcutta Turf Club, the Maharajah of Burdwan, an exceptionally tall and extremely old gentleman, was so captivated by the British punters that he gave a wonderful party for us at the Turf Club. It was the most elegant party imaginable, and nobody who was there will ever forget it.

As we walked back to our hotel through the streets of Calcutta that night we saw huddled figures dying of starvation in the gutters. The punters walked in shocked silence, emptying their wallets and handbags as they went. Nobody spoke.

The following day we moved on to Darjeeling. There we encountered for the first time somebody who did not treat us as prodigal sons. The manager of the hotel was a retired Indian Army officer who clearly felt that his high-class establishment was being invaded by a platoon of Other Ranks. He listened to their accents and sniffed. Not *comme il faut*. He thought they must be poor people and spoke to them condescendingly.

On the morning after our arrival we were all called before dawn, and drove in a fleet of Land Rovers to the foothills of the Himalayas to see the sun rise over Everest. On the way back we stopped at a settlement for Tibetan refugees that had been set up by the Anglo-American Commission after the rape of Tibet by China.

The Tibetans were quiet, courteous people. During the years since they had arrived in the settlement they had spent their lives pursuing their traditional arts and crafts, making beautiful carpets and rugs, jackets and hats of fur, exquisite pottery, tapestries, fine lace, wonderful embroidery, all made by hand. Some of the carpets had taken years to make. It was like Aladdin's cave.

Our punters were staggered by what they saw. The Tibetans offered us tea, but there was no question of payment. We were their guests. The punters went wandering round, looking wide-eyed at the artefacts, accompanied by two Tibetans who could speak English. All the things were for sale, but when they heard the prices their reaction was surprising. It was summed up by a man called Joe.

'It's a bloody scandal that these nice people should be selling their stuff so cheap, just because they don't understand,' he said. 'These are fifty-years-ago prices. I know because I've got a stall in the market, haven't I? If we buy any of this gear we've got to give these poor buggers more than they are asking.'

All the punters began telling the Tibetans, through the interpreters, that they were not asking nearly enough for their goods. The Tibetans simply smiled. They were not interested in money, and merely wished to live their lives enjoying what they did. By the time we left the punters had bought nearly everything in the place. None of them had nearly enough money on them to pay on the spot, so it was arranged that all the goods would be labelled with the buyers' names and we would return with the money on the following day.

I had bought a few presents to take home, so next morning I went to the front desk of the hotel, where the manager was standing, and took out my book of travellers cheques.

'I am sorry, Mr Whitcomb,' said the manager, with a puzzled look on his face, 'we have no money at all in the hotel. The members of your group have cashed travellers cheques for all we had, which was a substantial sum. All I can suggest is that you should go to Grindlay's Bank. It is only just down the hill.'

So I strolled down to the bank, went up to the counter and took out my travellers cheques.

'Excuse me, sir,' said the cashier, 'before you sign any of those I must advise you that we have run out of money. There is an English group in town, sir, and they have cleaned us out this morning. It has never happened before. We have sent to Calcutta for fresh supplies.'

The purchasing power of the punters never ceased to surprise me, and its significance was certainly not lost on the *Daily Mirror*'s advertisers, who paid increasingly high rates to advertise luxury goods that would previously have been considered too expensive for the mass-circulation market. Not that the punters were all well off, by any means, but they spent their money with a joyous abandon. Racing people tend to be like that – enjoy today and let tomorrow take care of itself.

When I think back to those happy days I have a seemingly endless line of smiling faces running before my eyes and I feel like Mr Chips calling the school roll – all of them familiar faces, all remembered with affection. But there is one face that is always in the front of the passing throng. Miss Craig.

Not that Miss Craig was beautiful. She was, frankly, of a forbidding demeanour. She was a shortish, thick-set woman who usually wore Donegal tweeds with a round tweed hat to match. Before she even spoke to me for the first time I knew where she came from, because I had worked in Northern Ireland, and I recognized that challenging air which gives advance notice that there is to be no compromise – no surrender. At the start Miss Craig was clearly by no means sure that this club she had joined was of a high enough class for her. She was a living symbol of respectability, as umistakable as the Union Jack. Just one word out of place from anyone and her resignation would have been on the doormat.

She looked to be about sixty, but one thing you had to say about Miss Craig was that she was real good goer – tireless. When the rest of us were longing to put our feet up after a day's racing abroad, Miss Craig could be seen marching round purposefully and talking to members of the hotel staff or local people.

Not for some time did I realize that what she was after was racing tips. Racing was Miss Craig's passion. Behind that craggy exterior lurked a heart that loved nothing better than a quid on a horse. But she was notoriously unlucky. When Miss Craig backed a horse you could bet your boots that it would either be beaten a short head or lose the race on an objection. There are some people like that.

One spring when we were down in the South of France for the racing at Cagnes-sur-Mer, staying at the Carlton in Cannes, Miss Craig's luck changed. It was a beautiful Sunday. The weather was superb. We had our usual luncheon on the lawn at the racecourse before racing began. One of the trainers who had a horse running in the first race told me he expected it would win. I passed the information round and the horse duly trotted up at 6-1. A good start to the day.

As I walked down from the stands I asked one of our members, 'Did you back it?'

'Not half,' he said. 'We all did. And I'll tell you something extraordinary – even Miss Craig had a tickle!' We both laughed, because we were all very fond of the old lady.

Miss Craig backed the winner of the next race as well. It was a talking point. Everyone was pleased. My wife and I left the racecourse shortly after that and drove back to the Carlton, but when the punters came streaming into the foyer from their coach they all came rushing up to tell me the amazing news. Miss Craig had backed all eight winners! Miss Craig had knocked it off at last.

That night we had arranged a club dinner at the casino. David Johnson's assistant, André Caizergues, had booked a private room and hired a band. It was all very elegant. Most of the punters wore black ties for the occasion. Miss Craig arrived looking radiant, in a new evening dress. After dinner she danced every dance with the excitement of a young girl. Every man in our party danced with Miss Craig. It was her day.

After the dinner-dance all the punters went up to the gaming rooms. Miss Craig took a seat at the roulette table, and the members all gathered round behind her. She placed a fiver – a big bet for her – on number 20. A straight bet – all on one number to win.

'*Faites vos jeux, messieurs,*' called the croupier. '*Rien ne va plus.*'

The little white ball whirled on its clicking way round, slowing down gradually until finally plopping into number 20.

The croupier began to push Miss Craig's £175 winnings across the green baize towards her, but she signalled to him to leave her original stake on number 20.

The punters piled their money on to number 20. There was a mountain on that single number. Hardly a chip for anything else.

When the little white ball plopped again into number 20 a cheer went up. Most of them picked up their winnings but Miss Craig told the croupier to put her stake on number 36.

You could have heard a pin drop as he spun the wheel and the little white ball clicked round. A sigh of incredulity went up as the ball limped round on the last turn of the wheel, wavered between two numbers and finally fell into number 36.

Miss Craig was sitting there, quiet as ever, with the most wonderful smile on her face. But it was a fixed smile.

Miss Craig was dead.

It turned out subsequently, to everyone's surprise, that Hilda Craig had been well over seventy. She had worked for a solicitor in Belfast, and he cabled me to say that she had left instructions that she was to be buried wherever she died, with no fuss. I read the solicitor's cable out to the assembled members. Typically she had added a further demand: 'No flowers.'

This brought an awkward silence, because there had been a whip-round for a wreath which had resulted in a large sum, many of the members having put in all their winnings.

One woman said, 'I'm sure she would not mind us taking just a simple bunch of flowers.' So they took a bunch of the mimosa that grows all over the hills, and gave the rest of the money to a local orphanage.

They buried Miss Craig in a churchyard on the hillside looking down upon the racecourse. Afterwards they all went down to the little bar just across the road from the racecourse. Everyone stood and raised a glass as one of the punters spoke the simple valediction: 'Miss Craig – eight winners on the trot.'

Year by year the Punters Club progressed from strength to strength, its membership consistently rising as its activities at home and abroad became ever more popular; and the profits it made out of travel and merchandizing rose to cover the club's race sponsorships, its charitable donations and its prizes to encourage young people in the racing industry. It was only a small department with a tiny but efficient staff inside a big newspaper, yet its fame and acclaim spread far and wide.

The *Daily Mirror* itself, however, was fighting for its life during all this time, struggling hopelessly to get out of the strangling grip of the print unions. Restrictive practices and nonsensical pay demands were choking Fleet Street to death.

It is a historical fact that the British press undergoes a major structural change every forty years. From the 1660s when John Milton published the *Areopagitica* on the liberty of the press and the beginning of Queen Anne's reign in 1702 when the first daily newspaper was published in Fleet Street, our press has undergone a cataclysmic change at the end of every span of forty years. Francis Williams traced this pattern in his anatomy of newspapers, *Dangerous Estate*; every forty years we have a journalistic *volte-face*. It always comes with a bang, never with a whimper. And it so happened that I worked in Fleet Street throughout the whole of the most recent of these forty-year periods, and stayed on long enough to watch my era explode in my face. Fleet Street and I retired together – both, as they say in cricket, retired hurt.

Towards the end the proprietors of my time were falling like green bottles off a wall, clearing the way for the imminent new epoch; the Berry brothers, Viscounts Kemsley and Camrose, the Beaverbrook family, the Harmsworth dynasty (with the exception of the present Lord Rothermere), the Astors, the Cadburys, the Hultons – all the old guard who had dominated the industry for forty years were either heading for the exit or had departed already. Even the rapid succession of *Mirror* chairmen during those last declining years (the *Daily Mirror* had nine chairmen during my time) had become sub-standard, with the outstanding exception of Sir Edward Pickering. No Cecil Kings among them. It was all downhill.

The last chairman of the *Mirror* under the old regime was Clive Thornton, an odd choice for the job because he had formerly been running the Abbey National Building Society, but he had been brought in to stop the financial rot on the advice of the *Mirror*'s City editor, Bob Head. Bob Head is a devout Roman Catholic, and so is Thornton, but the power of prayer did not help Thornton on the day Robert Maxwell took over at the *Mirror*. Maxwell fired him on the spot.

That was the beginning of the end for me, too. I expected short shrift from Maxwell, and that was what I got. The Punters Club that I was running at the time for the *Daily Mirror* had reached its zenith of public popularity and with over 600,000 members – still increasing at the rate of 1,000 a week – it was the biggest sporting association of its kind in the world. But Maxwell, a keen football fan, was not an *aficionado* of horse racing. He decided to close down the club.

In describing what happened to me after that I need to tread with extreme delicacy and caution. Maxwell was so urgently busy with matters of far greater importance at that time that it is possible, even probable, that after he decided to close the Punters Club he knew nothing about the details of what happened to the people concerned. Doubtless his executives devised the means for implementing his decisions, and in some cases it is possible that they may have used methods of which he would have disapproved if he had been consulted.

At all events, I was called in by Maxwell's newly appointed editorial manager, Duncan Lamont, who told me that my job was to disband the Punters Club, without telling anyone who did not need to know and without disclosing in the newspaper the fact that the club was to be discontinued. That point was stressed. In fact, to the best of my belief no announcement ever appeared in the *Daily Mirror* about the demise of the Punters Club.

Another matter about which secrecy was – understandably – required was the disposal of the *Mirror*'s old racehorses, Even Up and Heidelberg. This was a potentially emotive subject because both horses had been very popular with the readers. My tardiness in arranging for these old *Mirror* pensioners to be humanely destroyed was part of a series of events that made me the subject of controversy, which arose largely because the *Mirror* executives concerned with the cost-cutting exercise knew nothing – and did not pretend to know anything – about racehorses or about the way in which people in racing traditionally behave. I expect they were doing their duty as they saw it, but nevertheless it caused me great anguish. Perhaps I was too sensitive – certainly I was boiling over with a sense of outrage. After having been a reputable columnist on the paper for the best part of forty years I felt that I was being viewed as an antagonist. It was very unpleasant.

Rumours swept swiftly through the building that I was out of favour, and some of my old colleagues began to avoid me because they felt it might not be safe to be seen talking to a man who was not smiled upon by the new management. Although this was hurtful it was clearly understandable because many of them had young families to support and mortgages to pay, and employment prospects throughout Fleet Street were bleak. I began to feel that I was learning what it would be like to live in Albania.

My office was closed and I returned the keys. For a while I was a displaced person, carting my office baggage and files around with me. Then the new managing editor, a competent journalist called Alan Shillum who had the difficult task of finding office accommodation for staff who were being redeployed under the new regime, took me up to a vast empty room like a warehouse and pointed to a long row of desks with ancient upright typewriters chained to them.

'From now on,' he said, 'you can sit where you like along there. There will probably be another chap joining you up here in time.'

'His name wouldn't by any chance be Kafka?' I asked.

'I wouldn't try to be funny if I were you,' he said. 'Jokes aren't in fashion any more.'

I went on with the clearing up and closing down of the Punters Club. It was impossible to keep it a secret because members of the club were ringing up in hundreds every day to find out why all news of club activities had suddenly disappeared from the paper. Many were angry when they heard that the club was defunct. Some said it was the main reason they had taken the paper, and among these there were many who said that they would never buy the *Daily Mirror* again.

Perhaps some of them carried out their threat because the *Daily Mirror* circulation was falling fast at that time, and at one point it was down by a figure slightly less than the membership of the club.

Of course there is no doubt that it was necessary for Maxwell to take a hatchet to the *Mirror*'s heavily over-manned staff. It was a measure for survival. But experience shows that such exercises in stringent staff-reduction tend to result in an atmosphere of anger and fear – fear of the scrap heap and the dole queue. Employees who had long service with the former management found themselves faced with the destruction of their careers and no more than what they considered a pittance in compensation to take away with them. I knew one man whose marriage was wrecked and others who had nervous breakdowns. An outcome of that sort is not unfamiliar in companies that are part of an industry in turmoil, and sometimes it is economically inevitable, but it is never a pretty sight to watch. Human misery is always sad to see, no matter what the cause.

As I pressed on with the work of dismantling the department that had been my last useful contribution to the *Daily Mirror*, I had the feeling that

371

what I was doing was unconnected with the new regime – that I was merely fulfilling an obligation to the past.

Few people had reason to come into the vast area of empty floorspace in which I worked. One day an old colleague came through, a man who used to take my column on the telephone when I was filing from abroad. He came across to find out who was sitting there alone.

'My God – it's Noel,' he said. 'What are you doing here in Siberia?'

'*Sic transit* Gloria Swanson,' I said laughing.

But laughing was becoming less easy. Although I was taking care not to develop a persecution complex, I had to admit that I was beginning to feel like Winston Smith in Orwell's *1984*.

I finally finished the job of clearing up all the club affairs and leaving everything shipshape on the evening of the day upon which my contract with the *Daily Mirror* expired. As I took the lift down to the lobby I was smiling. I was thinking of the cocky young fool – a particular kind of fool – who had taken a taxi to Fleet Street all those years ago with the idea of working for a short while in the land of his fathers.

I was still wondering whether it had been a good idea.

As I walked across the lobby towards the main door to leave the *Daily Mirror* building for the last time, the doorman called out, 'Good night, Mr Whitcomb.'

Nobody said goodbye.

Index